Think Like a Data Scientist

TACKLE THE DATA SCIENCE PROCESS STEP-BY-STEP

BRIAN GODSEY

MANNING

SHELTER ISLAND

For online information and ordering of this and other Manning books, please visit www.manning.com. The publisher offers discounts on this book when ordered in quantity. For more information, please contact

> Special Sales Department
> Manning Publications Co.
> 20 Baldwin Road
> PO Box 761
> Shelter Island, NY 11964
> Email: orders@manning.com

Manning Publications Co.
20 Baldwin Road
PO Box 761
Shelter Island, NY 11964

Development editor:	Karen Miller
Review editor:	Aleksandar Dragosavljević
Technical development editor:	Mike Shepard
Project editor:	Kevin Sullivan
Copy editor:	Linda Recktenwald
Proofreader:	Corbin Collins
Typesetter:	Dennis Dalinnik
Cover designer:	Marija Tudor

ISBN: 9781633430273
Printed in the United States of America

Get the eBooks FREE!
(PDF, ePub, Kindle, and liveBook all included)

We believe that once you buy a book from us, you should be
able to read it in any format we have available. To get electronic
versions of this book at no additional cost to you, purchase and
then register this book at the Manning website.

Go to https://www.manning.com/freebook and follow the
instructions to complete your pBook registration.

That's it!
Thanks from Manning!

*To all thoughtful, deliberate problem-solvers
who consider themselves scientists first
and builders second*

*For everyone everywhere
who ever taught me anything*

brief contents

v

contents

preface

In 2012, an article in the *Harvard Business Review* named the role of data scientist "the sexiest job of the 21st century." With 87 years left in the century, it's fair to say they might yet change their minds. Nevertheless, at the moment, data scientists are getting a lot of attention, and as a result, books about data science are proliferating. There would be no sense in adding another book to the pile if it merely repeated or repackaged text that is easily found elsewhere. But, while surveying new data science literature, it became clear to me that most authors would rather explain how to use all the latest tools and technologies than discuss the nuanced problem-solving nature of the data science process. Armed with several books and the latest knowledge of algorithms and data stores, many aspiring data scientists were still asking the question: *Where do I start?*

And so, here is another book on data science. This one, however, attempts to lead you through the data science process as a path with many forks and potentially unknown destinations. The book warns you of what may be ahead, tells you how to prepare for it, and suggests how to react to surprises. It discusses what tools might be the most useful, and why, but the main objective is always to navigate the path—the data science process—intelligently, efficiently, and successfully, to arrive at practical solutions to real-life data-centric problems.

acknowledgments

I would like to thank everyone at Manning who helped to make this book a reality, and Marjan Bace, Manning's publisher, for giving me this opportunity.

I'd also like to thank Mike Shepard for evaluating the technical aspects of the book, and the reviewers who contributed helpful feedback during development of the manuscript. Those reviewers include Casimir Saternos, Clemens Baader, David Krief, Gavin Whyte, Ian Stirk, Jenice Tom, Łukasz Bonenberg, Martin Perry, Nicolas Boulet-Lavoie, Pouria Amirian, Ran Volkovich, Shobha Iyer, and Valmiky Arquissandas.

Finally, I extend special thanks to my teammates, current and former, at Unoceros and Panopticon Labs for providing ample fodder for this book in many forms: experiences and knowledge in software development and data science, fruitful conversations, crazy ideas, funny stories, awkward mistakes, and most importantly, willingness to indulge my curiosity.

about this book

Data science still carries the aura of a new field. Most of its components—statistics, software development, evidence-based problem solving, and so on—descend directly from well-established, even old, fields, but data science seems to be a fresh assemblage of these pieces into something that is new, or at least *feels* new in the context of current public discourse.

Like many new fields, data science hasn't quite found its footing. The lines between it and other related fields—as far as those lines matter—are still blurry. Data science may rely on, but is not equivalent to, database architecture and administration, big data engineering, machine learning, or high-performance computing, to name a few.

The core of data science doesn't concern itself with specific database implementations or programming languages, even if these are indispensable to practitioners. The core is the interplay between data content, the goals of a given project, and the data-analytic methods used to achieve those goals. The data scientist, of course, must manage these using any software necessary, but which software and how to implement it are details that I like to imagine have been abstracted away, as if in some distant future reality.

This book attempts to foresee that future in which the most common, rote, mechanical tasks of data science are stripped away, and we are left with only the core: applying the scientific method to data sets in order to achieve a project's goals. This, the process of data science, involves software as a necessary set of tools, just as a traditional scientist might use test tubes, flasks, and a Bunsen burner. But, what matters is what's happening on the inside: what's happening to the data, what results we get, and why.

In the following pages, I introduce a wide range of software tools, but I keep my descriptions brief. More-comprehensive introductions can always be found elsewhere, and I'm more eager to delve into what those tools can do for you, and how they can aid you in your research and development. Focus always returns to the key concepts and challenges that are unique to each project in data science, and the process of organizing and harnessing available resources and information to achieve the project's goals.

To get the most out of this book, you should be reasonably comfortable with elementary statistics—a college class or two is fine—and have some basic knowledge of a programming language. If you're an expert in statistics, software development, or data science, you might find some parts of this book slow or trivial. That's OK; skip or skim sections if you must. I don't hope to replace anyone's knowledge and experience, but I do hope to supplement them by providing a conceptual framework for working through data science projects, and by sharing some of my own experiences in a constructive way.

If you're a beginner in data science, welcome to the field! I've tried to describe concepts and topics throughout the book so that they'll make sense to just about anyone with some technical aptitude. Likewise, colleagues and managers of data scientists and developers might also read this book to get a better idea of how the data science process works from an inside perspective.

For every reader, I hope this book paints a vivid picture of data science as a process with many nuances, caveats, and uncertainties. The power of data science lies not in figuring out what *should* happen next, but in realizing what *might* happen next and eventually finding out what *does* happen next. My sincere hope is that you enjoy the book and, more importantly, that you learn some things that increase your chances of success in the future.

Roadmap

The book is divided into three parts, representing the three major phases of the data science process. Part 1 covers the preparation phase:

- Chapter 1 discusses my process-oriented perspective of data science projects and introduces some themes and concepts that are present throughout the book.
- Chapter 2 covers the deliberate and important step of setting good goals for the project. Special focus is given to working with the project's customer to generate practical questions to address, and also to being pragmatic about the data's ability to address those questions.
- Chapter 3 delves into the exploration phase of a data science project, in which we try to discover helpful sources of data. I cover some helpful methods of data

discovery and data access, as well as some important things to consider when choosing which data sources to use in the project.

- Chapter 4 gives an overview of data wrangling, a process by which "raw," unkempt, or unstructured data is brought to heel, so that you can make good use of it.
- Chapter 5 discusses data assessment. After you've discovered and selected some data sources, this chapter explains how to perform preliminary examinations of the data you have, so that you're more informed while making a subsequent project plan, with realistic expectations of what the data can do.

Part 2 covers the building phase:

- Chapter 6 shows how to develop a plan for achieving a project's goals based on what you've learned from exploration and assessment. Special focus is given to planning for uncertainty in future outcomes and results.
- Chapter 7 takes a detour into the field of statistics, introducing a wide variety of important concepts, tools, and methods, focusing on their principal capabilities and how they can help achieve project goals.
- Chapter 8 does the same for statistical software; the chapter is intended to arm you with enough knowledge to make informed choices when choosing software for your project.
- Chapter 9 gives a high-level overview of some popular software tools that are not specifically statistical, but that might make building and using your product easier or more efficient.
- Chapter 10 brings chapters 7, 8, and 9 together by discussing the execution of your project plan, given the knowledge gained from the previous detours into statistics and software, while considering some hard-to-identify nuances as well as the many pitfalls of dealing with data, statistics, and software.

Part 3 covers the finishing phase:

- Chapter 11 looks at the advantages of refining and curating the form and content of the product to concisely convey to the customer the results that most effectively solve problems and achieve project goals.
- Chapter 12 discusses some of the things that can happen shortly after product delivery, including bug discovery, inefficient use of the product by the customer, and the need to refine or modify the product.
- Chapter 13 concludes with some advice on storing the project cleanly and carrying forward lessons learned in order to improve your chances of success in future projects.

Exercises are included near the end of every chapter except chapter 1. Answers and example responses to these exercises appear in the last section of the book, before the index.

Author Online

Purchase of *Think Like a Data Scientist* includes free access to a private web forum run by Manning Publications where you can make comments about the book, ask technical questions, and receive help from the author and from other users. To access the forum and subscribe to it, point your web browser to www.manning.com/books/think-like-a-data-scientist. This page provides information on how to get on the forum once you're registered, what kind of help is available, and the rules of conduct on the forum.

Manning's commitment to our readers is to provide a venue where a meaningful dialog between individual readers and between readers and the author can take place. It is not a commitment to any specific amount of participation on the part of the author, whose contributions to the AO forum remain voluntary (and unpaid). We suggest you ask the author challenging questions, lest his interest stray!

About the author

Brian Godsey, PhD, worked for nearly a decade in academic and government roles, applying mathematics and statistics to fields such as bioinformatics, finance, and national defense, before changing focus to data-centric startups. He led the data science team at a local Baltimore startup—seeing it grow from seed to series A funding rounds and seeing the product evolve from prototype to production versions—before helping launch two startups, Unoceros and Panopticon Labs, and their data-centric products.

about the cover illustration

The figure on the cover of *Think Like a Data Scientist* is captioned "A soldier of the Strelitz guards under arms," or *Soldat du corps des Strelits sous les armés*. The Strelitz guards were part of the Muscovite army in Czarist Russia through the eighteenth century. The illustration is taken from Thomas Jefferys' *A Collection of the Dresses of Different Nations, Ancient and Modern*, published in London between 1757 and 1772. The title page states that these are hand-colored copperplate engravings, heightened with gum arabic. Thomas Jefferys (1719–1771) was called "Geographer to King George III." He was an English cartographer who was the leading map supplier of his day. He engraved and printed maps for government and other official bodies and produced a wide range of commercial maps and atlases, especially of North America. His work as a mapmaker sparked an interest in local dress customs of the lands he surveyed and mapped; they are brilliantly displayed in this four-volume collection.

Fascination with faraway lands and travel for pleasure were relatively new phenomena in the eighteenth century, and collections such as this one were popular, introducing both the tourist and the armchair traveler to the inhabitants of other countries. The diversity of the drawings in Jefferys' volumes speaks vividly of the uniqueness and individuality of the world's nations centuries ago. Dress codes have changed, and the diversity by region and country, so rich at one time, has faded away. It is now often hard to tell the inhabitant of one continent from another. Perhaps, trying to view it optimistically, we have traded a cultural and visual diversity for a more varied personal life—or a more varied and interesting intellectual and technical life.

At a time when it is hard to tell one computer book from another, Manning celebrates the inventiveness and initiative of the computer business with book covers based on the rich diversity of national costumes from centuries ago, brought back to life by Jefferys' pictures.

Part 1

Preparing and gathering data and knowledge

The process of data science begins with preparation. You need to establish what you know, what you have, what you can get, where you are, and where you would like to be. This last one is of utmost importance; a project in data science needs to have a purpose and corresponding goals. Only when you have well-defined goals can you begin to survey the available resources and all the possibilities for moving toward those goals.

Part 1 of this book begins with a chapter discussing my process-oriented perspective of data science projects. After that, we move along to the deliberate and important step of setting good goals for the project. The subsequent three chapters cover the three most important data-centric steps of the process: exploration, wrangling, and assessment. At the end of this part, you'll be intimately familiar with the data you have and relevant data you can get. More important, you'll know if and how it can help you achieve the goals of the project.

Philosophies of data science

1

This chapter covers

- The role of a data scientist and how it's different from that of a software developer
- The greatest asset of a data scientist, awareness, particularly in the presence of significant uncertainties
- Prerequisites for reading this book: basic knowledge of software development and statistics
- Setting priorities for a project while keeping the big picture in mind
- Best practices: tips that can make life easier during a project

In the following pages, I introduce data science as a set of processes and concepts that act as a guide for making progress and decisions within a data-centric project. This contrasts with the view of data science as a set of statistical and software tools and the knowledge to use them, which in my experience is the far more popular perspective taken in conversations and texts on data science (see figure 1.1 for a humorous take on perspectives of data science). I don't mean to say that these two perspectives contradict each other; they're complementary. But to neglect one in favor of the other would be foolish, and so in this book I address the less-discussed side: process, both in practice and in thought.

Figure 1.1   Some stereotypical perspectives on data science

To compare with carpentry, knowing how to use hammers, drills, and saws isn't the same as knowing how to build a chair. Likewise, if you know the process of building a chair, that doesn't mean you're any good with the hammers, drills, and saws that might be used in the process. To build a good chair, you have to know how to use the tools as well as what, specifically, to do with them, step by step. Throughout this book, I try to discuss tools enough to establish an understanding of how they work, but I focus far more on when they should be used and how and why. I perpetually ask and answer the question: what should be done next?

In this chapter, using relatively high-level descriptions and examples, I discuss how the thought processes of a data scientist can be more important than the specific tools used and how certain concepts pervade nearly all aspects of work in data science.

1.1 Data science and this book

The origins of data science as a field of study or vocational pursuit lie somewhere between statistics and software development. Statistics can be thought of as the schematic drawing and software as the machine. Data flows through both, either conceptually or actually, and perhaps it was only in recent years that practitioners began to give data top billing, though data science owes much to any number of older fields that combine statistics and software, such as operations research, analytics, and decision science.

In addition to statistics and software, many folks say that data science has a third major component, which is something along the lines of subject matter expertise or domain knowledge. Although it certainly is important to understand a problem before you try to solve it, a good data scientist can switch domains and begin contributing relatively soon. Just as a good accountant can quickly learn the financial nuances of a new industry, and a good engineer can pick up the specifics of designing various types of products, a good data scientist can switch to a completely new domain and begin to contribute within a short time. That is not to say that domain knowledge has little value, but compared to software development and statistics, domain-specific knowledge usually takes the least time to learn well enough to help solve problems involving data. It's also the one interchangeable component of the three. If you can do data science, you can walk into a planning meeting for a brand-new data-centric project, and almost everyone else in the room will have the domain knowledge you need, whereas almost no one else will have the skills to write good analytic software that works.

Throughout this book—perhaps you've noticed already—I choose to use the term *data-centric* instead of the more popular *data-driven* when describing software, projects, and problems, because I find the idea of data *driving* any of these to be a misleading concept. Data should drive software only when that software is being built expressly for moving, storing, or otherwise handing the data. Software that's intended to address project or business goals should not be driven by data. That would be putting the cart before the horse. Problems and goals exist independently of any data, software, or other resources, but those resources may serve to solve the problems and to achieve the goals. The term *data-centric* reflects that data is an integral part of the solution, and I believe that using it instead of *data-driven* admits that we need to view the problems not from the perspective of the data but from the perspective of the goals and problems that data can help us address.

Such statements about proper perspective are common in this book. In every chapter I try to maintain the reader's focus on the most important things, and in times of uncertainty about project outcomes, I try to give guidelines that help you decide which are the most important things. In some ways, I think that locating and maintaining focus on the most important aspects of a project is one of the most valuable skills that I attempt to instruct within these pages. Data scientists must have many hard skills—knowledge of software development and statistics among them—but I've found this soft skill of maintaining appropriate perspective and awareness of the many moving parts in any data-centric problem to be very difficult yet very rewarding for most data scientists I know.

Sometimes data quality becomes an important issue; sometimes the major issue is data volume, processing speed, parameters of an algorithm, interpretability of results, or any of the many other aspects of the problem. Ignoring any of these at the moment it becomes important can compromise or entirely invalidate subsequent results. As a data scientist, I have as my goal to make sure that no important aspect of a project goes awry unnoticed. When something goes wrong—and something will—I want to notice it so that I can fix it. Throughout this chapter and the entire book, I will continue to stress the importance of maintaining awareness of all aspects of a project, particularly those in which there is uncertainty about potential outcomes.

The lifecycle of a data science project can be divided into three phases, as illustrated in figure 1.2. This book is organized around these phases. The first part covers preparation, emphasizing that a bit of time and effort spent gathering information at the beginning of the project can spare you from big headaches later. The second part covers building a product for the customer, from planning to execution, using what you've learned from the first section as well as all of the tools that statistics and software can provide. The third and final part covers finishing a project: delivering the product, getting feedback, making revisions, supporting the product, and wrapping up a project neatly. While discussing each phase, this book includes some self-reflection,

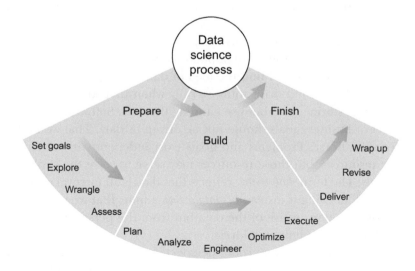

Figure 1.2   The data science process

in that it regularly asks you, the reader, to reconsider what you've done in previous steps, with the possibility of redoing them in some other way if it seems like a good idea. By the end of the book, you'll hopefully have a firm grasp of these thought processes and considerations when making decisions as a data scientist who wants to use data to get valuable results.

1.2 Awareness is valuable

If I had a dollar for every time a software developer told me that an analytic software tool "doesn't work," I'd be a wealthy man. That's not to say that I think all analytic software tools work well or at all—that most certainly is not the case—but I think it motivates a discussion of one of the most pervasive discrepancies between the perspective of a data scientist and that of what I would call a "pure" software developer—one who doesn't normally interact with raw or "unwrangled" data.

A good example of this discrepancy occurred when a budding startup founder approached me with a problem he was having. The task was to extract names, places, dates, and other key information from emails related to upcoming travel so that this data could be used in a mobile application that would keep track of the user's travel plans. The problem the founder was having is a common one: emails and other documents come in all shapes and sizes, and parsing them for useful information is a challenge. It's difficult to extract this specific travel-related data when emails from different airlines, hotels, booking websites, and so on have different formats, not to mention that these formats change quite frequently. Google and others seem to have good tools for extracting such data within their own apps, but these tools generally aren't made available to external developers.

Both the founder and I were aware that there are, as usual, two main strategies for addressing this challenge: manual brute force and scripting. We could also use some mixture of the two. Given that brute force would entail creating a template for each email format as well as a new template every time the format changed, neither of us wanted to follow that path. A script that could parse any email and extract the relevant information sounded great, but it also sounded extremely complex and almost impossible to write. A compromise between the two extreme approaches seemed best, as it usually does.

While speaking with both the founder and the lead software developer, I suggested that they forge a compromise between brute force and pure scripting: develop some simple templates for the most common formats, check for similarities and common structural patterns, and then write a simple script that could match chunks of familiar template HTML or text within new emails and extract data from known positions within those chunks. I called this *algorithmic templating* at the time, for better or for worse. This suggestion obviously wouldn't solve the problem entirely, but it would make some progress in the right direction, and, more importantly, it would give some insight into the common structural patterns within the most common formats and highlight specific challenges that were yet unknown but possibly easy to solve.

The software developer mentioned that he had begun building a solution using a popular tool for natural language processing (NLP) that could recognize and extract dates, names, and places. He then said that he still thought the NLP tool would solve the problem and that he would let me know after he had implemented it fully. I told him that natural language is notoriously tricky to parse and analyze and that I had less confidence in NLP tools than he did but I hoped he was right.

A couple of weeks later, I spoke again with the founder and the software developer, was told that the NLP tool didn't work, and was asked again for help. The NLP tool could recognize most dates and locations, but, to paraphrase one issue, "Most of the time, in emails concerning flight reservations, the booking date appears first in the email, then the departure date, the arrival date, and then possibly the dates for the return flight. But in some HTML email formats, the booking date appears between the departure and arrival dates. What should we do then?"

That the NLP tool doesn't work to solve 100% of the problem is clear. But it did solve some intermediate problems, such as recognizing names and dates, even if it couldn't place them precisely within the travel plan itself. I don't want to stretch the developer's words or take them out of context; this is a tough problem for data scientists and a *very* tough problem for others. Failing to solve the problem on the first try is hardly a total failure. But this part of the project was stalled for a few weeks while the three of us tried to find an experienced data scientist with enough time to try to help overcome this specific problem. Such a delay is costly to a startup—or any company for that matter.

The lesson I've learned through experiences like these is that awareness is incredibly valuable when working on problems involving data. A good developer using good tools to address what seems like a very tractable problem can run into trouble if they haven't considered the many possibilities that can happen when code begins to process data.

Uncertainty is an adversary of coldly logical algorithms, and being aware of how those algorithms might break down in unusual circumstances expedites the process of fixing problems when they occur—and they will occur. A data scientist's main responsibility is to try to imagine all of the possibilities, address the ones that matter, and reevaluate them all as successes and failures happen. That is why—no matter how much code I write—awareness and familiarity with uncertainty are the most valuable things I can offer as a data scientist. Some people might tell you not to daydream at work, but an imagination can be a data scientist's best friend if you can use it to prepare yourself for the certainty that something will go wrong.

1.3   *Developer vs. data scientist*

A good software developer (or engineer) and a good data scientist have several traits in common. Both are good at designing and building complex systems with many interconnected parts; both are familiar with many different tools and frameworks for building these systems; both are adept at foreseeing potential problems in those systems before they're actualized. But in general, software developers design systems consisting of many well-defined components, whereas data scientists work with systems wherein at least one of the components isn't well defined prior to being built, and that component is usually closely involved with data processing or analysis.

The systems of software developers and those of data scientists can be compared with the mathematical concepts of logic and probability, respectively. The logical statement "if A, then B" can be coded easily in any programming language, and in some sense every computer program consists of a very large number of such statements within various contexts. The probabilistic statement "if A, then *probably* B" isn't nearly as straightforward. Any good data-centric application contains many such statements— consider the Google search engine ("These are *probably* the most relevant pages"), product recommendations on Amazon.com ("We *think* you'll *probably* like these things"), website analytics ("Your site visitors are *probably* from North America and each views *about* three pages").

Data scientists specialize in creating systems that rely on probabilistic statements about data and results. In the previous case of a system that finds travel information within an email, we can make a statement such as "If we know the email contains a departure date, the NLP tool can *probably* extract it." For a good NLP tool, with a little fiddling, this statement is likely true. But if we become overconfident and reformulate the statement without the word *probably*, this new statement is much less likely to be true. It might be true some of the time, but it certainly won't be true all of the time. This confusion of probability for certainty is precisely the challenge that most software developers must overcome when they begin a project in data science.

When, as a software developer, you come from a world of software specifications, well-documented or open-source code libraries, and product features that either work or they don't ("Report a bug!"), the concept of uncertainty in software may seem foreign. Software can be compared to a car: loosely speaking, if you have all of the right pieces, and you put them together in the right way, the car works, and it will take you where you want it to go if you operate it according to the manual. If the car isn't working correctly, then quite literally something is broken and can be fixed. This, to me, is directly analogous to pure software development. Building a self-driving car to race autonomously across a desert, on the other hand, is more like data science. I don't mean to say that data science is as outrageously cool as an autonomous desert-racing vehicle but that you're never sure your car is even going to make it to the finish line or if the task is even possible. So many unknown and random variables are in play that there's absolutely no guarantee where the car will end up, and there's not even a guarantee that *any* car will ever finish a race—until a car does it.

If a self-driving car makes it 90% of the way to the finish line but is washed into a ditch by a rainstorm, it would hardly be appropriate to say that the autonomous car doesn't work. Likewise if the car didn't technically cross the finish line but veered around it and continued for another 100 miles. Furthermore, it wouldn't be appropriate to enter a self-driving sedan, built for roads, into a desert race and to subsequently proclaim that the car doesn't work when it gets stuck on a sand dune. That's precisely how I feel when someone applies a purpose-built data-centric tool to a different purpose; they get bad results, and they proclaim that it doesn't work.

For a more concrete example, suppose you've been told by a website owner, "The typical user visits four pages of our site before leaving." Suppose you do an analysis of a new data set of site usage and find that the average user is visiting eight pages before leaving. Does that mean there's an error? Are you using the mean user when you should be using the median user? Does this new data include a different type of user or usage? These are questions that a data scientist, not a software developer, typically answers, because they involve data exploration and uncertainty. Implementing a software solution based on these questions and their answers can certainly benefit from the expertise of a software developer, but the exploration itself—necessarily involving statistics—falls squarely within the realm of a data scientist. In chapter 5, we'll look at data assessment and evaluation as a useful tool for preventing and diagnosing problems and for helping avoid the case where a seemingly finished software product fails in some way.

It's worth noting that, though I've seemed to pit data scientists and software developers against each other, this conflict (if I can call it that) can also be internal to a single person. While working on data science projects, I often find myself trading my data scientist hat for that of a software developer, particularly when writing production code. The reason I conceive of them as two different hats is that there can be conflicts of interest at times, because priorities can differ between the two. Openly discussing these conflicts, as I do in this book, can be helpful in illustrating the resolution of these differences, whether they occur between two or more people or within an individual who may wear either hat.

1.4   *Do I need to be a software developer?*

Earlier, I discussed the difference between data scientists and software developers, often as if those are the only two options. Certainly, they are not. And you don't need to be either in order to gain something from this book.

Knowledge of a statistical software tool is a prerequisite for doing practical data science, but this can be as simple as a common spreadsheet program (for example, the divisive but near-ubiquitous Microsoft Excel). In theory, someone could be a data scientist without ever touching a computer or other device. Understanding the problem, the data, and relevant statistical methods could be enough, as long as someone else can follow your intentions and write the code. In practice, this doesn't happen often.

Alternatively, you may be someone who often works with data scientists, and you'd like to understand the process without necessarily understanding the technology. In this case, there's also something in this book for you. One of my primary goals is to enumerate the many considerations that must be taken into account when solving a data-centric problem. In many cases, I'll be directing explanations in this book toward some semi-fictionalized colleagues from my past and present: biologists, finance executives, product owners, managers, or others who may have given me data and asked me a single question: "Can you analyze this for me?" For that last case, perhaps if I write it down here, in detail and with plenty of examples, I won't have to repeat (yet again) that it's never that simple. An analysis demands a question, and I'll discuss both of those in depth on these pages.

This book is about the process of thinking about and doing data science, but clearly software can't be ignored. Software—as an industry and its products—is the data scientist's toolbox. The tools of the craft are the enablers of work that's beyond the capabilities of the human mind and body alone. But in this book, I'll cover software only as much as is necessary to explore existing strengths and limitations of the software tools and to provide concrete examples of their use for clarification. Otherwise, I'll try to write abstractly about software—without being impractical—so that the explanations are accessible by as many people as possible, technical or not, and years from now, the explanations may still be valuable, even after we've moved on to newer (and better?) software languages and products.

1.5 Do I need to know statistics?

As with software, expert knowledge of statistics certainly helps but isn't necessary. At my core, I'm a mathematician and statistician, and so I'm most likely to veer into an overly technical tangent in these fields. But I despise jargon and presumed knowledge more than most, and so I'll try hard to include accessible conceptual explanations of statistical concepts; hopefully, these are sufficient to any reader with a little imagination and perseverance. Where I fall short, I'll try to direct you to some resources with more thorough explanations. As always, I'm an advocate of using web searches to find more information on topics that interest you, but at least in some cases, it may be better to bear with me for a few pages before heading down a rabbit hole of web pages about statistics.

In the meantime, to get you started conceptually, consider the field of statistics as the theoretical embodiment of the processes that generate the data you encounter on a daily basis. An anonymous website user is a random variable who might click any number of things depending on what's going on in their head. Social media data reflects the thoughts and concerns of the populace. Purchases of consumer goods depend on both the needs of the consumers as well as marketing campaigns for the goods. In each of these cases, you must theorize about how intangible thoughts, needs, and reactions are eventually translated into measurable actions that create data. Statistics provides a framework for this theorizing. This book will spend less time on complex theoretical justifications for statistical models and more on formulating mental models of data-generating processes and translating those mental models into statistical terminology, equations, and, ultimately, code.

1.6   *Priorities: knowledge first, technology second, opinions third*

This section title is an adage of mine. I use it to help settle disputes in the never-ending battle between the various concerns of every data science project—for example, software versus statistics, changing business need versus project timeline, data quality versus accuracy of results. Each individual concern pushes and pulls on the others as a project progresses, and we're forced to make choices whenever two of them disagree on a course of action. I've developed a simple framework to help with that.

Knowledge, technology, and opinions are typically what you have at the beginning of any project; they are the three things that turn data into answers. *Knowledge* is what you know for a fact. *Technology* is the set of tools you have at your disposal. *Opinions* are those little almost facts you want to consider true but shouldn't quite yet. It's important to establish a hierarchy for your thought processes so that less-important things don't steamroll more-important ones because they're easier or more popular or because someone has a hunch.

In practice, the hierarchy looks like this:

- *Knowledge first*—Get to know your problem, your data, your approach, and your goal before you do anything else, and keep those at the forefront of your mind.
- *Technology second*—Software is a tool that serves you. It both enables and constrains you. It shouldn't dictate your approach to the problem except in extenuating circumstances.
- *Opinions third*—Opinions, intuition, and wishful thinking are to be used only as guides toward theories that can be proven correct and not as the focus of any project.

I'm not advocating that knowledge should always take precedence over technology in every decision—and likewise for technology over opinion—but if the hierarchy is to be turned upside down, you should be doing it deliberately and for a very good reason. For instance, suppose you have a large amount of data and a statistical model for which you would like to estimate parameters. Furthermore, you already have a tool for loading that data into a system that performs a type of statistical parameter optimization called *maximum likelihood estimation* (MLE). You know that your data and statistical model are complex enough, possibly, to generate many reasonable parameter values, and so using MLE to find a single most likely parameter value might give unpredictable results. There exist more robust alternatives, but you don't currently have one implemented. You have two options:

A. Build a new tool that can do robust parameter estimation.
B. Use the tool you have to do MLE.

Your knowledge says you should do A, if you had unlimited time and resources, but the technology indicates that you should do B because A requires a tremendous outlay of resources. The pragmatic decision is probably B, but that inverts the hierarchy.

As mentioned earlier, you can do this but only deliberately and for a very good reason. The good reason might be the difference in time and money that you'll need to spend on A and B. By *deliberately*, I mean that you should not make the decision lightly and you should not forget it. If you choose B, you should pass along with any results the knowledge that you made a sacrifice in quality in the interest of a cost savings, and you should make note of this in documentation and technical reports. You should appropriately intensify quality control and perform tests that check specifically for the types of optimization errors/biases to which MLE is prone. Making the decision and then forgetting the reasoning is a path to underwhelming or misleading results.

Opinion presents an even fuzzier challenge. Sometimes people are blinded by the potential of finding truly amazing results and forget to consider what might happen if those results aren't evident in the data. In the heyday of big data, any number of software startups attempted to exploit social media—particularly Twitter and its "firehose"—to determine trends within various business markets, and they often ran into obstacles much larger than they expected. Scale of computation and data, parsing of natural language in only 140 characters, and inferring random variables on messy data are often involved. Only the very best of these firms were able to extract meaningful, significant knowledge from that data and earn a profit with it. The rest were forced to give it up or change their focus. Each of these startups, at some point, had to decide whether they wanted to spend even more time and money chasing a goal that was based mainly on hope and not on evidence. I'm sure many of them regretted how far they'd gone and how much money they'd spent when they did decide to pack it in.

Often people are blinded by what they think is possible, and they forget to consider that it might not be possible or that it might be much more expensive than estimated. These are opinions—guesses—not knowledge, and they shouldn't play a primary role in data analysis and product development. Goals are not certain to be achieved but are required for any project, so it's imperative not to take the goal and its attainability for granted. You should always consider current knowledge first and seek to expand that knowledge incrementally until you either achieve the goal or are forced to abandon it. I've mentioned this uncertainty of attainability as a particularly stark difference between the philosophies of software development and data science. In data science, a goal is much less likely to be achievable in exactly its original form. In a room full of software developers or inexperienced data scientists, be particularly wary of anyone presupposing without evidence that a goal is 100% achievable.

Remember: knowledge first, then technology, and then opinion. It's not a perfect framework, but I've found it helpful.

1.7   Best practices

In my years of analyzing data and writing code as an applied mathematician, PhD student researcher, bioinformatics software engineer, data scientist, or any of the other titles I've had, I've run into a few problems involving poor project management on my part. When I worked for years on my own research projects, which no one else touched or looked at, I frequently managed to set poorly documented code aside for long enough that I forgot how it worked. I'd also forgotten which version of the results was the most recent. I'd managed to make it nearly impossible for anyone else to take up my projects after I left that position. None of this was intentional; it was largely negligence but also ignorance of the usual ways in which people ensure that their project's materials and code can survive a long while on the shelf or in another's hands.

When working on a team—in particular, a team of experienced software developers—someone has usually established a set of best practices for documentation and preservation of project materials and code. It's usually important that everyone on the team abides by the team's strategies for these things, but in the absence of a team strategy, or if you're working by yourself, you can do a few things to make your life as a data scientist easier in the long run. The following subsections cover a few of my favorite ways to stay organized.

1.7.1 Documentation

Can you imagine what one of your peers might have to go through to take over your project if you left suddenly? Would taking over your project be a horrible experience? If you answer yes, please do these future peers—and yourself—a favor by staying current on your documentation. Here are some tips:

- Comment your code so that a peer unfamiliar with your work can understand what the code does.
- For a finished piece of software—even a simple script—write a short description of how to use it and put this in the same place (for example, the same file folder) as the code.
- Make sure everything—files, folders, documents, and so on—has a meaningful name.

1.7.2 Code repositories and versioning

Some software products have been built specifically to contain and manage source code for software. These are called *source code repositories* (or *repos*), and they can help you immensely, for a number of reasons.

First, most modern repos are based on versioning systems, which are also great. A versioning system tracks the changes you make in your code, allows you to create and compare different versions of your code, and generally makes the process of writing and modifying code much more pleasant once you get used to it. The drawback of repos and versioning is that they take time to learn and incorporate into your normal workflow. They're both worth the time, however. At the time of this writing, both Bitbucket.org and GitHub.com provide free web hosting of code repos, although both websites host both public and private repos, so make sure you don't accidentally make all of your source code public. Git is currently the most popular versioning system, and it incorporates nicely into both repo hosts mentioned. You can find tutorials on how to get started on the hosts' web pages.

Another reason why I find a remote repo-hosting service nearly indispensable is that it functions as a backup. My code will be safe even if my computer is accidentally crushed by an autonomous desert-race vehicle (though that hasn't happened to me yet). I make it a habit to *push* (send or upload) my latest code changes to the remote host almost every day, or about as often as I might schedule an automatic backup on a standard data-backup service.

Some code-hosting services have great web interfaces for looking through code history, various versions, development status, and the like, which has become standard practice for collaborating on teams and large projects. It's helpful for individuals and small projects as well, particularly when returning to an old project or trying to figure out which changes you made since a particular time in the past.

Finally, remote repos let you access your code from any place with web access. You don't need a computer with the appropriate editor and environment to browse through code. No, you normally can't do much except browse code (and maybe do simple editing) from these web interfaces, but the best ones have good language-specific code highlighting and a few other features that make browsing easy and useful.

Here are some tips on repos and versioning:

- Using a remote source code repo is now standard practice for most groups that write code; use one!
- It's absolutely worth the effort to learn Git or another versioning system; learn it!
- Commit your code changes to the repo often, perhaps daily or whenever you finish a specific task. Push those changes to a remote repo, so they're backed up and shared with others on your team.
- If your next code changes will break something, do the work in a location that won't affect the production version or the development by other team members. For example, you could create a new branch in Git.
- Use versioning, branching, and forking (tutorials abound on the internet) instead of copying and pasting code from one place to another and therefore having to maintain/modify the same code in multiple places.
- Most software teams have a Git guru. Ask them whenever you have questions about best practices; the time spent learning now will pay off in the end.

1.7.3   Code organization

Many books detail good coding practices, and I don't intend to replicate or replace them here. But a few guidelines can be very helpful, particularly when you try to share or reuse code. Most people who have been programming for some time will be familiar with these, but I've found that many people—particularly in academia and other work environments without much coding collaboration—don't always know about them or adhere to them.

Here are the guidelines:

- Try to use coding patterns that are common for the particular programming language. Python, R, and Java, for instance, all have significant differences in the way developers typically organize their code. Any popular resource for the language contains examples and guidelines for such coding patterns.
- Use meaningful names for variables and other objects. This makes your code much more understandable for new collaborators and your future self.
- Use plenty of informative comments, for the reasons just mentioned.
- Don't copy and paste code. Having the same code active in two places means twice as much work for you when you want to change it. Encapsulating that code in a function, method, object, or library makes sure that later modifications happen in only one place.
- Try to code in chunks with specific functionalities. For scripts, this means having well-commented snippets (optionally in separate files or libraries) that each accomplish a specific task. For applications, this means having relatively simple functions, objects, and methods so that each does specific things. A good general rule is if you can't name your snippet, function, or method in such a way that the name generally describes everything the chunk of code accomplishes, you should probably break the chunk into smaller, simpler chunks.
- Don't optimize prematurely. This is a common mantra for programmers everywhere. Make sure you code your algorithm in a logical, coherent fashion, and only if you find out later that your implementation is inefficient should you try to shave off compute cycles and bytes of memory.
- Pretend that someone else will, at some point, join your project. Ask yourself, "Could they read my code and figure out what it does?" If not, spend a little time organizing and commenting sooner rather than later.

1.7.4 *Ask questions*

This may sound obvious or trivial, but it's so important that I include it here. I've already discussed how awareness is one of the greatest strengths of a good data scientist; likewise, the unwillingness to gain awareness via any and all means can be a great weakness. The stereotype of an introverted academic being too shy to ask for help may be familiar to you, but have you heard of the know-it-all PhD data scientist who was too proud to admit he didn't know something? I certainly have. Pride is perhaps a bigger pitfall to data scientists these days than shyness, but you should be wary of both.

Software engineers, business strategists, sales executives, marketers, researchers, and other data scientists all know more than you do about their particular domains or projects, and it would be a shame to ignore the wealth of knowledge they possess, due to shyness, pride, or any other reason. A business setting wherein nearly everyone else has a role different from yours provides ample opportunity to learn about the company and the industry. This is the subject matter expertise, or domain knowledge, that I've mentioned already. Nontechnical business folks, in my experience, have a tendency to treat you, the data scientist, as the smart one in the conversation, but don't forget that they tend to know a lot more than you about project goals and business problems, two extremely important concepts. Never hesitate to have a lengthy discussion with someone who knows the business side of the project and problems you're working on. I often find that such conversations illuminate projects in new ways, sometimes causing strategy changes but always contributing to the domain knowledge that's necessary for me to finish a project successfully.

1.7.5 *Stay close to the data*

Being "close to the data" means making sure that the methods and algorithms that you're applying to the data aren't so dense as to obscure it. Another way to phrase this would be "don't use methods that are more complex than needed, and always be conscious of the possibility of mistakes."

Many people will argue with this piece of advice, and I agree with these detractors that many complex methods have proven their worth. The field of machine learning is a perfect example of a source of such methods. In the cases where complex methods (*black box* methods, in some cases) give considerable advantage, the concept of being close to the data can be adapted: make sure that some results from complex methods can be verified, justified, or supported by simpler methods that are close to the data. This could include a glorified form of spot-checking, whereby you can pick some results at random, extract the raw data that's relevant to these results, and use logic and/or simple statistics to make sure that the results make sense intuitively. Straying too far from the data without a safety line can get you in trouble, because these problems are the hardest to diagnose. Throughout the book, and in each example, I'll return to this concept and give more specifics.

1.8 *Reading this book: how I discuss concepts*

It has been my experience—over and over—that complex concepts appear vastly more complex at the point when you begin to learn about them, as compared to later, after you've begun to understand them. This is not only because all concepts seem less complex once you begin to understand them, but also because people, in general, who might be explaining a concept to you or who are writing about it revel in the complexities that they understand and often have little patience or sympathy for those who don't understand. For example, it's difficult for most statistics professors to explain a simple statistical test to a layperson. This inability to explain in simple terms extends across all fields and industries, I've found. Part of this problem is that most people love to use jargon, and they love to prove their knowledge of it. This is, perhaps, a fault of human nature. But from this I've learned to ignore my frustrations at the beginning of learning a new, complex concept and not to get hung up on any specific point until I've gone through the concept as a whole.

Throughout this book, I try to explain new concepts in simple terms before getting into specifics. This is the way I prefer to learn and the way I prefer to explain. Despite this, you'll still have moments when you get stuck. I implore you suspend your frustration, stick with it to the end of the chapter, and then review the concept as a whole. At that point, if something still doesn't make sense, perhaps rereading the paragraphs in question can help, and if not, feel free to consult other resources. I employ conceptual thought processes, and I intend to focus on the whole before the parts. Knowing this in advance may help you while reading.

Before diving into the practical steps of the data science process in the next chapter and beyond, I'd like to note that this book is intended to be accessible for non-experts in data science, software, and statistics. If you're not a beginner, you may occasionally find some sections that cover material you already know. I'd like to think that every section of this book provides a useful or even fresh perspective on its topic, even for experts, but if you're pressed for time, feel free to skip ahead to something of more use to you. On the other hand, I'd like to discourage skipping whole chapters of this book when reading it for the first time. Each chapter describes a step in the data science process, and skipping one of them could break the continuity of the process and how it's presented. Rather than skipping, it would be better to read at least the beginning and the end of the chapter and to skim section by section in order to gain important context for subsequent chapters.

As a final disclaimer, throughout the book I pull many practical examples from my own experience. Several of my early, formative data science projects were in the field of bioinformatics, and so sometimes I delve into discussions of genetics, RNA, and other biological concepts. This may seem heavy to some people, and that's OK. It's not necessary to understand the biology as long as you're able to understand the data-oriented aspects such as project goals, data sources, and statistical analysis. This is also true for examples from other fields, but I rely particularly heavily on bioinformatics because I can still remember well what it was like to encounter various challenges of data science at that early phase of my career. Furthermore, I won't shy away from using highly specified examples because it's always good practice for a data scientist to learn the basics of a new field and attempt to apply experience and knowledge to problems therein. I do, however, try to present all examples in a way that anyone can understand.

Summary

- Awareness is perhaps the biggest strength of a good data scientist, particularly in the face of uncertainty.
- Dealing with uncertainty is often what separates the role of a data scientist from that of a software developer.
- Setting priorities and balancing them with limitations and requirements can be done using a helpful framework that I've outlined.
- Using some of the best practices that I suggest can spare you from headaches later.
- I'm a conceptual learner and teacher who loves talking about things abstractly before delving into practical examples, so please keep that in mind throughout the book.

Setting goals
by asking good questions

This chapter covers

- Putting yourself in the customer's shoes
- Asking specific, useful questions of the data
- Understanding the strengths and limitations of the data in answering those questions
- Connecting those questions and answers to project goals
- Planning backward from the desired goal, not forward from data and software tools

Figure 2.1 shows where we are in the data science process: setting goals, which is the first step of the preparation phase. In a data science project, as in many other fields, the main goals should be set at the beginning of the project. All the work you do after setting goals is making use of data, statistics, and programming to move toward and achieve those goals. This chapter emphasizes how important this initial phase is and gives some guidance on how to develop and state goals in a useful way.

19

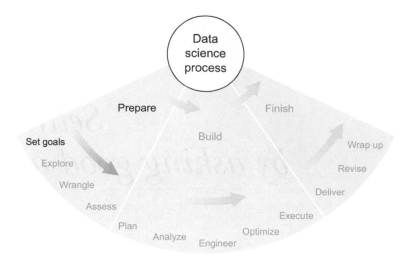

Figure 2.1   **The first step of the preparation phase of the data science process: setting goals**

2.1   *Listening to the customer*

Every project in data science has a customer. Sometimes the customer is someone who pays you or your business to do the project—for example, a client or contracting agency. In academia, the customer might be a laboratory scientist who has asked you to analyze their data. Sometimes the customer is you, your boss, or another colleague. No matter who the customer might be, they have some expectations about what they might receive from you, the data scientist who has been given the project. Often, these expectations relate to the following:

- Questions that need to be answered or problems that need to be solved
- A tangible final product, such as a report or software application
- Summaries of prior research or related projects and products

Expectations can come from almost anywhere. Some are hopes and dreams, and others are drawn from experience or knowledge of similar projects. But a typical discussion of expectations boils down to two sides: what the customer wants versus what the data scientist thinks is possible. This could be described as wishes versus pragmatism, with the customer describing their desires and the data scientist approving, rejecting, or qualifying each one based on apparent feasibility. On the other hand, if you'd like to think of yourself, the data scientist, as a genie, a granter of wishes, you wouldn't be the only one to do so!

2.1.1   *Resolving wishes and pragmatism*

With regard to the customer's wishes, they can range from completely reasonable to utterly outlandish, and this is OK. Much of business development and hard science is driven by intuition. CEOs, biologists, marketers, and physicists alike use their experience and knowledge to develop theories about how the world works. Some of these theories are backed by solid data and analysis, but others come more from intuition, which is a conceptual framework that the person has developed while working extensively in their field. A notable difference between many fields and data science is that in data science, if a customer has a wish, even an experienced data scientist may not know whether it's possible. Whereas a software engineer usually knows what tasks software tools are capable of performing, and a biologist knows more or less what the laboratory can do, a data scientist who has not yet seen or worked with the relevant data is faced with a large amount of uncertainty, principally about what specific data is available and about how much evidence it can provide to answer any given question. Uncertainty is, again, a major factor in the data scientific process and should be kept at the forefront of your mind when talking with customers about their wishes.

For example, during the few years that I worked with biologists and gene expression data, I began to develop my own conceptual ideas about how RNA is transcribed from DNA and how strands of RNA float around in a cell and interact with other molecules. I'm a visual person, so I often found myself picturing a strand of RNA comprising hundreds or maybe thousands of nucleotides, each one appearing like one of four letters representing a base compound (A, C, G, or T; I'll use *T* in place of *U* for convenience) and the whole strand looking like a long, flexible chain, a sentence that makes sense only to the machinery within the cell. Because of the chemistry of RNA and its nucleotides, complementary sequences like to bind to one another; A likes to bind to T, and C likes to bind to G. When two strands of RNA contain near-complementary sequences, they may very well stick to each other. A single strand of RNA might also fold in upon and stick to itself if it's flexible enough and contains mutually complementary sequences. I've used this conceptual framework on many occasions to make guesses about the types of things that can happen when a bunch of RNA is floating around in a cell.

When I began to work with microRNA data, it made sense to me that microRNA—short sequences of about 20 nucleotides—might bind to a section of a genetic mRNA sequence (RNA transcribed directly from a strand of DNA corresponding to a specific gene, which is typically much longer) and inhibit other molecules from interacting with the gene's mRNA, effectively rendering that gene sequence useless. It makes conceptual sense to me that one bit of RNA can stick to a section of genetic RNA and end up blocking another molecule from sticking to the same section. This concept is supported by scientific journal articles and hard data showing that microRNA can inhibit expression or function of genetic mRNA if they have complementary sequences.

A professor of biology I was working with had a much more nuanced conceptual framework describing how he saw this system of genes, microRNA, and mRNA. In particular, he had been working with the biology of *Mus musculus*—a common mouse—for decades and could list any number of notable genes, their functions, related genes, and physical systems, and characteristics that are measurably affected if one begins to do experiments that knock out those genes. Because the professor knew more than I will ever know about the genetics of mice, and because it would be impossible for him to share all of his knowledge with me, it was incredibly important for us to talk through the goals and expectations of a project prior to spending too much time working on any aspect of the project. Without his input, I would be guessing at what the biologically relevant goals were. If I was wrong, which was likely, that work would be wasted. For example, certain specific microRNAs have been well studied and are known to accomplish basic functions within a cell and little more. If one of the goals of the project was to discover new functions of little-studied microRNAs, we would probably want to exclude certain families of microRNAs from the analysis. If we didn't exclude them, they would most likely add to the noise of an already very noisy genetic conversation within a cell. This is merely one of a large number of important things that the professor knew that I didn't, making a lengthy discussion of goals, expectations, and caveats necessary before starting the project in earnest.

In some sense, and it is a very common one, a project can be deemed successful if and only if the customer is satisfied with the results. There are exceptions to this guideline, but nevertheless it's important always to have the expectations and goals in mind during every step of a data science project. Unfortunately, in my own experience, expectations aren't usually clear or obvious at the very beginning of a project, or they're not easy to formulate concisely. I've settled on a few practices that help me figure out reasonable goals that can guide me through each step of a project involving data science.

2.1.2   *The customer is probably not a data scientist*

A funny thing about customer expectations is that they may not be appropriate. It's not always—or even usually—the customer's fault, because the problems that data science addresses are inherently complex, and if the customer understood their own problem fully, they likely wouldn't need a data scientist to help them. That's why I always cut customers some slack when they're unclear in their language or understanding, and I view the process of setting expectations and goals as a joint exercise that could be said to resemble conflict resolution or relationship therapy.

You—the data scientist—and the customer share a mutual interest in completing the project successfully, but the two of you likely have different specific motivations, different skills, and, most important, different perspectives. Even if you are the customer, you can think of yourself as having two halves, one (the data scientist) who is focused on getting results and another (the customer) who is focused on using those results to do something real, or external to the project itself. In this way, a project in data science begins by finding agreement between two personalities, two perspectives, that if they aren't conflicting are at the very least disparate.

Although there is not, strictly speaking, a conflict between you and the customer, sometimes it can seem that way as you both muddle your way toward some semblance of a set of goals that are both achievable (for the data scientist) and helpful (for the customer). And, as in conflict resolution and relationship therapy, feelings are involved. These feelings can be ideological and driven by personal experience, preference, or opinion and may not make sense to the other party. A little patience and understanding, without too much judgment, can be extremely beneficial to both of you and, more importantly, to the project.

2.1.3 *Asking specific questions to uncover fact, not opinions*

When a customer is describing a theory or hypothesis about the system that you're about to investigate, they are almost certainly expressing a mixture of fact and opinion, and it can be important to distinguish between the two. For example, in a study of cancer development in mice, the biology professor told me, "It is well known which genes are cancer related, and this study is concerned with only those genes and the microRNAs that inhibit them." One might be tempted to take this statement at face value and analyze data from only the cancer-related genes, but this could be a mistake, because there is some ambiguity in the statement. Principally, it's not clear whether other supposedly non-cancer-related genes can be involved in auxiliary roles within the complex reactions incited by the experiments or whether it is well known and proven that the expression of cancer-related genes is entirely independent of other genes. In the case of the former, it wouldn't be a good idea to ignore the data corresponding to non-cancer-related genes, whereas in the case of the latter, it might be a good idea. Without resolving this issue, it's not clear which is the appropriate choice. Therefore, it's important to ask.

It's also important that the question itself be formulated in a way that the customer understands. It wouldn't be wise to ask, for example, "Should I ignore the data from the non-cancer-related genes?" This is a question about the practice of data science in this specific case, and it falls under your domain, not a biologist's. You should ask, rather, something similar to, "Do you have any evidence that the expression of cancer-related genes is independent, in general, of other genes?" This is a question about biology, and hopefully the biology professor would understand it.

In his answer, it is important to distinguish between what he thinks and what he knows. If the professor merely thinks that the expression of these genes is independent of others, then it's certainly something to keep in mind throughout the project, but you shouldn't make any important decisions—such as ignoring certain data—based on it. If, on the other hand, the professor can cite scientific research supporting his claim, then it's advisable to use this fact to make decisions.

In any project, you, the data scientist, are an expert in statistics and in software tools, but the principal subject-matter expert is very often someone else, as in the case involving the professor of biology. In learning from this subject matter expert, you should ask questions that give you some intuitive sense of how the system under investigation works and also questions that attempt to separate fact from opinion and intuition. Basing practical decisions on fact is always a good idea, but basing them on opinion can be dangerous. The maxim "Trust but confirm" is appropriate here. If I had ignored any of the genes in the data set, I may very well have missed a crucial aspect of the complex interaction taking place among various types of RNA in the cancer experiments. Cancer, it turns out, is a very complex disease on the genetic level as well as on the medical one.

2.1.4 Suggesting deliverables: guess and check

Your customer probably doesn't understand data science and what it can do. Asking them "What would you like to appear in the final report?" or "What should this analytic application do?" can easily result in "I don't know" or, even worse, a suggestion that doesn't make sense. Data science is not their area of expertise, and they're probably not fully aware of the possibilities and limitations of software and data. It's usually best to approach the question of final product with a series of suggestions and then to note the customer's reaction.

One of my favorite questions to ask a customer is "Can you give me an example of a sentence that you might like to see in a final report?" I might get responses such as "I'd like to see something like, 'MicroRNA-X seems to inhibit Gene Y significantly,'" or "Gene Y and Gene Z seem to be expressed at the same levels in all samples tested." Answers like these give a great starting point for conceiving the format of the final product. If the customer can give you seed ideas like these, you can expand on them to make suggestions of final products. You might then ask, "What if I gave you a table of the strongest interactions between specific microRNAs and genetic mRNAs?" Maybe the customer would say that this would be valuable—or maybe not.

It's most likely, however, that a customer makes less-clear statements, such as "I'd like to know which microRNAs are important in cancer development." For this you'll need clarification if you hope to complete the project successfully. What does *important* mean in a biological sense? How might this importance manifest itself in the available data? It's vital to get answers to these questions before proceeding; if you don't know how microRNA importance might manifest itself in the data, how will you know when you've found it?

One mistake that many others and I have made on occasion is to conflate correlation with significance. Some people talk about the confusion of correlation and causation; here's an example: a higher percentage of helmet-wearing cyclists are involved in accidents than non-helmet-wearing cyclists. It might be tempting to conclude that helmets cause accidents, but this is probably fallacious. The correlation between helmets and accidents doesn't imply that helmets cause accidents; nor does it imply that accidents cause the wearing of helmets (directly). In reality, cyclists who ride on busier and more dangerous roads are more likely to wear helmets and also are more likely to get into accidents. The act of riding on more dangerous roads causes both. In the question of helmets and accidents, there's no direct causation despite the existence of correlation. Causation, in turn, is merely one example of a way that correlation might be significant. If you're conducting a study on the use of helmets and the rates of accidents, then this correlation might be significant even if it doesn't imply causation. I should stress that *significance*, as I use the term, is determined by the project's goals.

This knowledge of a helmet–accident correlation could lead to considering (and modeling) the level of traffic and danger on each road as part of the project. Significance, also, is not guaranteed by correlation. I'm fairly certain that more cycling accidents happen on sunny days, but this is because more cyclists are on the road on sunny days and not because of any other significant relationship (barring rain). It's not immediately clear to me how I might use this information to further my goals, and so I wouldn't spend much time exploring it. The correlation doesn't seem to have any significance in this particular case.

In gene/RNA expression experiments, thousands of RNA sequences are measured within only 10–20 biological samples. Such an analysis with far more variables (expression levels for each RNA sequence or gene) than data points (samples) is called *high-dimensional* or often *under-determined* because there are so many variables that some of them are correlated by random chance, and it would be fallacious to say that they're related in a real biological sense. If you present a list of strong correlations to the biology professor, he'll spot immediately that some of your reported correlations are unimportant or, worse, contrary to established research, and you'll have to go back and do more analyses.

2.1.5 *Iterate your ideas based on knowledge, not wishes*

As it's important, within your acquired domain knowledge, to separate fact from opinion, it's also important to avoid letting excessive optimism make you blind to obstacles and difficulties. I've long thought that an invaluable skill of good data scientists is the ability to foresee potential difficulties and to leave open a path around them.

It's popular, in the software industry today, to make claims about analytic capabilities while they're still under development. This, I've learned, is a tactic of salesmanship that often seems necessary, in particular for young startups, to get ahead in a competitive industry. When I work with a startup, it always makes me nervous when a colleague is actively selling a piece of analytic software that I said I *think* I can build but that I'm not 100% sure will work exactly as planned, given some limitation of the data I have available. When I make bold statements about a hypothetical product, I try to keep them, as much as possible, in the realm of things that I'm almost certain I can do. In the case that I can't, I try to have a backup plan that doesn't involve the trickiest parts of the original plan.

Imagine you want to develop an application that summarizes news articles. You'd need to create an algorithm that can parse the sentences and paragraphs in the article and extract the main ideas. It's possible to write an algorithm that does this, but it's not clear how well it will perform. Summaries may be successful in some sense for a majority of articles, but there's a big difference between 51% successful and 99% successful, and you won't know where your particular algorithm falls within that range until you've built a first version at least. Blindly selling and feverishly developing this algorithm might seem like the best idea; hard work will pay off, right? Maybe. This task is hard. It's entirely possible that, try as you might, you never get better than 75%

success, and maybe that's not good enough from a business perspective. What do you do then? Do you give up and close up shop? Do you, only after this failure, begin looking for alternatives?

Good data scientists know when a task is hard even before they begin. Sentences and paragraphs are complicated, random variables that often seem designed specifically to thwart any algorithm you might throw at them. In case of failure, I always go back to first principles, in a sense. I ask myself: what problem am I trying to solve? What is the end goal, beyond summarization?

If the goal is to build a product that makes reading news more efficient, maybe there's another way to address the problem of inefficient news readers. Perhaps it's easier to aggregate similar articles and present them together to the reader. Maybe it's possible to design a better news reader through friendlier design or by incorporating social media.

No one ever wants to declare failure, but data science is a risky business, and to pretend that failure never happens is a failure in itself. There are always multiple ways to address a problem, and formulating a plan that acknowledges a likelihood of obstacles and failure can allow you to gain value from minor successes along the way, even if the main goal isn't achieved.

A far greater mistake would be to ignore the possibility of failure and also the need to test and evaluate the performance of the application. If you assume that the product works nearly perfectly, but it doesn't, delivering the product to your customer could be a huge mistake. Can you imagine if you began selling an untested application that supposedly summarized news articles, but soon thereafter your users began to complain that the summaries were completely wrong? Not only would the application be a failure, but you and your company might gain a reputation for software that doesn't work.

2.2 Ask good questions—of the data

It may seem at first glance that this section could be included with the previous one, and I've even mentioned a few ways in which good questions may be asked of the customer. But in this section I discuss the question as an inquiry not only into the knowledge of the customer but also into the capabilities of the data. A data set will tell us no more than what we ask of it, and even then, the data may not be capable of answering the question. These are the two most dangerous pitfalls:

- Expecting the data to be able to answer a question it can't
- Asking questions of the data that don't solve the original problem

Asking questions that lead to informative answers and subsequently improved results is an important and nuanced challenge that deserves much more discussion than it typically receives. The examples of good, or at least helpful, questions I've mentioned in previous sections were somewhat specific in their phrasing and scope, even if they can apply to many types of projects. In the following subsections, I attempt to define and describe a good question with the intent of delivering a sort of framework or thought process for generating good questions for an arbitrary project. Hopefully you'll see how it might be possible to ask yourself some questions in order to arrive at some useful, good questions you might ask of the data.

2.2.1 Good questions are concrete in their assumptions

No question is quite as tricky to answer as one that's based on faulty assumptions. But a question based on unclear assumptions is a close second. Every question has assumptions, and if those assumptions don't hold, it could spell disaster for your project. It's important to think about the assumptions that your questions require and decide whether these assumptions are safe. And in order for you to figure out if the assumptions are safe, they need to be *concrete*, meaning well defined and able to be tested.

For a brief while I worked at a hedge fund. I was in the quantitative research department, and our principal goal was, as with any hedge fund, to find patterns in financial markets that might be exploited for monetary benefit. A key aspect of the trading algorithms that I worked with was a method for model selection. Model selection is to mathematical modeling what trying on pants is to shopping: we try many of them, judge them, and then select one or a few that seem to work well for us, hoping that they serve us well in the future.

Several months after I began working at this hedge fund, another mathematician was hired, fresh out of graduate school. She began working directly with the model selection aspect of the algorithms. One day, while walking to lunch, she began to describe to me how a number of the mathematical models of the commodities markets had begun to diverge widely from their long-term average success rates. For example, let's assume that Model A has correctly predicted whether the daily price of crude oil has gone up or down 55% of the time over the last three years. But in the past four weeks, Model A had been correct only 32% of the time. My colleague informed me that because the success rate of Model A had fallen below its long-term average, it was bound to pick back up over the next several weeks, and we should bet on the predictions of Model A.

Frankly, I was disappointed with my colleague, but hers was an easy mistake to make. When a certain quantity—in this case the success rate of Model A—typically returns to its long-term mean, it's known as *mean reversion*, and it's a famously contested assumption of many real-life systems, not the least of which are the world's financial markets.

Innumerable systems in this world don't subscribe to mean reversion. Flipping a standard coin is one of them. If you flip a coin 100 times and you see heads only 32 times, do you think you're going to see more than 50 heads in the next 100 tosses? I certainly don't, at least to the point that I would bet on it. The history of a (fair) coin being tossed doesn't affect the future of the coin, and commodities markets are in general the same way. Granted, many funds find exploitable patterns in financial markets, but these are the exceptions rather than the rule.

The assumption of mean reversion is a great example of a fallacious assumption in a question that you might ask the data. In this case, my colleague was asking "Will Model A's success rate return to its long-term average?" and, based on the assumption of mean reversion, the answer would be yes: mean reversion implies that Model A will be correct more often when it has recently been on a streak of incorrectness. But if you don't assume mean reversion in this case, the answer would be "I have no idea."

It's extremely important to acknowledge your assumptions—there are always assumptions—and to make sure that they are true, or at least to make sure that your results won't be ruined if the assumptions turn out not to be true. But this is easier said than done. One way to accomplish this is to break down all of the reasoning between your analysis and your conclusion into specific logical steps and to make sure that all of the gaps are filled in. In the case of my former colleague, the original steps of reasoning were these:

1 The success rate of Model A has recently been relatively low.
2 Therefore, the success rate of Model A will be relatively high in the near future.

The data tells you 1, and then 2 is the conclusion you draw. If it isn't obvious that a logical step is missing here, it might be easier to see it when you replace the success rate of Model A with an arbitrary quantity X that might go up or down over time:

1 X has gone down recently.
2 Therefore, X will go up soon.

Think of all of the things X could be: stock price, rainfall, grades in school, bank account balance. For how many of these does the previous logic make sense? Is there a missing step? I would argue that there is indeed a missing step. The logic should be like this:

1 X has gone down recently.
2 Because X always corrects itself towards a certain value, V,
3 X will go up soon, toward V.

Note that the data has told you 1, as before, and you'd like to be able to draw the conclusion in 3, but 3 is dependent on 2 being true. Is 2 true? Again, think of all of the things X could be. Certainly, 2 is not true for a bank account balance or rainfall, so it can't always be true. You must ask yourself if it's true for the particular quantity you're examining: do you have any reason to believe that, for an arbitrary period, Model A should be correct in its prediction 55% of the time? In this case, the only evidence you have that Model A is correct 55% of the time is that Model A historically has been correct 55% of the time. This is something like circular reasoning, which isn't enough real evidence to justify the assumption. Mean reversion shouldn't be taken as truth, and the conclusion that Model A should be correct 55% of the time (or more) in the near future isn't justified.

As a mathematician, I've been trained to separate all analysis, argument, and conclusion into logical steps, and this experience has proven itself invaluable in making and justifying real-life conclusions and predictions through data science. Formal reasoning is probably the skill I value the most among those I learned through my mathematics course work in college. One important fact about reasoning is—to again emphasize the point I'm trying to make in this section—a false or unclear assumption starts you out in a questionable place, and you should make every effort to avoid relying on such false assumptions.

2.2.2 Good answers: measurable success without too much cost

Perhaps shifting focus to the answers to good questions can shed more light on what the good question comprises as well as help you decide when your answers are sufficient. The answer to a good question should measurably improve the project's situation in some way. The point is that you should be asking questions that, whatever the answer, make your job a little easier by moving you closer to a practical result.

How do you know if answering a question will move you closer to a useful, practical result? Let's return to the idea that one of a data scientist's most valuable traits is their awareness of what might occur and their ability to prepare for that. If you can imagine all (or at least most) possible outcomes, then you can follow the logical conclusions from them. If you know the logical conclusions—the additional knowledge that you can deduce from your new outcome—then you can figure out whether they will help you with the goals of your project.

There can be a wide range of possible outcomes, many of which can be helpful. Though this is not an exhaustive list, you can move closer to the goals of your project if you ask and answer questions that lead to positive or negative results, elimination of possible paths or conclusions, or increasing situational awareness.

Both positive and negative results can be helpful. What I call *positive* results are those that confirm what you suspected and/or hoped for when you initially asked the question. These are helpful, obviously, because they fit into your thought processes about the project and also move you directly toward your goals. After all, goals are yet-unrealized positive results that, if confirmed, give some tangible benefit to your customer.

Negative results are helpful because they inform you that something that you thought is probably true is indeed false. These results usually feel like setbacks but, practically speaking, they're the most informative of all possible results. What if you found out that the sun was not going to rise tomorrow, despite all of the historical evidence to the contrary? This is an extreme example, but can you imagine how informative that would be, if it were confirmed true? It would change everything, and you would be very likely one of very few people who knew it, given that it was so counterintuitive. In that way, negative results can be the most helpful, though often they require you to readjust your goals based on the new information. At the very least, negative results force you to rethink your project to account for those results, a process that leads to more informed choices and a more realistic path for your project.

As I mentioned in chapter 1, data science is fraught with uncertainty. There are always many possible paths to a solution, many possible paths to failure, and even more paths to the gray area between success and failure. Evidence of improbability or outright elimination of any of these possible paths or conclusions can be helpful to inform and focus the next steps of the project. A path can be eliminated or deemed improbable in many ways, which might include the following:

- New information making a path far less likely
- New information making other paths far more likely
- Technical challenges that make exploring certain paths very difficult or impossible

If eliminating a path doesn't seem like it's helping—maybe it was one of the only paths that might have succeeded—keep in mind that your situation has become simpler regardless, which can be good. Or take the chance to rethink your set of paths and your knowledge of the project. Maybe there's more data, more resources, or something else that you haven't thought of yet that might help you gain a new perspective on the challenges.

In data science, increasing situational awareness is always good. What you don't know can hurt you, because an unknown quantity will sneak into some aspect of your project and ruin the results. A question can be good if it helps you gain insight into how a system works or what peripheral events are occurring that affect the data set. If you find yourself saying "I wonder if..." at some point, or if a colleague does the same, ask yourself if that thought relates to a question that can help you gain some context for the project—if not answer some larger, more direct question. Being introspective in this way brings some formality and procedure to the often fuzzy task of looking for good results.

2.3 *Answering the question using data*

You have good questions, and now you want answers. Answers that provide solutions to problems are, after all, the goal of your entire project. Getting an answer from a project in data science usually looks something like the formula, or recipe, in figure 2.2. Although sometimes one of the ingredients—good question, relevant data, or insightful analysis—is simpler to obtain than the others, all three are crucial to getting a useful answer. Also, the four adjectives I chose, one in each ingredient (*good, relevant, insightful*) and one in the result (*useful*), should not be ignored, because without them the formula doesn't always work. The product of any old question, data, and analysis

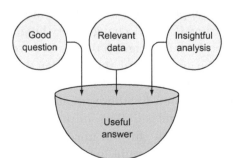

Figure 2.2 The recipe for a useful answer in a data science project

isn't always an answer, much less a useful one. It's worth repeating that you always need to be deliberate and thoughtful in every step of a project, and the elements of this formula are not exceptions. For example, if you have a good question but irrelevant data, an answer will be difficult to find.

2.3.1   Is the data relevant and sufficient?

It's not always easy to tell whether data is relevant. For example, let's say that you're building a beer recommendation algorithm. A user will choose a few beers that they like, and the algorithm will recommend other beers that they might like. You might hypothesize that a beer drinker typically likes certain types of beer but not others, and so their favorites tend to cluster into their favorite beer types. This is the good question: do beer drinkers like beers of certain types significantly more than others? You have access to a data set from a popular beer-rating website, composed of one- to five-star ratings by thousands of site users. You'd like to test your hypothesis using this data; is this data relevant?

Fairly soon, you realize that the data set is a CSV file containing only three columns: USER_NAME, BEER_NAME, and RATING. (Drat! No beer types.) A data set that seemed immensely relevant before now seems less so for this particular question. Certainly, for a question about beer types, you need to know, for each beer, what type it is. Therefore, to answer the question you must either find a data set matching beers to beer types or try to infer the beer types from the data you already have, perhaps based on the name of the beer.

Either way, it should be apparent that the data set that at first glance seemed perfectly capable of answering the question needs some additional resources in order to do so. A data scientist with some foresight and awareness can anticipate these sorts of problems before they cost you or your colleagues time and/or money. The first step is to outline specifically how data will help you answer your question. In the case of the investigation of affinity for beer types, such a statement might suffice:

> *In order to find out whether beer drinkers like certain types of beers significantly more than others, we need data containing beer name, beer type, user names, and their individual ratings for the beers. With this data, we can perform a statistical test, such as an analysis of variance (ANOVA), with each beer type as a variable, and examine whether beer type is a significant influencer of rating for individual users.*

Disregarding the lack of specific detail in the description of the statistical test (it's not important here, but we'll return to it in a later chapter), you have here a basic outline of what might be done to answer the question using data you believe to be available. There may be other such outlines that serve the purpose equally well or better, but a good outline states what data you would need and how you would use that data to answer the question. By stating what specific properties the data set should have, you—or anyone you're working with—can check quickly to see if a data set (or more than one) fulfills the requirements.

I (like many people I know) have on occasion begun creating algorithms based on data I *thought* I had instead of the data I *actually* had. When I realized my mistake, I had wasted some time (thankfully not much) on code that was worthless. By making a short outline of how you're going to answer a question using data, it would be very easy to check to make sure that a data set you're considering using contains all the information you've listed as a requirement—before you start coding. If the data set is lacking a vital piece of information, you can then adjust your plan either to find the missing piece elsewhere or to devise another plan/outline that doesn't require it. Planning during this stage of a data science project can save you quite a lot of time and effort later. Having to modify code heavily at a late stage of a project or scrap it altogether is not usually an efficient use of time.

In the following subsections, I outline some steps you can use to develop a solid but detailed plan to find and use data to answer a specific question. In later chapters, I'll discuss gathering and using data in detail, but here I'd like to cover the basic ideas of what to note and keep in mind throughout the project. You usually have many choices to make, and if those choices later turn out to be inefficient—or plain wrong—then it helps to have a record of other choices you could have made instead.

2.3.2   *Has someone done this before?*

This should always be the first step in developing a plan: check the internet for blog posts, scientific articles, open-source projects, research descriptions from universities, or anything else you can find related to the project you're starting. If someone else has done something similar, you may gain a lot of insight into the challenges and capabilities that you haven't yet encountered. Again, awareness is very helpful.

Regarding similar projects that others have done, you're likely to encounter similar problems and similar solutions in your project, so it's best to learn as much as you can about what you should watch out for and how to handle it.

Sometimes, a little searching will lead you to useful data sets you hadn't seen yet, analytic methods you may not have considered, or, best of all, results or conclusions that you can use in your own project. Presuming that the analyses were rigorous—but it's always best to verify—someone else may have done a lot of your work for you.

2.3.3   *Figuring out what data and software you could use*

Now that you've searched around, both for prior similar projects and for relevant data sets, you should take stock of what you have and what you still need.

DATA

If you can imagine a data set that would help you tremendously, but that data set doesn't exist anywhere, it often helps to make a note about it in case you realize something can be done later. For instance, if you're missing the beer type labels in the data set of beer ratings, you may find that many breweries have the types listed on their websites or that other web pages do. This provides the opportunity to collect them yourself, potentially at a cost of time and effort. If you make a note of this need and this potential solution, then at any point in the future you can reevaluate the costs and benefits and make a decision about how to proceed. Because of the many uncertainties associated with data-centric projects, costs and benefits of possible choices may change in scope or scale at virtually any time.

SOFTWARE

Most data scientists have a favorite tool for data analysis, but that tool may not always be appropriate for what you intend to do. It's usually a good idea to think about the analysis you want to do conceptually before you try to match that concept to a piece of software that can turn the concept into a reality. You may decide that a statistical test can provide a good answer if the data supports it, that machine learning can figure out the classifications you need, or that a simple database query can answer the question. In any of these cases, you may know of a good way to use your favorite tool to perform the analysis, but first you might want to consider the format of your data, any data transformations that might have to take place, the amount of data you have, the method of loading the data into analytic tools, and finally the manner of the analysis in the tools. Thinking through all of these steps before you perform them and considering how they might work in practice can certainly lead to better choice of software tools.

If you aren't familiar with many software tools and techniques, you can skip this step for now and continue reading, because I cover these in later chapters. But for now I merely want to emphasize the importance of thinking through—deliberately—various options before choosing any. The decision can have large implications and should not be taken lightly.

2.3.4 *Anticipate obstacles to getting everything you want*

Here are some questions you might want to ask yourself at this planning stage of the project:

- Is the data easily accessed and extracted?
- Is there anything you might not know about the data that could be important?
- Do you have enough data?
- Do you have too much data? Will it take too long to process?
- Is there missing data?
- If you're combining multiple data sets, are you sure everything will integrate correctly? Are names, IDs, and codes the same in both data sets?
- What happens if your statistical test or other algorithm doesn't give the result you expect?
- Do you have a way to spot-check your results? What if the checks show errors somewhere?

Some of these may seem obvious, but I've seen enough people—data scientists, software engineers, and others—forget to consider these things, and they paid for their negligence later. It's better to remind you to be skeptical at the very beginning so that the uncertainty of the task doesn't cost you nearly as much later.

2.4   Setting goals

I've mentioned goals several times in this chapter, but I haven't yet addressed them directly. Though you probably began the project with some goals in mind, now is a good time to evaluate them in the context of the questions, data, and answers that you expect to be working with.

Typically, initial goals are set with some business purpose in mind. If you're not in business—you're in research, for example—then the purpose is usually some external use of the results, such as furthering scientific knowledge in a particular field or providing an analytic tool for someone else to use. Though goals originate outside the context of the project itself, each goal should be put through a pragmatic filter based on data science. This filter includes asking these questions:

- What is possible?
- What is valuable?
- What is efficient?

Applying this filter to all putative goals within the context of the good questions, possible answers, available data, and foreseen obstacles can help you arrive at a solid set of project goals that are, well, possible, valuable, and efficient to achieve.

2.4.1   What is possible?

Sometimes it's obvious what is possible, but sometimes it's not. In the following chapters, I'll describe how some tasks that might seem easy are not. For instance, finding appropriate data, wrangling the data, exploiting the data to get answers, designing software to perform the analysis, and confronting any other obstacle such as those I referenced in the previous section may affect your ability to achieve a certain goal. The more complex a task becomes and the less you know about the tasks beforehand, the less likely it is that the task is possible. For example, if you think a certain data set exists but you haven't confirmed it yet, then achieving any goal requiring that data set might not be possible. For any goal with uncertainties, consider the possibility that achieving the goal might be impossible.

2.4.2   What is valuable?

Some goals give more benefit than others. If resources are scarce, everything else being equal, it's better to pursue the more beneficial goal. In business, this might mean pursuing the goal(s) that are expected to give the highest profit increase. In academia, this might mean aiming for the most impactful scientific publication. Formally considering the expected value of achieving a goal, as I suggest here, creates a deliberate context and framework for project planning.

2.4.3   *What is efficient?*

After considering what is possible and what is valuable, you can consider the effort and resources it might take to achieve each goal. Then you can approximate efficiency via this equation:

$$efficiency = value \ / \ effort \ * \ possibility$$

The overall efficiency of achieving a goal is the value of achieving it divided by the effort it took to achieve it (the value gained per unit of effort) multiplied by the possibility (the probability that it will be achieved at all). Efficiency goes up with the value of the goal, down if more effort is required, and also down if the goal seems less possible of being achieved. This is only a rough calculation, and it means more to me conceptually than it does practically, but I do find it helpful.

2.5   *Planning: be flexible*

Given all your knowledge of the project, all the research you've done so far, and all the hypothetical questions you've asked yourself about the data and the software tools you might use, it's time to formulate a plan. This should not be a plan containing sequential steps with outcomes that are presumed beforehand. The uncertainty of data and data science virtually guarantees that something won't turn out the way you expect. It's a good strategy to think of a few different ways that you might achieve your goals. Even the goals themselves can be flexible.

These alternative paths might represent different overarching strategies, but in most cases two paths in the plan will diverge wherever there's an anticipated uncertainty, where the two most likely scenarios indicate two different strategies for addressing the outcome of the uncertainty. It's definitely advisable to make a plan from the beginning to the first major uncertainty. If you want to stop there, it might save you some planning time now, but it's even better to map out all of the most likely paths, in particular if you're working with multiple people. That way, everyone can see where the project is headed and knows from the very beginning that there will be problems and detours, but you don't yet know which ones they will be. Such is the life of a data scientist!

Last, the plans you formulate here will be revisited periodically throughout the project (and this book), so the early stages of the plans are the most important ones. A good goal is to plan the next steps to put you in the best position to be well informed the next time you revisit plans and goals. Increasing knowledge and reducing uncertainty are always good things.

Exercises

Consider the following scenario:

You're working at a firm that consolidates personal finance data for its customers, which are primarily individual consumers. Let's call this firm Filthy Money, Inc, or FMI. Through FMI's primary product, a web application, customers can view all their data in one place instead of needing to log into the websites of each of their financial accounts separately. The typical customer has connected several of their accounts, such as bank accounts and credit cards, to the FMI app.

One of FMI's lead product designers has asked you to help build a new product component called Filthy Money Forecasting, which was conceived to provide users of the FMI app with near-term forecasts of their accounts and overall financial status based on their spending and earning habits. The product designer wants to collaborate with you to figure out what is possible and what some good product features might be:

1 What are three questions you would ask the product designer?
2 What are three good questions you might ask of the data?
3 What are three possible goals for the project?

Summary

- Stay aware: experience, domain experts, and knowledge of other related projects help you plan and anticipate problems before they arise.
- Be aware of the customer's perspective and potential lack of data science knowledge.
- Make sure the project focuses on answering questions that are good.
- Take time to think through all possible paths to answering those good questions.
- Set goals using a pragmatic perspective of what the customer wants, the questions you've developed, and the possible paths to getting answers.

Data all around us: the virtual wilderness

3

This chapter covers

- Discovering data you may need
- Interacting with data in various environments
- Combining disparate data sets

This chapter discusses the principal species of study of the data scientist: data. Having possession of data—namely, useful data—is often taken as a foregone conclusion, but it's not usually a good idea to assume anything of the sort. As with any topic worthy of scientific examination, data can be hard to find and capture and is rarely completely understood. Any mistaken notion about a data set that you possess or would like to possess can lead to costly problems, so in this chapter, I discuss the treatment of data as an object of scientific study.

3.1 Data as the object of study

In recent years, there has been a seemingly never-ending discussion about whether the field of data science is merely a reincarnation or an offshoot—in the Big Data Age—of any of a number of older fields that combine software engineering and data analysis: operations research, decision sciences, analytics, data mining, mathematical modeling, or applied statistics, for example. As with any trendy term or topic, the discussion over its definition and concept will cease only when the popularity of the term dies down. I don't think I can define *data science* any better than many of those who have done so before me, so let a definition from Wikipedia (https://en.wikipedia.org/wiki/Data_science), paraphrased, suffice:

> *Data science is the extraction of knowledge from data.*

Simple enough, but that description doesn't distinguish data *science* from the many other similar terms, except perhaps to claim that *data science* is an umbrella term for the whole lot. On the other hand, this era of data science has a property that no previous era had, and it is, to me, a fairly compelling reason to apply a new term to the types of things that data scientists do that previous applied statisticians and data-oriented software engineers did not. This reason helps me underscore an often-overlooked but very important aspect of data science, as shown in figure 3.1.

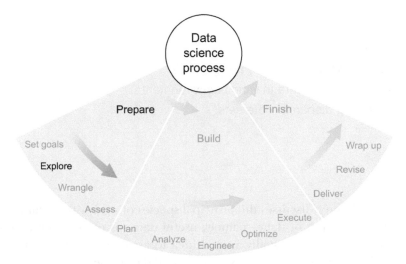

Figure 3.1   The second step of the preparation phase of the data science process: exploring available data

3.1.1   *The users of computers and the internet became data generators*

Throughout recent history, computers have made incredible advances in computational power, storage, and general capacity to accomplish previously unheard-of tasks. Every generation since the invention of the modern computer nearly a century ago has seen ever-shrinking machines that are orders of magnitude more powerful than the most powerful supercomputers of the previous generation.

The time period including the second half of the twentieth century through the beginning of the twenty-first, and including the present day, is often referred to as the Information Age. The Information Age, characterized by the rise to ubiquity of computers and then the internet, can be divided into several smaller shifts that relate to analysis of data.

First, early computers were used mainly to make calculations that previously took an unreasonable amount of time. Cracking military codes, navigating ships, and performing simulations in applied physics were among the computationally intensive tasks that were performed by early computers.

Second, people began using computers to communicate, and the internet developed in size and capacity. It became possible for data and results to be sent easily across a large distance. This enabled a data analyst to amass larger and more varied data sets in one place for study. Internet access for the average person in a developed country increased dramatically in the 1990s, giving hundreds of millions of people access to published information and data.

Third, whereas early use of the internet by the populace consisted mainly of consuming published content and communication with other people, soon the owners of many websites and applications realized that the aggregation of actions of their users provided valuable insight into the success of their own product and sometimes human behavior in general. These sites began to collect user data in the form of clicks, typed text, site visits, and any other actions a user might take. Users began to produce more data than they consumed.

Fourth, the advent of mobile devices and smartphones that are connected to the internet made possible an enormous advance in the amount and specificity of user data being collected. At any given moment, your mobile device is capable of recording and transmitting every bit of information that its sensors can collect (location, movement, camera image and video, sound, and so on) as well as every action that you take deliberately while using the device. This can potentially be a huge amount of information, if you enable or allow its collection.

Fifth—though this isn't necessarily subsequent to the advent of personal mobile devices—is the inclusion of data collection and internet connectivity in almost everything electronic. Often referred to as the Internet of Things (IoT), these can include everything from your car to your wristwatch to the weather sensor on top of your office building. Certainly, collecting and transmitting information from devices began well before the twenty-first century, but its ubiquity is relatively new, as is the availability of the resultant data on the internet in various forms, processed or raw, for free or for sale.

Through these stages of growth of computing devices and the internet, the online world became not merely a place for consuming information but a data-collection tool in and of itself. A friend of mine in high school in the late 1990s set up a website offering electronic greeting cards as a front for collecting email addresses. He sold the resulting list of millions of email addresses for a few hundred thousand dollars. This is a primitive example of the value of user data for purposes completely unrelated to the website itself and a perfect example of something I'm sorry to have missed out on in my youth. By the early 2000s, similar-sized collections of email addresses were no longer worth nearly this much money, but other sorts of user data became highly desirable and could likewise fetch high prices.

3.1.2   *Data for its own sake*

As people and businesses realized that user data could be sold for considerable sums of money, they began to collect it indiscriminately. Very large quantities of data began to pile up in data stores everywhere. Online retailers began to store not only everything you bought but also every item you viewed and every link you clicked. Video games stored every step your avatar ever took and which opponents it vanquished. Various social networks stored everything you and your friends ever did.

The purpose of collecting all of this data wasn't always to sell it, though that happens frequently. Because virtually every major website and application uses its own data to optimize the experience and effectiveness of users, site and app publishers are typically torn between the value of the data as something that can be sold and the value of the data when held and used internally. Many publishers are afraid to sell their data because that opens up the possibility that someone else will figure out something lucrative to do with it. Many of them keep their data to themselves, hoarding it for the future, when they supposedly will have enough time to wring all value out of it.

Internet juggernauts Facebook and Amazon collect vast amounts of data every minute of every day, but in my estimation, the data they possess is largely unexploited. Facebook is focused on marketing and advertising revenue, when they have one of the largest data sets comprising human behavior all around the world. Product designers, marketers, social engineers, and sociologists alike could probably make great advances in their fields, both academic and industrial, if they had access to Facebook's data. Amazon, in turn, has data that could probably upend many beloved economic principles and create several new ones if it were turned over to academic institutions. Or it might be able to change the way retail, manufacturing, and logistics work throughout the entire industry.

These internet behemoths know that their data is valuable, and they're confident that no one else possesses similar data sets of anywhere near the same size or quality. Innumerable companies would gladly pay top dollar for access to the data, but Facebook and Amazon have—I surmise—aspirations of their own to use their data to its fullest extent and therefore don't want anyone else to grab the resulting profits. If these companies had unlimited resources, surely they would try to wring every dollar out of every byte of data. But no matter how large and powerful they are, they're still limited in resources, and they're forced to focus on the uses of the data that affect their bottom lines most directly, to the exclusion of some otherwise valuable efforts.

On the other hand, some companies have elected to provide access to their data. Twitter is a notable example. For a fee, you can access the full stream of data on the Twitter platform and use it in your own project. An entire industry has developed around brokering the sale of data, for profit. A prominent example of this is the market of data from various major stock exchanges, which has long been available for purchase.

Academic and nonprofit organizations often make data sets available publicly and for free, but there may be limitations on how you can use them. Because of the disparity of data sets even within a single scientific field, there has been a trend toward consolidation of both location and format of data sets. Several major fields have created organizations whose sole purpose is to maintain databases containing as many data sets as possible from that field. It's often a requirement that authors of scientific articles submit their data to one of these canonical data repositories prior to publication of their work.

In whichever form, data is now ubiquitous, and rather than being merely a tool that analysts might use to draw conclusions, it has become a purpose of its own. Companies now seem to collect data as an end, not a means, though many of them claim to be planning to use the data in the future. Independent of other defining characteristics of the Information Age, data has gained its own role, its own organizations, and its own value.

3.1.3 *Data scientist as explorer*

In the twenty-first century, data is being collected at unprecedented rates, and in many cases it's not being collected for a specific purpose. Whether private, public, for free, for sale, structured, unstructured, big, normal size, social, scientific, passive, active, or any other type, data sets are accumulating everywhere. Whereas for centuries data analysts collected their own data or were given a data set to work on, for the first time in history many people across many industries are collecting data first and then asking, "What can I do with this?" Still others are asking, "Does the data already exist that can solve my problem?"

In this way data—all data everywhere, as a hypothetical aggregation—has become an entity worthy of study and exploration. In years past, data sets were usually collected deliberately, so that they represented some intentional measurement of the real world. But more recently the internet, ubiquitous electronic devices, and a latent fear of missing out on hidden value in data have led us to collect as much data as possible, often on the loose premise that we *might* use it later.

Figure 3.2 shows an interpretation of four major innovation types in computing history: computing power itself, networking and communication between computers, collection and use of big data, and rigorous statistical analysis of that big data. By *big data*, I mean merely the recent movement to capture, organize, and use any and all data possible. Each of these computing innovations begins with a problem that begs to be addressed and then goes through four phases of development, in a process that's similar to the technological surge cycle of Carlota Perez (*Technological Revolutions and Financial Capital*, Edward Elgar Publishing, 2002) but with a focus on computing innovation and its effect on computer users and the general public.

Innovation type	The stages of computing innovation				
	Problem	Innovation	Proof/ recognition	Adoption	Refinement
Computing	Cracking codes High-powered physics Ship navigation	Pre-1950s • Purpose-built computing machines	~1950s • Enigma • ENIAC	~1970s • First PCs • Computers in schools and libraries	~1980s • Supercomputers • Consumer PCs
Networking	Communicating and sending text and files	~1970s • pre-internet • ARPANET	~1980s • Academic networks • IRC	1990s • Prodigy • Compuserve • AOL	2000s • Mobile devices • Social networks • Cloud services
Big data collection and use	Too much useful data being thrown away	~2000 • Web crawling • Click tracking • Early, big social networks	2000s • Google search • Big retailers tracking users	2010s • Twitter firehose • Hadoop	2015+ • Massive API development • Format standardization
Big data statistical analysis	Even basic statistics are hard to calculate on large data sets	2000s • Google search • Amazon streamlining processes	2010s • Netflix challenge • Kaggle.com	2015+ • Google Analytics • Budding analytics start-ups	2025+? • Ubiquitous intelligent, integrated systems

Figure 3.2   We're currently in the refinement phase of big data collection and use and in the widespread adoption phase of statistical analysis of big data.

For each innovation included in the figure, there are five stages:

1   *Problem*—There is a problem that computers can address in some way.
2   *Invention*—The computing technology that can address that problem is created.
3   *Proof/recognition*—Someone uses the computing technology in a meaningful way, and its value is proven or at least recognized by some experts.
4   *Adoption*—The newly proven technology is widely put to use in industry.
5   *Refinement*—People develop new versions, more capabilities, higher efficiency, integrations with other tools, and so on.

Because we're currently in the refinement phase of big data collection and the widespread adoption phase of statistical analysis of that data, we've created an entire data ecosystem wherein the knowledge that has been extracted is only a very small portion of the total knowledge contained. Not only has much of the knowledge not been extracted yet, but in many cases the full extent and properties of the data set are not understood by anyone except maybe a few software engineers who set up the system; the only people who might understand what's contained in the data are people who are probably too busy or specialized to make use of it. The aggregation of all of this underutilized or poorly understood data to me is like an entirely new continent with many undiscovered species of plants and animals, some entirely unfamiliar organisms, and possibly a few legacy structures left by civilizations long departed.

There are exceptions to this characterization. Google, Amazon, Facebook, and Twitter are good examples of companies that are ahead of the curve. They are, in some cases, engaging in behavior that matches a later stage of innovation. For example, by allowing access to its entire data set (often for a fee), Twitter seems to be operating within the *refinement* stage of big data collection and use. People everywhere are trying to squeeze every last bit of knowledge out of users' tweets. Likewise, Google seems to be doing a good job of analyzing its data in a rigorous statistical manner. Its work on search-by-image, Google Analytics, and even its basic text search are good examples of solid statistics on a large scale. One can easily argue that Google has a long way to go, however. If today's ecosystem of data is like a largely unexplored continent, then the data scientist is its explorer. Much like famous early European explorers of the Americas or Pacific islands, a good explorer is good at several things:

- Accessing interesting areas
- Recognizing new and interesting things
- Recognizing the signs that something interesting might be close
- Handling things that are new, unfamiliar, or sensitive
- Evaluating new and unfamiliar things
- Drawing connections between familiar things and unfamiliar things
- Avoiding pitfalls

An explorer of a jungle in South America may have used a machete to chop through the jungle brush, stumbled across a few loose-cut stones, deduced that a millennium-old temple was nearby, found the temple, and then learned from the ruins about the religious rituals of the ancient tribe. A data scientist might hack together a script that pulls some social networking data from a public API, realize that a few people compose major hubs of social activity, discover that those people often mention a new photo-sharing app in their posts on the social network, pull more data from the photo-sharing app's public API, and in combining the two data sets with some statistical analysis learn about the behavior of network influencers in online communities. Both cases derive previously unknown information about how a society operates. Like an explorer, a modern data scientist typically must survey the landscape, take careful note of surroundings, wander around a bit, and dive into some unfamiliar territory to see what happens. When they find something interesting, they must examine it, figure out what it can do, learn from it, and be able to apply that knowledge in the future. Although analyzing data isn't a new field, the existence of data everywhere—often regardless of whether anyone is making use of it—enables us to apply the scientific method to discovery and analysis of a pre-existing world of data. This, to me, is the differentiator between data science and all of its predecessors. There's so much data that no one can possibly understand it all, so we treat it as a world unto itself, worthy of exploration.

This idea of data as a wilderness is one of the most compelling reasons for using the term *data science* instead of any of its counterparts. To get real truth and useful answers from data, we must use the scientific method, or in our case, the *data scientific method*:

1 Ask a question.
2 State a hypothesis about the answer to the question.
3 Make a testable prediction that would provide evidence in favor of the hypothesis if correct.
4 Test the prediction via an experiment involving data.
5 Draw the appropriate conclusions through analyses of experimental results.

In this way, data scientists are merely doing what scientists have been doing for centuries, albeit in a digital world. Today, some of our greatest explorers spend their time in virtual worlds, and we can gain powerful knowledge without ever leaving our computers.

3.2   *Where data might live, and how to interact with it*

Before we dive in to the unexplored wilderness that is the state of data today, I'd like to discuss the forms that data might take, what those forms mean, and how we might treat them initially. Flat files, XML, and JSON are a few data formats, and each has its own properties and idiosyncrasies. Some are simpler than others or more suited to certain purposes. In this section, I discuss several types of formats and storage methods, some of their strengths and weaknesses, and how you might take advantage of them.

Although plenty of people will object to this, I decided to include in this section a discussion of databases and APIs as well. Commingling a discussion of file formats with software tools for data storage makes sense to me because at the beginning of a data science project, any of these formats or data sources is a valid answer to the question "Where is the data now?" File, database, or API, what the data scientist needs to know is "How do I access and extract the data I need?" and so that's my purpose here.

Figure 3.3 shows three basic ways a data scientist might access data. It could be a file on a file system, and the data scientist could read the file into their favorite analysis tool. Or the data could be in a database, which is also on a file system, but in order to access the data, the data scientist has to use the database's interface, which is a software layer that helps store and extract data. Finally, the data could be behind an application programming interface (API), which is a software layer between the data scientist and some system that might be completely unknown or foreign. In all three cases, the data can be stored and/or delivered to the data scientist in any format I discuss in this section or any other. Storage and delivery of data are so closely intertwined in some systems that I choose to treat them as a single concept: getting data into your analysis tools.

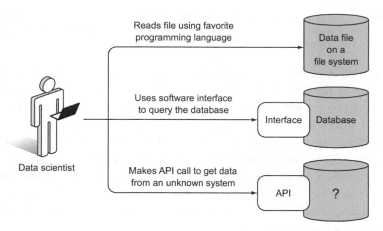

Figure 3.3   Three ways a data scientist might access data: from a file system, database, or API

In no way do I purport to cover all possible data formats or systems, nor will I list all technical details. My goal here is principally to give descriptions that would make a reader feel comfortable talking about and approaching each one. I can still remember when extracting data from a conventional database was daunting for me, and with this section I'd like to put even beginners at ease. Only if you're fairly comfortable with these basic forms of data storage and access can you move along to the most important part of data science: what the data can tell you.

3.2.1   Flat files

Flat files are plain-vanilla data sets, the default data format in most cases if no one has gone through the effort to implement something else. Flat files are self-contained, and you don't need any special programs to view the data contained inside. You can open a flat file for viewing in a program typically called a text editor, and many text editors are available for every major operating system. Flat files contain ASCII (or UTF-8) text, each character of text using (most likely) 8 bits (1 byte) of memory/storage. A file containing only the word DATA will be of size 32 bits. If there is an end-of-line (EOL) character after the word DATA, the file will be 40 bits, because an EOL character is needed to signify that a line has ended. My explanation of this might seem simplistic to many people, but even some of these basic concepts will become important later on as we discuss other formats, so I feel it's best to outline some basic properties of the flat file so that we might compare other data formats later.

There are two main subtypes of the flat file: plain text and delimited. *Plain text* is words, as you might type them on your keyboard. It could look like this:

```
This is what a plain text flat file looks like. It's just plain ASCII text.
Lines don't really end unless there is an end-of-line character, but some
text editors will wrap text around anyway, for convenience.
```

```
Usually, every character is a byte, and so there are only 256 possible
characters, but there are a lot of caveats to that statement, so if you're
really interested, consult a reference about ASCII and UTF-8.
```

This file would contain seven lines, or technically eight if there's an end-of-line character at the end of the final line of text. A plain text flat file is a bunch of characters stored in one of two (or so) possible very common formats. This is not the same as a text document stored in a word processor format, such as Microsoft Word or Open-Office Writer. (See the subsection "Common bad formats.") Word processor file formats potentially contain much more information, including overhead such as style formats and metadata about the file format itself, as well as objects like images and tables that may have been inserted into a document. Plain text is the minimal file format for containing words and only words—no style, no fancy images. Numbers and some special characters are OK too.

But if your data contains numerous entries, a delimited file might be a better idea. A *delimited file* is plain text but with the stipulation that every so often in the file a delimiter will appear, and if you line up the delimiters properly, you can make something that looks like a table, with rows, columns, and headers. A delimited file might look like this:

```
NAME       ID     COLOR      DONE
Alison     1      'blue'     FALSE
Brian      2      'red'      TRUE
Clara      3      'brown'    TRUE
```

Let's call this table JOBS_2015, because it represents a fictional set of house-painting jobs that started in 2015, with the customer name, ID, paint color, and completion status.

This table happens to be tab-delimited—or tab-separated value (TSV)—meaning that columns are separated by the tab character. If opened in a text editor, such a file would usually appear as it does here, but it might optionally display the text \t where a tab would otherwise appear. This is because a tab, like an end-of-line character, can be represented with a single ASCII character, and that character is typically represented with \t, if not rendered as variable-length whitespace that aligns characters into a tabular format.

If JOBS_2015 were stored as a comma-separated value (CSV) format, it would appear like this in a standard text editor:

```
NAME,ID,COLOR,DONE
Alison,1,'blue',FALSE
Brian,2,'red',TRUE
Clara,3,'brown',TRUE
```

The commas have taken the place of the tab characters, but the data is still the same. In either case, you can see that the data in the file can be interpreted as a set of rows and columns. The rows represent one job each for Alison, Brian, and Clara, and the column names on the header (first) line are NAME, ID, COLOR, and DONE, giving the types of details of the job contained within the table.

Most programs, including spreadsheets and some programming languages, require the same number of delimiters on each line (except possibly the header line) so that when they try to read the file, the number of columns is consistent, and each line contributes exactly one entry to each column. Some software tools don't require this, and they each have specific ways of dealing with varying numbers of entries on each line.

I should note here that delimited files are typically interpreted as tables, like spreadsheets. Furthermore, as plain text files can be read and stored using a word processing program, delimited files can typically be loaded into a spreadsheet program like Microsoft Excel or OpenOffice Calc.

Any common program for manipulating text or tables can read flat files. Popular programming languages all include functions and methods that can read such files. My two most familiar languages, Python (the csv package) and R (the read.table function and its variants), contain methods that can easily load a CSV or TSV file into the most relevant data types in those languages. For plain text also, Python (readlines) and R (readLines) have methods that read a file line by line and allow for the parsing of the text via whatever methods you see fit. Packages in both languages—and many others—provide even more functionality for loading files of related types, and I suggest looking at recent language and package documentation to find out whether another file-loading method better suits your needs.

Without compressing files, flat files are more or less the smallest and simplest common file formats for text or tables. Other file formats contain other information about the specifics of the file format or the data structure, as appropriate. Because they're the simplest file formats, they're usually the easiest to read. But because they're so lean, they provide no additional functionality other than showing the data, so for larger data sets, flat files become inefficient. It can take minutes or hours for a language like Python to scan a flat file containing millions of lines of text. In cases where reading flat files is too slow, there are alternative data storage systems designed to parse through large amounts of data quickly. These are called *databases* and are covered in a later section.

3.2.2 HTML

A *markup language* is plain text marked up with tags or specially denoted instructions for how the text should be interpreted. The very popular Hypertext Markup Language (HTML) is used widely on the internet, and a snippet might look like this:

```
<html>
    <body>
        <div class="column">
            <h1>Column One</h1>
            <p>This is a paragraph</p>
        </div>
```

```
        <div class="column">
            <h1>Column Two</h1>
            <p>This is another paragraph</p>
        </div>
    </body>
</html>
```

An HTML interpreter knows that everything between the <html> and </html> tags should be considered and read like HTML. Similarly, everything between the <body> and </body> tags will be considered the body of the document, which has special meaning in HTML rendering. Most HTML tags are of the format <TAGNAME> to begin the annotation and </TAGNAME> to end it, for an arbitrary TAGNAME. Everything between the two tags is now treated as being annotated by TAGNAME, which an interpreter can use to render the document. The two <div> tags in the example show how two blocks of text and other content can be denoted, and a class called column is applied to the div, allowing the interpreter to treat a column instance in a special way.

HTML is used primarily to create web pages, and so it usually looks more like a document than a data set, with a header, body, and some style and formatting information. HTML is not typically used to store raw data, but it's certainly capable of doing so. In fact, the concept of *web scraping* usually entails writing code that can fetch and read web pages, interpreting the HTML, and scraping out the specific pieces of the HTML page that are of interest to the scraper.

For instance, suppose we're interested in collecting as many blog posts as possible and that a particular blogging platform uses the <div class="column"> tag to denote columns in blog posts. We could write a script that systematically visits a blog, interprets the HTML, looks for the <div class="column"> tag, captures all text between it and the corresponding </div> tag, and discards everything else, before proceeding to another blog to do the same. This is web scraping, and it might come in handy if the data you need isn't contained in one of the other more friendly formats. Web scraping is sometimes prohibited by website owners, so it's best to be careful and check the copyright and terms of service of the site before scraping.

3.2.3 *XML*

Extensible Markup Language (XML) can look a lot like HTML but is generally more suitable for storing and transmitting documents and data other than web pages. The previous snippet of HTML can be valid XML, though most XML documents begin with a tag that declares a particular XML version, such as the following:

```
<?xml version="1.0" encoding="UTF-8"?>
```

This declaration helps ensure that an XML interpreter reads tags in the appropriate way. Otherwise, XML works similarly to HTML but without most of the overhead associated with web pages. XML is now used as a standard format for offline documents such as the OpenOffice and Microsoft Office formats. Because the XML specification is designed to be machine-readable, it also can be used for data transmission, such as through APIs. For example, many official financial documents are available publicly in the Extensible Business Reporting Language (XBRL), which is XML-based.

This is a representation of the first two rows of the table JOBS_2015 in XML:

```
<JOB>
     <NAME>Alison</NAME>
     <ID>1</ID>
     <COLOR>'blue'</COLOR>
     <DONE>FALSE</DONE>
</JOB>
<JOB>
     <NAME>Brian</NAME>
     <ID>2</ID>
     <COLOR>'red'</COLOR>
     <DONE>TRUE</DONE>
</JOB>
```

You can see that each row of the table is denoted by a <JOB> tag, and within each JOB, the table's column names have been used as tags to denote the various fields of information. Clearly, storing data in this format takes up more disk space than a standard table because XML tags take up disk space, but XML is much more flexible, because it's not limited to a row-and-column format. For this reason, it has become popular in applications and documents using non-tabular data and other formats requiring such flexibility.

3.2.4   *JSON*

Though not a markup language, JavaScript Object Notation (JSON) is functionally similar, at least when storing or transmitting data. Instead of describing a document, JSON typically describes something more like a data structure, such as a list, map, or dictionary in many popular programming languages. Here's the data from the first two rows of the table JOBS_2015 in JSON:

```
[
     {
          NAME: "Alison",
          ID: 1,
          COLOR: "blue",
          DONE: False
     },
     {
          NAME: "Brian",
          ID: 2,
          COLOR: "red",
          DONE: True
     }
]
```

In terms of structure, this JSON representation looks a lot like the XML representation you've already seen. But the JSON representation is leaner in terms of the number of characters needed to express the data, because JSON was designed to represent data objects and not as a document markup language. Therefore, for transmitting data, JSON has become very popular. One huge benefit of JSON is that it can be read directly as JavaScript code, and many popular programming languages including Python and Java have natural representations of JSON as native data objects. For interoperability between programming languages, JSON is almost unparalleled in its ease of use.

3.2.5 *Relational databases*

Databases are data storage systems that have been optimized to store and retrieve data as efficiently as possible within various contexts. Theoretically, a relational database (the most common type of database) contains little more than a set of tables that could likewise be represented by a delimited file, as already discussed: row and column names and one data point per row-column pair. But databases are designed to search—or *query*, in the common jargon—for specific values or ranges of values within the entries of the table.

For example, let's revisit the JOBS_2015 table:

```
NAME      ID      COLOR     DONE
Alison    1       'blue'    FALSE
Brian     2       'red'     TRUE
Clara     3       'brown'   TRUE
```

But this time assume that this table is one of many stored in a database. A database query could be stated in plain English as follows:

```
From JOBS_2015, show me all NAME in rows where DONE=TRUE
```

This query should return the following:

```
Brian
Clara
```

That's a basic query, and every database has its own language for expressing queries like this, though many databases share the same basis query language, the most common being Structured Query Language (SQL).

Now imagine that the table contains millions of rows and you'd like to do a query similar to the one just shown. Through some tricks of software engineering, which I won't discuss here, a well-designed database is able to retrieve a set of table rows matching certain criteria (a query) much faster than a scan of a flat file would. This means that if you're writing an application that needs to search for specific data very often, you may improve retrieval speed by orders of magnitude if you use a database instead of a flat file.

The main reason why databases are good at retrieving specific data quickly is the database index. A *database index* is itself a data structure that helps that database software find relevant data quickly. It's like a structural map of the database content, which has been sorted and stored in a clever way and might need to be updated every time data in the database changes. Database indexes are not universal, however, meaning that the administrator of the database needs to choose which columns of the tables are to be indexed, if the default settings aren't appropriate. The columns that are chosen to be indexed are the ones upon which querying will be most efficient, and so the choice of index is an important one for the efficiency of your applications that use that database.

Besides querying, another operation that databases are typically good at is joining tables. Querying and joining aren't the only two things that databases are good at, but they're by far the most commonly utilized reasons to use a database over another data storage system. *Joining*, in database jargon, means taking two tables of data and combining them to make another table that contains some of the information of both of the original tables.

For example, assume you have the following table, named CUST_ZIP_CODES:

```
CUST_ID   ZIP_CODE
1         21230
2         45069
3         21230
4         98033
```

You'd like to investigate which paint colors have been used in which ZIP codes in 2015. Because the colors used on the various jobs are in JOBS_2015 and the customers' ZIP codes are in CUST_ZIP_CODES, you need to join the tables in order to match colors with ZIP codes. An inner join matching ID from table JOBS_2015 and CUST_ID from table CUST_ZIP_CODES could be stated in plain English:

JOIN tables JOBS_2015 and CUST_ZIP_CODES where ID equals CUST_ID, and show me ZIP_CODE and COLOR.

You're telling the database to first match up the customer ID numbers from the two tables and then show you only the two columns you care about. Note that there are no duplicate column names between the two tables, so there's no ambiguity in naming. But in practice you'd normally have to use a notation like CUST_ZIP_CODES.CUST_ID to denote the CUST_ID column of CUST_ZIP_CODES. I use the shorter version here for brevity.

The result of the join would look like this:

```
ZIP_CODE   COLOR
21230      'blue'
45069      'red'
21230      'brown'
```

Joining can be a very big operation if the original tables are big. If each table had millions of different IDs, it could take a long time to sort them all and match them up. Therefore, if you're joining tables, you should minimize the size of those tables (primarily by number of rows) because the database software will have to shuffle all rows of both tables based on the join criteria until all appropriate combinations of rows have been created in the new table. Joins should be done sparingly and with care.

It's a good general rule, if you're going to query *and* join, to query the data *first* before joining. For example, if you care only about the COLOR in ZIP_CODE 21230, it's usually better to query CUST_ZIP_CODES for ZIP_CODE=21230 first and join the result with JOBS_2015 instead of joining first and then querying. This way, there might be far less matching to do, and the execution of the operation will be much faster overall. For more information and guidance on optimizing database operations, you'll find plenty of practical database books in circulation.

You can think of databases in general as well-organized libraries, and their indexes are good librarians. A librarian can find the book you need in a matter of seconds, when it might have taken you quite a long time to find it yourself. If you have a relatively large data set and find that your code or software tool is spending a lot of time searching for the data it needs at any given moment, setting up a database is certainly worth considering.

3.2.6   *Non-relational databases*

Even if you don't have tabular data, you might still be able to make use of the efficiency of database indexing. An entire genre of databases called *NoSQL* (often interpreted as "Not only SQL") allows for database schemas outside the more traditional SQL-style relational databases. Graph databases and document databases are typically classified as NoSQL databases.

Many NoSQL databases return query results in familiar formats. Elasticsearch and MongoDB, for instance, return results in JSON format (discussed in section 3.2.4). Elasticsearch in particular is a document-oriented database that's very good at indexing the contents of text. If you're working with numerous blog posts or books, for example, and you're performing operations such as counting the occurrences of words within each blog post or book, then Elasticsearch is typically a good choice, if indexed properly.

Another possible advantage of some NoSQL databases is that, because of the flexibility of the schema, you can put almost anything into a NoSQL database without much hassle. Strings? Maps? Lists? Sure! Why not? MongoDB, for instance, is extremely easy to set up and use, but then you do lose some performance that you might have gained by setting up a more rigorous index and schema that apply to your data.

All in all, if you're working with large amounts of non-tabular data, there's a good chance that someone has developed a database that's good at indexing, querying, and retrieving your type of data. It's certainly worth a quick look around the internet to see what others are using in similar cases.

3.2.7   *APIs*

An *application programming interface* (API) in its most common forms is a set of rules for communicating with a piece of software. With respect to data, think of an API as a gateway through which you can make requests and then receive the data, using a well-defined set of terms. Databases have APIs; they define the language that you must use in your query, for instance, in order to receive the data you want.

Many websites also have APIs. Tumblr, for instance, has a public API that allows you to ask for and receive information about Tumblr content of certain types, in JSON format. Tumblr has huge databases containing all the billions of posts hosted on its blogging service. But it has decided what you, as a member of the public, can and can't access within the databases. The methods of access and the limitations are defined by the API.

Tumblr's API is a REST API accessible via HTTP. I've never found the technical definition of *REST API* to be helpful, but it's a term that people use when discussing APIs that are accessible via HTTP—meaning you can usually access them from a web browser—and that respond with information in a familiar format. For instance, if you register with Tumblr as a developer (it's free), you can get an API key. This API key is a string that's unique to you, and it tells Tumblr that you're the one using the API whenever you make a request. Then, in your web browser, you can paste the URL http://api.tumblr.com/v2/blog/good.tumblr.com/info?api_key=API_KEY, which will request information about a particular blog on Tumblr (replacing API_KEY with the API key that you were given). After you press Enter, the response should appear in your browser window and look something like this (after some reformatting):

```
{
    meta:
    {
        status: 200,
        msg: "OK"
    },
    response:
    {
        blog:
        {
            title: "",
            name: "good",
            posts: 2435,
            url: "http://good.tumblr.com/",
            updated: 1425428288,
            description: "<font size="6">
                    GOOD is a magazine for the global citizen.
                    </font>",
            likes: 429
        }
    }
}
```

This is JSON with some HTML in the description field. It contains some metadata about the status of the request and then a response field containing the data that was requested. Assuming you know how to parse JSON strings (and likewise HTML), you can use this in a programmatic way. If you were curious about the number of likes of

Tumblr blogs, you could use this API to request information about any number of blogs and compare the numbers of likes that they have received. You wouldn't want to do that, though, from your browser window, because it would take a very long time.

In order to capture the Tumblr API response programmatically, you need to use an HTTP or URL package in your favorite programming language. In Python there is urllib, in Java HttpUrlConnection, and R has url, but there are many other packages for each of these languages that perform similar tasks. In any case, you'll have to assemble the request URL (as a string object/variable) and then pass that request to the appropriate URL retrieval method, which should return a response similar to the previous one that can be captured as another object/variable. Here's an example in Python:

```
import urllib

requestURL = \
    'http://api.tumblr.com/v2/blog/good.tumblr.com/info?api_key=API_KEY'

response = urllib.urlopen(requestURL)
```

After running these lines, the variable response should contain a JSON string that looks similar to the response shown.

I remember learning how to use an API like this one from Python, and I was a bit confused and overwhelmed at first. Getting the request URL exactly right can be tricky if you're assembling it programmatically from various parts (for example, base URL, parameters, API key, and so on). But being adept at using APIs like this one can be one of the most powerful tools in data collection, because so much data is available through these gateways.

3.2.8 Common bad formats

It's no secret that I'm not a fan of the typical suites of office software: word processing programs, spreadsheets, mail clients. Thankfully, I'm not often required to use them. I avoid them whenever possible and never more so than when doing data science. That doesn't mean that I won't deal with those files; on the contrary, I wouldn't throw away free data. But I make sure to get away from any inconvenient formats as quickly as possible. There usually isn't a good way to interact with them unless I'm using the highly specialized programs that were built for them, and these programs typically aren't capable of the analysis that a data scientist usually needs. I can't remember the last time I did (or saw) a solid bit of data science in Microsoft Excel; to me, Excel's methods for analysis are limited, and the interface is unwieldy for anything but looking at tables. But I know I'm biased, so don't mind me if you're convinced you can do rigorous analysis within a spreadsheet. OpenOffice Calc and Microsoft Excel both allow you to export individual sheets from a spreadsheet into CSV formats. If a Microsoft Word document contains text I'd like to use, I export it either into plain text or maybe HTML or XML.

A PDF can be a tricky thing as well. I've exported lots of text (or copied and pasted) from PDFs into plain text files that I then read into a Python program. This is one of my favorite examples of *data wrangling*, a topic I devote an entire chapter to, and so for now it will suffice to say that exporting or scraping text from a PDF (where possible) is usually a good idea whenever you want to analyze that text.

3.2.9 *Unusual formats*

This is the umbrella category for all data formats and storage systems with which I'm unfamiliar. All sorts of formats are available, and I'm sure someone had a good reason to develop them, but for whatever reason they're not familiar to me. Sometimes they're archaic; maybe they were superseded by another format, but some legacy data sets haven't yet been updated.

Sometimes the formats are highly specialized. I once participated in a project exploring the chemical structure of a compound and its connection to the way the compound smelled (its aroma). The RDKit package (www.rdkit.org) provided a ton of helpful functionality for parsing through chemical structures and substructures. But much of this functionality was highly specific to chemical structure and its notation. Plus the package made heavy use of a fairly sophisticated binary representation of certain aspects of chemical structure that greatly improved the computational efficiency of the algorithms but also made them extremely difficult to understand.

Here's what I do when I encounter a data storage system unlike anything I've seen before:

1 Search and search (and search) online for a few examples of people doing something similar to what I want to do. How difficult might it be to adapt these examples to my needs?

2 Decide how badly I want the data. Is it worth the trouble? What are the alternatives?

3 If it's worth it, I try to generalize from the similar examples I found. Sometimes I can gradually expand from examples by fiddling with parameters and methods. I try a few things and see what happens.

Dealing with completely unfamiliar data formats or storage systems can be its own type of exploration, but rest assured that someone somewhere has accessed the data before. If no one has ever accessed the data, then someone was completely mistaken in creating the data format in the first place. When in doubt, send a few emails and try to find someone who can help you.

3.2.10 *Deciding which format to use*

Sometimes you don't have a choice. The data comes in a certain format, and you have to deal with it. But if you find that format inefficient, unwieldy, or unpopular, you're usually free to set up a secondary data store that might make things easier, but at the additional cost of the time and effort it takes you to set up the secondary data store. For applications where access efficiency is critical, the cost can be worth it. For smaller projects, maybe not. You'll have to cross that bridge when you get there.

I'll conclude this section with a few general rules about what data formats to use, when you have a choice, and in particular when you're going to be accessing the data from a programming language. Table 3.1 gives the most common good format for interacting with data of particular types.

Table 3.1   Some common types of data and formats that are good for storing them

Type of data	Good, common format
Tabular data, small amount	Delimited flat file
Tabular data, large amount with lots of searching/querying	Relational database
Plain text, small amount	Flat file
Plain text, large amount	Non-relational database with text search capabilities
Transmitting data between components	JSON
Transmitting documents	XML

And here are a few guidelines for choosing or converting data formats:

- For spreadsheets and other office documents, export!
- More common formats are usually better for your data type and application.
- Don't spend too much time converting from a certain format to your favorite; weigh the costs and benefits first.

Now that I've covered many of the forms in which data might be presented to you, hopefully you'll feel somewhat comfortable in a high-level conversation about data formats, stores, and APIs. As always, never hesitate to ask someone for details about a term or system you haven't heard of before. New systems are being developed constantly, and in my experience, anyone who recently learned about a system is usually eager to help others learn about it.

3.3   *Scouting for data*

The previous section discussed many of the common forms that data takes, from file formats to databases to APIs. I intended to make these data forms more approachable, as well as to increase awareness about the ways you might look for data. It's not hard to find data, much like it's not hard to find a tree or a river (in certain climates). But finding the data that can help you solve your problem is a different story. Or maybe you already have data from an internal system. It may seem like that data can answer the major questions of your project, but you shouldn't take it for granted. Maybe a data set out there will perfectly complement the data you already have and greatly improve results. There's so much data on the internet and elsewhere; some part of it should be able to help you. Even if not, a quick search is certainly worth it, even for a long-shot possibility.

In this section, I discuss the act of looking for data that might help you with your project. This is the exploration I talked about at the beginning of this chapter. Now that you have some exposure to common forms of data from the previous section, you can focus less on the format and more on the content and whether it can help you.

3.3.1 First step: Google search

This may seem obvious, but I still feel like mentioning it: Google searches are not perfect. To make them work as well as possible, you have to know what to search for and what you're looking for in the search results. Given the last section's introduction to data formats, you now have a little more ammunition for Google searches than before.

A Google search for "Tumblr data" gives different results from a search for "Tumblr API." I'm not sure which I prefer, given that I don't have a specific project involving Tumblr at the moment. The former returns results involving the term *data* as used on Tumblr posts as well as third parties selling historical Tumblr data. The latter returns results that deal almost exclusively with the official Tumblr API, which contains considerable up-to-the-minute information about Tumblr posts. Depending on your project, one might be better than the other.

But it's definitely worth keeping in mind that terms such as *data* and *API* do make a difference in web searches. Try the searches "social networking" and "social networking API." There's a dramatic difference in results.

Therefore, when searching for data related to your project, be sure to include modifying terms like *historical, API, real time*, and so on, because they do make a difference. Likewise, watch out for them in the search results. This may be obvious, but it makes a considerable difference in your ability to find what you're looking for, and so it's worth repeating.

3.3.2 Copyright and licensing

I've talked about searching for, accessing, and using data, but there's another very important concern: are you *allowed* to use it?

As with software licenses, data may have licensing, copyright, or other restrictions that can make it illegal to use the data for certain purposes. If the data comes from academic sources, for example (universities, research institutions, and the like), then there's often a restriction that the data can't be used for profit. Proprietary data, such as that of Tumblr or Twitter, often comes with the restriction that you can't use the data to replicate functionality that the platform itself provides. You may not be able to make a Tumblr client that does the same things as the standard Tumblr platform, but perhaps if you offer other functionality not included in the platform, there would be no restriction. Restrictions like these are tricky, and it's best to read any legal documentation that the data provider offers. In addition, it's usually good to search for other examples of people and companies using the data in a similar way and see if there are any references to legal concerns. Precedent is no guarantee that a particular use of the data is legally sound, but it may provide guidance in your decision to use the data or not.

All in all, you should remain keenly aware that most data sets not owned by you or your organization come with restrictions on use. Without confirming that your use case is legal, you remain at risk of losing access to the data or, even worse, a lawsuit.

3.3.3   *The data you have: is it enough?*

Let's say you've found data and confirmed that you're allowed to use it for your project. Should you keep looking for more data, or should you attack the data you have immediately? The answer to this question is—like pretty much everything in data science—tricky. In this case, the answer is tricky because data sets aren't always what they seem to be or what you want them to be. Take the example of Uber, the taxi service app publisher. I recently read that Uber was compelled (upon losing an appeal) to turn over trip data to New York City's Taxi and Limousine Commission (TLC). Suppose you're an employee of the TLC, and you'd like to compare Uber with traditional taxi services in regard to the number of trips taken by riders over many specific routes. Given that you have data from both Uber and traditional taxis, it may seem straightforward to compare the number of trips for similar routes between the two types of car services. But once you begin your analysis, you realize that Uber had provided pick-up and drop-off locations in terms of ZIP codes, which happen to be the minimum specificity required by the TLC. ZIP codes can cover large areas, though admittedly less so in New York City than anywhere else. Addresses, or at least city blocks, would have been considerably better from a data analysis perspective, but requiring such specificity presents legal troubles regarding the privacy of personal data of the users of taxi services, so it's understandable.

So what should you do? After the first waves of disappointment wear off, you should probably check to see whether your data will suffice after all or if you need to supplement this data and/or amend your project plans. There's often a simple way to accomplish this: can you run through a few specific examples of your intended analyses and see if it makes a significant difference?

In this taxi-versus-Uber example, you'd like to find out whether the relative nonspecificity of ZIP code can still provide a useful approximation for the many routes you'd like to evaluate. Pick a specific route, say Times Square (ZIP code: 10036) to the Brooklyn Academy of Music (ZIP code: 11217). If a car travels between 10036 and 11217, what other specific routes might the rider have taken? In this case, those same ZIP codes could also describe a trip from the Intrepid Sea, Air & Space Museum to Grand Army Plaza, or likewise a trip from a restaurant in Hell's Kitchen to an apartment in Park Slope. These probably don't mean much to people outside the New York City area, but for our purposes it suffices to say that these other locations are up to a kilometer from the origin and destination of the chosen route, a distance that's about a ten-minute walk and, by NYC standards, not very short. It's up to you, the data scientist, to make a decision about whether these other locations in the same ZIP codes are close enough or too far from their intended targets. And this decision, in turn, should be made based on the project's goals and the precise questions (from chapter 2) that you're hoping to answer.

3.3.4 Combining data sources

If you find that your data set is insufficient to answer your questions, and you can't find a data set that is sufficient, it might still be possible to combine data sets to find answers. This is yet another point that seems obvious at times but is worth mentioning because of its importance and because of a few tricky points that might pop up.

Combining two (or more) data sets can be like fitting puzzle pieces together. If the puzzle is, metaphorically, the complete data set you wish you had, then each piece of the puzzle—a data set—needs to cover precisely what the other pieces don't. Sure, unlike puzzle pieces, data sets can overlap in some sense, but any gap left after all the present pieces have been assembled is an obstacle that needs to be overcome or circumvented, either by changing the plan or some other reevaluation of how you're going to answer your questions.

Your multiple data sets might be coming in multiple formats. If you're adept at manipulating each of these formats, this doesn't usually present a problem, but it can be tough to conceptualize how the data sets relate to one another if they're in vastly different forms. A database table and a CSV file are similar to me—they both have rows and columns—and so I can typically imagine how they might fit together, as in the database example earlier in this chapter, with one data set (one of the tables) providing the customer's color choice and another data set (the other table) providing the customer's ZIP code. These two can be combined easily because both data sets are based on the same set of customer IDs. If you can imagine how you might match up the customer IDs between the two data sets and then combine the accompanying information—a *join*, in database parlance—then you can imagine how to combine these two data sets meaningfully.

On the other hand, combining data sets might not be so simple. During my time as the lead data scientist at a Baltimore analytic software firm, I took part in a project in which our team was analyzing email data sets as part of a legal investigation. The collection of emails was delivered to us in the form of a few dozen files in PST format, which is Microsoft Outlook's archival format. I'd seen this format before, because I'd worked previously with the now-public and commonly studied Enron email data set. Each archive file comprised the email from one person's computer, and because the people under investigation often emailed each other, the data sets overlapped. Each email, excepting deleted emails, was present in each of the senders' and recipients' archives. It's tempting to think that it would be easy to combine all of the email archives in to a single file—I chose a simple, large CSV file as the goal format—and then analyze this file. But it wasn't so easy.

Extracting individual emails from each archive and turning each of them into a row of a CSV file was, comparatively, the easy part. The hard part, I quickly realized, was making sure I could keep all of the senders and recipients straight. As it turns out, the names listed in the sender and recipient fields of emails are not standardized— when you send an email, what appears in the SENDER field isn't always the same as what appears in the RECIPIENT field when someone writes an email to you. In fact, even within each of these two fields, names are not consistent. If Nikola Tesla sent an email to Thomas Edison (names have been changed to protect the innocent), the SENDER and RECIPIENT fields might be any of the following:

```
SENDER                            RECIPIENT
Nikola Tesla <nikola@ac.org>      Thomas Edison, CEO <thomas@coned.com>
Nikola <nikola.tesla@ac.org>      thomas.edison@dc.com
ntesla@gmail.com                  tommyed@comcast.com
nikola@tesla.me                   Tom <t@coned.com>
wirelesspower@@tesla.me           litebulbz@hotmail.com
```

Some of these would be recognizable as Tesla or Edison, even out of context, but others would not. To be sure each email is attributed to the right person, you'd also need a list of email addresses matched to the correct names. I didn't have that list, so I did the best I could, made some assumptions, and used some fuzzy string matching with spot-checking (discussed more in the next chapter on data wrangling) to match as many emails as possible with the appropriate names. I thought the multiple email data sets would merge nicely together, but I soon found out that this was not the case.

Data sets can differ in any number of ways; format, nomenclature, and scope (geographic, temporal, and so on) are a few. As in section 3.3.3 on finding out whether your data is enough, before you spend too much time manipulating your multiple data sets or diving into analyses, it's usually extremely helpful and informative to spot-check a few data points and attempt a quick analysis on a small scale. A quick look into a few PST files in the email example made me aware of the disparate naming schemes across files and fields and allowed me to plan within the project for the extra time and inevitable matching errors that arose.

Now imagine combining this email data set with internal chat messages in a JSON format—potentially containing a different set of user names—with a set of events/ appointments in a proprietary calendar format. Assembling them into a single timeline with unambiguous user names is no simple task, but it might be possible with care and awareness of the potential pitfalls.

3.3.5   *Web scraping*

Sometimes you can find the information you need on the internet, but it's not what you might call a data set in the traditional sense. Social media profiles, like those on Facebook or LinkedIn, are great examples of data that's viewable on the internet but not readily available in a standard data format. Therefore, some people choose to scrape it from the web.

I should definitely mention that web scraping is against the terms of service for many websites. And some sites have guards in place that will shut down your access if they detect a scraper. Sometimes they detect you because you're visiting web pages much more quickly than a human being can, such as several thousand pages in few minutes or even a few hours. Regardless, people have used scraping techniques to gather useful data they wouldn't have otherwise, in some cases circumventing any guards by adapting the scraper to act more human.

Two important things that a web scraper must do well are visit lots of URLs programmatically and capture the right information from the pages. If you wanted to know about your friend network on Facebook, you could theoretically write a script that visits the Facebook profiles of all of your friends, saves the profile pages, and then parses the pages to get lists of their friends, visits their friends' profiles, and so on. This works only for people who have allowed you to view their profiles and friend lists, and would not work for private profiles.

An example of web scraping that became popular in early 2014 is that of mathematician Chris McKinlay, who used a web scraper to capture data from thousands of profiles on the popular dating website OKCupid. He used the information he gathered—mostly women's answers to multiple-choice questions on the site—to cluster the women into a few types and subsequently optimize a separate profile for himself for each of the types he found generally attractive. Because he optimized each profile for a certain cluster/type of women, women in that cluster had a high matching score (according to OKCupid's own algorithms) for the respective profile and were therefore more likely to engage him in conversation and ultimately to go out on a date with him. It seems to have worked out well for him, earning him dozens of dates before he met the woman with whom he wanted to start a monogamous relationship.

For more on the practicalities of building a web scraper, see the documentation for the HTTP- and HTML-related utilities of your favorite programming language and any number of online guides, as well as section 3.2 on data formats, particularly the discussion of HTML.

3.3.6 *Measuring or collecting things yourself*

Contrary to the principal way I've presented data in this chapter—a product of a culture that wants data for its own sake, existing regardless of whether someone intends to use it—you sometimes have the opportunity to collect data the old-fashioned way. Methods could be as simple as personally counting the number of people crossing a street at a particular crosswalk or perhaps emailing a survey to a group of interest. When starting a new project, if you ever ask yourself, "Does the data I need exist?" and find that the answer is "No" or "Yes, but I can't get access to it," then maybe it would be helpful to ask, "*Can* the data exist?"

The question "Can the data exist?" is intended to draw attention to the potential for simple measures you can take that can create the data set you want. These include the following:

- *Measuring things in real life*—Using tape measures, counting, asking questions personally, and so on may seem outmoded, but it's often underrated.

- *Measuring things online*—Clicking around the internet and counting relevant web pages, numbers of relevant Google search results, and number of occurrences of certain terms on certain Wikipedia pages, among others, can benefit your project.
- *Scripting and web scraping*—Repeated API calls or web scraping of certain pages over a period of time can be useful when certain elements in the API or web page are constantly changing but you don't have access to the history.
- *Data-collection devices*—Today's concept of the Internet of Things gets considerable media buzz partially for its value in creating data from physical devices, some of which are capable of recording the physical world—for example, cameras, thermometers, and gyroscopes. Do you have a device (your mobile phone?) that can help you? Can you buy one?
- *Log files or archives*—Sometimes jargonized into *digital trail* or *exhaust*, log files are (or can be) left behind by many software applications. Largely untouched, they're usually called to action only in exceptional circumstances (crashes! bugs!). Can you put them to good use in your project?

For that last bullet, much like web scraping, the primary tasks are to identify manually whether and where the log files contain data that can help you and to learn how to extract this useful data programmatically from a set of log files that contain, in most cases, a bunch of other data that you'll never need. This, perhaps, is the frontier of the data wilderness: creating conceptually new data sets using other data that exists for an entirely different purpose. I believe *data alchemy* has been put forth as a possible name for this phenomenon, but I'll leave you to judge whether your own data extractions and transformations merit such a mystical title.

3.4   *Example: microRNA and gene expression*

When I was a PhD student, most of my research was related to quantitative modeling of gene expression. I mentioned working in genetics previously, but I haven't delved deeply until now. I find it to be an incredibly interesting field.

Genetics is the study of the code from which all living things are built. This code is present in every organism's genome, which is composed of DNA or RNA, and copies of it are present in every cell. If an organism's genome has been sequenced, then its genome has been parsed into genes and other types of non-gene sequences. Here I focus only on the genes and their expression. Biologists' concept of *gene expression* involves the activity of known genes within a biological sample, and we measure gene expression using any of several tools that can measure the *copy number*, or concentration of specific RNA sequence fragments that are related directly to these genes. If an RNA fragment contains a sequence that's known to match a certain gene but not other genes, then that sequence can be used as an indicator of the expression of the gene. If that RNA sequence occurs very often (high copy number or concentration) in the biological sample, then the expression of the corresponding gene is said to be high, and a sequence that occurs rarely indicates that its associated gene is expressed at a low level.

Two technologies, known as *microarrays* and *sequencing*, are common methods for measuring gene expression via the concentration or copy number of RNA sequences found in biological samples. Sequencing tends to be favored now, but at the time of my PhD research, I was analyzing data from microarrays. The data had been given to me by a collaborator at the University of Maryland School of Medicine, who had been studying the stem cells of *Mus musculus*—a common mouse—through various stages of development. In the earliest stages, stem cells are known to be of a general type that can subsequently develop into any of a number of *differentiated*, or specialized, cell types. The progression of cells through these stages of undifferentiated and then specific differentiated stem cell types isn't fully understood, but it had been hypothesized by my collaborators and others that a special class of RNA sequences called microRNA might be involved.

MicroRNAs (or miRs) are short RNA sequences (about 20 base pairs, vastly shorter than most genes) that are known to be present in virtually all organisms. To help determine whether miRs help regulate the development of stem cells and differentiation, my collaborators used microarrays to measure the expression of both genes and miRs throughout the early stages of development of stem cells.

The data set consisted of microarray data for both genes and miRs for each of the seven stem cell types. A single microarray measures several thousand genes or, alternatively, a few hundred miRs. And for each stem cell type, there were two to three replicates, meaning that each biological sample was analyzed using two to three gene-oriented microarrays and two to three miR-oriented microarrays. Replicates are helpful for analyzing variance between samples as well as identifying outliers. Given 7 stem cell types and 2 to 3 replicates each for genes and miRs, I had 33 microarrays in total.

Because miRs are thought mainly to inhibit expression of genes—they apparently bind to complementary sections of genetic RNA and block that RNA from being copied—the main question I asked of the data set was "Can I find any evidence of specific miRs inhibiting the expression of specific genes?" Is the expression of any certain gene routinely low whenever the expression of a specific miR is high? In addition, I wanted to know whether the expression and inhibiting activity of any miRs could be highly correlated with particular stages of stem cell development and differentiation.

Though no one had previously studied this specific topic—the effect of miRs in mouse stem cell development—a fair amount of work had been done on related topics. Of particular note was the class of statistical algorithms that attempted to characterize whether a particular miR would target (inhibit) a specific section of genetic RNA, based solely on the sequence information alone. If a miR's base sequence looks like this

ACATGTAACCTGTAGATAGAT

(again, I use *T* in place of *U* for convenience), then a perfectly complementary genetic RNA sequence would be

TGTACATTGGACATCTATCTA

because, within an RNA sequence, the nucleotide A is complementary to T, and C is complementary to G. Because these miRs are floating around in a cell's cytoplasm, as are genetic RNA sequences, there's no guarantee that even a perfect match will bind and inhibit gene expression. Under perfect conditions, such complementary sequences will bind, but nothing in biology is perfect. It's also likely that a miR and its perfect match will float past each other like two ships passing in the night, as they say. Also, it's a funny quirk of all RNA sequences that sometimes they bend a little too much and get stuck to themselves—for miRs the result is known as a *hairpin* because of the shape that's easy to imagine. In any case, it's not a foregone conclusion that perfectly complementary sequences will bind; nor is it true that imperfect matches won't bind. Many researchers have explored this and developed algorithms that assign miR-gene pairs matching scores based on complementarity and other features of the sequences. These are generally referred to as *target prediction* algorithms, and I made use of two such algorithms in my work: one called TargetScan (www.targetscan.org) and another called miRanda (www.microrna.org).

Both TargetScan and miRanda are widely viewed as the products of solid scientific research, and both of these algorithms and their predictions are freely available on the internet. For any miR-gene pair in my microarray data sets, I had at least two target prediction scores indicating whether the miR is likely to inhibit expression of the gene. The files I obtained from TargetScan look like this (with some columns removed for clarity):

```
Gene ID     miRNA          context+ score    percentile
71667       xtr-miR-9b     -0.259            89
71667       xtr-miR-9      -0.248            88
71667       xtr-miR-9a     -0.248            88
```

As you can see, for each gene and miR/miRNA, TargetScan has given a score representing the likelihood that the miR will target the genetic RNA. miRanda provides similar files. These scores are known to be imperfect, but they are informative, so I decided to include them as evidence but not certainty of inhibition of the gene's expression by the miR.

My main data set was still the set of microarrays I had from my collaborators' lab, and from these I would be able to analyze all expression values of genes and miRs and determine positive and negative correlations between them. Also, I could use the target predictions as further evidence in favor of certain miR-gene target pairs. In the framework of Bayesian statistics—discussed more in chapter 8—the target predictions can be considered a priori knowledge, and I could adjust that knowledge based on the new data I collected—the new microarray data I received from my collaborators. In this way, neither the prediction nor the noisy data set was taken as truth, but both informed the final estimates of which miR-gene pairs are most likely true targeting interactions.

So far in this section, I've talked about combining gene expression data with microRNA data to search for targeting interactions between them and to analyze the effects of miRs on stem cell development. In addition, I included two target prediction data sets as further evidence that certain miRs target certain genes. As I completed analysis based on these data sets, I needed to be able to show that the miRs and genes that my models indicated as being related to stem cell development made sense in some way. There were two ways I might typically do this: ask my biologist collaborators to test some of my results in the lab to confirm that they were correct, or find more data sets online somewhere that were already validated and that supported my results in some way.

If I'd had no experience working with this sort of data, I might have Googled "validated microRNA targeting" or "stem cell development gene annotations," but because I knew from past projects that a large public set of annotations of genes known as Gene Ontology (GO) terms was available, as well as a database of validated miR-gene targeting interactions already reported in scientific publications, I didn't have to search much. GO term annotation can be accessed via a few web-based tools (geneontology.org) as well as a package for the R language, among others. I had previously used these annotations for analyzing groups of genes to see whether they have some things in common. In the case of this project, it would help to confirm my results if any group of genes found significant within my model with respect to stem cell development also had a significant number of GO annotations related to stem cells and stem cell development.

Also, I obviously preferred that any miR-gene target pairs that my model found significant would have already been validated in some other reliable way. This is where the data set of *validated* targeting interactions on www.microrna.org comes in. It's certainly a useful data set, but one important aspect of it is that, although some miR-gene target pairs have been confirmed, just because a pair *hasn't* been confirmed doesn't mean that it *isn't* a true target pair. If my model found a particular target pair significant, but it hadn't been validated yet, that didn't indicate at all that the model was wrong. On the other hand, if a validated target pair did not appear significant according to my model, then there was some reason for concern. Overall, in the validation step of my project, I hoped that all or most of the validated target pairs appeared significant according to the model, but I didn't necessarily need to see validations for my most significant results.

Lastly, my collaborators had some interest in which families of microRNAs (groups of miRs with partially matching sequences) contributed to which stages of stem cell development. It turned out that TargetScan provided a nicely formatted file matching miRs with their families. In addition to the gene expression microarrays, the microRNA expression microarrays, two target prediction algorithm results, a set of gene annotations, and some validated miR-gene target pairs, I added a miR family data set.

Needless to say, there were many moving parts in this project. Also, as happens quite often in academia, the resulting scientific papers couldn't include every piece of analysis. There's one paper describing the model and application to a public data set ("Inferring MicroRNA Regulation of mRNA with Partially Ordered Samples of Paired Expression Data and Exogenous Prediction Algorithms," PloS ONE, 2012) and another paper describing the application to the mouse data set ("Correlated miR-mRNA Expression Signatures of Mouse Hematopoietic Stem and Progenitor Cell Subsets Predict 'Stemness' and 'Myeloid' Interaction Networks," PLoS ONE, 2014).

I won't describe all results here in detail, but I was quite satisfied with the project. After matching miRs and genes from their respective expression data sets with their predicted target pairs from TargetScan and miRanda, I analyzed them via a Bayesian model incorporating all of this data and validated it using GO annotations and known target pair validations, with some miR family analysis tacked on. The results weren't perfect; bioinformatics is notoriously complex, not to mention imperfect in its data quality. But most validated target pairs were significant, and some relevant GO annotations were overrepresented in significant groups of genes. In later chapters, I'll delve more deeply into statistical models, their significance, and drawing conclusions from results, but for now I'd like to leave this example as one in which various data sets have been combined in ways that make new analyses possible.

Exercises

Continuing with the Filthy Money Forecasting personal finance app scenario from the last chapter's exercises, try these exercises:

1   List three potential data sources that you expect would be good to examine for this project. For each, also list how you would expect to access the data (for example, database, API, and so on).

2   Consider the three project goals you listed in exercise 3 in the last chapter. What data would you need in order to achieve them?

Summary

- Data science treats *data* as something that might exist independently of any specific purpose. Much like nature itself, and all of the organisms and species that exist within it, discovered or undiscovered, the realm of data is worth exploration and study.

- Data can be found in many places with varying accessibility, complexity, and reliability.

- It's best to become familiar with some of the forms that data might take, as well as how to view and manipulate these forms.

- Before assuming that a data set contains what you want, it's best to evaluate data extent and quality.

- Finding and recognizing data sets that are useful for your project aren't always straightforward, but some preliminary investigation can help.

Data wrangling: from capture to domestication

One definition of *wrangling* is "having a long and complicated dispute." That sounds about right.

Data wrangling is the process of taking data and information in difficult, unstructured, or otherwise arbitrary formats and converting it into something that conventional software can use. Like many aspects of data science, it's not so much a process as it is a collection of strategies and techniques that can be applied within the context of an overall project strategy. Wrangling isn't a task with steps that can be prescribed exactly beforehand. Every case is different and takes some problem solving to get good results. Before I discuss specific techniques and strategies of data wrangling, as shown in figure 4.1, I'll introduce a case study that I'll use to illustrate those techniques and strategies throughout the chapter.

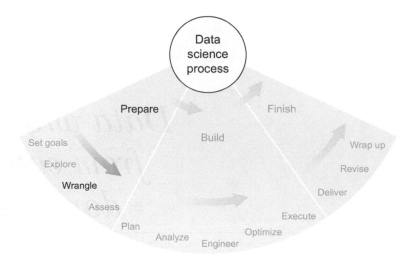

Figure 4.1   **The third step of the preparation phase of the data science process: data wrangling**

4.1   *Case study: best all-time performances in track and field*

While I was in graduate school, the Jamaican sprinter Usain Bolt began to astonish the world with amazing performances in both the 100 m and 200 m dashes. In the 2008 Olympic Games in Beijing, Bolt ran a world record 9.69 seconds in the 100 m dash despite celebrating his victory with outstretched arms well before he crossed the finish line. A few days later, Bolt's time of 19.30 sec in the 200 m final broke Michael Johnson's world record, which had been widely considered one of the best marks in the entire sport of track and field. Usain Bolt had claimed his position as the greatest sprinter in history, but he continued to improve.

At the 2009 World Championships in Berlin, Usain Bolt broke both of his own world records. He ran 9.58 sec in the 100 m dash and 19.19 sec in the 200 m dash, making all of his competitors, the fastest people in the world, appear average. Specifically, in the 100 m dash, American Tyson Gay set a national record—and the USA is traditionally good at sprinting—but was meters behind Bolt at the finish line. I was so impressed by Bolt's performances, and so ubiquitous were discussions of "How good are Usain Bolt's marks compared to other world records?" and "No other athlete has dominated like Bolt has," that I decided to quantify the improbability of what Bolt had done. I wanted to settle the score for all of the armchair track and field enthusiasts out there who mostly made guesses and used anecdotes and heuristic methods to show how rare a given performance is.

4.1.1   *Common heuristic comparisons*

Armchair track and field enthusiasts tend to compare world records in different events by how old they are or how close anyone else has come to breaking them.

Michael Johnson's 200 m dash world record was 12 years old when Usain Bolt broke it, whereas the 100 m world record was less than a year old when Usain Bolt broke it the first time in early 2008, before breaking it again at the 2008 Olympics and the 2009 World Championships. The age of a world record probably does indicate some amount of strength of the record, but it's certainly not a perfect measure. Was Bolt's 19.19 sec mark for the 200 m worse than his 19.30 sec mark because the previous record was younger? Certainly not.

Sometimes people will cite the percentage improvement of a mark over the second-best mark as evidence that it's good. The world record javelin throw by Jan Zelezný of 98.48 m is 2.9% farther than his second-best throw and 5.8% farther than anyone else's ever. Usain Bolt's still-current world record of 9.58 sec was 1.1% faster than his second-best time and 1.3% faster than the fastest mark by another person, which happened to be the second-place finisher in the same race, Tyson Gay. Again, this is a reasonable indicator of a good performance but is nowhere near perfect because of the high variance of those second-best performances. If, for some reason, the second-best performance had never happened, the percentage could change dramatically.

4.1.2   *IAAF Scoring Tables*

More sophisticated methods existed at the time I began this project in 2009, but they also had their shortcomings. The most widely accepted method for comparing performances between events in track and field among coaches, fans, and many others is a set of points tables called the IAAF Scoring Tables of Athletics. Typically every few years, an updated set of points tables is published by the International Association of Athletics Federations (IAAF). The IAAF also publishes the *combined events* points tables that are used in the multidiscipline events such as the men's decathlon and women's heptathlon, in which competitors are given points for their performances in each of the disciplines, and the winner is the athlete with the most total points. In combined events, the points tables are the basis for the competition itself. The Scoring Tables for individual events have little effect on competition, with the exception of certain track and field meetings that award prizes based on the tables.

The 2008 Scoring Tables, the most recent tables at the time Usain Bolt ran 9.58 sec in the 100 m dash, gave the world-record performance a score of 1374 (the tables' highest score listed is 1400 points). In the next update to the Scoring Tables, in 2011, Usain Bolt's 2009 performance received a score of 1356. This was quite a dramatic change in score, and such a large change did not occur in most events. For reference, according to the 2008 tables, 9.58 sec 100 m was equivalent to a 42.09 sec 400 m dash, whereas according to the 2011 tables, it was equivalent to a 42.37 sec 400 m. In an Olympic 400 m final, 0.28 sec is easily the difference between a gold medal and no medal. According to the Scoring Tables, Usain Bolt's world record was getting worse.

There is a reason for this. The IAAF's Combined Scoring Tables are known to be based on a relatively small set of the best performances in each event. The small set might be the top 10 or top 25, but I'm merely guessing, because the methods aren't fully disclosed. If the tables are based heavily on a small set of the top performances, then a dramatic change in this set will dramatically affect the scores in the next update to the tables. The 2008 and 2009 track and field seasons produced some incredible 100 m performances, even without Usain Bolt. These performances affected the next set of scores, released in 2011. In some sense, through the Scoring Tables, Usain Bolt's world-record performances and the strong performances of his rivals eventually made themselves less impressive.

By recounting all of this, I mean only to show how basing models on too little data can significantly distort results and conclusions. In the Scoring Tables, a few great performances within two or three years of great results drastically changed our impression of how good such performances are. I made it my goal to use all data I could find to generate a scoring method that would not only be less sensitive to changes in the best performances but would also be a good predictor of future level of performance, which represents a good set of out-of-sample data.

4.1.3   *Comparing performances using all data available*

My biggest question when starting out: how much data can I find? All manner of searching the internet and asking friends led me to conclude that alltime-athletics.com provides the most complete set of elite track and field performances available. The site provides lists of the top performances ever in all Olympic track and field events; for some events, the lists contain thousands of performances. I felt that if I used all of this data and a little statistical knowledge, I could improve on the robustness and predictive power of the IAAF's Scoring Tables.

The first step was to wrangle the data. The lists of the top performances were on a website but weren't available in a convenient format such as CSV, so I'd have to resort to web scraping in some way. In addition to that, I'd need to compare my scores and results with those from my leading competitor, the IAAF Scoring Tables, which were available only in PDF. Neither web pages nor PDFs are ideal for programmatic parsing, and both can get quite messy when considering HTML structure in web pages and page headers, footers, and numbers in PDFs. Simply put, it would take some wrangling.

Throughout the following sections, I'll continue to refer to the two wrangling tasks in this track and field project:

- Wrangling the lists of top performances from the website alltime-athletics.com
- Wrangling the IAAF Scoring Tables from the PDF that contains them

4.2   *Getting ready to wrangle*

Some people like to dive in immediately and start throwing data around, but that's not my style. I'm a bit more deliberate. I like to look around a bit before I write any code or commit to trying any strategies. I do a few things to gather some good information about the data that can help me wrangle more effectively.

In this section, first I show you what it might look like to have messy data that needs to be wrangled. Then I list a few steps that you can take before you begin to wrangle that are helpful for figuring out what you have, what you should do, and how much trouble you might be in.

4.2.1 Some types of messy data

The thing about messy data sets is that each set is messy in its own way. If all messy data looked the same, we would find a way to parse it and use it quickly and efficiently. Although I can't possibly enumerate every way that data is messy and in need of wrangling, I can describe a few ways and hope that it helps you get an idea of the ways things can go wrong as you dive into a new data set and how you might be able to prepare for it.

If you've been working in data science for a few years, I'm sure you've seen cases like these—or worse. As of 2016, we still haven't entered the Era of Clean Data, and I'm beginning to wonder if we'll ever get there.

DATA TO BE SCRAPED

I mentioned web scraping in chapter 3, but you might also scrape data from PDFs and other unconventional sources. *Scraping* is the process of programmatically pulling selected elements from sources that weren't designed to be accessed programmatically. The data to be scraped is usually poorly structured. But if you write a sophisticated scraper, the data may be neat and tidy at the end.

CORRUPTED DATA

Sometimes you may find data that's not only poorly formatted but downright corrupted. This usually means that some aspect of the file is either missing or has been obfuscated because of a disk error or other low-level problem. It can be like losing the instructions for building a model plane or accidentally mixing up a stack of index cards that are supposed to be kept in order. A commonly corrupted file format is PST, an email archive. But thankfully we have many tools for recovering most of the data from such a corrupted file. (That's one of the few benefits of having a file format that's often corrupted: someone developed an anti-corruption tool!)

POORLY DESIGNED DATABASES

Databases have growing pains too, and sometimes that means that two databases that weren't intended to be used together are now your best sources of information. Sources of error include database values or keys that don't match each other and incongruences in scope, depth, APIs, or schemas.

4.2.2 Pretend you're an algorithm

I've already discussed web scraping in general, and given that the data I wanted for my track and field project was available on a website, scraping seemed like a good choice. In the Google Chrome browser I used the option View Page Source to see the raw HTML that composes the page that lists the top men's 100 m dash results of all time. This is what a programmatic scraper will be reading.

Sometimes it's easy to parse through HTML to extract the elements you want, but sometimes it takes a bit of imagination. I tend toward role playing; pretending to be a wrangling script—a bit of code that programmatically turns messy data into nice data—helps me figure out how I might write a script later, and it gives me a good idea of how difficult that task might be and what problems I might encounter.

The first step in wrangling, and in pretending to be a script, is to look at the raw data (for example, using View Page Source on a web page or looking at HTML in a text editor). This is what any code that you write will be seeing, and so it's what you should look at when figuring out how to deal with it. Some header lines and other material at the top of the page, a section of the page containing the men's 100 m dash data, look like this:

```
...
<A HREF="#7">faulty wind gauge - possibly wind assisted</a><br></FONT>
<center><p>
<A name="1"><H1>All-time men's best 100m </H1></a><P>
<PRE>
1    9.58    Usain Bolt     JAM    Berlin      16.08.2009
2    9.63    Usain Bolt     JAM    London      05.08.2012
3    9.69    Usain Bolt     JAM    Beijing     16.08.2008
3    9.69    Tyson Gay      USA    Shanghai    20.09.2009
3    9.69    Yohan Blake    JAM    Lausanne    23.08.2012
6    9.71    Tyson Gay      USA    Berlin      16.08.2009
...
```

This is the section of the page where the list of the best men's 100 m performances starts. Because I'm writing this in 2016, there are performances on this list now that were not there when I first analyzed this data in 2011. But the format is the same.

Stepping into my role as a wrangling script, I imagine what I would do if I encountered this chunk of HTML. Nothing before this section is useful to me, so the main goal is to start capturing the top marks at this point. I recognize the line containing Usain Bolt's 9.58 sec performance as the world record and beginning of the data I want to capture, but how will a script recognize it?

One way to recognize an athlete's performance is to test each line of the file to see if it looks like this:

```
[INTEGER]    [NUMBER]    [NAME]    [COUNTRY]    [CITY]    [DATE]
```

Any method that tries to match each line of this HTML would have to be able to recognize integers, numbers, names, countries, and the like. This task is often more complex than it initially may seem. How, for example, would you test for a name in the third column? Would you test for capitalized words? Two words separated by a space? Would Joshua J. Johnson meet your criteria? What about Leonard Miles-Mills or the city Kuala Lumpur? All of these appear in the list. This process is less simple than it looks, and so I usually try a different strategy before resorting to pattern recognition.

Document structure, particularly in HTML or XML, can provide good clues to wrangling scripts about where the valuable data starts. What comes right before the data? In this case, the data is preceded by a <PRE> tag. Regardless of what this tag means, it's worth checking to see if it appears often on the page or only right before the data set starts. Investigating this, I see that in the page, the first time the <PRE> tag appears is right before the data. And, thankfully, this is true of the pages for all track and field events, so I could safely use the <PRE> tag to denote the beginning of the data set for each of the events.

Imagining myself as a wrangling script, I would begin reading the HTML line by line, and I'd look for a <PRE> tag. When I find a <PRE> tag, I know that the next line will be a row of data in the particular table format, where the second column is the measured performance, the third column is the name, the fourth is the country, and so on. The text parser in your favorite scripting language can read that line, separate the columns into fields using either tab characters or multiple consecutive spaces, and store each text field in a variable or data structure.

4.2.3   *Keep imagining: what are the possible obstacles and uncertainties?*

Now that you know where the valuable data starts within each HTML page and how to begin capturing lines of data, you still have to continue playing the role, in your mind, of the wrangling script, as it continues line by line through the file.

As I scroll downward through the raw HTML of men's 100 m performances, most lines look like they should: performance, name, country, and so on, all in their appropriate places. But every now and then there's a funny character sequence. Sometimes in the city column I see the text ü or é between some other letters. These entries seem weird, and I worry that a script (wait, that's me!) might not know what to do. I look for the corresponding places in the rendered HTML (the web page itself) and realize that these character sequences are the HTML representations of ü and é, respectively. I also could perform an internet search to figure out what those character sequences mean.

Zürich and San José occur fairly often in the list of locations for some of the top performances, so it's obvious I need to worry about characters that are represented by special character sequences in HTML. Are there others I haven't seen yet? Should I be wary whenever an ampersand occurs in any field? The answers to each of these questions is likely yes, but I'd like to draw attention to the fact that *I don't know yet.*

This is an important point in data wrangling: lots of things can happen that you might not expect. Therefore, if there is one tenet of wrangling, it is this:

Double-check everything.

A manual second check is preferred, but a programmatic check can work, too, if you're careful. If I don't have an absurd amount of data, as a second check I like to scroll through the post-wrangle, supposedly clean data files. Sometimes a quick scroll-through can reveal some obvious mistakes that an hour of software debugging would reveal. What if a column of data shifted somewhere? One extra tab character can mess up a lot of parsing algorithms, including some standard R packages and the occasional Excel import, among others.

What else might go wrong while trying to wrangle some data programmatically? What in the file(s) looks a little weird? What checks can you do afterward that might uncover some important mistakes in your wrangling? Every case is different, but every case deserves careful and deliberate thought about any of the possibilities for parsing error. Yet again, awareness is the most important thing a data scientist can have at this point.

4.2.4   *Look at the end of the data and the file*

If I'm pretending to be a wrangling script, I'm going to start at the beginning of the file and finish at the end. Many unexpected things can happen in the middle, so there are no guarantees that I'll arrive at the end of the file in the expected state. I may have wrangled people's names in the place of cities and dates in the place of countries of origin. Who knows, unless I've had the amazing luck to write a bugless script for a data set without irregularities? Does such a script or such a data set exist? Assuming that's not the case—and assuming I've made at least one mistake in my current conception of a wrangling script—I probably should examine the wrangled data file(s) at the beginning, at the end, and at least a few places in the middle.

It takes a lot of scrolling through the list of men's 100 m performances to find the first line of HTML that doesn't belong in the data set. It took me an embarrassingly long time before I realized that there were additional, nonstandard lists of best performances at the bottom of the pages. For the men's 100 m page, there are lists for running start and manual timing after the main list. These lists look identical to the main list but are separated from the main list by a few tags of HTML. The transition from the main list to the first auxiliary list looks like this:

```
. . .
2132   10.09    Richard Thompson    TTO    Glasgow      11.07.2014
2132   10.09    Kemarley Brown      JAM    Sundsvall    20.07.2014
2132   10.09    Keston Bledman      TTO    Stockholm    21.08.2014
</pre></center>
2401 total
<p><center>
<A name="2"><H3>rolling start</H3></A><P>
<PRE>
1      9.91     Dennis Mitchell     USA    Tokyo        25.08.1991
2      9.94     Maurice Greene      USA    Berlin       01.09.1998
3      9.98     Donovan Bailey      CAN    Luzern       27.06.2000
. . .
```

The HTML tag that denoted the beginning of the desired data, <PRE>, is closed at the end of the main list with the </pre> tag closure. (Note that HTML tags are generally not case sensitive.) This would be a good way to end the parsing of the data set. As a wrangling script, that's what I'd do, unless I want to capture the auxiliary lists as well. Do I? In this case, no I don't. I want only completely legal marks that abide by all world-record-eligible rules, because I want to compare world records and every performance that came close. It's probably not helpful to consider performances under conditions that are nonstandard and inherently different from the core set of legal performances.

If my wrangling script ignored the end of the useful data set, in this case the </pre> tag closure, and assumed that the data continued until the end of the file, the script would probably collect the nonstandard results at the bottom of the page. Or the script wouldn't know what to do when the data stopped fitting the appropriate column format that was established. In this case and many others, looking at the end of the wrangled data file is crucial to determining whether the data wrangling was successful. It's up to you, the data scientist, to decide which aspects of wrangling are most important and to make sure those aspects are completed properly. But it's almost always important to scan the file to the end, if for no other reason than to make sure that nothing weird happened right before the script finished.

4.2.5 *Make a plan*

Now that I've discussed the process of imagining yourself as a wrangling script, parsing through raw data and extracting the parts that are needed, the next step is to consider all the information that you've gathered so far and to make a plan for wrangling.

Based on what you've seen in the track and field data, a good option would be to download all the web pages containing all the Olympic track and field events and to parse them as we discussed, using HTML structure as appropriate, double-checking everything. One complication of this that I haven't yet mentioned—if you're going to use a pure web-scraping strategy—is that you need a list of all of the web addresses of the pages for individual events in order to download all of them programmatically. Sometimes such a list of site addresses to scrape is easy to generate, but each of the 48 individual pages (24 Olympic events each, for men and women) has a unique address that needs to be copied or typed manually. Therefore, you might need to manually create a list of 48 web addresses that needed to be scraped, plus you'd need to write the wrangling script that parses the HTML, as already discussed. That's one potential plan that could wrangle the data you need. But because each page address needs to be copied or typed manually, I don't think you'd save much time by programmatically visiting each of the manually typed page addresses when compared to downloading each of the pages manually. Those were two good options, but they weren't the only ways to wrangle the data I needed.

In the end, I decided not to go with web scraping. Parsing through HTML structure wouldn't have been incredibly hard, as you've seen, but I realized there was another way. The pages of alltime-athletics.com aren't heavy with HTML. The HTML and the text that appears on the web page as rendered HTML aren't too different. There's not much styling on the page, particularly in the part of the page containing the data I needed. In both cases, the top performances were given as a whitespace-separated table, with one performance per line. In that way, there was little difference between raw HTML and rendered HTML. As I've already mentioned, however, some individual characters appeared differently in raw HTML than they did in rendered HTML. For example, in raw HTML, a city might appear as `Z&uuml;rich` but in rendered HTML it would appear as `Zürich`.

I decided to take the post-HTML, already rendered web page version so I didn't have to worry about character rendering or any other HTML-parsing issues. I needed data from 48 pages, and instead of writing (or pretending to be) a script that would download each of these pages and parse the HTML for each Olympic event, I decided to copy the text from each of the web pages myself.

I would visit each of the 48 web pages with Chrome, my web browser, press Ctrl-A to select all text on each page, press Ctrl-C to copy the text, and then press Ctrl-V to paste the text from each event's page into a separate flat file. It was some manual work to copy the pages, but I wouldn't have to worry about translating HTML or scripting the downloading of the pages. That was the plan I settled on: skip the HTML parsing, copy all the pages manually, and then write a simple script that would pull the track and field performance data into a usable format. It might not be the best plan for every project, but it's certainly good in this scenario.

In general, the choice of data wrangling plan should depend heavily on all of the information you discover while first investigating the data. If you can imagine parsing the data or accessing it in some hypothetical way—I try to play the role of a wrangling script—then you can write a script that does the same thing. Pretend you're a wrangling script, imagine what might happen with your data, and then write the script later. Data wrangling is such an uncertain process that it's always best to explore a bit and to make a wrangling plan based on what you've seen.

4.3   Techniques and tools

Data wrangling is an incredibly abstract process with uncertain outcomes at nearly every step. There's no one way or one tool to accomplish the goal of making messy data clean. If someone tells you they have a tool that can wrangle any data, then either that tool is a programming language or they're lying. Many tools are good for doing many things, but no one tool can wrangle arbitrary data. Honestly, I don't think that will ever be possible, though we can certainly make progressively better tools. Data exists in so many forms and for so many purposes that it's likely that no one application can ever exist that's able to read arbitrary data with an arbitrary purpose. Simply put, data wrangling is an uncertain thing that requires specific tools in specific circumstances to get the job done.

4.3.1   File format converters

Among HTML, CSV, PDF, TXT, and any other common formats a file might take, it's helpful to know when it's possible to convert from one file format directly to another.

The IAAF Scoring Tables are published as a PDF, a format that's not conducive to data analysis. But there are file format converters that can take PDFs and produce other file formats, such as text files and HTML. The Unix application pdf2txt extracts text from PDFs and saves it to a text file. pdf2html is another useful format converter and something that might be useful to most data scientists.

Many file format converters are available—many of them are free or open source—and it's certainly worth a Google search to figure out whether the format you have is easily convertible to a format you want.

4.3.2 *Proprietary data wranglers*

In 2016, there's no shortage of companies that want to wrangle your data for you—for a price. In some ways, it's unsettling how many software products claim to be able to do this, when I know from personal experience that many of them are severely limited. On the other hand, some of these products work well.

If you can find any proprietary products that can convert the data you have into the data you want, then they're well worth the consideration. Spending a little money on these proprietary tools may be worth it if your project gets done much earlier, but the industry is young and changing too fast for me to give any sort of meaningful survey here.

4.3.3 *Scripting: use the plan, but then guess and check*

Earlier in this chapter, I talked about pretending that I was a wrangling script and described what I would do in that role. This is exactly the basis for writing a real script for wrangling data.

As you imagine being a script and reading through files, recognizing where useful data begins and ends and how to parse that data, you should get an idea of how complex the task is and what the main features might be. For simpler tasks, simple tools are often useful for accomplishing them. The Unix command line, for instance, is helpful for tasks like these:

- Extracting all lines from a file that contain a certain word (grep is one such tool)
- Converting occurrences of a certain word or character into another (tr, sed, awk)
- Cutting files into smaller chunks (split)

Those are a few, but if your wrangling plan entails a few such simple steps, the command line might be the way to go.

But if you have a more complex set of operations to perform, and none of the aforementioned file format converters or proprietary wranglers fits the bill, then a scripting language is usually your best bet. Both Python and R are common languages for writing wrangling scripts, and it's usually best to choose whichever language you're most comfortable with, because you'll probably be trying several different techniques in a short amount of time.

Writing a wrangling script, at least the first version, is usually not a well-orchestrated affair. In fact, it fits nicely with a current usage of the word *hacking* to mean trying a bunch of things until you find a few that get the job done. Being able to load, manipulate, write, and transform data quickly is the most important capability you should strive for when choosing your scripting languages or tools.

Because you've already imagined being a script and parsing the data, you should have a good general idea what the final script will do, but I'm sure that some of the details are still unclear. You can make some informed decisions about how best to wrangle, or you can guess and check if that seems more time efficient. Now is also a good time to revisit the manual-versus-automate question: can you wrangle manually in a shorter time than you can write a script? And will you reuse the script? Go ahead and take whichever path seems like the biggest payoff for the lowest cost in time and effort.

Awareness is important while writing a wrangling script. This includes staying aware of the status of the data, the script, the results, what the goals are, and what each of the potentially many wrangling steps and tools is gaining you.

4.4   Common pitfalls

With messy data, any wrangling script conceived based on looking at only part of that data is bound to have omitted something important. Even if you were observant and thorough in considering all possibilities, there's still a risk that something might go wrong. In this section, I outline a few of these pitfalls and give some noticeable symptoms that your wrangling script may have fallen into one.

4.4.1   Watch out for Windows/Mac/Linux problems

When I first began wrangling data, in 2005 or so, major data incompatibilities between the most popular operating systems were a problem that I didn't think would still exist in 2016. But the three major OSs still haven't agreed on a single way to denote line endings in text files. Any day now, all specs for text files might magically be unified across OSs, but until then there will be issues with conversion from files on one operating system to another.

Since time immemorial (since the 1970s), Unix—and later, by inheritance, Linux—has used the line feed (LF) denotation of a new line, whereas versions of Mac OS before version 9.0 used the carriage return (CR) character for a new line. Since 1999, Mac OS has joined the other Unix derivatives in using the line feed to denote a newline, but Microsoft Windows continues to use a hybrid CR+LF line ending.

I won't attempt to address any specific problems here; they can be varied and nuanced. But I should stress that they can sneak up on you. Improperly parsing line endings can lead to various problems, so it pays to be wary of the output of the parsing. In addition to this and other OS complexities, each programming language has its own faculties for reading files of various types. Depending on which package or native method you choose to read files, make sure you pay attention to how it parses text, line endings, and other special characters. This information should be present in the language documentation.

When looking at your newly wrangled data, some signs that you may have encountered an issue with OS files formats include the following:

- You seem to have far more lines of text than you think you should have.
- You seem to have far too few lines of text.
- Weird-looking characters are interspersed through the file.

4.4.2 Escape characters

When dealing with text, some characters have special meaning. For example, on the most common Unix (or Linux) shells (command-line interpreters), the character * is a wildcard that represents all files in the current directory. But if you precede it with the common escape character \ as in *, then the special meaning is removed, representing only the simple asterisk character. The line

```
rm *
```

removes all files in the current directory, whereas

```
rm \*
```

removes the file named simply *, if it exists. In this case, the backslash character is said to *escape* the wildcard character.

Such escape characters can occur in text files and text/string variables in programming languages. For instance, let's say you want to read a text file that looks like this in a text editor:

```
this is line 1
this is line 2
A    B    C    D
```

This is three lines of text, followed by a line containing no characters. The third line contains tab characters in between the letters.

Many common programming languages, including Python and R, upon reading this file with the simplest file reader (or file stream), would see this:

```
this is line 1\nthis is line 2\nA\tB\tC\tD\n
```

Notice that the line breaks have been replaced by \n and the tab characters by \t. This contains the same information as before, but it's encoded in a single string, simply by using ASCII characters (n and t) with escape characters (backslash) to represent whitespace elements like the newline and the tab.

Another complication: creating string variables in languages such as Python or R includes the use of quotation marks, and quotation marks can affect escaping in various ways. Let's put the previous string in double quotes, assign it to a variable in Python (the >>> represents the Python interpreter prompt), and then check the contents of the variable, first by entering only the variable name itself and then by using the print command:

```
>>> s = "this is line 1\nthis is line 2\nA\tB\tC\tD\n"

>>> s
'this is line 1\nthis is line 2\nA\tB\tC\tD\n'

>>> print s
this is line 1
this is line 2
A    B    C    D
```

Note that the two checks of the variable contents confirm that it's a string (first shown in single quotation marks) and that this string renders as in the original file when making use of the print command, which translates the escaped characters as the appropriate newline and tab characters. In this way, a single string variable can represent the data from an entire file, with each line separated by the escaped newline character.

The fun begins when using escape characters within quotations or quotations within quotations. Let's say you have a second file that looks like this in a text editor:

```
I call this "line 1"
I call this "line 2"
There are tabs in this quote: "A    B    C"
```

Storing this file in a single Python variable and then checking its contents looks like this:

```
>>> t = "I call this \"line 1\"\nI call this \"line 2\"\nThere are Tabs in
this quote: \"A\tB\tC\""

>>> t
'I call this "line 1"\nI call this "line 2"\nThere are Tabs in this quote:
"A\tB\tC"'

>>> print t
I call this "line 1"
I call this "line 2"
There are Tabs in this quote: "A    B    C"
```

That's clearly a bit more complicated than the previous example. Because the text itself contains quotation marks, these need to be escaped within the string variable.

As a final example of escape characters, let's assume you have a data set containing some emails. People could have written anything they want in the emails, including quotation marks, tabs, or anything else. For an unspecified reason, you want to store the email data in a text file, with one email per line. One email reads:

```
Dear Edison,

I dislike "escaped characters" .

-N
```

This this email could be encoded as the following string:

```
Dear Edison,\n\nI dislike "escaped characters".\n\n-N\n
```

And it could be stored in Python as a string variable like this, escaping the internal quotations:

```
>>> s = "Dear Edison,\n\nI dislike \"escaped characters\".\n\n-N\n"
```

Now you want to write this email to one line of a file, so you check the contents of the variable and then print/render them (the `print` command replicates in the terminal what would be written to a file):

```
>>> s
'Dear Edison,\n\nI dislike "escaped characters".\n\n-N\n'
>>> print s
Dear Edison,

I dislike "escaped characters".

-N
```

This isn't what you intended. The `print` process is rendering the newlines, and this data is no longer on a single row. It looks like you have to escape the newline characters again, as shown here:

```
>>> s = "Dear Edison,\\n\\nI dislike \"escaped characters\".\\n\\n-N\\n"
>>> print a
Dear Edison,\n\nI dislike "escaped characters".\n\n-N\n
```

Now it's printing on a single line, as intended, because you used double backslashes. Keep in mind that in the variable s, the sequence \\n represents a literal backslash (only one—the first of the pair is the escaping one) and the character n. Sometimes this can be confusing, so it's best to be careful when dealing with complex escapes.

It doesn't have to stop at two backslashes. The backslash is a common escape character, and you may not have to worry much about it if you're using smart file readers and writers, but if you're using many nested quotation marks and newlines, escaping can be problematic. One time in R, I was using five or six backslashes in a row because of some nuanced escaping. It was quite astonishing for me to realize that I had to use \\\\\\n to accomplish my task, because none of the file reader's parameters seemed to get everything right.

Symptoms that you might have a problem with escaping may include the following:

- Some lines or strings are too long or too short.
- You try to read a file line by line but end up with one long line.
- You find text inside quotation marks that doesn't belong there.
- You get errors while reading or writing files.

4.4.3   *The outliers*

Sometimes a data point contains a perfectly valid value, from a logical perspective, but that value isn't realistic from the perspective of a subject matter expert. In our track and field example, at some point on the list of top 100 m dash times, the number 8.9 may have appeared. Now 8.9 is a perfectly logical number from a statistical perspective, but anyone who knows anything about track knows that no one has ever run 8.9 seconds in the 100 m dash. It might be that the 8.9 resulted in a typo somewhere along the line, or perhaps one row wasn't formatted right, or any other imaginable reason for a data point to be in the wrong place. But the point is that sometimes incorrect data can sneak its way into your project without causing an error or otherwise making itself obvious. This is where summary statistics and exploratory graphs can be helpful.

In this case, merely checking the range of values—minimum to maximum—could have caught the error. During this project I plotted histograms of all of the data, not only to check for errors but also to gain some awareness about what the data sets looked like. A histogram probably would have highlighted a data error like this, though. It's usually a good idea to spend a little time generating some summaries— statistical or visual—even if they don't seem necessary. They can prevent errors and promote awareness. I cover data assessment, including basic descriptive statistics, summaries, and diagnostics, in chapter 5, and some of those techniques can be used here as well, to make sure the wrangling has been successful.

4.4.4   *Horror stories around the wranglers' campfire*

Any seasoned data scientist has a story or two to tell: data ghost stories that haunt a data scientist for years, The One That Got Away, the near-miss when disaster was averted by a last-minute detection of The Bug, the time "the data was SO bad... (how bad was it?)." I have nothing more to add here; you'll get most of my stories throughout this book, but don't be afraid to ask your local veteran data scientists about theirs. The stories are probably pretty nerdy, but hey, aren't we all?

Exercises

Continuing with the Filthy Money Forecasting personal finance app scenario first described in chapter 2, and relating to previous chapters' exercises, imagine these scenarios:

1   You're about to begin pulling data from FMI's internal database, which is a relational database. List three potential problems that you would be wary of while accessing and using the data.

2   In the internal database, for each financial transaction you find that a field called `description` containing a string (plain text) seems to provide some useful information. But the string doesn't seem to have a consistent format from entry to entry, and no one you've talked to can tell you exactly how that field is

generated or any more information about it. What would be your strategy for trying to extract information from this field?

Summary

- Data wrangling is the process of capturing the useful parts of raw and unkempt data under some bad conditions.
- Think like a computer program in order to create a good data-wrangling script.
- It helps to familiarize yourself with some typical tools and strategies and some common wrangling pitfalls.
- Good wrangling comes down to solid planning before wrangling and then some guessing and checking to see what works.
- Spending a little extra time on data wrangling can save you a lot of pain later.

Data assessment: poking and prodding

This chapter covers

- Descriptive statistics and other techniques for learning about your data
- Checking assumptions you have about your data and its contents
- Sifting through your data for examples of things you want to find
- Performing quick, rough analyses to gain insight before spending a lot of time on software or product development

Figure 5.1 shows where we are in the data science process: assessing the data available and the progress we've made so far. In previous chapters we've searched for, captured, and wrangled data. Most likely, you've learned a lot along the way, but you're still not ready to throw the data at the problem and hope that questions get answered. First, you have to learn as much as you can about what you have: its contents, scope, and limitations, among other features.

It can be tempting to start developing a data-centric product or sophisticated statistical methods as soon as possible, but the benefits of getting to know your data are well worth the sacrifice of a little time and effort. If you know more about your data—and if you maintain awareness about it and how you might analyze it—you'll make more informed decisions at every step throughout your data science project and will reap the benefits later.

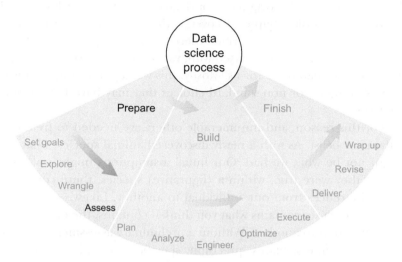

Figure 5.1 The fourth and final step of the preparation phase of the data science process: assessing available data and progress so far

5.1 Example: the Enron email data set

In my first job at a software company—after years of research-oriented, academic data science—I was helping to build software that would analyze communication patterns of employees of large, heavily regulated organizations in order to detect anomalous or problematic behavior. My employer, a Baltimore startup, developed software that helps make sense of massive amounts of employee data, which in many cases must be archived for a number of years according to current law and often contains evidence of wrongdoing that can be useful in investigations of known infractions as well as in the detection of yet-unknown ones. Two good examples of potential customers are compliance officers at large financial institutions and security departments at government agencies. Both of these have the express responsibility to prevent anyone from divulging or mishandling privileged or secret information. The monitoring of employees' use of internal networks is often mandated or highly recommended by regulating agencies. Needless to say, we needed to do a thorough statistical analysis of employee communications and other activity while still being extremely careful regarding points of ethics and privacy.

But privacy was not much of a concern for one of the first data sets we used for demonstration purposes. The set of emails that were collected by investigators after the Enron scandal in the early 2000s is now a matter of public record and is well documented and studied by researchers (www.cs.cmu.edu/~./enron). Because it's one of the most comprehensive and relevant public data sets available, we wanted to use the Enron emails to test and demonstrate the capabilities of our software.

Several versions of the Enron data set are available, including text versions in CSV format as well as the original proprietary format, PST, which can be generated by Microsoft Outlook. Chapter 4 covered the basics of data wrangling, and all of the problems and warnings described there certainly applied here. Depending on which version of the data set we started with, various preprocessing and wrangling steps may have already been done for us. Mostly, this was a good thing, but we always had to be wary of mistakes or non-standard choices that may have been made before the data got to us.

For this reason, and innumerable others, we needed to treat our data set like an unfamiliar beast. As with a newly discovered animal species, what we thought we had might not be what we had. Our initial assumptions might not have been true, and even if they were true, within a (figurative) species, there could have been tremendous differences from one individual to another. Likewise, even if you're confident that your data set contains what you think it contains, the data itself surely varies from one data point to another. Without a preliminary assessment, you may run into problems with outliers, biases, precision, specificity, or any number of other inherent aspects of the data. In order to uncover these and get to know the data better, the first step of post-wrangling data analysis is to calculate some descriptive statistics.

5.2   *Descriptive statistics*

Descriptive statistics are what you might think:

- Descriptions of a data set
- Summaries of a data set
- Maximum values
- Minimum values
- Average values
- A list of possible values
- A range of time covered by the data set
- And much more

Those are examples; for a definition, let's look at one from Wikipedia:

> *Descriptive statistics is the discipline of quantitatively describing the main features of a collection of information, or the quantitative description itself.*

Descriptive statistics is both a set of techniques and the description of the data sets that are produced using those techniques.

It's often hard to discuss descriptive statistics without mentioning inferential statistics. *Inferential statistics* is the practice of using the data you have to deduce—or infer—knowledge or quantities of which you don't have direct measurements or data. For example, surveying 1000 voters in a political election and then attempting to predict the results of the general population (presumably far larger than 1000 individuals) uses inferential statistics. Descriptive statistics concerns itself with only the data you have, namely the 1000 survey responses. In this example, the generalization step from sample to population separates the two concepts.

With respect to a data set, you can say the following:

- Descriptive statistics asks, "What do I have?"
- Inferential statistics asks, "What can I conclude?"

Although descriptive and inferential statistics can be spoken of as two different techniques, the border between them is often blurry. In the case of election surveys, as in many others, you would have to perform descriptive statistics on the 1000 data points in order to infer anything about the rest of the voting populace that wasn't surveyed, and it isn't always clear where the description stops and where the inference starts.

I think most statisticians and businesspeople alike would agree that it takes inferential statistics to draw most of the cool conclusions: when the world's population will peak and then start to decline, how fast a viral epidemic will spread, when the stock market will go up, whether people on Twitter have generally positive or negative sentiment about a topic, and so on. But descriptive statistics plays an incredibly important role in making these conclusions possible. It pays to know the data you have and what it can do for you.

5.2.1 Stay close to the data

I mentioned staying *close to the data* in chapter 1 as well, but it's certainly worth repeating and is perhaps more important to mention here. The purpose of calculating descriptive statistics at this stage in a data science project is to learn about your data set so that you understand its capabilities and limitations; trying to do anything but learn about your data at this point would be a mistake. Complex statistical techniques such as those in machine learning, predictive analytics, and probabilistic modeling, for example, are completely out of the question for the moment.

Some people would argue with me, saying that it's OK to dive right in and apply some machine learning (for example) to your data, because you'll get to know the data as you go along, and if you're astute, you'll recognize any problems as they come and then remedy them. I wholeheartedly disagree. Complex methods like most of those used in machine learning today are not easily dissected or even understood. Random forests, neural networks, and support vector machines, among others, may be understood in theory, but each of these has so many moving parts that one person (or a team) can't possibly comprehend all of the specific pieces and values involved in obtaining a single result. Therefore, when you notice an incorrect result, even one that's grossly incorrect, it's not straightforward to extract from a complex model exactly which pieces contributed to this egregious error. More importantly, complex models that involve some randomness (again, most machine learning techniques) may not reproduce a specific error if you rerun the algorithm. Such unpredictability in sophisticated statistical methods also suggests that you should get to know your own data before you allow any random processes or black boxes to draw conclusions for you.

The definition I use for *close to the data* is this:

> *You are close to the data if you are computing statistics that you are able to verify manually or that you can replicate exactly using another statistical tool.*

In this phase of the project, you should calculate descriptive statistics that you can verify easily by some other means, and in some cases you should do that verification to be sure. Therefore, because you're doing simple calculations and double-checking them, you can be nearly 100% certain that the results are correct, and the set of close-to-the-data descriptive statistics that you accumulate becomes a sort of inviolable canon of knowledge about your data set that will be of great use later. If you ever run across results that contradict these or seem unlikely in relation to these, then you can be nearly certain that you've made a significant error at some point in producing those results. In addition, which results within the canon are contradicted can be hugely informative in diagnosing the error.

Staying close to the data ensures that you can be incredibly certain about these preliminary results, and keeping a set of good descriptive statistics with you throughout your project provides you an easy reference to compare with subsequent more relevant but more abstruse results that are the real focus of your project.

5.2.2   *Common descriptive statistics*

Examples of helpful and informative descriptive statistics methods include but are not limited to mean, variance, median, sum, histogram, scatter plot, tabular summaries, quantiles, maximum, minimum, and cumulative distributions. Any or all of these might be helpful in your next project, and it's largely a matter of both preference and relevance when deciding which ones you might calculate in order to serve your goals.

In the Enron email data set, here's the first line of statistical questioning that occurs to me:

1 How many people are there?
2 How many messages are there?
3 How many messages did individual people write?

A short paper called "Introducing the Enron Corpus" (2004) by Brian Klimt and Yiming Yang gives a good summary that answers these questions.

In the Enron email corpus, there are 619,446 messages from the accounts of 158 employees. But by removing mass emails and duplicate emails appearing in multiple accounts, Klimt and Yang reduced the data to 200,399 emails in a clean version of the data set. In the clean version, the average user sent 757 emails. These are useful facts to know. Without them, it may not be obvious that there is a problem if, later, a statistical model suggests that most people send dozens of emails per day. Because this data set spans two years, roughly speaking (another descriptive statistic!), we know that two to three emails per day is much more typical.

Speaking of ranges of time, in the Enron data set and others, I've seen dates reported incorrectly. Because of the way dates are formatted, a corrupted file can easily cause dates to be reported as 1900 or 1970 or another year, when that's obviously erroneous. Enron didn't exist until much later, and for that matter neither did email as we know it. If you want to use time as an important variable in your later analyses, having a few emails a century before the rest may be a big problem. It would have been helpful to recognize these issues while wrangling the data, as described in chapter 4, but it may have slipped past unnoticed, and some descriptive statistics can help you catch it now.

For example, let's say you're interested in analyzing how many emails are sent from year to year, but you skipped descriptive statistics, and you jumped straight into writing a statistical application that begins in the year of the earliest email (circa 1900) and ends at the latest (circa 2003). Your results would be heavily biased by the many years in the middle of that range that contained no messages. You might catch this error early and not lose much time in the process, but for larger, more complex analyses, you might not be so lucky. Comparing the real date range with your presumed one beforehand could have uncovered the erroneous dates more quickly. In today's big data world, it wouldn't be uncommon for someone to write an application that does this—analyzes quantities of emails over time—for billions of emails, which would probably require using a computing cluster and would cost hundreds or thousands of dollars per run. Not doing your homework—descriptive statistics—in that case could be costly.

5.2.3 *Choosing specific statistics to calculate*

In the paper describing the Enron corpus, Klimt and Yang make it clear that they're primarily focused on classifying the emails into topics or other groups. In their case, dates and times are less important than subjects, term frequencies, and email threads. Their choice of descriptive statistics reflects that.

We were concerned mainly with users' behavior over time, and so we calculated descriptive statistics such as these:

- Total number of emails sent per month
- Most prolific email senders and the number they sent
- Number of emails sent each month by the most prolific senders
- Most prolific email recipients and the number they received
- Most prolific sender-recipient pairs and the number of emails they exchanged

It's not always obvious which statistics would be the best choice for your particular project, but you can ask yourself a few questions that will help lead you to useful choices:

1 How much data is there, and how much of it is relevant?
2 What are the one or two most relevant aspects of the data with respect to the project?

3 Considering the most relevant aspects, what do typical data points look like?

4 Considering the most relevant aspects, what do the most extreme data points look like?

Question 1 is usually fairly straightforward to answer. For the Enron data set, you find the total number of emails, or the total number of email accounts, both of which I've mentioned already. Or if the project concerns only a subset of the data—for example, emails involving Ken Lay, the CEO who was later convicted of multiple counts of fraud, or maybe only emails sent in 2001—then you should find the totals for that subset as well. Is there enough relevant data for you to accomplish the goals of the project? Always be wary that prior data wrangling may not have been perfect, and so obtaining the precise subset may not be as easy as it seems. Errors in name or date formatting, among other things, could cause problems.

Question 2 concerns the focus of the project. If you're studying the rise and fall of Enron as an organization, then time is a relevant aspect of the data. If you're looking mainly at email classification, as Klimt and Yang were, then email folders are important, as are the subject and body text from the emails. Word counts or other language features may be informative at this point. Think about your project, look at a few individual data points, and ask yourself, "Which part do I care about the most?"

For question 3, take the answer to question 2 and calculate some summary statistics on the values corresponding to those aspects. If a time variable is important to you, then calculate a mean, median, and maybe some quantiles of all of the email timestamps in the data set (don't forget to convert timestamps to a numerical value—for example, Unix time—and then back again for a sanity check). You might also calculate the number of emails sent each week, month, or year. If email classification is important to you, then add up the emails that appear in each of the folders and find the folders that contain the most emails across all accounts. Or look at how different people have different numbers and percentages of their emails in different folders. Do any of these results surprise you? Given your project goals, can you foresee any problems occurring in your analysis?

Question 4 is similar to question 3, but instead of looking at typical values, looks at extreme values such as maximum and minimum. The earliest and latest timestamps, as well as some extreme quantiles such as 0.01 and 0.99, can be useful. For email classifications, you should look at the folders containing the most emails as well as folders that may contain few—it's likely many folders contain one or a few emails and are possibly mostly useless for analysis. Perhaps for later stages of the project you would consider excluding these. When looking at extreme values, are there any values so high or so low that they don't make sense? How many values are outside a reasonable range? For categorical or other non-numeric data, what are the most common and least common categories? Are all of these meaningful and useful to subsequent analysis?

5.2.4 *Make tables or graphs where appropriate*

Beyond calculating the raw values of these statistics, you might find value in formatting some of the data as tables, such as the quantities of emails for the various categories of most prolific, or as graphs, such as the timelines of monthly quantities of email sent and received.

Tables and graphs can convey information more thoroughly and more quickly at times than pure text. Producing tables and graphs and keeping them for reference throughout your project is a good idea.

Figure 5.2 shows two plots excerpted from Klimt and Yang's paper. They're graphical representations of descriptive statistics. The first shows a cumulative distribution of users versus the number of messages they sent within the data set. The second plots the number of messages in Enron employees' inboxes versus the number of folders that were present in those email accounts. If you're interested in the number of

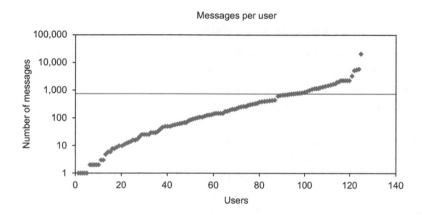

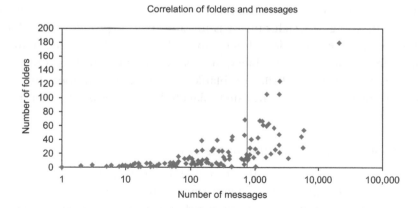

Figure 5.2   Two graphs redrawn from Klimt and Yang's "The Enron Corpus: A New Dataset for Email Classification Research"(published by Springer in *Machine Learning: ECML 2004*).

emails sent by the various employees or in how the employees used folders, it might be good to keep these graphs handy and compare them with all subsequent results. It's possible that they'll either help verify that your results are reasonable or indicate that your results are not reasonable and then help you diagnose the problem.

The types of descriptive graphs or tables that are appropriate for your project might be different from these, but they similarly should address the aspects of the data that are relevant to your goals and the questions you hope to answer.

5.3 Check assumptions about the data

Whether we like to admit it or not, we all make assumptions about data sets. As implied in the previous section, we might assume that our data is contained within a particular time period. Or we might assume that the names of the folders that contain emails are appropriate descriptors of the topics or classifications of those emails. These assumptions about the data can be expectations or hopes, conscious or subconscious.

5.3.1 Assumptions about the contents of the data

Let's consider the element of time in the Enron data. I certainly assumed, when I began looking at the data, that the emails would span the few years between the advent of email in the late 1990s and the demise of the firm in the early 2000s. I would have been mistaken, because of the potential errors or corruption in the date formatting that I've already mentioned. In practice, I saw dates far outside the range that I assumed as well as some other dates that were questionable. My assumption about the date range certainly needed to be checked.

If you want to use the folder names in the email accounts to inform you about the contents of emails within, there's an implied assumption that these folder names are indeed informative. You definitely would want to check this, which would likely involve a fair amount of manual work, such as reading a bunch of emails and using your best judgment about whether the folder name describes what's in the email.

One specific thing to watch out for is missing data or placeholder values. Most people tend to assume—or at least hope—that all fields in the data contain a usable value. But often emails have no subject, or there is no name in the From field, or in CSV data there might be NA, NaN, or a blank space where a number should be. It's always a good idea to check whether such placeholder values occur often enough to cause problems.

5.3.2 Assumptions about the distribution of the data

Beyond the contents and range of the data, you may have further assumptions about its distribution. In all honesty, I know many statisticians who will get excited about the heading of this section but then disappointed with its contents. Statisticians *love* to check the appropriateness of distribution assumptions. Try Googling "normality test" or go straight to the Wikipedia page and you'll see what I mean. It seems there are about a million ways to test whether your data is normally distributed, and that's one statistical distribution.

I'll probably be banned from all future statistics conferences for writing this, but I'm not usually that rigorous. Generally, plotting the data using a histogram or scatter plot can tell you whether the assumption you want to make is at all reasonable. For example, figure 5.3 is a graphic from one of my research papers in which I analyzed performances in track and field. Pictured is a histogram of the best men's 400 m performances of all time (after taking their logarithms), and overlaid on it is the curve of a normal distribution. That the top performances fit the tail of a normal distribution was one of the key assumptions of my research, so I needed to justify that assumption. I didn't use any of the statistical tests for normality, partially because I was dealing with a tail of the distribution—only the best performances, not all performances in history—but also because I intended to use the normal distribution unless it was obviously inappropriate for the data. To me, visually comparing the histogram with a plot of the normal distribution sufficed as verification of the assumption. The histogram was similar enough to the bell curve for my purposes.

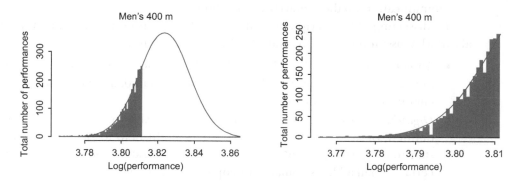

Figure 5.3   The logarithms of the best men's 400 m performances of all time seem to fit the tail of a normal distribution.

Although I may have been less than statistically rigorous with the distribution of the track and field data, I don't want to be dismissive of the value of checking the distributions of data. Bad things can happen if you assume you have normally distributed data and you don't. Statistical models that assume normal distributions don't handle outliers well, and the vast majority of popular statistical models make some sort of assumption of normality. This includes the most common kinds of linear regression, as well as the t-test. Assuming normality when your data isn't even close can make your results appear significant when in fact they're insignificant or plain wrong.

This last statement is valid for any statistical distribution, not only the normal. You may have categorical data that you think is uniformly distributed, when in fact some categories appear far more often than others. Social networking statistics, such as the kind I've calculated from the Enron data set—number of emails sent, number of people contacted in a day, and so on—are notoriously non-normal. They're typically something like exponentially or geometrically distributed, both of which you should also check against the data before assuming them.

All in all, although it might be OK to skip a statistical test for checking that your data fits a particular distribution, do be careful and make sure that your data matches any assumed distribution at least roughly. Skipping this step can be catastrophic for results.

5.3.3   *A handy trick for uncovering your assumptions*

If you feel like you don't have assumptions, or you're not sure what your assumptions are, or even if you think you know all of your assumptions, try this: describe your data and project to a friend—what's in the data set and what you're going to do with it—and write down your description. Then, dissect your description, looking for assumptions.

For example, I might describe my original project involving the Enron data like this: "My data set is a bunch of emails, and I'm going to establish organization-wide patterns of behavior over the network of people using techniques from social network analysis. I'd like to draw conclusions about things like employee responsiveness as well as communication up the hierarchy, with a boss."

In dissecting this description, you should first identify phrases and then think about what assumptions might underlie them, as in the following:

- *My data set is a bunch of emails*—That's probably true, but it might be worth checking to see whether there might be other non-email data types in there, such as chat messages or call logs.
- *Organization-wide*—What is the organization? Are you assuming it's clearly defined, or are there fuzzy boundaries? It might help to run some descriptive statistics regarding the boundaries of the organization, possibly people with a certain email address domain or people who wrote more than a certain number of messages.
- *Patterns of behavior*—What assumptions do you have about what constitutes a pattern of behavior? Does everyone need to engage in the same behavior in order for it to be declared a pattern, or do you have a set of patterns and you're looking for individual examples that match those patterns?
- *Network of people*—Does everyone in the network need to be connected? Can there be unconnected people? Are you planning to assume a certain statistical model from social network analysis literature? Does it require certain assumptions?
- *Responsiveness*—What do you assume this term means? Can you define it statistically and verify that the data supports such a definition by using the basic definition along with some descriptive statistics?
- *Hierarchy*—Are you assuming you have complete knowledge of the organization's hierarchy? Do you assume that it's rigid, or does it change?

Realizing when you're making assumptions—by dissecting your project description and then asking such questions—can help you avoid many problems later. You wouldn't want to find out that a critical assumption was false only after you had completed your analysis, found odd results, and then gone back to investigate. Even more, you wouldn't want a critical assumption to be false and never notice it.

5.4   *Looking for something specific*

Data science projects have all sorts of goals. One common goal is to be able to find entities within your data set that match a certain conceptual description. Here, I'm using the term *entity* to represent any unique individual represented in your data set. An entity could be a specific person, place, date, IP address, genetic sequence, or other distinct item.

If you're working in online retailing, you might consider customers as your main entities, and you might want to identify those who are likely to purchase a new video game system or a new book by a particular author. If you're working in advertising, you might be looking for people who are most likely to respond to a particular advertisement. If you're working in finance, you might be looking for equities on the stock market that are about to increase in price. If it were possible to perform a simple search for these characterizations, the job would be easy and you wouldn't need data science or statistics. But although these characterizations aren't inherent in the data (can you imagine a stock that tells you when it's about to go up?), you often can recognize them when you see them, at least in retrospect. The main challenge in such data science projects is to create a method of finding these interesting entities in a timely manner.

In the Enron email data set, we were looking for suspicious behavior that might somehow be connected to the illegal activity that we now know was taking place at the company. Although suspicious behavior in an email data set can take many forms, we can name a few: in general, employees discussing illegal activity, trying to cover something up, talking to suspicious people, or otherwise communicating in an abnormal fashion.

We already had statistical models of communication across social/organizational networks that we wanted to apply to the Enron data set, but there were any number of ways in which we could configure the model and its parameters in order to find suspicious behavior in its various forms. There was no guarantee that we would find the kind we were looking for, and there was also no guarantee that we would find any at all. One reason we might not find any was that there might not have been any.

5.4.1   *Find a few examples*

If you're looking for something fairly specific, something interesting in your data, try to find something. Go through the data manually or use some simple searches or basic statistics to locate some examples of these interesting things. You should stay close to the data and be able to verify that these examples are indeed interesting. If you have a lot of data—if it's hard even to browse through it—it's OK to take a subset of the data and look for some good examples there.

If you can't find any interesting examples, you might be in trouble. Sometimes, interesting things are rare or don't exist in the form you think they do. In fact, the Enron data, as published, doesn't contain a trail of clues or a smoking gun of any kind. It often helps to dig deeper, to change the way you're searching, to think differently about the data and what you're looking for, or otherwise to exhaust all possible ways to find the good, interesting examples in the data.

Sometimes brute force works. A team of a few people could theoretically read all of the Enron emails in a few days. It wouldn't be fun—and I'm sure more than a few lawyers have done it—but it is possible and would be the most thorough way of finding what you're looking for. I feel fairly confident in saying that over the course of the several months that I worked with the Enron data, I read most of the emails in that data set. This would have been a hallmark of a data science project gone wrong had the goal of the project not extended far beyond the Enron data set. We were developing software whose entire purpose was to make reading all emails unnecessary. We wanted to use the Enron data to characterize what suspicious communications look like so that we could use those characterizations to find such communications in other data sets. That's why brute force made sense for us at the time. Depending on your data, looking through all your data manually might make sense for you, too.

You might also use brute force on a subset of your data. Think of it this way: if 1 in 1000 entities—data points, people, days, messages, whatever—is supposed to be interesting, then you should find one if you manually look at more than 0.1% of a data set consisting of a million entities.

You should probably look at more data than that to be sure you haven't had bad luck, but if you've covered 1% of the data and you still haven't found any, you know the interesting entities are rarer than you thought or nonexistent. You can adjust these percentages for rarer or more common entities.

If it turns out that you can't find any interesting entities via any means, the only options are to look for another type of interesting thing, following another of your project's goals, or to go back to all your data sources and find another data set that contains some trace of something you find interesting. It's not fun to have to do that, but it's a real possibility and not that rare in practice. Let's be optimistic, though, and assume you were successful in finding some interesting entities within your data set.

5.4.2 Characterize the examples: what makes them different?

Once you've found at least a few examples of interesting things, take a close look and see how they're represented within your data. The goal in this step is to figure out which features and attributes of the data could help you accomplish your goal of finding even more examples of these interesting things. Often you may be able to recognize by simple inspection some pattern or value that the interesting examples share, some aspect of their data points that could identify them and differentiate them from the rest of the data set.

For email data, is it the email text that has interesting content and terms, or is it the time at which the email was sent? Or is it possibly that the sender and recipient(s) themselves are interesting? For other data types, have a look at the various fields and values that are present and make note of the ones that seem to be most important in differentiating the interesting things from everything else. After all, that's the foundation of most statistics (in particular, machine learning) projects: differentiating two (or more) groups of things from one another. If you can get a rough idea of how you can do this manually, then it's far easier to create a statistical model and implement it in code that will help you find many more of these examples, which I cover in a later chapter.

Often there's nothing quantitative about a data point that's remarkable or easily differentiable from typical data points, but it's interesting nonetheless. Take, for instance, a single email from Andrew Fastow, the CFO of Enron in its final years and one of the main perpetrators of the fraudulent activity that later landed him and others in jail. In the data set, none of the emails from Fastow contains any sign of fraud or secrecy, but what's interesting is that there are only nine emails from him in the entire corpus. As CFO, one would think his role would include communicating with others more often than once every couple of months. Therefore, either he avoided email or he did a good job of deleting his emails from all servers and others' personal inboxes and archives. In any case, an email from Fastow might be remarkable not because of any inherent information but only within the context of its rarity.

In a similar way, interesting things in your data might be characterizable by their context or by something I might call their neighborhood. *Neighborhood* is a term I'm borrowing from topology, a branch of mathematics:

> *The* neighborhood *of a [data] point is, loosely speaking, a set of other points that are similar to, or located near, the point in question.*

Similarity and location can take on many meanings. For the Enron data, we could define one type of neighborhood of a particular email as "the set of emails sent by this email's sender." Or we could define a neighborhood as "the set of emails sent during the same week." Both of these definitions contain a notion of similarity or nearness. By the first definition, an email sent by Andrew Fastow has a small neighborhood indeed: only eight other emails. By the second definition of neighborhood, the neighborhoods are much larger, often with several hundred emails in a given week.

In addition to aspects of a data point itself, you can use its neighborhood to help characterize it. If emails from Andrew Fastow are interesting to you, maybe all emails sent by people who seldom write emails are interesting. In that case, one quantitative characterization of *interesting* uses the same-sender definition of neighborhood and can be stated like this:

> *An email might be interesting if it's sent by someone who rarely sends emails.*

You can incorporate this statement into a statistical model. It is quantitative (rarity can be quantified) and it can be determined by information contained within the data set that you have.

Likewise, you could use a time-based neighborhood to create another characterization of *interesting*. Maybe, hypothetically, you found during your search an email that was sent in the middle of the night, from a work account to a private email address, asking to meet at an all-night diner. No such email exists in the Enron data set, but I like to pretend that the case was much more dramatic than it was—data science's version of cloak and dagger, perhaps.

This concept of middle of the night, or odd hours, can be quantified in a few ways. One way is to choose hours of the day that represent middle of the night. Another way is to characterize odd hours as those hours in which almost no emails were written. You could use a time neighborhood of a few hours and characterize some interesting emails like this:

> *An email might be interesting if there are few other emails sent from within two hours both before and after the email in question.*

This characterization, like the previous one, is both quantitative (*few* can be quantified empirically) and answerable within the data set you have.

A good characterization of an interesting entity or data point is one that is quantitative, that is present in or calculable from the data you have, and that in some way helps differentiate it from normal data, if only a little. We'll use these characterizations, and I'll talk about them more, in later sections on preliminary analyses and choosing statistical models.

5.4.3   Data snooping (or not)

Some might call it *data snooping* to poke around in the data, find examples of something you find interesting, and then tailor subsequent analyses to fit the examples. Some might say that this will unfairly bias the results and make them appear better than they are. For example, if you're looking to estimate the number of blue pickup trucks in your neighborhood, and you happen to know that there's usually a blue pickup truck parked a few blocks away, you'll probably walk in that direction, counting trucks along the way, and that one truck that you already know about could skew your results upward, if only slightly. Or, at best, you'll walk around randomly, but being close to your house and on one of your typical routes, you're more likely to walk past it.

You want to avoid significant bias in your results, so you want to be careful not to let the preliminary characterizations I'm suggesting affect that. Data snooping can be a problem, and astute critics are right to say you should avoid it sometimes. But snooping is a problem only when assessing the accuracy or quality of your results. In particular, if you already know about some of the things your methods are attempting to discover again, you're likely to be successful in those cases, and your results will be unfairly good.

But you're not at the assessment phase yet. Right now, while trying to find and characterize data points, entities, and other things within the data set that are interesting and rare, you should do everything you can to be successful, because it's a hard task. Later, though, all this useful snooping can complicate assessment of results, so I bring it up now to make you take note of a potential complication and to address potential critics who might say that you shouldn't snoop around in your data.

5.5　*Rough statistical analysis*

Already in this chapter I've discussed basic descriptive statistics, validating assumptions, and characterizing some types of interesting things you're looking for. Now, in terms of statistical sophistication, it's time to take the analysis up one notch, but not two. I cover full-fledged statistical modeling and analysis in chapter 7, but before you get that far, it's better to take only a single step in that direction and see how it works out.

Most sophisticated statistical algorithms take a while to implement; sometimes they take a while to run or compute on all your data. And as I've mentioned, a lot of them are quite fragile or difficult when it comes to understanding how and why they give a specific result and if it's correct, in some sense. That's why I prefer to approach such sophisticated analyses slowly and with care, particularly with a new or unfamiliar data set.

If some of the statistical concepts in this section are unfamiliar to you, feel free to skip ahead for now and come back to this section after you finish the rest of the book—or at least chapter 7. If you're already familiar with most sophisticated statistical methods, this section can help you decide whether your planned statistical method is a good choice. Or if you don't know yet what method you might use, this section can help you figure it out.

5.5.1　*Dumb it down*

Most statistical methods can be translated into rough versions that can be implemented and tested in a fraction of the time when compared to the full method. Trying one or a few of these now, before you begin the full implementation and analysis, can provide tremendous insight into what statistical methods will be useful to you and how.

If, for your final analysis, all you intend to do is a linear regression or a t-test, by all means charge right in. This section concerns primarily those projects that will likely include some sort of classification, clustering, inference, modeling, or any other statistical method that has more than a few parameters, fixed or variable.

CLASSIFICATION

If you plan to do some classification as part of your analysis, there are numerous statistical models designed for the task, from random forests to support vector machines to gradient boosting. But one of the simplest methods of classification is logistic regression.

The task of classification is, in its simplest form, assigning one of two class labels to entities based on a set of entity features that you've chosen and whose values you've calculated from the data. Typically, the labels are 0 and 1, where 1 represents interesting in the same sense I've used previously, and 0 is normal. You can have more classes and more complicated classification, but I'll save that for later.

The most sophisticated methods in classification have many moving parts and therefore have the potential to perform much better than logistic regression. But as I've mentioned, they're much harder to understand and debug. Logistic regression is a relatively simple method that works like linear regression, except the output values (the predictions, for new data) are between 0 and 1.

Compared to classification methods from machine learning, logistic regression is much faster to calculate and has virtually no parameters that you need to fiddle with. On the other hand, it carries a few assumptions—such as a certain type of normality—so if you have profoundly skewed or otherwise weird data values, it might not be the best choice.

If you have a favorite entity feature that you think will help classify yet-unknown entities, try it as the only feature/parameter in your logistic regression model. Your software tool can tell you whether the feature does indeed help, and then you can proceed to try another feature, either by itself or in addition to the first. Starting simple is generally the best choice, then increasing complexity, and checking to see if it helps.

One good candidate for an informative feature for finding suspicious emails in the Enron data set is the time of day at which the email was sent. Late-night emails might prove suspicious. Another feature might be the number of recipients of the email.

Another, more general method for investigating the usefulness of features for classification is to look at the distributions of feature values for each of the two classes (0 or 1). Using a couple of plots, you can see whether there seems to be a significant difference between the feature values of the two classes. Figure 5.4 is a two-dimensional plot of data points from three classes, designated by shape. The x- and y-axes represent two feature values for the data points. If your goal is to make statistical software that can find data points that are square—without knowing the true shape—you'd probably be in good shape; square data points have high x- and y-values. It would be easy to find a statistical model that correctly identifies square data points. The tough part might be finding the features that, when plotted, give neatly grouped classes such as these. Creating plots can help you find those good, useful features by giving you a sense of where the classes fall in the space of all data points and can help you figure out how to develop or tweak features to make them better.

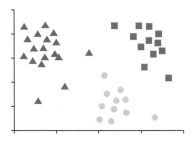

Figure 5.4   A plot of three classes, given by shape, in two dimensions[1]

---

[1] From https://en.wikipedia.org/wiki/Cluster_analysis (public domain)

Lastly, if you have a favorite statistical method for classification that you understand, and you know how to adjust its parameters in your statistical software to make it simple and easy to understand, then that's also a good way to perform a rough and fast classification. For example, you might use a random forest with 10 trees and a maximum depth of 2. Or a support vector machine with linear kernel functions can be reasonably easy to understand if you know the theory behind it. Both of these might be good choices if you're familiar with how those techniques work. If you do choose this route, it's important that you understand how to evaluate the results of your method, check the contributions of the various features, and make sure that the method is working the way you expect it to.

CLUSTERING

Clustering is conceptually a lot like classification—there are entities with feature values that are intended to fall into groups—except there are no explicit, known labels. The process of clustering is often called *unsupervised learning* because the results are groups of similar entities—but because there are no labels, it may not immediately be clear what each group, or cluster, represents. It often takes manual inspection or descriptive statistics to figure out what kinds of entities are in each cluster.

As a rough version of clustering, I like to plot various values pertaining to entities and use plain visual inspection to determine whether the entities tend to form clusters. For data or entities with many aspects and values, it may take a while to visually inspect plots of one or two dimensions/variables at a time. But if you believe that a few key features should differentiate groups of entities from one another, you should be able to see that in a two-dimensional plot. If you can't, you may want to revisit some assumptions that you've made. Blindly assuming that two entities are similar merely because they fall into the same cluster can lead to problems later. For example, even without labels/colors, the data points in figure 5.4 seem to cluster well into three groups. A clustering algorithm should be able to find them, if you know there are three clusters. On the other hand, if your data doesn't group together so nicely, clustering might give poor results.

Beyond visual inspection, the simplest versions of clustering contain few variables and few clusters (most of the time, you have to set the number of clusters beforehand). If you can choose, say, three or four of your favorite entity features, and they cluster nicely using one of the simplest clustering algorithms, perhaps k-means, then you're off to a good start and can proceed to more sophisticated clustering methods or configurations. It may also help to plot the results of your clustering algorithm within your software tool to make sure everything looks like it makes sense.

INFERENCE

Statistical inference is the estimation of a quantitative value that you haven't observed directly. For instance, in the case of the Enron project I've mentioned, at one point we wanted to estimate the probability that each employee would send an email to their boss as opposed to any other potential recipient. We intended to include this probability as a latent variable in a statistical model of communication, a complex model whose optimal parameter values could be found only via a complex optimization technique. For a lot of data, it could be slow.

But we could approximate the inference of this particular latent parameter value by counting the number of times each employee wrote an email to their boss and how many times they didn't. It's a rough approximation, but later, if the full model's optimal parameter is found to be something quite different, we'd know that something may have gone wrong. If the two values differ, it doesn't mean that something definitely did go wrong, but if we don't understand and can't figure out why they differ, it definitely shows that we don't know how the model works on our data.

We could approach other latent variables in our statistical model in the same way: find a way to get a rough approximation and make note of it for later comparison with the estimated value within the full model. Not only is this a good check for possible errors, but it also tells us things about our data that we may not have learned while calculating descriptive statistics, as discussed earlier in this chapter—and, even better, these new pieces of information are specific to our project's goals.

OTHER STATISTICAL METHODS

I certainly haven't covered how to do a rough approximation of every statistical method here, but hopefully the previous examples give you the idea. As with almost everything in data science, there's no one solution; nor are there 10 or 100. There are an infinite number of ways to approach each step of the process.

You have to be creative in how you devise and apply quick-and-dirty methods because every project is different and has different goals. The main point is that you shouldn't apply sophisticated statistical methods without first making sure they're reasonably appropriate for your project's goals and your data and that you're using them properly. Applying a simple version of the statistical analysis first gives you a feeling for how the method interacts with your data and whether it's appropriate. Chapter 7 discusses several types of statistical methods in far more detail, and from it you should be able to gather more ideas for your own analyses.

5.5.2 *Take a subset of the data*

Often you have too much data to run even a simple analysis in a timely fashion. At this stage of doing many rough preliminary analyses, it might be OK to use subsets of data for testing the applicability of simple statistical methods.

If you do apply the rough statistical methods to subsets of the full data set, watch out for a few pitfalls:

- Make sure you have enough data and entities for the statistical methods to give significant results. The more complicated the method is, the more data you need.
- If the subset is not representative of the full data set, your results could be way off. Calculate descriptive statistics on this subset and compare them to the relevant descriptive statistics on the full data set. If they're similar in ways that matter—keep your projects goals in mind—then you're in good shape.

- If you try only one subset, you may unknowingly have chosen a highly specialized or biased subset, even if you run some descriptive statistics. But if you take three distinct subsets, do a quick analysis on them all, and get similar results, you can be reasonably certain the results will generalize to the full data set.
- If you try different subsets and get different results, it might not be a bad thing. Try to figure out why. Data inherently has variance, and different data might give different results, slightly or greatly. Use descriptive statistics and diagnosis of these simple statistical methods to make sure you understand what's happening.

5.5.3 *Increasing sophistication: does it improve results?*

If you can't get at least moderately good or promising results from a simple statistical method, proceeding with a more sophisticated method is dangerous. Increasing the sophistication of your method should improve results, but only if you're on the right track. If the simple version of the method isn't appropriate for your data or project, or if the algorithm isn't configured properly, chances are that stepping up the sophistication isn't going to help. Also, it's harder to fix the configuration of a more sophisticated method, so if you begin with an improper configuration of a simple method, your configuration of the more sophisticated version will probably be as improper—or even more so—and harder to fix.

I like to make sure I have a solid, simple method that I understand and that clearly gives some helpful if not ideal results, and then I check the results as I step up the sophistication of the method. If the results improve with each step, I know I'm doing something right. If the results don't improve, I know I'm either doing something wrong or I've reached the limit of complexity that the data or my project's goals can handle.

Applying methods that are too complex for the data or setting goals that can't handle it is generally called *over-fitting*. Specifically, this implies that the methods have too many moving parts, and all these moving parts work perfectly on your data, but then when you give the method new data, the accuracy of the results isn't nearly as good. I cover over-fitting in more detail in chapter 7, but for now let it suffice to say that sophistication should lead to better results—to a point—and if you're not experiencing that, there's likely a problem somewhere.

Exercises

Continuing with the Filthy Money Forecasting personal finance app scenario first described in chapter 2, and relating to previous chapters' exercises, try these exercises:

1 Given that a main goal of the app is to provide accurate forecasts, describe three types of descriptive statistics you would want to perform on the data in order to understand it better.

2 Assume that you're strongly considering trying to use a statistical model to classify repeating and one-time financial transactions. What are three assumptions you might have about the transactions in one of these two categories?

Summary

- Instead of jumping straight into a sophisticated statistical analysis, be intentionally deliberate during the exploratory phase of data science, because most problems can be avoided—or fixed quickly—through knowledge and awareness.

- Before analyzing data, state your prior assumptions about the data and check that they're appropriate.

- Before assuming there are needles in your haystack, sift through the data, manually if necessary, and find some good examples of the types of things you want to find more of during the project.

- Perform rough statistical analyses on subsets of the data to guarantee you're on the right track before you devote too much time to a full software implementation.

- Record any exploratory results somewhere handy; they might be of use later when making follow-up decisions.

Part 2

Building a product with software and statistics

The main object of any data science project is to produce something that helps solve problems and achieve goals. This might take the form of a software product, report, or set of insights or answers to important questions. The key tool sets for producing any of these are software and statistics.

Part 2 of this book begins with a chapter on developing a plan for achieving goals based on what you learned from the exploration and assessment covered in part 1. Then chapter 7 takes a detour into the field of statistics, introducing a wide variety of important concepts, tools, and methods, focusing on their principal capabilities and how they can help achieve project goals. Chapter 8 does the same for statistical software; the chapter is intended to arm you with enough knowledge to make informed software choices for your project. Chapter 9 then gives a high-level overview of some popular software tools that are not specifically statistical but that might make building and using your product easier or more efficient. Finally, chapter 10 brings all these chapters together by considering some hard-to-foresee nuances of executing your project plan given the knowledge gained from the previous detours into statistics and software, as well as the many pitfalls of dealing with data, statistics, and software.

Developing a plan

6

This chapter covers

- Assessing what you've learned in the preliminary phases of the project
- Revising the goals of the project based on new information
- Realizing when you should redo prior work
- Communicating new information to the customer and getting feedback
- Developing a plan for the execution phase

Figure 6.1 shows where we are in the data science process: beginning the build phase by formal planning. Throughout this book, I've stressed that uncertainty is one of the principle characteristics of data science work. If nothing were uncertain, a data scientist wouldn't have to explore, hypothesize, assess, discover, or otherwise apply scientific methods to solve problems. Nor would a data scientist need to apply statistics—a field founded on uncertainty—in projects consisting only of absolute certainties. Because of this, every data science project comprises a series of open questions that are subsequently answered—partially or wholly—via a scientific process.

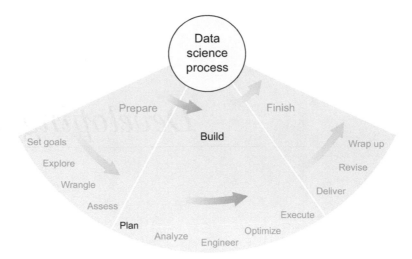

Figure 6.1   The first step of the build phase of the data science process: planning

It would be a mistake not to consider these new answers as they arrive. That would be comparable to continuing to drive along a specific road even after you've been informed that the road is closed ahead and the best detour requires you to turn. Within the past decade, internet-connected navigation devices, most often smartphones, have become ubiquitous. These devices are constantly being updated with new information, notably traffic and accident information, and they use this information to try to optimize the route suggested to the driver. This is also what a data scientist needs to do as uncertainties fade or disappear.

I like to stop periodically throughout a project, take stock of everything that I've learned, and consider it in the larger context of the major goals, similar to how I described the formulation of good questions and goals in chapter 2. But each time I do this, new information arises that can influence decisions. It may not be necessary to pause a project deliberately and formally consider all new information, but it's often useful, because many people have a tendency to plow ahead with a prior plan that may no longer be the best plan. This relates to the concept of awareness, which I emphasize that every data scientist should maintain, and a formal periodic review of new knowledge can help share this awareness with a team if you're working on one. Even when working by yourself, a somewhat formal review can be helpful for organization as well as for communicating progress to customers or other stakeholders of the project.

The types of progress assessment and planning described in this chapter can also be done continually or periodically instead of all at once, and this is preferred in some cases. But it should absolutely be performed sometime between the preliminary phases of the project, which I've covered in previous chapters, and what I call the *execution phase*, which I'll discuss beginning in the next chapter, and which includes most of a typical project's formal statistical modeling and software development time and effort. Because the execution phase is labor intensive, you want to make sure the plan is good and will address the major goals of the project. You don't want to have to redo the execution phase.

6.1 What have you learned?

After asking some questions and setting some goals in chapter 2, you surveyed the world of data in chapter 3, wrangled some specific data in chapter 4, and got to know that data in chapter 5. In each step, you learned something, and now you may already be able to answer some of the questions that you posed at the beginning of the project.

For instance, while searching for data, did you find everything you needed, or is a critical chunk of data still missing? After assessing the data, did it contain everything you expected it to? Did the descriptive statistics you calculated turn out as expected, or were there any surprises?

6.1.1 Examples

Because the answers to each of these questions will depend greatly on the details of the project, it's difficult for me to formalize the process of asking and answering them. Instead I'll consider the examples I've already presented in this book and describe some of my experiences at this stage of those projects. Later in this chapter, I'll return to these examples and discuss how I used the new information to make subsequent decisions about the projects.

BEER RECOMMENDATION ALGORITHM

In chapter 2, I briefly described a hypothetical project whose goal was to recommend beers to users of a beer website based on ratings that those users provided for other beers. Because it's a hypothetical project that I've never undertaken (though lots of others have), I can take some liberties in answering "what have I learned?" from the preliminary stages of the project, but I think it's illustrative nonetheless.

In particular, I mentioned that the data set we started with, a CSV file containing users' beer ratings, didn't contain the specific type of beer as one of the columns. This was a problem because the type or style of beer is usually informative in determining whether a person will like it or not. Knowing that the types are missing, my initial plan was either to find a data set containing the data types or infer the types from the name of the beer. If neither of these was possible, I would have to do the project without the types. There were, then, three different paths for analyzing and recommending beers, and determining the optimal path required some preliminary data science.

In surveying the world of data, as in chapter 2, I may have found a list of beers matched with their types. If I did, then that particular uncertainty would become a certainty (if I trusted it), and I would make use of the given beer types in my recommendation algorithm. If I didn't find that list of beer types, then, as I was assessing my data as described in chapter 4, I may have written a script, hopefully quickly, designed to parse the name of each beer and determine which style it is. If it seemed to work well, I would have made a plan to tweak it to improve it as much as possible, and that particular path would have been realized.

If I couldn't find a data set with beer types and I also couldn't manage to write a script that successfully inferred the beer types, then only one possible path would be left: I'd have to go without. Without knowing the beer types, the statistical challenge would be significantly greater but not impossible, and so I'd have to develop a plan with that in mind.

In all three cases I've described, I've gained new knowledge from the process of searching for data, wrangling it, and then assessing it. This new knowledge influences the optimal plan for continuing along in the project.

BIOINFORMATICS AND GENE EXPRESSION

In chapter 3, I introduced a project I worked on as part of my PhD research, which involved analyzing the relationship between the expression of specific microRNAs and individual genes.

While searching for more data and information that could be useful in public bioinformatics data repositories and publications, I found a few databases containing algorithmic predictions of which microRNAs (miRs) are expected to regulate the expression of certain genes. I also found some other analytic tools that achieved some of the same goals that I pursued but in a different way from that which I intended.

For each data set of algorithmic predictions, which were based solely on RNA sequences, I would have to decide if they could be helpful to my project and also if that helpfulness justified the work required to take advantage of the data. Each new data set would require some amount of effort to access, parse, and transform the data into a useful form. In two cases, I decided to put in the work to take advantage of these predictions to inform my statistical models, which I had not yet built.

But while wrangling and assessing the data, I realized that the names of the miRs and the genes didn't match exactly with the ones in my main data set, which was microarray expression data. Different scientific organizations have developed different naming schemes for genes based on particular needs, and they haven't yet been unified, but name-conversion tools do exist. If I hoped to take advantage of these prediction data sets, I'd have to include in my plan something that would convert names from one scheme into another so I could match predictions with specific values in the microarray data that are, in some sense, realizations of the results that are predicted.

In addition to that new knowledge concerning naming schemes, in assessing the data I learned something about the distributions of the microarray expression data. Because I used replicate microarrays of most of the biological samples—I put the same biological RNA sample onto multiple microarrays—I could calculate what's called a technical variance. A *technical variance* is the variance induced solely by the technology (a microarray) and that has nothing to do with biological processes. What I found was that in a majority of the 10,000 or so genes, the technical variance was greater than the biological variance. This meant that in those cases the measured expression level of the gene had more to do with the randomness of measuring a microscopic chemical compound than it did with biological effects. I had to decide whether I wanted to include those high-technical-variance (or low-biological-variance) genes in my analysis or to ignore them. Some statistical methods don't handle variance well, and others do, so I would have to choose wisely.

TOP PERFORMANCES IN TRACK AND FIELD

In chapter 4, I discussed how I once analyzed lists of best-ever performances in track and field to score and compare marks across events for both men and women. In particular, I wanted to compare the world records for all events and find out which one was the best.

One of the first choices I had to make in this project was whether I wanted to use the best available no-cost data set, at www.alltime-athletics.com, or pay for what is, supposedly, a more complete data set on another website. I'm a fan of open-access data, so I opted for the free data set, but if I had later realized that I didn't have enough data to inform my statistical models, I would have had to reconsider my choice.

While examining my data set, I checked the lengths of each of the performance lists, finding that some events, such as the women's one-mile run, contained only a couple hundred performances, whereas other events, such as the women's steeplechase, were on the order of 10,000 entries in length. It wasn't immediately clear whether this vast difference in performance list lengths would cause a problem, but it was definitely new information that I'd have to consider while planning.

Another bit of information that I hadn't foreseen was that some events, such as high jump, pole vault, and the 100 m and 200 m dashes, produced performance values that were more discrete values than continuous ones. In the high jump and pole vault, the bar is raised progressively to higher heights, and the athletes either jump that high or they don't, meaning that on each day many athletes have the same performance. On the list of best-ever high jump performances, more than 10 are tied at 2.40 m, more than 30 at 2.37 m, and at lower heights the numbers are larger. Looking at a distribution of performances, such as in a histogram or something comparable, a good argument can be made that a continuous distribution such as the log-normal distribution may not be the best choice. While planning, I'd have to decide whether and how I could compare these events to the others, such as the distance-running events, that produce marks that are obviously continuous because almost no one on the best all-time list is tied with anyone else.

ENRON EMAIL ANALYSIS

In chapter 5, I talked about the set of Enron emails that have been made public and how I, along with my colleagues at the time, was using social network analysis techniques to try to detect suspicious behavior.

This was an open-ended project. We knew that some bad, criminal things happened at Enron, but we didn't know how they would manifest themselves in the data, if they did at all. We did know that we wanted to treat the email data as a set of communications across a social network, and so the first step to any analysis would be to enable the construction of a social network from the data.

One of the first surprising and disappointing realizations was that, across the 100+ PST files containing the emails, the same email sender (or recipient) could be represented in many different ways. For instance, one of the most prolific emailers in the data set, Jeff Dasovich, might appear in the email's Sender field as Jeff Dasovich, Jeffrey Dasovich, jeff.dasovich@enron.com, or even DASOVICH, and those are only a few of the many possibilities. This may not seem like a big problem at first glance, but it was. Dasovich himself wasn't tough to recognize, but there were multiple people named Davis, Thomas, and so on that weren't so easy.

As part of the data-wrangling process, I ended up writing a script that would try to parse whatever name appeared and determine whether the name had already been encountered, with preference for nicely formatted names and email addresses, but the script was by no means perfect. In some cases, we had two or more different people in the constructed social network who were, in fact, the same person, but we had failed to combine them because the script hadn't recognized the names as matching each other. We had checked the most prolific senders and recipients manually, but past the top 100 or 200 people, there were no guarantees that the script had matched names correctly. In planning, we had to take into account this uncertainty in the matching of emails with named senders and recipients.

Needless to say, at the beginning of the project we didn't know that matching names to one another would be one of the biggest challenges that we faced. The task of writing a reasonably successful script consumed a larger portion of my effort than any other aspect of the project, if I recall correctly. The uncertainty of the task and awareness of the complexity of the problem were crucial to the assessment and planning for the execution phase of the project.

After we had a reasonable solution to the name-matching problem, we ran some descriptive statistics on the Enron data set. Surprising or not, we quickly realized that certain people, such as Jeff Dasovich, had sent several thousand emails over the course of a couple of years, whereas key executives such as Ken Lay had sent almost none. Clearly, personal behavior, at least as it relates to email, would have to be considered in our statistical models. We had made an implicit assumption that all significant employees at Enron wrote enough emails for us to model their behavior, but clearly this wasn't true. Whatever analyses we did later would have to allow for vastly differing general behaviors while still detecting specific behaviors that were anomalous in some sort of criminal sense. This was no small problem and yet was another thing to consider during planning.

6.1.2 *Evaluating what you've learned*

I've provided examples but little concrete guidance regarding what you may have learned on your specific project. Concrete guidance would be hard to come by, because every project is different, and it also doesn't seem possible to group projects into types that will generally produce the same types of lessons and new information. This evaluative phase embodies the uncertainty of data science projects and emphasizes how and why data scientists need to be—first and foremost—always aware, technology-enabled problem solvers. For the real problems in data science, there are no canned solutions. The only solutions are awareness and creativity while applying tools, off-the-shelf or custom, and intelligent interpretation of results. During the preliminary phases of any data science project, you learn some things, and you should take these as seriously as any other information, particularly because they precede and are in a position to inform the main execution phase of the project, and because they are the most project-specific information you have. Because of the possible significance of this new information, performing the evaluation phase described in this chapter can be helpful.

This evaluation phase is a retrospective phase of the project. If you're someone who takes copious notes, remembering what you've done and what the results were won't be a problem, but if you're like me and you rarely take notes on your own work, the task of remembering might be more difficult. I've begun to tend toward technologies that automatically record my work. Git, in yet another use it wasn't explicitly designed for, provides some functionality that can help me remember what has happened in the recent history of my project. If my commit messages are informative, sometimes I can reconstruct a project history from them, but this is clearly not ideal. An email trail can also be a memory aid. For that reason, I also now tend toward more wordy emails and Git commit messages; I never know when I'm going to need to remember something and which specific details will be helpful.

In any case, if you're able to collect and summarize what you've learned since the beginning of the project, you're in good shape. People often begin projects with unrealistic expectations and define their goals in accordance with these expectations, but then they wait too long to readjust their expectations based on new information that proves them unreasonable. That's the point of this section: every data scientist should pause sometimes and consider whether any new information changes the fundamental expectations and assumptions that underlie the goals that had been formulated when far less project-specific information was available. Reconsidering goals and expectations in light of this new information is the topic of the next section.

6.2 Reconsidering expectations and goals

The summary of new information that we've collected according to the previous section could be substantial, insignificant, unsurprising, transformative, bad, good, or of any other description you might care to think up. But you won't know how to describe the new information until you have it. Principally, however, the new information possesses some quality that colors how you think about the project, its progress, its usefulness, and so on, even if that quality is to confirm some things that you previously believed to be true. As I discussed in chapter 5, confirmation of assumptions is important, and the same is true here for the project's expectations. It may feel like little progress has been made if you've done considerable work only to have your expectations unchanged, but in fact progress was made in the removal of uncertainty. Removal of uncertainty is a form of strengthening the foundation of the project, upon which other more deliberate progress is built.

On the other hand, if your expectations weren't fulfilled by the project's new information, then you're in a different boat entirely. Some folks are emboldened by having their expectations confirmed, whereas others prefer the opposite—they enjoy having their expectations challenged, because it means they're learning and discovering new things. In the case where the expectations for your project are challenged, or even disproved entirely, it's an opportunity to put various data science skills to use at once.

6.2.1   *Unexpected new information*

Discovering something new during the preliminary stages of a data science project isn't unusual, and you might be tempted to think, "Of course! Given new information, I obviously will take it in stride and make full use of it from then on." But it's often not that simple.

Sometimes people so desperately want something to be true that they continue believing it even after it has been proven false. I found that the field of bioinformatics had many such hopefuls (that's not to say there's anything wrong with the field as a whole). It must be something about the nexus of two different types of cutting-edge technologies—machines that can extract and measure molecular-biological activity on a cellular level, as well as some of the most sophisticated statistical methods in existence—that makes some people believe that one can save the other.

More than once in the course of my work, I have been presented with a data set produced by a laboratory experiment that took days or even weeks to prepare, and at some point during my analysis I came to the realization that the data was of low quality. This happens sometimes in bioinformatics; even the smallest contamination or slip of the hand can ruin a droplet of dissolved RNA that's the entire basis for the experiment. Understandably, though, given the large amount of laboratory work involved in creating some data sets, biologists are reluctant to discard them. In one case, I found that the technical variance of a microarray data set was far larger than the biological variance, meaning that the measurements more closely resembled a random number generator than meaningful gene expression values. In another case, we used a time-intensive process that's considered the gold standard in measuring the expression of individual genes, and the resulting data set was self-contradictory. In both of these cases, in my estimation, the data had been proven virtually worthless, and the experiments would need to be redone (this happens all the time in bioinformatics, which is why it's important to check the data quality). But in both cases, someone involved with the project wasn't able to admit that fact and spent a week or more trying to figure out how to salvage the data or how to analyze it in a clever way so that the shortcomings didn't matter. This, to me, is irrational. It was the scientific equivalent of a sunk cost from financial accounting terminology: the experiment is done and it ended up being a bad investment. Instead of worrying about the money, time, and effort wasted, researchers should find a way to move forward that maximizes the chance of getting good results later. That isn't to say there aren't lessons to learn in failures—figuring out why it happened is usually helpful—but the main goal is to optimize the future, not justify the past.

In cases where new information runs contrary to expectations, though uncertainty is reduced, it isn't reduced in the way expected, so it could feel like uncertainty is added, because those involved probably haven't yet thought through all implications. Consider a close battle for an election in which a huge underdog has only recently made it into widespread attention. If the underdog wins, all the uncertainty is removed in the moment the result is announced. But because that result was not expected, it feels less certain than the case where the expected candidate wins, because most people would have been mentally prepared for the expected win of the heavy favorite and many of its implications.

This may not seem like data science, but this line of thinking has certainly played a role in my work. When I deal with expectations—and with them being proven right, wrong, or somewhere in between—feelings often get involved. Feelings are not data science, but if feelings affect how I react to new information, they become relevant. Although handling uncertainty is one of the principal skills of a data scientist, it's human to react emotionally to uncertainty and to being right or wrong. Data scientists are, after all, only human.

The solution to all of this, if there is one, is to do everything to take all emotion out of the decision-making process. This is easier said than done, for me as well as almost everyone I've ever worked with. Everyone enjoys being right, and few data scientists or software engineers enjoy changing a plan midway through, in particular for large projects. Here are a few strategies for eliminating emotion from data science decision making:

- *Formality*—Make lists, create flow charts, or write logical if-then statements showing the new information directly affecting future results. The most important task is to write these down so that you have a permanent record of why you chose a certain new path based on this new information.
- *Consult a colleague*—A colleague who isn't invested in the project might be best, but certainly consult others on the project as well. Talking the new information through often helps, but having an outsider who listens well think through your new information and your plans to handle it can be invaluable.
- *Search the internet*—This may not apply in some cases, but the world's data scientists and statisticians have seen a *lot* of unexpected results. If you're clever with a search engine and can whittle your result and pending decision into somewhat generic terms, the internet can be a big help.

Once you've reduced the problem to its core facts, including all the new information that you have and all the work you've done so far, making any new goals or adjusting any old goals based on the new information is a rational process that has no emotional penalties for ditching prior work that ended up being worthless.

6.2.2   *Adjusting goals*

Regardless of whether your expectations were met or whether you were completely surprised by preliminary results, it's often worthwhile to evaluate and possibly adjust your project's goals. Chapter 2 described a process for gathering initial information, asking good questions, and planning some ways to answer those questions that lead to fulfillment of the project's goals. You want to revisit that same process here, in the presence of the new information you have as a result of the early exploratory stages of the project, to answer these questions again:

- What is possible?
- What is valuable?
- What is efficient?

The practical limit of "What is possible?" is the counterbalance of the business-oriented daydreamer's question "What is valuable?" and both are extremes that frame the pragmatic inquiry "What is efficient?" which ends up possibly being an important amalgam of the prior two.

WHAT IS POSSIBLE?

While asking yourself what is possible at this stage of the project, you should consider the same things you did at the beginning of the project: data, software, obstacles, and many others. But because you know more now than you did then, some things that seemed impossible earlier may seem possible now, and some things that you thought would be possible may now appear quite the opposite.

Usually at this point, it's the data sets that make things seem less possible. There's a tendency to be overly optimistic about the capability and content of data before you dig in and explore a little. By now you know a lot more and can draw far more informed conclusions about possibility.

WHAT IS VALUABLE?

Most likely, the values of the goals of the project haven't changed much, but it's often worth considering them again for reference. On the other hand, in some fast-moving industries, the value estimates of various goals may indeed have changed. In those cases, it's probably best to go through the list of goals with the customer to see what has changed and how.

WHAT IS EFFICIENT?

Data and software details in particular might have made some paths and goals seem easier or harder, more or less resource intensive, or otherwise different from before. Running the numbers again conceptually can help you reoptimize the plans to get the most benefit from the resources you have.

6.2.3 *Consider more exploratory work*

Sometimes during this evaluative stage, it becomes obvious that you haven't learned as much as you would have liked from the earlier exploratory phase. But you may have more informed ideas about what specific exploration would have led to more and better knowledge.

For example, consider the beer recommendation algorithm project I've already discussed. Perhaps during the exploratory phase you wrote a script that tried to infer the beer type from the name of the beer, a possible tactic I discussed earlier in this chapter. The script seemed to work pretty well, but someone asks you, "How good is it?" and you realize you didn't explicitly evaluate the script's performance. In this case, it would be good to measure the performance in an objective way, so you can be reasonably sure it works well. A decent strategy for measuring performance is to spot-check a bunch of beer types that were inferred by the script. Randomly picking 20, 50, or even 100 beers and checking the inferred type against, say, the brewer's web page would be a reliable way to get a statistic—probably the percentage of correctly inferred types—that tells you how well your script is doing. A good statistic can lend a lot of credibility to what you've done, and a bad one means you might have to improve the script.

Similarly, questions and concerns during this evaluative and planning stage can often indicate the usefulness of other exploratory work that you haven't done yet. It's OK—and sometimes good—to go back and do more exploring if it seems like it will be beneficial.

6.3 *Planning*

As in chapter 2, evaluating and setting goals immediately precedes creating a plan. Some folks might like to do them at the same time, but I like to separate them, at least conceptually, because planning involves a lot of details—specifics about time, resources, people, schedules, monetary costs, for example—that aren't usually directly relevant to the setting of goals. Which team member will be working on which aspect of the project and when shouldn't play a large role in setting the principal goals of the project. But that does have a role in planning.

As in the earlier planning phase, uncertainties and flexible paths should be in the forefront of your mind. You know more about your project now, so some of the uncertainties that were present before are no longer there, but certain new ones have popped up.

Think of your plan as a tentative route through a city with streets that are constantly under construction. You know where you'd like to go and a few ways to get there, but at every intersection there might be a road closed, bad traffic, or pavement that's pocked and crumbling. You'll have to make decisions as you arrive at these obstacles, but for now it's enough to have a backup plan or two.

6.3.1   *Examples*

Earlier, I discussed four projects and some specific things that I learned or might have learned from them during their prior exploratory phases. I'd like to discuss them again now within the context of setting goals and planning. As with lessons learned, the processes of setting goals and planning are project specific and don't lend themselves well to concrete if-then statements, so examples can be illustrative and invaluable.

BEER RECOMMENDATION ALGORITHM

The goal of a beer recommendation algorithm is possibly singular: make good beer recommendations. But you probably want to be more specific than that. Do you want to make a top-10 list of beers for each user, or do you want to have the user select a beer or a style before recommending something similar that the user would like? This is one case where the job of a data scientist wanders into the typical duties of a product designer. Think back to chapter 2's discussion of listening to and understanding the customer: what will the customer be doing with the product of your project? Let's assume that—after much deliberation and consulting both the project team and some prospective users—a goal should be to make a top-10 list of beers that each user should try.

Let's go back to the goal-setting filter I proposed: possible, valuable, and efficient. Making such a top-10 list is possible; depending on the quality of the statistical methods employed, the list could range from good to bad, but regardless of that, making a list is certainly possible. The list is also valuable in some sense; the project is predicated on the fact that someone somewhere wants to discover some new beers that they would like, so let's assume that it's valuable; otherwise, the project itself is not valuable. The goal seems efficient; it seems 100% possible, and it's difficult to think of a related goal that provides more value for less effort. In terms of possibility, value, and efficiency, this goal is straightforward: alternatives can be considered, but few arguments can be made against a top-10 list.

That's the main goal, then: a list of beers that a user will probably like if they try them. What about a plan? I've talked about a *plan* as a set of contingencies intertwined with a set of uncertainties. The uncertainties of building a beer recommendation algorithm lie mainly in the statistical methods as well as in the data set's ability to support those methods. Even the best statistical methods won't give good results when the data set is too small or unreliable. Therefore, the largest uncertainty in the project is the quality of the output of the algorithm itself. You don't know the probability that a user of the algorithm will like a beer that's recommended.

A good plan would consider that the algorithm might not be as good as you hope it will be. If you have a perfect algorithm, all users will love the beers that are recommended, but if the algorithm gets some of them wrong, what should you do? As a statistician, I would first suggest that you diagnose some of the bad recommendations and modify the algorithm to account for these. A few iterations of this might solve the problem, or it might not.

Another alternative is to develop a product that is error friendly. Depending on how the users interact with the algorithm, they may be expecting perfect beer recommendations, or they may fully understand that mistakes can be made. A scoring system is a possible solution that comes more from a product design perspective than an analytic one. If the algorithm makes mistakes, but it gives a recommendation score that indicates how reliable the recommendation is (and this score is itself reliable), then the users would tolerate some erroneous recommendations in the interest of taking a risk for finding a good beer.

With those two alternatives, a good plan is forming. If the algorithm produces reliable results, then you can trust the top-10 lists, and you can feel assured in presenting the lists to users. But if the lists aren't that reliable, you should either revise the statistical methods to make the lists more reliable or generate a recommendation reliability score that conveys to users that not every recommendation is guaranteed to be enjoyed. Therefore, in the future, there are two possible paths and a choice to make. But how will you make that choice? The process of making the choice should also be included in the plan, insofar as it is possible.

In this case, in the future, the choice between the two paths depends on the reliability of the recommendations generated by the algorithm, so you need a way to evaluate the reliability of recommendations, and you need to include this in the plan. I'll discuss these statistical methods in more detail in later chapters, but a good way to check the accuracy of predictions from a statistical algorithm is to withhold some of the data set from the algorithm while it is training or learning and then test the algorithm by checking to see whether it predicts that data correctly. In this project, you would probably withhold a few beer recommendations for each user during training of the statistical methods and then check to see if the beers that were highly rated by a user but withheld during training were indeed recommended by the algorithm. Likewise, you can check to see if low-rated beers were kept off the recommendation lists. In any case, recommendations by the algorithm should corroborate the user ratings that were withheld; if they don't, then the algorithm isn't that good, and you'll need to choose one of the remedial paths just mentioned.

That, in aggregate, is a good if basic plan. Figure 6.2 shows the plan in the form of a flow chart. Notice that this plan consists of a set of steps that are to be followed, but also there is a major uncertainty regarding the algorithm performance. Depending on the outcome of the performance evaluation, different paths can be taken. Acknowledging beforehand that this uncertainty exists and that it plays a major role in determining what happens next is hugely informative during this planning phase, both for you as a data scientist as well as the customers who are depending on you. I discuss communicating revised goals and plans to your customers in the next section, after I've covered the rest of the examples.

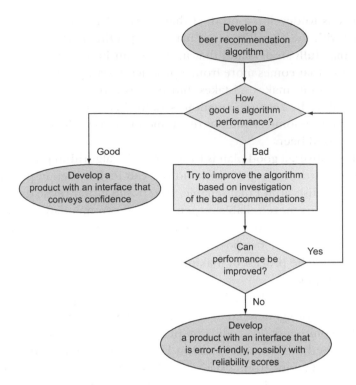

Figure 6.2   A flowchart showing a possible plan for developing a beer recommendation application

BIOINFORMATICS AND GENE EXPRESSION

The purpose of this project, in general, was to figure out whether miRs affected the expression levels of genes, specifically within the context of stem cell development in mice. Possible goals included the following:

1 Discovery of miR–gene pairs that are most likely to interact with each other
2 Discovery of miRs that regulate stem cell development
3 Discovery of pathways (sequences of causes and effects) among miRs and genes affecting stem cell development and regulation

Goal 1 included a statistical analysis of specific correlations between miRs and genes within the time-series data that I already had. There were no guarantees of how reliable the results would be, but the analysis was certainly possible. Likewise, goal 2 required a statistical analysis of the expression levels of miRs throughout the stages of stem cell development. Again, this was entirely possible, though it wasn't certain that the results of the statistical methods would be correct in terms of functional biology. Goal 3 was a bit more complicated. Pathways involve more than two miRs or genes, and so discovering a single pathway required proving multiple correlations among the three-plus constituents, plus the added work of showing that the multiple correlations were connected by more than coincidence. A biological scientific journal would expect substantial evidence of the connections between the individual parts before it would publish my article on the discovery of pathways. Goal 3, though possible, was far more complicated and harder to justify than the other two possible goals. Also, the work required to analyze a pathway statistically is greater than a simple miR–gene interaction.

The value of each of these goals was somewhat uncertain. Definitely, discoveries of new miR–gene interactions, miRs that regulate stem cell development, or stem cell pathways are all valuable, but the value of each would depend on the genes involved and how strongly I could justify the results. If I discovered a novel interaction or pathway that could be related, convincingly, to a popular biological phenomenon such as genetic disease or sexual differentiation, then I would have a much better chance of publishing the research in a high-impact journal. But all three goals had approximately the same chance of giving such valuable results, so I considered the value of each to be equal.

While evaluating the efficiency of the goals, it was immediately obvious that goal 3, being more complicated, would require vastly more work than the others. Goals 1 and 2 demanded roughly the same amount of work and were also roughly equal in their chance of giving meaningful results. The only tiebreaker between those two goals was that determining specific miRs that interacted with specific genes seemed to be slightly more interesting to the scientific community than discovering stem cells that could only generally be associated with stem cell development.

So with goal 1 being slightly more valuable and efficient than goal 2, I chose goal 1 as my main goal, with goal 2 a close second and goal 3 a distant third, to be done only if I had plenty of extra time after achieving the first two.

Given these goals, the plan would necessarily include developing statistical methods that aimed to discover the miR–gene pairs of goal 1 while possibly taking into account the regulating miRs of goal 2. The correlations discovered in trying to achieve those two goals might then be assembled in such a way as to construct plausible pathways as in goal 3.

A flow chart describing my plan appears in figure 6.3. As you can see, this plan is fairly straightforward. Scientific research tends toward this structure: you work on improving methods and results until you have a result that the scientific community will appreciate, at which point you write an article about your research and then submit it for publication. This contrasts with typical business projects, in which stricter constraints on time usually, to some extent, require data scientists to compromise the quality of results in order to meet a deadline. On the other hand, although academic researchers don't usually have a strong time constraint other than conference application deadlines, they're usually held to a higher standard of statistical rigor and significance of discovery than in industry. An academic data scientist's plan will probably look different from the plan of a data scientist in a comparable private industry, which is another factor in settling on a specific plan for your particular project.

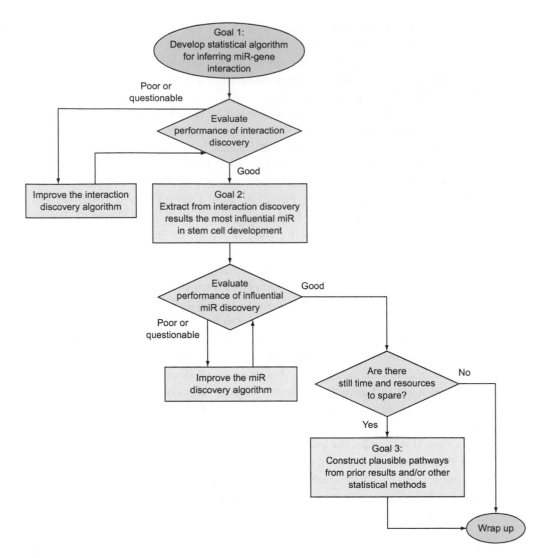

Figure 6.3   A flowchart showing the basic plan for my gene interaction project

TOP PERFORMANCES IN TRACK AND FIELD

In chapter 4, I discussed one of my projects in which I analyzed lists of best-ever perfor-mances in the various events of track and field. As I mentioned earlier in this chapter, two of the main uncertainties remaining in the project concerned the quality and com-pleteness of the data as related to the power of the statistical methods I applied to them.

The first uncertainty could be stated: is there enough data? Because I had lists of the best performances by elite athletes and not complete lists of all performances ever, I would be looking only at data from the tail of the statistical distributions, which makes estimating parameters even more difficult. To determine whether there is enough data—something I'll cover in more depth in later chapters—I check to see if the estimation variance of the estimated parameters is small enough, and I also check the estimation variance of predictions generated by the model to make sure that it's not making predictions that vary wildly with only small changes of the inputs. Most important, I wouldn't know if I had enough data until I wrote the code that applies the statistical model to the data and generates estimates. If I didn't have enough data, I would have to consider purchasing more data from another website (though I'm not sure how much more data it would have, if any) or, possibly, making the model simpler so that it requires less data.

The second main uncertainty concerned the statistical distribution I would use. I wanted to use a log-normal distribution within the statistical model, but before writing the statistical code, I couldn't know for sure whether the distribution was appropriate. During the exploratory phase described in chapter 5, I did generate some histograms of the data, and the histograms seemed to follow the tail of a bell curve like the normal curve, but it wasn't until later that I wrote the code that estimated optimal parameters for such a curve and compared them to the data, so, for our purposes in this section, that uncertainty still exists.

Finally, there's the uncertainty that's ever present in statistical challenges: will the results be good enough? There's almost never a guarantee that you'll get good results, and this project was no exception. For academic purposes—and this was an academic project I intended to publish in a scientific journal—"good enough" usually implies "better than the next guy." By that I mean that I would have to demonstrate that the scoring system I developed was more reliable, in some sense, than other existing methods that were designed for the same purpose. My principal competitor was the set of IAAF Scoring Tables of Athletics. I chose to compare predictions that are implied by their scoring tables and my scoring tables to see which ones predicted better. If I fell short, then I pretty much had nothing I could publish. I would have to improve the model and the predictions or—keep in mind this is the shady, no-good, Evil Statistician way of doing it—I'd change the way I compare the two scoring systems to work in my favor. I mention the second, very, very bad way of improving results not because I would suggest it, but because people do that, and anyone who is reading a comparison of statistical methods should keep in mind!

Given these three uncertainties, I made the plan that appears in figure 6.4. There are two checkpoints—data fitting the distribution and then the quality of the predictions—and if I didn't get to the checkpoints without problems, I had one or two possible solutions for each. At the distribution checkpoint, if something looked wrong, I would find a better distribution, and at the quality of predictions checkpoint I could optionally get more data or improve the model, whichever seemed more reasonable to me at the time. If I had wanted to write an even more thorough plan, I could

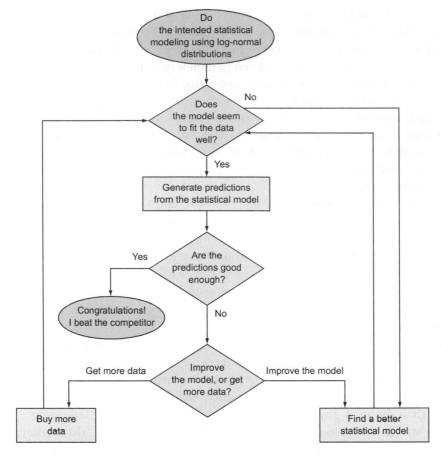

Figure 6.4   A flowchart showing the basic plan for my project involving the analysis of track and field performances

include specific criteria that would convince me to take the data route over the model quality route, or vice versa.

By now you've probably noticed that the primary sources of uncertainty are closely related to data and statistics. This is usually true, and it's true for me because I'm more of a statistician than a software developer, and wherever there is a statistical model, uncertainty is guaranteed.

ENRON EMAIL ANALYSIS

In chapter 5, I introduced a project that was intended to find and analyze criminal, suspicious, or negligent behavior within the public set of Enron emails and to apply concepts from the field of social network analysis to describe them. Nearly everything about the project was an uncertainty. Not only did we have the data challenges I mentioned near the beginning of this chapter, but we also did not know of any specific examples of criminal or suspicious behavior within the data set itself. We mostly assumed they were there somewhere—a lot of bad stuff went on at Enron—but with more than 100,000 emails, it would be hard to find them.

Because we had plenty of news stories and research about the Enron scandal, and we had on hand a few experts in the area of corporate fraud, we thought it might be a reasonable idea to develop a few coarse statistical analyses to filter the data, after which we could read through the top-scoring 100 emails or so, looking for good examples of suspicious behavior. If we did this a few times, it might be more efficient than trying to read all the emails until we found some that were suspicious.

Another suggestion was to build a full-fledged statistical model of social network behavior and try to use it to find suspicious behavior. This, to me, seemed like putting the cart before the horse. Or at the least it would leave us open to some serious confirmation bias in the event that we happened to find some interesting emails—did the methods work, or did we stumble into the results we were looking for?

Because almost nothing was concrete or guaranteed about this project, our plan would be more concerned with time and resource management than with a specific set of steps. Given that we had a deadline, even though it was a fuzzy one, we had to keep in mind that we needed to produce *some* results by the end of the project. We couldn't use the academic strategy of working until there are good results and then submitting them, so we used a strategy that some people call *time boxing*. It's not as exciting as it sounds—sorry. It's placing a somewhat-arbitrary time limit on an open-ended task to remind yourself that you have to move on.

For a 10-day project time line, our loosely defined plan looked something like the flow chart that appears in figure 6.5. It's definitely a fuzzy plan, but at least it's something to start from, and it makes sure the whole team knows how you expect the time line to work out, even if it doesn't work out exactly that way. Even the plan itself can change, given new information or other changes to the goals, priorities, or other aspects of the situation. The most notable characteristic of this example, when compared to the others, is that it shows how to create a schedule even in the face of near-absolute uncertainty, wide-open goals, and a deadline.

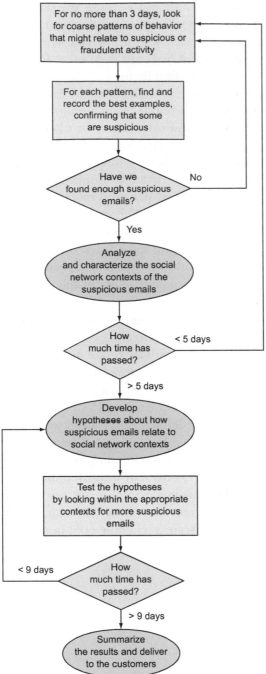

Figure 6.5   A flowchart showing the basic plan for the Enron project

6.4 Communicating new goals

Plans and goals can change at any moment, given new information or new constraints or for any other reason. You must communicate significant changes to everyone involved with the project, including the customer. The project's customer obviously has a vested interest in what the final product of the project should be—otherwise the project wouldn't exist—so the customer should be made aware of any changes to the goals. Because most customers like to be kept informed, it's often advisable to inform them of your plans, new or old, for how you will achieve those goals. A customer might also be interested in a progress report including what preliminary results you have so far and how you got them, but these are of the lowest priority.

I mention priority in this context because what's often interesting or important to a data scientist isn't interesting or important to a customer who is not a data scientist. For example, I've been to many talks at biological conferences in which the presenter seems more interested in telling the story of how they got their results than in present-ing the results themselves and their impact. For a data scientist, the story of the proj-ect—typically including every twist, turn, and obstacle—represents the intrigue of the work that has been done, the difficulty, and the ultimate victory. But non–data scien-tists are most interested in whether you got good results and whether they can trust that your good results weren't a fluke. Explaining that data wrangling took a full week, for example, serves only to say, "My job can be tough at times," and might justify a missed deadline but little else.

Focus on what the customer cares about: progress has been made, and the current expected, achievable goals are X, Y, and Z. They may have questions, which is great, and they may be interested in hearing about all aspects of your project, but in my experience most are not. My one and only must-have conclusion for a meeting with the customer at this stage is that I communicate clearly what the new goals are and that they approve them. Everything else is optional.

You may consider communicating your basic plan to the customer, particularly if you're using any of their resources to complete the project. They may have sugges-tions, advice, or other domain knowledge that you haven't experienced yet. If their resources are involved, such as databases, computers, other employees, then they will certainly be interested in hearing how and how much you'll be making use of them.

Finally, as I mentioned, preliminary results and the story of how you got them are of the lowest priority. In my experience, sharing these can be helpful, but only for a few reasons, such as when doing so serves the following purposes:

- To bolster the customer's confidence in the case of promising preliminary results
- To gain the customer's trust by showing that your methods are sound
- To make the customer feel like a data scientist on the team in the case of a good story that the customer can understand

All of these can be desirable under various circumstances, but in communication with the customer it's best to ensure that you don't lose sight of the main intersection between your project role and theirs: the goals.

Exercises

Continuing with the Filthy Money Forecasting personal finance app scenario first described in chapter 2 and relating to previous chapters' exercises, try these:

1 Suppose that your preliminary analyses and descriptive statistics from the previous chapter lead you to believe that you can probably generate some reliable forecasts for active users with financial accounts that have many transactions, but you don't think you can do the same for users and accounts with relatively few transactions. Translate this finding into the "What is possible? What is valuable? What is efficient?" framework for adjusting goals.

2 Based on your answer to the previous question, describe a general plan for generating forecasts within the app.

Summary

- An explicit and formal evaluation phase such as I suggest here can help you organize your progress, your goals, your plan, and your knowledge of the project.
- Before proceeding, ask, "What have I learned?"
- Adjust expectations and goals based on preliminary findings.
- Make a plan based on any new information and new goals, while taking into account the inevitable uncertainties.
- Communicate to the customer the new goals, plans, and progress.

Statistics and modeling: concepts and foundations

7

This chapter covers

- Statistical modeling as a core concept in data science
- Mathematics as a foundation of statistics
- Other useful statistical methods such as clustering and machine learning

Figure 7.1 shows where we are in the data science process: statistical analysis of data. Statistical methods are often considered as nearly one half, or at least one third, of the skills and knowledge needed for doing good data science. The other large piece is software development and/or application, and the remaining, smaller piece is subject matter or domain expertise. Statistical theory and methods are hugely important to data science, but I've said relatively little about them so far in this book. In this chapter, I attempt to present a grand overview.

Statistics is a big field. I wouldn't presume to be able to cover all of statistics in one book, let alone one chapter. Hundreds of textbooks, thousands of journal articles, and even more web pages have been written on the subject, so you'll find plenty of references if you have specific questions. What I haven't yet seen in another written work, however, is a conceptual description of statistics and its most important ideas that provides a solid theoretical foundation for someone aspiring to data science who doesn't have formal statistical training or education. In this chapter I'll introduce the field of statistics as a collection of related tools, each with pros and cons, for accomplishing the goals of data science. The aim of such an introduction is to enable you to begin to consider the range of possible statistical methods that might be applied in a project, to the point where you're able to feel comfortable seeking more specific information from more detailed, technical references.

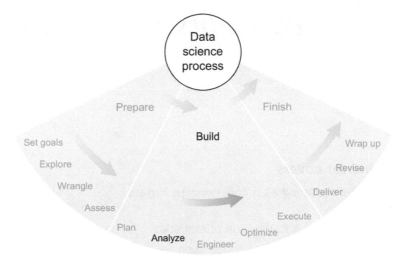

Figure 7.1   An important aspect of the build phase of the data science process: statistical data analysis

7.1   *How I think about statistics*

You may already feel comfortable with statistics and technical references describing how to apply its complex techniques, and in that case this chapter may seem unnecessary. But unless you've had much formal statistical education, there are likely many areas that you haven't yet seen. Or you may not be familiar with how various statistical areas are related to each other. I do feel that even experienced data scientists can benefit from thinking about the field of statistics as a whole, how its components relate to each other, and how the methods of statistics are distinct from both the software that performs them and the data upon which they're used. I don't intend to present a definitive description of any of these concepts, but I do intend to initiate a discussion of these concepts, how they relate to each other, and how each can be important.

Throughout this chapter, I'll continue to emphasize the distinctness of the methods, the software, and the data. Using a machine learning library isn't the same thing as applying a type of machine learning to your data set. One is a tool; the other is an action. Likewise, a database isn't the same thing as the data contained within it, no matter how intertwined they may be. Therefore, because I want to focus on statistical methods in this chapter, I'll often mention software and data only abstractly, though I will refer to concrete examples at times when it seems appropriate.

Finally, before we dive in, I'd like to say that I think and write conceptually about the world of statistical methods. I imagine scenarios in which I'm grabbing data with my hands and stuffing it into the pipes of a machine that will somehow learn about this data, and my job is to tweak the pipes and the dials of the machine so that good, useful information comes out the other end. Or in the case of classifying data points, I picture myself drawing a line with chalk that best divides the red points from the blue points and then considering how I might draw another line to correct for some of the red points that fell on the blue side and vice versa. I think in that way, and I'm warning you in case you were expecting a chapter filled with differential equations and correlation coefficients. To the contrary, it's going to be a big-picture chapter with lots of conceptual and imaginative passages. I like thinking about this stuff, so I hope I can present it in a way that's fun for you, too.

7.2   *Statistics: the field as it relates to data science*

The Oxford Dictionary of Statistical Terms (OUP, 2006) describes statistics as "the study of the collection, analysis, interpretation, presentation, and organization of data." For our purposes in this chapter, we're going to skip the collection, presentation, and organization and focus on the analysis and interpretation. I'll assume that you've already collected and organized your data, as described in previous chapters, and I'll discuss presentation in a later chapter.

Analysis and interpretation, from my perspective, are the scientific aspects of statistics. They're concerned with wringing knowledge from data and recognizing whether there's enough evidence to support a given hypothesis or putative conclusion. In the face of much uncertainty—which is always the case for highly statistical projects in data science—good analysis and interpretation are important, and so I'd like to dedicate most of this chapter to discussing some of the methods by which statistics helps to achieve them.

7.2.1   *What statistics is*

Statistics lies between the theoretical field of mathematics and the reality of observable data. Mathematics, surprisingly to most people, has little if anything to do with data. Despite this, it has much to do with data science. Data scientists need mathematics in order to do meaningful statistical analyses, so I'd be remiss if I didn't begin a discussion about statistics in data science with a discussion of mathematics. In the next section, I'll write about mathematics, the main concepts it depends on, and how it's useful in real-world applications.

On the one side of statistics is mathematics, and on the other side is data. Mathematics—particularly, *applied mathematics*—provides statistics with a set of tools that enables the analysis and interpretation that are the main focus of this chapter. In addition to mathematics, statistics possesses its own set of techniques that are primarily data centric.

Descriptive statistics, introduced in chapter 5, is a generally intuitive or simple kind of statistics that can provide a good overview of the data without being overly complex or difficult to understand. Descriptive statistics usually stays close to the data, in a sense.

Inferential statistics is inherently one or more steps removed from the data. *Inference* is the process of estimating unknown quantities based on measurable, related quantities. Typically, inferential statistics involves a statistical model that defines quantities, measurable and unmeasurable, and their relationships to each other. Methods from inferential statistics can range from quite simple to wildly complex, varying also in their precision, abstractness, and interpretability.

Statistical modeling is the general practice of describing a system using statistical constructs and then using that model to aid in analysis and interpretation of data related to the system. Both descriptive and inferential statistics rely on statistical models, but in some cases an explicit construction and interpretation of the model itself plays a secondary role. With statistical modeling, the primary focus is on understanding the model and the underlying system that it describes. Mathematical modeling is a related concept that places more emphasis on model construction and interpretation than on its relationship to data. Statistical modeling focuses on the model's relationship to data.

Farthest from the raw data is a set of statistical techniques that are often called, for better or worse, black box methods. The term *black box* refers to the idea that some statistical methods have so many moving pieces with complex relationships to each other that it would be nearly impossible to dissect the method itself because it was applied to specific data within a specific context. Many methods from machine learning and artificial intelligence fit this description. If you attempt to classify individuals appearing in a data set into one of several categories, and you apply a machine learning technique such as a random forest or neural network, it will often be difficult to say, after the fact, why a certain individual was classified in a certain way. Data goes into the black box, a classification comes out, and you're not usually certain what exactly happened in between. I'll discuss this concept more later in this chapter.

In the following sections, I'll cover the various concepts in statistics in more detail. I'll usually favor high-level descriptions over specific applications so as to be widely applicable in many cases, but I'll use illustrative examples when they seem helpful. There are many excellent technical resources that can provide more detail about each particular topic, and I'll try to provide enough detail, including key words and common method names, so that you're able to find additional resources quickly, on the internet or elsewhere.

7.2.2   *What statistics is not*

The most common misconception about what I do as a data scientist usually appears when I talk to a recruiter or other hiring agent for a company or institution. On occasion, the misconception appears later, after I've already taken a job and I'm midway through a project. The misconception is that I, as a data scientist, can set up, load, and administer a number of data stores serving a large number of people in various ways. I've explained many times to many people that data science is not data management, and it is definitely not database administration. There's absolutely nothing wrong with those two roles—in fact, I am forever thankful when I get the chance to work with a highly competent database administrator (DBA)—but those roles are quite the opposite of scientific.

Science is the endeavor to discover the unknown. Moving data around and improving reliability and query speed is an incredibly important job that has nothing to do with discovering the unknown. I'm not sure why, exactly, some people confuse these two data-oriented jobs, but it's happened to me on more than one occasion. It's particularly funny to me when someone asks me to set up a database for a large organization, because, of all of the most common data science tasks, database administration is probably the one in which I have the least experience. I can set up a database that serves me well, but I definitely wouldn't count on myself to build a data management solution for a large organization.

Maybe it's because I'm a mathematician, but I consider data management among those skills that are useful to me but that are peripheral to the main task. I want to get to the analysis. Anything that enables good data analysis is undeniably good, but I'll suffer passable database performance for a long time before I feel the need to take control of it—and all of its administrative headaches—in the name of optimal performance. I'm all about the statistics, however long they take.

Data management is to statistics as a food supplier is to a chef: statistics is an art that depends deeply on reliable data management, as a restaurant famous for their bacon-encrusted salmon relies heavily on timely, high-quality raw materials from local pig and salmon farms. (Apologies to my vegetarian readers and fans of wild salmon.) To me, statistics *is* the job; everything else is only helping. Restaurant-goers want, first and foremost, good food with good ingredients; secondarily, they might want to know that the source of their food was reliable and fast. Consumers of statistical analysis— the customers of data science projects—want to know that they've gleaned reliable information in some way. Then and only then would they care if the data store, software, and workflow that uses both are reliable and fast. Statistical analysis is the product, and data management is a necessary part of the process.

The role that statistics plays in data science is not a secondary, peripheral function of dealing with data. Statistics is the slice of data science that provides the insights. All of the software development and database administration that data scientists do contribute to their ability to do statistics. Web development and user interface design— two other tasks that might be asked of a data scientist—help deliver statistical analysis to the customer. As a mathematician and statistician, I might be biased, but I think statistics is the most intellectually challenging part of a data scientist's job.

On the other hand, some of the biggest challenges I've dealt with in data science involve getting various software components to play nicely with one another, so I may be underestimating software engineering. It all depends on where you stand, I suppose. The next chapter will cover the basics of software, so I'll put off further discussion of it until then.

7.3   Mathematics

The field of mathematics, though its exact boundaries are disputed, is based wholly on logic. Specifically, every mathematical concept can be deconstructed into a series of if-then statements plus a set of assumptions. Yes, even long division and finding the circumference of a circle can be boiled down to purely logical steps that follow from assumptions. It so happens that people have been doing math for so long that there are innumerable logical steps and assumptions that have been in common use for so long that we often take some of them for granted.

7.3.1   Example: long division

Long division—or plain division—as you learned it in elementary school, is an operation between two numbers that comes with a lot of assumptions. It's likely that everyone reading this book learned how to do long division as a set of steps, a sort of algorithm that takes as input two numbers, the dividend and divisor, and gives a result called the quotient. Long division can be quite useful (more so in the absence of a calculator or computer) in everyday life when, for example, you want to divide a restaurant bill equally among several people or share a few dozen cupcakes with friends.

Many people think the field of mathematics is composed of numerous such moderately useful algorithms for calculating things, and these people wouldn't be entirely wrong. But far more important than mathematical algorithms are the assumptions and logical steps that can be assembled into a proof that something is true or false. In fact, every mathematical algorithm is constructed from a series of logical statements that can end up proving that the algorithm itself does what it is supposed to do, given the required assumptions.

Take, for instance, three logical statements X, Y, and Z, each of which could be either true or false under various circumstances, as well as the following statements:

- If X is true, then Y must be false.
- If Y is false, then Z is true.

This is obviously an arbitrary set of statements that could be straight out of a logic text, but such statements lie at the heart of mathematics.

Given these statements, let's say that you find out that X is true. It follows that Y is false and also that Z is true. That's logic, and it doesn't seem exciting. But what if I put real-life meaning into X, Y, and Z in an example that includes a visitor, or potential customer, to a retail website:

- *Statement X*—The potential customer put more than two items into their online shopping cart.
- *Statement Y*—The customer is only browsing.
- *Statement Z*—The potential customer will buy something.

Those statements are all meaningful to an online retailer. And you know that the statement "Z is true" is exciting to any retailer that's trying to make money, so the logical statements shown previously imply that the statement "X is true" should also be exciting to the retailer. More practically, it might imply that if the retailer is able to get a potential customer to put more than two items into the shopping cart, then they will make a sale. This might be a viable marketing strategy on the website if other paths to making a sale are more difficult. Obviously, real life is rarely this purely logical, but if you make all of the statements fuzzier such that "is true" becomes "probably is true" and likewise for "is false," then this scenario might indeed be a realistic one in which a data scientist could help increase sales for the retailer. Such fuzzy statements are often best handled using statements of probability, which I cover later in this chapter.

Back to the example of long division: even the algorithms of basic arithmetic (as you probably learned in school) are predicated on assumptions and logical statements. Before getting into those, instead of boring you with a description of how I do long division, let's assume that you have a favorite way to do long division—correctly—with pencil and paper, and we'll refer to that way as *The Algorithm* hereafter in this example. The Algorithm must be the kind that gives decimal results and not the kind of long division that gives an almost answer plus a remainder. (You'll understand why in a few minutes.) Furthermore, let's assume that The Algorithm was originally developed by a mathematician and that this mathematician has already proven that The Algorithm results in correct answers under the appropriate conditions. Now let's explore some of the conditions that the mathematician requires in order for you to use The Algorithm properly.

First, you have to assume that the dividend, divisor, and quotient are elements of a set called the real numbers. The set of *real numbers* includes all the decimal and whole numbers you're used to but not others, such as the imaginary numbers you might get if, for example, you tried to take the square root of a negative number. There are all sorts of other sets of non-real numbers as well as sets not containing numbers at all, but I'll leave that to mathematics textbooks to discuss.

In addition to the assumption that you're dealing with the set of real numbers, you also assume that this particular set of real numbers is also a specific type of set called a field. A *field*, a central concept in abstract algebra, is a set that's defined by a number of properties, among which are the existence of two operations, commonly called addition and multiplication, which in an abstract sense are not guaranteed to work in the way they do in common arithmetic. You do know that these two operations in fields always operate on two elements of the field in certain specific ways, but the fact that addition and multiplication work in this one specific way is another assumption you have to make when doing long division. For more on fields, consult a reference on abstract algebra.

You're assuming you have a field composed of real numbers and that you have the operations addition and multiplication that work in the specific ways you learned in school. As part of the definition of a field, these two operations must both have *inverses.* As you can probably guess, you often call the inverse of addition *subtraction* and the inverse of multiplication *division*. The inverse of any operation must undo what the operation does. A number *A multiplied by B* gives a result *C* such that *C divided by B* gives the number *A* again. Division is defined to be the inverse of multiplication as you know it. That's not an assumption; it follows from the other assumptions and the definition of a field.

To summarize, here's what you have on long division:

- Assumptions:
  1 You have the set of real numbers.
  2 You have a field over the set of real numbers.
  3 The field operations addition and multiplication work as in arithmetic.

- Statements:
  1 If you have a field, then addition and multiplication have inverses: subtraction and division, respectively.
  2 If the field operations addition and multiplication work as in arithmetic, then subtraction and division also work as in arithmetic.
  3 If division works as in arithmetic, then The Algorithm will give correct answers.

Putting together these assumptions with these statements yields the following:

- Assumptions 1 and 2 together with statement 1 imply that the operations subtraction and division exist.
- Assumption 3 and statement 2 imply that subtraction and division work as in arithmetic.
- The previous two statements together with statement 3 imply that The Algorithm will give correct answers.

That example may seem trivial, and in some ways it is, but I think it's illustrative of the way that our knowledge of the world, in particular on quantitative topics, is built on specific instances of mathematical constructs. If the system of real numbers didn't apply for some reason, then long division with decimal results wouldn't work. If instead you were using the set of whole numbers or the integers, then a different algorithm for long division would be appropriate, possibly one that resulted in a sort of quotient plus a remainder. The reason long division can't work the same on whole numbers or integers as it does with the real numbers is that neither set—whole numbers or integers—forms a field. Knowledge of the underlying mathematics, such as when you have a field and when you don't, is the only definitive way to determine when The Algorithm is appropriate and when it is not. Extending that idea, knowledge of mathematics can be useful in choosing analytical methods for data science projects and in diagnosing eventual problems with those methods and their results.

7.3.2 *Mathematical models*

A *model* is a description of a system and how it works. A mathematical model describes a system using equations, variables, constants, and other concepts from mathematics. If you're trying to describe a system that exists in the real world, then you're venturing into *applied mathematics*, a phrase that generally implies that the work done can be applied to something outside mathematics, such as physics, linguistics, or data science. Applied mathematics is certainly often close to statistics, and I won't attempt to make a clear distinction between the two. But, generally speaking, applied math focuses on improving models and techniques, possibly without any data at all, whereas statistics concentrates on learning from data using mathematical models and techniques. The fields of mathematical modeling and applied mathematics are likewise not clearly distinguishable; the former focuses on the models, and the latter on some kind of real-world applications, but neither does so exclusively. The concept and use of mathematical models aren't intuitive to everyone, so I'll discuss them briefly here.

One of the simplest and most commonly used mathematical models is the linear model. A *linear model* is merely a line, described by a linear equation, that's intended to represent the relationship between two or more variables. When the relationship is linear, it's equivalent to saying that the variables are directly proportional, terminology that's used more often in some fields. A linear equation describing a linear model in two dimensions (two variables) can be written in slope-intercept form (remember from school!) as

$$y = Mx + B$$

where M is the slope and B is the y-intercept.

Linear models are used in many applications because they're easy to work with and also because many natural quantities can be reasonably expected to follow an approximately linear relationship with each other. The relationship between distance driven in a car and the amount of gasoline used is a good example. The farther you drive, the more gasoline you burn. Exactly how much gasoline was used depends on other factors as well, such as the type of car, how fast you were driving, and traffic and weather conditions. Therefore, although you can reasonably assume that distance and gasoline usage are approximately linearly related, other somewhat random variables cause variations in gasoline usage from trip to trip.

Models are often used to make predictions. If you had a linear model for gasoline usage based on distance traveled, you could predict the amount of gasoline you'd use on your next trip by putting the distance of the trip into the linear equation that describes your model. If you used the linear model

$$y = 0.032x + 0.0027$$

where y is the amount of gasoline (in liters) needed and x is the distance traveled (in kilometers), then the slope of the line, 0.032, implies that trips in your data set required on average 0.032 liters of gasoline per kilometer traveled. In addition to that, there appears to be an additional 0.0027 liters of gasoline used per trip, regardless of distance traveled. This might account for the energy needed to start the car and idle for a few moments before beginning the trip. Regardless, using this model, you can predict the gasoline usage for an upcoming trip of, say, 100 km by setting x = 100 and calculating y. The prediction according to the model would be y = 3.2027 liters. This is a basic example of how a linear model might be used to make predictions.

Figure 7.2 shows a graphical representation of a linear model without any axis labels or other context. I've included this graph without context because I'd like to focus on the purely conceptual aspects of the model and the mathematics, and the context can sometimes distract from those. In the graph, the line is the model, and the dots represent data that the line is attempting to model. The y-intercept seems to be approximately 5.0, the slope is about 0.25, and the line seems to follow the data reasonably well. But notice the dispersion of the data around the line. If, for example, you wanted to predict a y-value from a given x-value, the model probably wouldn't give a perfect prediction, and there would be some error. Based on the dots, the predictions of y-values appear to be within about three or four units of the linear model, which may be good or not, depending on the goals of the project. I'll discuss fitting models to data later, in the section on statistical modeling. The main idea here is the conceptual relationship between a model and data. Having an image such as this one in your mind—and the conceptual understanding it brings—while modeling data increases awareness and improves decision making throughout your analyses.

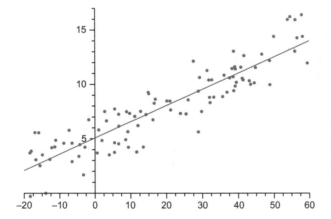

Figure 7.2   A representation of a linear model (line) and some data (dots) that the model attempts to describe. The line is a mathematical model, and its optimal parameters—slope and intercept—can be found using statistical modeling techniques.[1]

It's important to emphasize that mathematical models are fabricated things that don't have any inherent connection to the real-life system. Models are descriptions of what you think happens in those systems, and there's no guarantee that they work well. It's the responsibility of the data scientist (or mathematician or statistician) to find a model that's good enough to suit the purposes of the project and apply it correctly.

---

[1]   From https://en.wikipedia.org/wiki/Linear_regression, in the public domain.

Examples of mathematical models

Einstein's model of gravity, as described in his theory of general relativity, famously supplanted Newton's model of gravity. Newton's model is a simple equation that describes the forces of gravity quite accurately at normal masses and distances, but Einstein's model, which uses a mathematical model based on metric tensors (a sort of higher-order object describing linear relationships), is far more accurate at extreme scales.

The current Standard Model of particle physics, finalized in the 1970s, is a mathematical model based on quantum field theory that theorizes how physical forces and subatomic particles behave. It has survived a few experimental tests of its applicability as a model, most recently during the process of confirming the existence of the Higgs boson. The Higgs boson is an elementary particle predicted by the Standard Model for which, prior to 2012, there was little experimental proof of existence. Since then, experiments at the Large Hadron Collider at CERN have confirmed the existence of a particle consistent with the Higgs boson. Like any good scientist, the researchers at CERN won't say with certainty that they found the Higgs boson and only the Higgs boson, because some properties of the particle are still unknown, but they do say with certainty that nothing in the Standard Model has yet been contradicted by experimental evidence.

From my own experience, some of the more interesting applications of mathematical models happen in social network analysis. Social networks are composed of individuals and connections between them, making graph theory an excellent mathematical field in which to look for applicable models. Theories of connectedness, centrality, and in-betweenness, among others, can be nearly directly applied to real-life scenarios in which groups of people interact in various ways. Graph theory has numerous other applications, and frankly it has some quite interesting purely mathematical (non-applied) problems as well, but the recent advent of social networks on the internet provides a wealth of new phenomena to model as well as data to support it.

The geometric equivalent of a linear model is the concept of Euclidean geometry, which is the normal concept of how three-dimensional space works—length, height, width, all lines can extend to infinity without intersecting—extended to any number of dimensions. But other geometries exist, and these can be useful in modeling certain systems. Spherical geometry is the geometry that exists on the surface of a sphere. If you're standing on the Earth, a sphere (approximately), and you walk in a straight line, ignoring bodies of water, you'll arrive back where you started some time later. This doesn't happen in Euclidean geometry—where you'd be walking into infinity—and it's a property that can come in handy when modeling certain processes. Certainly, any model of airplane traffic could benefit from a spherical geometry, and I'm sure there are many more uses, such as manufacturing engineering, where precision milling a ball joint or other curved surface might need a model of a spherical geometry to get the shape exactly right.

Mathematical models are used in every quantitative field, explicitly or implicitly. Like some of the logical statements and assumptions that we must make in everyday arithmetic, some mathematical models are used so often for a given purpose that they're taken for granted. For example, surveys, democratic election polling, and medical

(continued)

testing make use of correlations between variables to draw informative conclusions. The common concept of correlation—specifically the Pearson correlation coefficient—assumes a linear model, but that fact is often taken for granted, or at least it's not common knowledge. The next time you're reading a forecast for an upcoming election, know that the predictions as well as the margins of error are based on a linear model.

7.3.3   *Mathematics vs. statistics*

Real math is made up of assumptions and logical statements, and only in specific instances does it involve numeric quantities. In that way, among all the topics that are taught in high school math classes in the United States, geometry—with its proofs of triangle congruence and parallelity of lines—comes the closest to the heart of mathematics. But everyday life obviously deals in numeric quantities quite often, so we tend to focus on the branches of mathematics that deal with quantities. Data science does this quite often, but it has also been known to bleed into not-so-quantitative, or pure, branches of mathematics such as group theory, non-Euclidean geometry, and topology, if they seem useful. In that way, knowledge of some pure mathematical topics can prove useful to a data scientist.

In any case, mathematics generally doesn't touch the real world. Based wholly on logic and always—always—starting with a set of assumptions, mathematics must first assume a world it can describe before it begins to describe it. Every mathematical statement can be formulated to start with an *if* (*if* the assumptions are true), and this *if* lifts the statement and its conclusion into abstractness. That is not to say that mathematics isn't useful in the real world; quite the contrary. Mathematics, rather than being a science, is more of a vocabulary with which we can describe things. Some of these things might be in the real world. As with vocabularies and the words they contain, rarely is a description perfectly correct. The goal is to get as close to correct as possible. The mathematician and statistician George Box famously wrote, "Essentially, all models are wrong, but some are useful." Indeed, if a model is reasonably close to correct, it can be useful.

The field of statistics shares these concerns about the correctness of models, but instead of being a vocabulary and a system of logic, statistics is a lens through which to see the world. Statistics begins with data, and though statistical models are mostly indistinguishable from mathematical models, the intent is quite different. Instead of seeking to describe a system from the inside out, a statistical model observes a system from the outside in by aggregating and manipulating relevant observable data.

Mathematics does, however, provide much of the heavy machinery that statistics uses. Statistical distributions are often described by complex equations with roots that are meaningful in a practical, scientific sense. Fitting statistical models often makes use of mathematical optimization techniques. Even the space in which a project's data is assumed to lie must be described mathematically, even if the description is merely "N-dimensional Euclidean space." Although the boundary is a bit blurry, I like to say that the point at which mathematics ends and statistics begins is the point at which real data enters an equation.

7.4   *Statistical modeling and inference*

In chapter 5, I mentioned statistical inference in the context of the rough statistical analysis I suggested as a part of data assessment. *Inference* is the task of estimating the value of a quantity you're not able to measure directly. Because you don't have direct measurements of the quantity, it's necessary to construct a model that, at the least, describes the relationship between the quantity you want and the measurements you have. Because of the existence of a model in inference, I've lumped statistical modeling and inference together in this section.

A statistical model is not that different from a mathematical model, which I've already covered in this chapter. As I've written, the difference is mainly the focus: mathematical modeling focuses on the model and its inherent properties, but statistical modeling focuses on the model's relationship to data. In both cases, the model is a set of variables whose relationships are described by equations and other mathematical relations. A linear model—which I've already introduced—between the quantities x and y might look like

$$y = Mx + B$$

whereas an exponential model might look like

$$y = Ae^x$$

where e is the exponential constant, also known as Euler's number. The model parameter values M, B, and A are probably unknown until they're estimated via some statistical inference technique.

Each of these two models is a description of how x and y might be related to one another. In the first case, the linear model, it is assumed that as x goes up a certain amount, y goes up (or down, depending on the value of M) the same amount no matter how large x gets. In the second case, the exponential one, if x increases a certain amount, then y will increase an amount that depends on the size of x; if x is larger, then an increase in x will increase y an even bigger amount than if x was smaller. In short, if x gets bigger, then bigger again, the second movement will cause a greater increase in y than the first.

A common example of exponential growth is unconstrained population growth. If resources aren't scarce, then populations—bacteria, plants, animals, even people—sometimes grow exponentially. The growth rate might be 5%, 20%, or larger, but the term *exponential* implies that percentages (or proportions), and not scalar numbers, describe the growth. For example, if a population has 100 individuals and is growing at a rate of 20% per year, then after one year the population will contain 120 individuals.

After two years, you expect to have 20% more than 120, which adds 24 individuals to the total, bringing it to 144. As you can see, the rate of increase grows as the population grows. That's one of the characteristics of an exponential growth model.

Both of these models, linear and exponential, can be described by a single equation. If you use one of these models in a project, the challenge is to find estimates of the parameters M, B, and/or A that represent the data well and can provide insight into the system you're modeling. But models can extend far beyond a single equation.

Now that you've seen a couple of simple examples, let's have a look at what statistical models are in general.

7.4.1 *Defining a statistical model*

A *statistical model* is a description of a set of quantities or variables that are involved in a system and also a description of the mathematical relationships between those quantities. So far, you've seen a linear model as well as an exponential one, both of which pertain only to two variables, x and y, whatever those quantities are. Models can be far more complex, consisting of variables of many dimensions as well as requiring many equations of various types.

Beyond linear and exponential equations, all sorts of function types are used in statistical modeling: polynomial, piecewise polynomial (spline), differential equations, nonlinear equations of various types, and many others. Some equation or function types have more variables (moving parts) than others, which affect the complexity of the model description as well as the difficulty of estimating all the model parameters.

Beyond these mathematical descriptions of models, a statistical model should have some explicit relationship to data that's relevant to the system being modeled. Usually, this means that the values for which data exists are included explicitly as variables in the model. For instance, if you consider the population growth example from the previous section, and your data set includes several measurements of population size over time, then you'll want to include the population size in your model as well as a variable for time. In this case, it can be straightforward, such as using the model equation

$$P = P_0 e^{rt}$$

where P is the population at time t, P_0 is the population at time zero—you can choose when time zero is, and then all other times are relative to that t = 0 point—and r is the growth rate parameter (e is still the exponential constant).

Presumably, one of the goals of modeling this data is that you'd like to be able to predict the population at some time in the future. The data set that you have, a set of population sizes over time, is a collection of value pairs for P and t. The task is then to use these past values to find good model parameters that help you make good predictions about the population in the future. In this model, P_0 is defined to be the population when t = 0, so the only remaining, unknown model parameter is r. Estimating a good value for r is one of the primary tasks of statistical modeling in this hypothetical project.

Once you have a good estimate of the model parameter r, and given that you would know the value for P_0 because it's defined by the data and the chosen definition for the time variable t, you'd then have a usable model of the growth of the population you're studying. You can then use it to make conclusions and predictions about the past, present, and future state of the population. That's the purpose of statistical modeling: to draw meaningful conclusions about the system you're studying based on a model of that system and some data.

In order to draw meaningful conclusions about a system via statistical modeling, the model has to be good, the data has to be good, and the relationship between them also has to be good. That's far easier said than done. Complex systems—and most real-life systems are quite complex—require special care in order to make sure that the model and its relationship to the data are good enough to draw those meaningful conclusions you seek. You often have to take into account many unknowns and moving parts in the system. Some unknowns can be included explicitly in the model, such as the growth rate in the exponential population model. These are called *latent variables* and are described in the next section.

7.4.2 *Latent variables*

When you create a model of a system, there are some quantities that you can measure and some you can't. Even among the measurable quantities, there are some for which you already have measurements in your data and others for which you don't. In the exponential growth model, it's fairly obvious that the growth rate is a quantity that exists, regardless of whether you can measure it. Even if you wanted to use a different model, such as a linear one, there would probably still be at least one variable or parameter that represents the rate of growth of the population. In any case, this growth parameter is probably not measurable. There might be some rare cases in which you could keep track of the new members of the population, and in that case you might be able to measure the population growth rate directly, but this seems unlikely. Let's assume that the growth rate isn't directly measurable or at least that you don't have direct measurements of it in the data. Whenever you know a variable or parameter exists but you don't have measurements of it, you call it a latent variable.

Latent variables, as in the case of the growth rate parameter in an exponential population growth model, are often based on an intuitive concept of how a system works. If you know that a population is growing, you know there must be a growth rate, and so creating a variable for that growth rate is an intuitive thing to do that helps explain your system and how other variables are related. Furthermore, if you can draw conclusions about that growth rate, then that might be helpful to your project's goals. Those are the two most common reasons to include a latent variable in a statistical model:

- The variable plays an intuitive role in how the system works.
- You'd like to draw statistical conclusions about this particular variable.

In either case, latent variables represent variables or quantities of which you'd like to know the value but can't measure or haven't measured for one reason or another. In order to use them, you have to infer them from what you know about other, related variables.

In the exponential population growth model, if you know about the population size P at multiple time points, then it's reasonably easy to get some idea of the rate of change of that population. One way would be to take the differences/changes in population between consecutive time points, which is pretty close to a direct measurement but not quite. Then the question is whether the absolute differences are constant over time, implying linear growth, or if they grow as the population grows, implying an exponential growth or something similar. If the population seems to be growing by a constant number every time period (for example, year, month, day), then linear seems better suited, but if the population seems to be growing by a certain percentage every time period, then an exponential model probably suits the system better.

I'll discuss model comparison later in this chapter—finding a good statistical model is important—but for now I'll focus on the fact that the nature of a quantity that seems intuitive—the population growth rate in our example—depends heavily on the choice of model. It's tempting to think that the population growth rate is directly measurable, but in reality, even if you could measure it, you'd still have to make at least the decision about whether the population grows by an absolute number each time period or whether it grows by a percentage each time period. In addition, many, many other models are also possible; linear (absolute) and exponential (percentage) are only the two most commonly used for population growth. The choice of model and the nature of its latent variables are closely related. Both are highly influenced by how the system works, intuitively, as well as the system's relationship to the data.

7.4.3 *Quantifying uncertainty: randomness, variance, and error terms*

There's always uncertainty in the estimated values of latent variables if you can't measure them directly, but also even if you can. Getting near-exact values for latent variables and model parameters is difficult, so it's often useful to explicitly include some variance and error terms in your model, which are typically represented by the notion of a probability distribution of values.

USING PROBABILITY DISTRIBUTIONS IN STATISTICAL MODELS

If a quantity described by your model has an expected value—estimated by some statistical method—then the variance of that quantity describes how far from the expected value an individual instance of that quantity might be. For example, if you're modeling the height of human beings, you might find the average height of men to be 179.0 cm. But each individual differs from that expected value by some amount; each man is probably a few centimeters taller or shorter than that, with some men almost exactly 179.0 cm tall, and then there are the extremely tall and extremely short, who are 20 or 30 cm taller or shorter. This concept of the dispersion of values around an expected value naturally evokes the idea of a bell curve, or normal distribution, with which most people are familiar.

Probability distributions, in general, describe precisely the dispersion of random values, across a range of possible values, that you'd get from a random process if you took a sample from it. If you observed values that are generated by a random process, the probability distribution for that process would tell you how often you'd expect to see certain values. Most people know how the normal distribution is shaped, and they might be able to say what percentage of values generated by a normally distributed random process would be above or below certain marks. Although the normal distribution is the most popular probability distribution, there are distributions of all shapes, continuous and discrete, and each of these carries with it a set of assumptions. The normal distribution in particular doesn't deal well with outliers, so in the presence of outliers, a more robust distribution or method might be better. Each specific distribution has its own advantages and caveats, and choosing an appropriate one can have significant implications for your results. All randomness is not created equal, so it's best do to a little investigation before settling on a particular distribution. Plenty of statistics literature exists for this purpose.

The normal distribution is a probability distribution with two parameters: mean and variance. In the case of modeling a single quantity like human height, the normal distribution could describe the entire model. In that case, the system you're modeling is, in some sense, a system that produces human beings of various heights. The mean parameter represents the height that the system is aiming for when it makes each human, and the variance represents how far from that mean height the system usually is.

Aiming for a value and missing it by some amount is the core idea of error terms in statistical models. An *error* in this sense is how far off the mark the instance (or measurement) of the quantity is. Conceptually, this implies that every man should be 179.0 cm tall, but that some error in the system caused some men to be taller and some shorter. In statistical models, these errors are generally considered as unexplainable noise, and the principal concern becomes making sure that all the errors across all the measurements are normally distributed.

FORMULATING A STATISTICAL MODEL WITH UNCERTAINTY

A possible version of the human height model involving an error term is the equation

$$h_i = h_p + \varepsilon_i$$

where h_p is the expected height of the human-producing system, and h_i is the height of the individual with the label i. The error terms are represented by the variables ε_i, which are assumed to be normally distributed with mean zero and independent of each other. The Greek letter epsilon is the favored symbol for errors and other arbitrarily small quantities. Note that the subscript i indicates that there's a different error for each individual. If you have a good estimate for h_p and the variance for ε_i, then you have a reliable model of male human height. This isn't the only way to model male human height.

Because you know from experience that the height of human males varies among individuals, you might consider the conceptual difference between the expected height within a human population and the heights of the individuals. Individuals can be considered different instances of the same quantity or set of quantities. There are two conceptual reasons why different instances of the same quantity might vary:

- The system or the measurement process is noisy.
- The quantity itself can vary from one instance to another.

Note a subtle difference between these two reasons. The first reason is embodied by the notion of error terms. The second corresponds to the notion of a random variable.

Random variables possess their own inherent randomness that generally wouldn't be considered noise. In the human height example, rather than calling the system noisy, you could assume that the system itself picks a height at random and then produces a human of that height, nearly exactly. This conceptual distinction does have benefits, particularly in more complex models. This version of the model might be described by

$$h_i \sim N(h_p, \sigma^2)$$

$$m_i = h_i + \varepsilon_i$$

where the first statement indicates that the height h_i of individual i is generated by a random process using a normal distribution with mean h_p and variance σ^2. The second statement indicates that the measurement of h_i is a noisy process resulting in a measurement m_i. In this case, the error term ε_i corresponds only to the real-life measurement process and so would probably be only a fraction of a centimeter.

It's probably bad form to mix probability distribution notation with error term notation in the same model description, because they describe practically the same random process, but I think it's illustrative of the conceptual difference between inherently random variables that are important to the model and the presumed-unexplained error term.

A good example of an inherently random variable that isn't an error term would appear if you were to generalize your model of male human height to also include women. Males around the world are consistently taller than local women, so it would likely be a mistake to lump men and women together in a model of human height. Let's say that one of the goals of the modeling task is to be able to generate predictions about the height of a randomly chosen human, regardless of whether they are male, female, or otherwise. You could construct a model for males, as you did previously, and a corresponding one for females. But if you're generating a prediction for the height of a randomly chosen human, you wouldn't know definitively which model is more applicable, so you should include a random variable representing the sex of the individual. It could be a binary variable that you assume gets chosen first, before you make a prediction about the height from the normally distributed height model appropriate for that sex. This model might be described by the equations

$$s_i \sim B(1, p)$$

$$h_i \sim N(h_p(s_i), \sigma^2(s_i))$$

where s_i is the sex of the individual, which according to the first statement is chosen randomly from a Bernoulli distribution (a common distribution with two possible outcomes), where the probability of choosing female is assumed to be p (for two sexes, the probability of male is assumed to be 1–p). Given the individual's sex s_i, the term $h_p(s_i)$ is intended to represent the mean height of the population of people matching the sex s_i, and $\sigma^2(s_i)$ is the variance for people matching the sex s_i. The second statement, in summary, describes how the predicted height is generated from a normal distribution with parameters that are determined by an individual's sex, which was randomly chosen from the Bernoulli distribution.

DRAWING CONCLUSIONS FROM MODELS INVOLVING UNCERTAINTY

Assuming that you've found some good estimates for the parameters in this model, you can predict heights of randomly chosen individuals. Such prediction is useful in analysis of small sample sizes; if you, for example, chose randomly a group of 10 people, and you found that they averaged 161 cm in height, you might want to know if you didn't have a sample that's representative of the whole population. By generating height predictions from your model, in groups of 10, you can see how often you'd get such a small average height. If it's a rare occurrence, then that would be evidence that your sample isn't representative of the whole population, and you might want to take action to improve your sample in some way.

Random variables can be helpful in statistical modeling for a number of reasons, not the least of which is that many real-life systems contain randomness. In describing such a system using a model, it's important never to confuse the expectations of the model with the distributions that the model relies on. For instance, even though the model of human male height expects individuals to be 179.0 cm tall, it doesn't mean that every human male is 179.0 cm. This may seem obvious, but I've seen many academic papers confuse the two and take a statistical shortcut because it would be convenient to assume that everyone is of average height. Sometimes it may not matter much, but sometimes it might, and it pays to figure out which situation you're in. If you're an architect or a builder, you certainly wouldn't want to build doorways that are 180 cm tall; probably 40% or more of the population would have to duck their head to walk through, even though the average man wouldn't. If you're going to make important decisions based on your project's conclusions, it's often best to admit uncertainty at various stages, including in the statistical model.

I hope that this discussion of random variables, variance, and error terms has been illustrative of how uncertainty—which is so pervasive in all of data science—also works its way into statistical models. That might be an understatement; in fact, I consider reducing uncertainty to be the primary job of statistics. But sometimes in order to reduce uncertainty in the way you want, you have to admit that uncertainty exists within the various pieces of the model. Treating uncertainties—randomness, variance, or error—as certainties can lead you to overly confident results or even false conclusions. Both of these are uncertainties themselves, but the bad kind—the kind you can't explain in a rigorous and useful manner. For that reason, I tend to treat every quantity as a random variable at first, only replacing it with a certain, fixed value after I've managed to convince myself rigorously that it's appropriate to do so.

7.4.4 *Fitting a model*

So far, I've discussed models in a mostly abstract sense, without saying much about the relationship between the model and the data. This was intentional, because I believe that it's beneficial to think about the system I intend to model and decide how I think the model should work before I try to apply it to data. *Fitting* a model to a data set is the process of taking the model that you've designed and finding the parameter values that describe the data the best. The phrase "fit a model" is synonymous with estimating values for a model's parameters.

Model fitting is optimization, among all possible combinations of parameter values, of a goodness-of-fit function. *Goodness of fit* can be defined in many ways. If your model is intended to be predictive, then its predictions should be close to the eventual outcome, so you could define a closeness-of-prediction function. If the model is supposed to represent a population, as in the model of human height discussed earlier in this chapter, then you might want random samples from the model to look similar to the population you're modeling. There can be many ways to imagine your model being close to representing the data you have.

Because there are many possible ways to define goodness of fit, deciding which one is best for your purposes can be confusing. But a few common functions are suitable for a large number of applications. One of the most common is called the *likelihood*, and in fact this type of function is so common and well studied that I recommend using it as your goodness-of-fit function unless you have a compelling reason not to do so. One such compelling reason is that likelihood functions are applicable only to models that are specified by probability distributions, so if you have a model that isn't based on probability, you can't use the likelihood. In that case, it would be best to check some statistical literature on model fitting for some more appropriate goodness-of-fit function for your model.

THE LIKELIHOOD FUNCTION

The word *likelihood* is used commonly in the English language, but it has a special meaning in statistics. It's much like probability but in reverse, in a way.

When you have a model with known parameter values, you can choose a possible outcome arbitrarily and calculate the probability (or probability density) of that outcome. That's evaluating the probability density function. If you have data and a model but you don't know the parameter values for the model, you can sort of do the same thing in reverse: use the same probability function and calculate the joint probability (or probability density) for all points in the data set but do so over a range of model parameter values. The input to a likelihood function is a set of parameter values, and the output is a single number, the likelihood, which could also be called (somewhat improperly) the *joint probability* of the data. As you move the input parameter values around, you get different values for the likelihood of the data.

Probability is a function of outcomes that's based on known parameters, and likelihood is a function of parameter values that's based on known outcomes in a data set.

MAXIMUM LIKELIHOOD ESTIMATION

The *maximum likelihood* solution for a model with respect to a data set is exactly what it sounds like: the model parameter set that produces the highest value from the likelihood function, given the data. The task of *maximum likelihood estimation* (MLE) is to find that optimal parameter set.

For linear models with normally distributed error terms, MLE has a quick and easy mathematical solution. But that's not the case for all models. Optimization is notoriously hard for large and complex parameter spaces. MLE and other methods that depend on optimization are searching for the highest point along a complex, multidimensional surface. I always picture it as a mountain-climbing expedition to find the highest peak in a large area that no one has ever explored. If no one has been to the area, and no aerial photos are available, then it's difficult to find the highest peak. From the ground, you probably can see the closest peaks but not much farther, and if you head to the one that looks the tallest, you'll usually see one that looks taller from where you are. Even worse, optimization is usually more akin to no-visibility mountain climbing. Along the mathematical surface that you're trying to optimize, there's usually no way to see beyond the immediate surroundings. Usually you know how high you are and maybe which direction the ground is sloping, but you can't see far enough to find a higher point.

Numerous optimization algorithms can help the situation. The simplest strategy is always to walk uphill; that's called a greedy algorithm and it doesn't work well unless you can guarantee that there's only one peak in the area. Other strategies incorporate some randomness and use some intelligent strategies that tentatively head in one direction before retracing their steps if it doesn't turn out as well as they hoped.

In any case, MLE tries to find the highest peak in the space of all possible parameter values. It's great if you know that the highest peak is what you want. But in some cases it might be better to find the highest plateau that has several very high peaks, or you might want to get a general idea of what the whole area looks like before you make a decision. You can use other model-fitting methods to accomplish that.

MAXIMUM A POSTERIORI ESTIMATION

Maximum likelihood estimation searches for the highest peak along the surface of all possible model parameter values. This might not be ideal for the purposes of your project. Sometimes you might be more interested in finding the highest collection of peaks than in finding the absolute highest one.

Take, for example, the Enron email data discussed at length in prior chapters and the project involving modeling behavior of the Enron employees based on social network analysis. Because social network analysis is based on a range of human behaviors that are, at best, fuzzy descriptions of tendencies of people to interact in certain ways with other people, I tend not to rely too much on any single behavior when making conclusions that are meaningful to the project. I would rather draw conclusions based on collections of behaviors, any of which could explain whatever phenomenon I'm looking at. Because of this, I'm also skeptical of quirky behavioral explanations that seem to be the best explanation of what has happened in the social network, when in fact if any aspect of the explanation wasn't true, even a little bit, then the whole explanation and conclusion would fall apart. Finding a collection of pretty-good explanations would be better than finding one seemingly very good but potentially vulnerable explanation.

If you're looking to find a collection of high peaks and not only the highest overall, then *maximum a posteriori* (MAP) methods can help. MAP methods are related to MLE methods, but by utilizing some values from Bayesian statistics (discussed later in this chapter), specifically the concept of prior distributions on variables of interest, MAP methods can help find a location in the model parameter space that's surrounded by points that fit the data well, though not quite as well as the single highest peak. The choice depends on your goals and assumptions.

EXPECTATION MAXIMIZATION AND VARIATIONAL BAYES

Whereas both MLE and MAP methods result in point estimates of parameter values, both *expectation maximization* (EM) and *variational Bayes* (VB) methods find optimal distributions of those parameter values. I lean pretty heavily toward Bayesian statistics rather than frequentist statistics (discussed later in this chapter, in case you're not familiar), and so methods like EM and VB appeal to me. Similar to how I like to treat every quantity as a random variable until I convince myself otherwise, I like to carry variance and uncertainty through all steps of modeling, including the estimated parameters and final results, if possible.

Both EM and VB are distribution centric in that they try to find the best probability distribution for each random variable in the model, with respect to describing the data. If MLE finds the highest peak, and MAP finds a point surrounded by many high areas, then EM and VB each find an area around which you can explore in every direction and always be in an area of fairly high altitude. In addition to that, EM and VB can tell you how far you can wander before you're in a much lower area. In a sense, they're the random variable versions of MAP—but they don't come for free. They can be computationally intensive and difficult to formulate mathematically.

The specific difference between EM and VB lies mainly in the algorithm used to optimize the latent variable distributions in the model. When optimizing the distribution of one variable, EM makes more simplifications to the assumptions about the other variables in the model, so EM can sometimes be less complicated than VB in terms of both the mathematics involved and the computational needs. VB considers the full estimated distributions of all random variables at all times, taking no shortcuts in that realm, but it does make some of the other assumptions that EM also does, such as independence of most variables from each other.

Like MLE and MAP, EM and VB are focused on finding areas within the parameter space that have high likelihood. The main differences are in their sensitivity to changes. Whereas MLE might walk off a cliff, MAP probably won't, but it can't make many guarantees beyond a single location. EM understands the surrounding area, and in addition to that, VB pays a little more attention to how walking in one direction affects the landscape in other directions. That's the hierarchy of some common parameter optimization methods in a nutshell.

MARKOV CHAIN MONTE CARLO

Whereas MLE, MAP, EM, and VB are all optimizations methods that focus on finding a point or an area in the parameter space that explains the data well, *Markov chain Monte Carlo* (MCMC) methods are designed to explore and document the entire space of possible parameter values in a clever way, so that you have a topographical map of the whole space and can draw conclusions or explore further based on that map.

Without getting into too much detail—you can find a considerable amount of literature on its behaviors and properties—a single MCMC sampler begins at a certain point in the parameter space. It then chooses at random a direction and a distance in which to step. Typically, the step should be small enough that the sampler doesn't step over important contours, such as an entire peak, and the step should be large enough that the sampler could theoretically traverse (usually within a few million steps, at the most) the whole region of the parameter space containing reasonable parameter values. MCMC samplers are clever in that they tend to step into areas of higher likelihood, but they don't always do so. After selecting a tentative place to step, they make a random decision based on the likelihood at the current location and the likelihood at the new, tentative location. Because they're clever, if a particular region of the parameter space has about twice the likelihood of another region, the MCMC sampler will tend to be located in that region about twice as often as in the other region, as it continues to traverse the space. A well-tuned MCMC sampler therefore finds itself in each region of the parameter space approximately as often as the likelihood function would predict. This means that the set of step locations (samples) is a good empirical representation of the optimal probability distributions of the model parameters.

To make sure that the set of samples does represent the distributions well, it's usually best to start several MCMC samplers—ideally many of them—in different locations around the parameter space and then watch to see if they all, after some number of steps, tend to give the same picture of the landscape based on their step locations. If all the samplers tend to be mingling around the same areas repeatedly and in the same proportions, then the MCMC samplers are said to have *converged*. Some heuristic convergence diagnostics have been developed specifically for judging whether convergence has occurred in a meaningful sense.

On the one hand, MCMC usually requires less software development than the other methods, because all you need is the goodness-of-fit function and a statistical software package that has MCMC implemented (of which there are many). The other model-fitting algorithms I've mentioned often require manipulations of the goodness-of-fit function and various other model-specific optimization functions in order to find their solution, but not MCMC. MCMC can be off and running as long as you have a model specified mathematically and a data set to operate on.

On the downside, MCMC generally needs considerably more computational power than the others, because it explores the model parameter space randomly—albeit cleverly—and evaluates the altitude at every point at which it lands. It tends to stick around higher peaks but doesn't stay there exclusively and commonly roves far enough to find another good peak. Another drawback of MCMC is that whether it is exploring the space cleverly or not is usually determined by a set of tuning parameters for the algorithm itself. If the tuning parameters aren't set correctly, you can get poor results, so MCMC needs some babysitting. On a brighter note, some good evaluation heuristics have been implemented in common software packages that can quickly give you a good idea about whether your tuning parameters are set adequately.

In general, MCMC is a great technique for fitting models that don't have another obviously better choice for fitting them. On the one hand, MCMC should be able to fit almost any model, at the cost of increased computation time as well as the babysitting and checking of evaluative heuristics. To be fair, other model-fitting methods also require some babysitting and evaluative heuristics but probably not quite as much as MCMC.

OVER-FITTING

Over-fitting is not a method of fitting a model, but it's related; it's something bad that can happen inadvertently while fitting a model. *Over-fitting* is the term most commonly used to refer to the idea that a model might seem to fit the data well, but if you get some new data that should be consistent with the old data, the model doesn't fit that data well at all.

This is a common occurrence in modeling the stock market, for example. It seems that right when someone finds a pattern in stock prices, that pattern ceases. The stock market is a complex environment that produces a ton of data, so if you take a thousand or a million specific price patterns and check to see whether they fit the data, at least one of them will seem to fit. This is especially true if you tune the parameters of the pattern (for example, "This stock price usually goes up for four days and then down for two days") to best explain past data. This is over-fitting. The pattern and the model might fit the data that you have, but they probably won't fit the data that comes in next.

Certainly, the model should fit the data well, but that's not the most important thing. The most important thing is that the model serves the purposes and goals of the project. To that end, I like to have a general idea of how a model should look and which aspects of it are indispensable to my project before I begin applying it to data.

Using previous exploratory data assessment to inform model design is a good idea, but letting the data design your model for you is probably not.

Over-fitting can happen for a few reasons. If you have too many parameters in your model, then the model's parameter values, after they've already explained the real phenomena in your data, will begin to explain fake phenomena that don't exist, such as peculiarities in your data set. Over-fitting can also happen when your data has some serious peculiarities that aren't present in most of the data you could expect to receive in the future. If you're modeling written language, then having a corpus full of Enron emails or children's books will result in models that fit your data set well but don't fit the entire body of the written English language well.

Two techniques that are valuable in checking for over-fitting of your model are train-test separation and cross-validation. In *train-test separation,* you train (fit) your model based on some of your data, the training data, and then you test your model on the rest of the data, the test data. If you're over-fitting your model to the training data, it should be pretty obvious when you make predictions about your test data that you're way off.

Likewise, *cross-validation* refers to the process of doing repeated train-test-separated evaluations based on different (often random) partitions of the data. If the predictions made based on training data match the outcomes on the test data in several replicates of cross-validation, you can be reasonably sure that your model will generalize to similar data. On the other hand, there can be many reasons why new data will be different from old data, and if you've cross-validated only on old data, you have no guarantee that new data will also fit the model. That's the curse of the stock market, among other systems, and it can be circumvented only by careful application and testing of models and understanding of data.

7.4.5 Bayesian vs. frequentist statistics

Although both have existed since at least the eighteenth century, frequentist statistics were far more popular than Bayesian statistics for most of the twentieth century. Over the last few decades, there has been a debate—I'll stop short of saying *feud*—over the merits of one versus the other. I don't want to fan the flames of the debate, but the two schools of statistics are mentioned in conversation and in literature often enough that it's helpful to have a decent idea of what they're about.

The primary difference between the two is a theoretically interpretive one that does have an impact on how some statistical models work. In *frequentist* statistics, the concept of confidence in a result is a measure of how often you'd expect to get the same result if you repeated the experiment and analysis many times. A 95% confidence indicates that in 95% of the replicates of the experiment, you'd draw the same conclusion. The term *frequentist* stems from the notion that statistical conclusions are made based on the expected frequency, out of many repetitions, of a particular event happening.

Bayesian statistics holds more closely to the concept of probability. Results from Bayesian statistical inference, instead of having a frequentist confidence, are usually described using probability distributions. In addition, Bayesian probabilities can be described intuitively as a degree of belief that a random event is going to happen. This is in contrast with frequentist probability, which describes probability as a relative frequency of certain random events happening in an infinite series of such events.

To be honest, for many statistical tasks it doesn't make a difference whether you use a frequentist or Bayesian approach. Common linear regression is one of them. Both approaches give the same result if you apply them in the most common way. But there are some differences between the two approaches that result in some practical differences, and I'll discuss those here.

Disclaimer: I'm primarily a Bayesian, but I'm not so one-sided as to say that frequentist approaches are bad or inferior. Mainly I feel that the most important factor in deciding on an approach is understanding what assumptions each of them carries implicitly. As long as you understand the assumptions and feel they're suitable, either approach can be useful.

PRIOR DISTRIBUTIONS

Bayesian statistics and inference require that you hold a prior belief about the values of the model parameters. This prior belief should technically be formulated before you begin analyzing your main data set. But basing your prior belief on your data is part of a technique called *empirical Bayes*, which can be useful but is frowned on in some circles.

A prior belief can be as simple as "I think this parameter is pretty close to zero, give or take one or two," which can be translated formally into a normal distribution or another appropriate distribution. In most cases, it's possible to create non-informative (or *flat*) priors, which are designed to tell your statistical model "I don't know," in a rigorous sense. In any case, a prior belief must be codified into a probability distribution that becomes part of the statistical model. In the microarray protocol comparison example from earlier in this chapter, the hyper-parameters that I described are the parameters of the prior distributions for some of the model parameters.

Some frequentist statisticians take exception to the necessity of formulating such a prior distribution. Apparently they think that you shouldn't have to formulate a prior belief if you know absolutely nothing about the model's parameter values prior to seeing the data. I'm tempted to agree with them, but the existence in most cases of non-informative prior distributions allows Bayesians to sidestep the requirement for a prior distribution by making it irrelevant. In addition, the frequentist statistics concept of having no prior belief, if you attempted to formalize it, would look a lot like a non-informative prior in Bayesian statistics. You might conclude that frequentist methods often have an implied prior distribution that isn't denoted explicitly. With this, I don't mean to say that frequentists are wrong and that Bayesian methods are better; instead, I intend to illustrate how the two approaches can be quite similar and to debunk the notion that the requirement of having a prior belief is somehow a disadvantage.

UPDATING WITH NEW DATA

I've explained how the existence of a prior distribution in Bayesian statistics isn't a disadvantage, because most of the time you can use a non-informative prior. Now I'll explain how priors are not only not bad but also good.

One of most commonly cited differences between frequentist and Bayesian statistics, along with "You have to have a prior," is "You can update your models with new data without having to include the old data as well." The way to accomplish this is quite simple in a Bayesian framework.

Let's assume that a while back you had a statistical model, and you received your first batch of data. You did a Bayesian statistical analysis and fit your model using non-informative priors. The result of fitting a Bayesian model is a set of parameter distributions called *posterior distributions* because they're formed after the data has been incorporated into the model. Prior distributions represent what you believe before you let the model see the data, and posterior distributions are the new beliefs based on your prior beliefs, plus the data that the model saw.

Now you're getting more data. Instead of digging up the old data and refitting the model to all the data at once, using the old non-informative priors you can take the posterior distributions based on the first set of data and use those as your prior distributions for fitting the model to the second set of data. If the size of your data sets or computational power is a concern, then this technique of Bayesian updating can save considerable time and effort.

Today, with so many real-time analytics services under development, Bayesian updating provides a way to analyze large quantities of data on the fly, without having to go back and reexamine all the past data every time you want a new set of results.

PROPAGATING UNCERTAINTY

Of all the differences between frequentist and Bayesian statistics, I like this one the most, though I haven't heard it mentioned that often. In short, because Bayesian statistics holds close the notion of probability—it begins with a prior probability distribution and ends with a posterior probability distribution—it allows uncertainty to propagate through quantities in the model, from old data sets into new ones and from data sets all the way into conclusions.

I've mentioned several times in this book that I'm a big fan of admitting when uncertainty exists and keeping track of it. By promoting probability distributions to first-class citizens, as Bayesian statistics does, each piece of the model can carry its own uncertainty with it, and if you continue to use it properly, you won't find yourself being overconfident in the results and therefore drawing false conclusions.

My favorite of the few academic papers that I published in the field of bioinformatics emphasizes this exact concept. The main finding of that paper, called "Improved Inference of Gene Regulatory Networks through Integrated Bayesian Clustering and Dynamic Modeling of Time-Course Expression Data" (PloS ONE, 2013)—the title rolls off the tongue, doesn't it?—showed how high technical variances in gene expression measurements can be propagated from the data, through the Bayesian model, and into the results, giving a more accurate characterization of which genes interact with which others. Most prior work on the same topic completely ignored the technical variances and assumed that each gene's expression level was merely the average of the values from the technical replicates. Frankly, I found this absurd, and so I set out to rectify it. I may not quite have succeeded in that goal, as implied by the paper having so few citations, but I think it's a perfect, real-life example of how admitting and propagating uncertainty in statistical analysis leads to better results. Also, I named the algorithm I presented in the paper *BAyesian Clustering Over Networks*, also known as BACON, so I have that going for me.

7.4.6 *Drawing conclusions from models*

With all this talk about designing models, building models, and fitting models, I feel I've almost lost track of the real purpose of statistical modeling: to learn about the system you're studying.

A good statistical model contains all of the system's variables and quantities that you're interested in. If you're interested in the worldwide average female height, that should be a variable in your model. If you're interested in the gene-expression differences between male and female fruit flies, that should be in your model. If it's important to you and your project to know about the responsiveness of Enron employees to incoming emails, you should have a variable that represents responsiveness in your model. Then the process of fitting the model, using whichever methods you choose, results in estimates for those variables. In the case of latent model parameters, fitting the model produces parameter estimates directly. In the case of predictive modeling, in which a prediction is a latent variable in the future (from the future?), the fitted model can generate an estimated value, or prediction.

Drawing conclusions based on your fitted model comes in many forms. First, you have to figure out what questions you want to ask of it. Consult the list of questions you generated during the planning phase of your project, discussed in the early chapters of this book. Which ones can the model help answer? A well-designed model, for the purposes of your project, should be able to answer many if not all of the project's questions regarding the system in question. If it can't, you may have to create a new model that can. It would be a shame to have to rebuild a model, but it's better than using a bad or unhelpful model. You can avoid this type of situation by maintaining awareness of the project's goals at all times, specifically the aspects of the project that this statistical model was intended to address.

Let's say that many of the questions from the project's planning phase involve variables and quantities that are represented in your model. For each of these variables, the model-fitting process has produced value estimates or probability distributions. You can ask two main types of questions of these estimates:

- What is the value of the variable, approximately?
- Is this variable greater/less than X?

I'll cover the techniques to address each of these questions in their own subsections.

WHAT'S THE VALUE? ESTIMATES, STANDARD ERROR, AND CONFIDENCE INTERVALS

All the model-fitting methods I described earlier produce best guesses—called *point estimates*—of variables and parameters in a model. Most but not all of them also give some measure of uncertainty of that value. Depending on which specific algorithm you're using, MLE may not produce such a measure of uncertainty automatically, so if you need it, you may have to find an algorithm that produces one. All the other model-fitting methods give the uncertainty as an inherent output of the model-fitting process.

If all you need is a point estimate, then you're good to go. But if, as is usually the case, you want some sort of guarantee that the value is approximately what you think it is, then you'll need either a probability distribution or a standard error. A *standard error* for a parameter estimate is the frequentist equivalent of a standard deviation (square root of variance) of a probability distribution. In short, you can be 95% confident that a parameter is within two standard errors of its point estimate or 99.7% confident that it's within three standard errors. These are *confidence intervals*, and if the standard error is relatively small, then the confidence intervals will be narrow, and you can be reasonably (whichever percentage you choose) sure that the true value falls within the interval.

The Bayesian equivalents of standard error and confidence intervals are *variance* and *credible intervals*, respectively. They work almost exactly the same but, as usual, differ on philosophical grounds. Given that a Bayesian parameter estimate is a probability distribution, you can naturally extract the variance and create credible intervals such that for a normal distribution, the probability is 95% that the true value is within two standard deviations of the mean, and 99.7% that it's within three standard deviations.

Sometimes reporting a value or an interval addresses one of the goals of your project. But other times you might want to know a little more—for example, whether the variable possesses a specific property, such as being greater or less than a certain amount. For this you need hypothesis testing.

IS THIS VARIABLE _____? HYPOTHESIS TESTING

Often you need to know more about a variable than merely a point estimate or a range of values that probably contain the true value. Sometimes it's important to know whether a variable possesses a certain property or not, such as these:

- Is the variable X greater than 10?
- Is the variable X less than 5?
- Is the variable X non-zero?
- Is the variable X substantially different from another variable Y?

Each of these questions can be answered by a hypothesis test. A *hypothesis test* consists of a null hypothesis, an alternative hypothesis, and then a statistical test that fits the two hypotheses.

A *null* hypothesis is kind of the status quo. If this hypothesis was true, it would be kind of boring. An alternative hypothesis is a hypothesis that, if true, would be exciting.

For instance, let's say you think that the variable X is greater than 10, and if this was true, it would have cool implications for the project (maybe X is the number of song downloads, in millions, that are expected to happen next week). "X is greater than 10" is a good alternative hypothesis. The null hypothesis would be the inverse: "X is not greater than 10." Now, because you want the alternative hypothesis to be true, you need to show beyond a reasonable doubt that the null hypothesis is not true. In statistics, you generally never prove that something is true so much as show that the other possibility, the null hypothesis, is almost certainly not true. It's a subtle distinction, linguistically, that has a fairly large impact mathematically.

To test the null and alternative hypotheses in the example and to reject the null, as they say, you need to show that the value of X almost certainly wouldn't venture below 10. Let's say that the posterior probability distribution for X based on your model is normally distributed with a mean of 16 and a standard deviation of 1.5. It's important to note that this is a one-sided hypothesis test, because you care only if X is too low (below 10) and not if it's too high. Choosing the correct version of the test (one-sided or two-sided) can make a difference in the significance of your results.

You need to check whether 10 is beyond a reasonable threshold of how low X might be. Let's choose a significance of 99% because you want to be sure that X isn't below 10. Consulting a reference for a one-sided test, the 99% threshold is 2.33 standard deviations. You'll notice that the estimate of 16 is 4.0 standard deviations above 10, meaning that you can be almost certain, and definitely more than 99% certain, that the value of X is above 10.

I could hardly talk about hypothesis testing without at least mentioning p-values. You can find much more thorough explanations elsewhere, but a *p-value* is the inverse of confidence (1 minus confidence, or 99% confidence, corresponds to $p<0.01$) and represents the frequentist concept of the chance that a hypothesis test ended up giving you an incorrect answer. It's important not to treat a p-value in frequentist statistics like a probability in Bayesian statistics. P-values should be used for thresholding of hypothesis test results and nothing else.

Another concept and potential pitfall happens when you run many hypothesis tests on the same data or the same model. Running a few might be OK, but if you run hundreds or more hypothesis tests, then you're bound to find at least one test that passes. For example, if you do 100 hypothesis tests, all at the 99% significance level, you'd still expect at least one test to pass (a null hypothesis getting rejected) even if none of them should. If you must perform many hypothesis tests, it's best to do *multiple testing correction,* in which the significance of the results is adjusted to compensate for the fact that some true null hypotheses will be rejected by random chance otherwise. There are a few different methods for multiple testing correction, and the differences between them are too nuanced to discuss in detail here, so I'll skip them. Yet again, consult a good statistical reference if you're interested!

7.5　*Miscellaneous statistical methods*

Statistical modeling is an explicit attempt to describe a system using mathematical and statistical concepts, with the aim of understanding how a system works inside and out. It's a holistic process, and I feel that understanding a system holistically—along with the project's data-to-goals process—is important, regardless of whether you end up implementing a statistical model in the strict sense. Many other statistical techniques fall at least partially outside my definition of a statistical model, and these can help inform your understanding of the system and possibly even be used in place of a formal model.

I've discussed descriptive statistics, inference, and other techniques that might be called *atomic statistics*—by that, I mean they form some of the core concepts and building blocks of statistics. If you move up the ladder of complexity, you can find statistical methods and algorithms that can't be said to be atomic—they have too many moving pieces—but they're so popular and often so useful that they should be mentioned in any overview of statistical analysis techniques. In the following subsections I'll give brief descriptions of a few such higher-complexity techniques, when they might be used effectively, and what to watch out for when using them.

7.5.1　*Clustering*

Sometimes you have a bunch of data points, and you know some patterns are in there, but you're not sure where they are exactly, so you can group the data points into clusters of generally similar data points in order to get the broad strokes of what's going on in the data. In that way, *clustering*, if it didn't usually have so many moving pieces that are somewhat hard to dissect and diagnose, could make a good technique for descriptive statistics.

Clustering can also be an integral part of a statistical model. I used clustering as a major aspect of the model of gene interactions—which I named BACON—mentioned earlier. The *C* in BACON stands for *clustering*. The full name is BAyesian Clustering Over Networks. In that model, I assumed that the expressions of some genes moved together in unison because they were involved in some of the same high-level processes. Much scientific literature supports this concept. I didn't specify beforehand which genes' expression moved together (literature is not often conclusive on this), but instead I incorporated a clustering algorithm into my model that allowed genes with similar expression movement to come together on their own, as the model was fit. Given that there were thousands of genes, clustering served to reduce the number of moving parts (called *dimensionality reduction*), which can be a goal unto itself, but in this particular case, academic literature provided some justification for the practice, and more importantly I found that the clustered model made better predictions than the unclustered model.

HOW IT WORKS

There are many different clustering algorithms—k-means, Gaussian mixture models, hierarchical—but all of them traverse the space of data points (all continuous numeric values) and group data points that are close to each other in some sense into the same cluster.

Both k-means and Gaussian mixture models are *centroid-based* clustering algorithms, meaning that each cluster has something like a center that generally represents the members of the cluster. In each of these algorithms, whichever cluster centroid a data point is closer to, roughly speaking, that cluster can be said to contain the data point. Clusters can be fuzzy or probabilistic, meaning that a data point can partially belong to one cluster and partially to others. Usually you have to define a fixed number of clusters before running the algorithm, but there are alternatives to this.

Hierarchical clustering is a bit different. It focuses on individual data points and their proximity to one another. To put it simplistically, hierarchical clustering looks for the two data points that are closest together and joins them into a cluster. Then it looks for the two data points (including the ones in the new cluster) that are the closest two yet-unjoined points, and it joins those two together. The process continues until all data points are joined together into a single mega-cluster. The result is a tree (most statistical software packages will gladly draw one of these for you) organized with close data points close to each other along the structure of the tree's branches. This is helpful for seeing which data points are close to which other data points. If you want multiple clusters instead of one big (tree) cluster, you can cut the tree at a depth that gives the number of (branch) clusters that you want—cutting the tree in this sense means separating the trunk and the largest limbs, at a certain height, from the smaller branches, each of which would remain a unified cluster.

WHEN TO USE IT

If you want to put your data points (or other variables) into groups for any reason, consider clustering. If you want to be able to describe the properties of each of the groups and what a typical cluster member looks like, try a centroid-based algorithm like k-means or a Gaussian mixture model. If you'd like to get an idea of which of your data points is closest to which other ones, and you don't care that much how close that is—if closer is more important than close in an absolute sense—then hierarchical clustering might be a good choice.

WHAT TO WATCH OUT FOR

With clustering algorithms, there are usually many parameters to tweak. You usually have no guarantees that all designated members of each cluster are represented well by each cluster or that significant clusters even exist. If dimensions (aspects, fields) of your data points are highly correlated, that can be problematic. To help with all this, most software tools have many diagnostic tools for checking how well the clustering algorithm performed. Use them, and clustering in general, with great care.

7.5.2   *Component analysis*

It can be difficult to make sense of data that has many dimensions. Clustering puts data points together into similarity groups in order to reduce the number of entities under scrutiny or analysis. Methods of *component analysis*—of which *principal component analysis* (PCA) and *independent component analysis* (ICA) are the most popular—do something similar, but they group together the dimensions of the data instead of data points, and they rank the groupings in order of how much of the data's variance they explain. In a sense, component analysis reduces the dimensionality of the data directly, and by ranking and evaluating the new dimensions that are built out of the old ones, you may be able to explain each data point in terms of only a few of those dimensions.

For example, let's say you're analyzing gasoline usage during car trips. In each data point, the fields include distance traveled, duration of the trip, type of car, age of the car, and a few others, and also the amount of gasoline used during the trip. If you were trying to explain gasoline usage using all of the other variables, there's a good chance that both the distance traveled and the trip duration could help explain how much gasoline was used. Neither is a perfect predictor, but they both can contribute largely, and in fact they're highly correlated. You'd have to be careful building a model that predicts gasoline usage with both of these variables in the face of high correlation; many models would confuse such highly correlated variables with one another. Component analysis manipulates dimensions—mixing them, combining them, and ranking them—to minimize correlations, loosely speaking. A model that was predicting gasoline usage based on dimensions generated by component analysis usually wouldn't confuse any of the dimensions.

The notion that distance traveled and trip duration are highly correlated is probably obvious, but imagine that you're working with a less-familiar system that you're studying, and you have dozens, hundreds, or even thousands of data dimensions. You know that some of the dimensions are probably correlated, but you don't know exactly which ones, and you also know that it would be generally beneficial to reduce the total number of dimensions in a clever way. That's what component analysis is good at.

HOW IT WORKS

Component analysis generally examines the data set as a sort of data cloud in many dimensions and then finds the component or angle along which the length of the data cloud is the longest. By *component* or *angle*, I mean a combination of dimensions, so that the dimension chosen might be diagonal, in some sense, when compared to the original dimensions. After the first component is chosen, that dimension is collapsed or disregarded in a clever way, and a second component is then selected, with the goal of finding the longest or widest component that has nothing in common with the first component. The process continues, finding as many components, in order of importance, as you'd like.

WHEN TO USE IT

If you have numerous dimensions in your data and you want fewer, component analysis is probably the best way to reduce the number of dimensions, and in addition to that, the resulting dimensions usually have some nice properties. But if you need the dimensions to be interpretable, you'll have to be careful.

WHAT TO WATCH OUT FOR

PCA, the most popular type of component analysis, is sensitive to the relative scale of the values along various dimensions of the data set. If you rescale a particular field in the data—say, you switch from kilometers to miles—then that will have a significant effect on the components that are generated by PCA. It's not only that rescaling can be a problem, but that the original (or any) scales of the variables can be problematic as well. Each of the dimensions should be scaled such that the same size change in any of them would be, in some sense, equally notable. It's probably best to consult a good reference before trying any stunts with component analysis.

7.5.3   *Machine learning and black box methods*

In the world of analytic software development, machine learning is all the rage these days. Not that it hasn't been popular for a long time now, but in the last few years I've seen the first few products come to market that claim to "bring machine learning to the masses," or something like that. It sounds great on some level, but on another level it sounds like they're asking for trouble. I don't think most people know how machine learning works or how to notice if it has gone wrong. If you're new to machine learning, I'd like to emphasize that machine learning, in most of its forms, is a tricky tool that shouldn't be considered a magic solution to anything. There's a reason why it takes years or decades of academic research to develop a completely new machine learning technique, and it's the same reason why most people wouldn't yet understand how to operate it: machine learning is extremely complex.

The term *machine learning* is used in many contexts and has a somewhat fluid meaning. Some people use it to refer to any statistical methods that can draw conclusions from data, but that's not the meaning I use. I use the term *machine learning* to refer to the classes of somewhat abstract algorithms that can make conclusions from data but whose models—if you want to call them that—are difficult to dissect and understand. In that sense, only the machine can understand its own model, in a way. Sure, with most machine learning methods, you can dig into the innards of the machine's generated model and learn about which variables are most important and how they relate to each other, but in that way the machine's model begins to feel like a data set unto itself—without reasonably sophisticated statistical analysis, it's tough to get a handle on how the machine's model even works. That's why many machine learning tools are called black box methods.

There's nothing wrong with having a black box that takes in data and produces correct answers. But it can be challenging to produce such a box and confirm that its answers continue to be correct, and it's nearly impossible to look inside the box after you've finished and debug. Machine learning is great, but probably more than any other class of statistical methods, it requires great care to use successfully.

I'll stop short of giving lengthy explanations of machine learning concepts, because countless good references are available both on the internet and in print. I will, however, give some brief explanations of some of the key concepts to put them in context.

Feature extraction is a process by which you convert your data points into more informative versions of themselves. To get the best results, it's crucial to extract good features every time you do machine learning—except, maybe, when doing deep learning. Each feature of a data point should be showing its best side(s) to a machine learning algorithm if it hopes to be classified or predicted correctly in the future. For example, in credit card fraud detection, one possible feature to add to a credit card transaction is the amount by which the transaction is above the normal transaction amount for the card; alternatively, the feature could be the percentile of the transaction size compared to all recent transactions. Likewise, good features are those that common sense would tell you might be informative in differentiating good from bad or any two classes from one another. There are also many valuable features that don't make common sense, but you always have to be careful in determining whether these are truly valuable or if they're artifacts of the training data set.

Here are a few of the most popular machine learning algorithms that you would apply to the feature values you extracted from your data points:

- *Random forest*—This is a funny name for a useful method. A decision tree is a series of yes/no questions that ends in a decision. A random forest is a collection of randomly generated decision trees that favors trees and branches that correctly classify data points. This is my go-to machine learning method when I know I want machine learning but I don't have a good reason to choose a different one. It's versatile and not too difficult to diagnose problems.

- *Support vector machine (SVM)*—This was quite popular a few years ago, and now it has settled into the niches where it's particularly useful as the next machine learning fads pass through. SVMs are designed to classify data points into one of two classes. They manipulate the data space, turning it and warping it in order to drive a wedge between two sets of data points that are known to belong to the two different classifications. SVMs focus on the boundary between the two classes, so if you have two classes of data points, with each class tending to stick together in the data space, and you're looking for a method to divide the two classes with maximal separation (if possible), then an SVM is for you.

- *Boosting*—This is a tricky one to explain, and my limited experience doesn't provide all the insights I probably need. But I know that boosting was a big step forward in machine learning of certain types. If you have a bunch of so-so machine learning models (*weak learners*), boosting might be able to combine them intelligently to result in a good machine learning model (a *strong learner*). Because boosting combines the outputs of other machine learning methods, it's often called a *meta-algorithm*. It's not for the faint of heart.

- *Neural network*—The heyday for the neural network seemed to be the last decades of the twentieth century, until the advent of deep learning. In their earlier popular incarnation, *artificial neural networks* (the more formal name) were perhaps the blackest of black boxes. They seemed to be designed not to be understood. But they worked well, in some cases at least. Neural networks consist of layers upon layers of one-way valves (or neurons), each of which transforms the inputs in some arbitrary way. The neurons are connected to each other in a large network that leads from the input data to the output prediction or classification, and all of the computational work for fitting the model involved weighting and reweighting each of the neurons in clever ways to optimize results.

- *Deep learning*—This is a new development in this millennium. Loosely speaking, deep learning refers to the idea that you might not need to worry much about feature extraction because, with enough computational power, the algorithm might be able to find its own good features and then use them to learn. More specifically, deep learning techniques are layered machine learning methods that, on a low level, do the same types of learning that other methods do, but then, on a higher level, they generate abstractions that can be applied generally to recognize important patterns in many forms. Today, the most popular deep learning methods are based on neural networks, causing a sort of revival in the latter.

- *Artificial intelligence*—I'm including this term because it's often conflated with machine learning and rightly so. There's no fundamental difference between machine learning and artificial intelligence, but with artificial intelligence comes the connotation that the machine is approaching the intellectual capabilities of a human. In some cases, computers have already surpassed humans in specific tasks—famously, chess or *Jeopardy!*, for instance—but they're nowhere near the general intelligence of an average human on a wide variety of day-to-day tasks.

HOW IT WORKS

Each specific machine learning algorithm is different. Data goes in, answers come out; you have to do much work to confirm that you didn't make any mistakes, that you didn't over-fit, that the data was properly train-test separated, and that your predictions, classifications, or other conclusions are still valid when brand-new data comes in.

WHEN TO USE IT

Machine learning, in general, can do things that no other statistical methods can do. I prefer to try a statistical model first in order to get an understanding of the system and its relationship to the data, but if the model falls short in terms of results, then I begin to think about ways to apply machine learning techniques without giving up too much of the awareness that I had with the statistical model. I wouldn't say that machine learning is my last resort, but I do usually favor the intuitiveness and insight of a well-formed statistical model until I find it lacking. Head straight for machine learning if you know what you're doing and you have a complex problem that's nowhere near linear, quadratic, or any of the other common variable relationships in statistical models.

WHAT TO WATCH OUT FOR

Don't trust the machine's model or its results until you've verified them—completely independently of the machine learning implementation—with test-train separation as well as some completely new data that you and the machine have never seen before.

Data snooping—the practice of looking at data before you formally analyze it and using what you see to bias how you analyze—can be a problem if you didn't already do test-train separation before you snooped.

Exercises

Continuing with the Filthy Money Forecasting personal finance app scenario first described in chapter 2, and relating to previous chapters' exercises, try these:

1 Describe two different statistical models you might use to make forecasts of personal financial accounts. For each, give at least one potential weakness or disadvantage.

2 Assume you've been successful in creating a classifier that can accurately put transactions into the categories *regular, one time,* and any other reasonable categories you've thought of. Describe a statistical model for forecasting that makes use of these classifications to improve accuracy.

Summary

- It's worthwhile to think about a project and a problem theoretically before you start into a software-building or full-analysis phase. There's much to be learned, in data science and elsewhere, by stopping and thinking about the problem for a while.
- Mathematics is a vocabulary and framework for describing how a system works.
- Statistical modeling is a process of describing a system and connecting it to data.
- A vast range of analytic methods and software that implements them is available; choosing from among them can be daunting, but it shouldn't be overwhelming.
- Machine learning and other complex statistical methods can be good tools for accomplishing the otherwise impossible, but only if you're careful with them.

Software:
statistics in action

8

This chapter covers

- The basics of some statistical software applications
- Introductions to a few useful programming languages
- Choosing the appropriate software to use or build
- How to think about getting statistics into your software

Figure 8.1 shows where we are in the data science process: building statistical software. In the last chapter, I introduced statistics as one of the two core concepts of data science. Knowledge of software development and application is the other. If statistics is the framework for analyzing and drawing conclusions from data, then software is the tool that puts this framework into action. In few cases would a data scientist be able to go without software during a project, but I suppose it's possible when the data set is very small.

Beyond going without, a data scientist must make many software choices for any project. If you have a favorite program, that's often a good choice, if for no other reason than your familiarity with it. But there can be good reasons to pick something

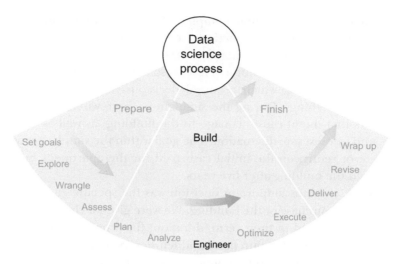

Figure 8.1   An important aspect of the build phase of the data science process: statistical software and engineering

else. Or if you're new to data science or statistical software, it can be hard to find a place to start. Therefore, in this chapter I give a broad overview of different types of software that might be used in data science before providing some guidelines for choosing from among them for a project. As in chapter 7, I intend to provide only a high-level description of relevant concepts plus some examples.

Experienced software developers probably won't like this chapter much, but if you're a statistician or a beginner with software, I think these high-level descriptions are a good way to start. For more information on any specific topic, many in-depth references are available both on the internet and in print.

8.1   Spreadsheets and GUI-based applications

To anyone who has spent significant time using Microsoft Excel or another spreadsheet application, this is often the first choice for performing any sort of data analysis. Particularly if the data is in a tabular form, such as CSV, and there's not too much of it, getting started with analysis in a spreadsheet can be easy. Furthermore, if the calculations you need to do aren't complex, a spreadsheet might even be able to cover all the software needs for the project.

8.1.1   Spreadsheets

For the few who may be uninitiated, a *spreadsheet* is a piece of software that represents data in a row-and-column tabular format. It typically allows analysis of that data via sets of functions—such as average, median, sum—that can operate on the data and answer some questions. Microsoft Excel, OpenOffice and LibreOffice Calc, and Google Sheets are popular examples of spreadsheet applications.

Spreadsheets can be quite complex when they contain multiple sheets, cross-references, table lookups, and functions/formulas. The most sophisticated spreadsheet I ever made was for a college finance class on the topic of real estate. As part of the class, we participated in a simulation of a real estate market in which each student owned an apartment building, which required decisions regarding financing and insurance, among other things. During the simulation, there would be random events such as disasters that might cause damage to the building, as well as operating costs, vacancies, and interest rate fluctuation. The goal within the simulation was to have the highest rate of return on the initial cash paid for the apartment building, assuming we then sold the building after five years.

By far, the most important decision was the specific choice of mortgage used to finance the purchase of the building. We were given a choice of eight mortgage structures that differed in their term/duration, fixed or variable interest rates and their margins, points paid at purchase, and temporary teaser rates. There was a stated purchase price for the apartment building, but as in real life, we had a choice about how much money we'd like to borrow for the purchase. The amount we didn't borrow via the mortgage was the cash outlay on which we'd be calculating the rate of return that measured our success.

With all the variables, random or chosen, included in the simulation, it was obvious that running through some calculations would be of great benefit when making decisions, particularly regarding financing. At the time, I had written programs only on my graphing calculator, and none of those analyzed data. Short of learning another tool for the purpose, using Microsoft Excel was my only choice. I have a mild dislike for Excel, as do many, but it got the job done.

For each of the 8 mortgage structures and 12 different possible amounts to borrow, I calculated cash flows for each of the 5 years of the simulation, and from these cash flows I also calculated an expected rate of return. I made use of several of Excel's formulas, including the standard SUM formula for addition, the PMT formula for calculating a mortgage payment, and the IRR formula for calculating an internal rate of return for cash flows. At that point, I could see the rates of return for all possibilities under the expected conditions. As I mentioned, though, there would be random events during each year of the simulation, and so the expected outcomes almost certainly wouldn't be the ones observed. To account for this, I added to the spreadsheet some values representing simulated disasters, interest rate fluctuations, and vacancies, among others. I then was able to enter some possible random outcomes and see how they affected the rates of return and the optimal choices.

Ultimately, my spreadsheet contained two sheets, one that did the heavy calculation and one that summarized results (shown in figure 8.2), random variables and their fluctuations, and the decisions that needed to be made. The sheet with the heavy calculations contained 96 different statements of cash flow, one for each of the eight mortgage types for 12 different amounts borrowed. Each statement of cash flow used the random variable values from the summary sheet to calculate five years of cash

B	C	D	E	F	G	H	I	J	K	L	M	N
						yr 1	yr 2	yr 3	yr 4	yr 5		
		number of units		18								
		rent per month		$425								
		vacancies/bad debts		=======> of PGI		0.05	0.06	0.07	0.05	0.03		
		operating expenses		=======> of EGI		0.4	0.42	0.43	0.41	0.38		
		land value		$125,000								
		building value		$425,000								
		tax rate		0.35		0.2 (capital gains)						
		net selling proceeds		$591,360								
		index interest rate		=======> =====>		0.06	0.0675	0.0575	0.0325	0.02		
		insurance expense		=======> =====>		-1600	0	0	-3700	-3400		
		extra principal? (0 or 1)		=======> =====>		0	1	1	0	0		

Amount Borrowed

	$275,000	$302,500	$324,500	$346,500	$368,500	$390,500	$412,500	$434,500	$456,500	$478,500	$500,500	$522,500
1	9.07%	9.33%	9.51%	9.71%	9.90%	10.11%	10.33%	10.14%	9.75%	9.03%	5.55%	-2.33%
2	9.08%	9.34%	9.52%	9.71%	9.91%	10.12%	10.34%	10.12%	9.69%	8.88%	4.93%	-4.90%
3	9.24%	9.53%	9.75%	9.98%	10.23%	10.51%	10.81%	10.72%	10.45%	9.90%	6.49%	-1.87%
4	9.24%	9.54%	9.76%	9.99%	10.25%	10.52%	10.83%	10.72%	10.43%	9.80%	5.90%	-4.78%
5	9.23%	9.52%	9.74%	9.97%	10.22%	10.50%	10.81%	10.69%	10.38%	9.71%	5.62%	-5.91%
6	9.23%	9.53%	9.75%	10.00%	10.25%	10.54%	10.85%	10.82%	10.66%	10.30%	7.76%	2.39%
7	9.17%	9.45%	9.66%	9.88%	10.12%	10.37%	10.65%	10.55%	10.29%	9.77%	6.76%	0.02%
8	9.47%	9.82%	10.10%	10.40%	10.73%	11.10%	11.54%	11.63%	11.63%	11.47%	8.70%	1.59%

Amount Borrowed				412500	extra margin			0.015				
				0.0875	0.1	0.09	0.075	0.06				
		buying		year 1	year 2	year 3	year 4	year 5	selling			
Income												
PGI				$91,800.00	$91,800.00	$91,800.00	$91,800.00	$91,800.00				
Vacancies				($4,590.00)	($5,508.00)	($6,426.00)	($4,590.00)	($4,590.00)				
EGI				$87,210.00	$86,292.00	$85,374.00	$87,210.00	$87,210.00				
Operating Exp												

Figure 8.2 First page of the spreadsheet I used to simulate the management of an apartment building in my college finance class

flows from several types of income and expenses based on that particular mortgage's parameters. Each cash flow calculation resulted in a rate of return figure that the summary sheet then referenced. Looking at all 96 rates of return—using Excel's conditional formatting option to highlight the highest among them—and how each of them changed if the random variables turned out differently, I then felt confident in choosing a mortgage that would result in not only one of the highest expected rates of return but that also wouldn't be too risky if a disaster hit.

I don't think my classmates spent as much time analyzing choices as I did. I don't believe any of them created a spreadsheet, either. I ended up winning the contest by more than a full percentage point, which the financially inclined among you will recognize as quite a large margin of victory. If I recall correctly, I earned over 9% on my initial investment, when everyone else earned less than 8%—a figure that would have amounted to several thousand dollars had the money been real. I did win real money also from the contest: $200 cash as the first prize, which, though not the thousands of dollars I earned on the fictional apartment building, was no small sum for me as a college student.

I probably learned more about spreadsheets during that single finance project than in the rest of my whole life. One advantage of spreadsheets, particularly Excel, became obvious: the number of built-in formulas is astronomical. For nearly any static calculation that you might care to apply to your data in a spreadsheet, there is a formula or a combination thereof that can accomplish it for you. Here, I use the word *static* to refer to calculations that happen in one step, without iteration or complex interdependency between values.

One major disadvantage of spreadsheets is that even moderately complex formulas might look something like this:

```
=-((-PMT((F15)/12,$B20*12,F$14,1))*12-(F$14-((1-((1+(F15)/12)^12-
1)/((1+(F15)/12)^($B20*12)-1))*F$14)))
```

Or worse. I took that one directly from my real estate simulation spreadsheet, though it's not immediately clear exactly how—even to me—this formula was once intended to calculate the interest expense for one year of the cash flow statement for one of the mortgages. Needless to say, this formula is difficult to read and understand—and it's nowhere near the worst that I've seen or written—mostly because the entire formula is on a single line, and all the variables are referenced by unhelpful combinations of letters and numbers. Don't get me started on the parentheses. Readability of such calculations can be a serious concern. Frankly, I'm not surprised that Excel formula errors have been implicated in many missteps by big banking organizations, such as the 2013 London Whale case at JP Morgan, in which, apparently, an Excel formula error caused dramatic underestimation of the risk of a particular investment portfolio, ultimately resulting in a $6 billion loss. That's an expensive mistake and a compelling reason to use a statistical tool with readable calculation instructions.

Spreadsheets aren't limited to rows, columns, and formulas. One other feature of note is the solver in Excel, a tool that can help you find the optimal solution for a complex equation or optimize parameters to meet some objective goal. To use it, you must tell the solver which values are allowed to change, and you also have to tell it which value is the objective that is to be maximized or minimized; the solver then uses optimization techniques to find the best solution. I used the solver, for example, during another college project in which I was trying to maximize the number of people a set of elevators could transport to their desired floors on a busy day. The optimal solution that I found involved limiting the floors that each elevator would visit; for example, one elevator would service floors 1–10 and another 10–15. By letting Excel's solver change the floors that each elevator might visit, it found a solution that maximized the total number of people transported.

Another significant feature of most spreadsheet applications is the macro. *Macros*, in applications like Excel, are mini-programs that users can write themselves. In Excel, macros are written in Visual Basic for Applications (VBA) and can generally accomplish anything that can be accomplished in Excel. Instead of pointing and clicking to do something, you could theoretically write a macro that does the same thing. This can be helpful if you typically do that thing many times. Running one macro can be much faster and easier than doing a set of steps manually, depending on the complexity of those steps. I created a macro for my real estate spreadsheet, one that copied changes that I had made to the first cash flow statement and pasted them into all of the 95 other cash flow statements. Notably, I didn't write the macro in VBA, but instead Excel was able to record me performing the manual steps of copying and pasting and then convert that recording into a macro I could use. This is a handy feature of Excel if you do a specific thing often, you want to create a macro for it, and you don't want to write code in VBA.

8.1.2   *Other GUI-based statistical applications*

I consider spreadsheet applications like Excel to be level 1 software for data analysis; even beginners aren't truly afraid to open a spreadsheet and poke around a little bit. Level 10 is writing your own flawless software from scratch; it's not for the faint of heart. The levels in between are populated by any number of software applications that possess varying amounts of ease of use, like spreadsheets, and versatility, like programming. If you're finding your favorite spreadsheet application lacking in sophistication, but you're not ready to jump head first into a programming language, then some in-between solutions might work for you.

I was at a big statistics conference recently and was surprised by the number of vendors offering mid-level statistical applications. I saw booths for SPSS, Stata, SAS (and its JMP product), and Minitab, among others. Each of these applications is popular in some circles, and I'd used three out of those four at some point in my life. I decided to play a bit of a game by visiting a couple of the booths when they weren't busy and asking each company's representatives to explain to me why their software product is better than the others. It was an honest question, more than anything, but I also thought it funny to ask the representatives, mostly statisticians themselves, so directly to disparage the competition. One rep was kind enough to admit straight away that the companies were all producing roughly equivalent products. That is not to say that they are equal, but only that none is vastly or definitely better than the others. Preference for one or the other is a matter of specific use and personal taste.

What unites the various companies' core products is a similar experience in doing statistical analysis. It seemed to me that the graphical user interface (GUI) of each application was based on that of a spreadsheet. If you take a typical spreadsheet application and divide the screen into panels, with one panel showing the data, one displaying some graph or visualization of the data, and one describing the results of a regression or component analysis, that's the basic experience of these mid-level statistical applications. I know I sound dismissive in my description, so please don't infer that I think these applications aren't worthwhile—quite the contrary. In fact, everything I know about them tells me that they're incredibly useful. But software companies, as companies will, sometimes use hyperbole to make you think that their product is head and shoulders above the competitors' and that it will solve your data problems in a jiffy. This is almost never true, though I'll admit we're doing much better in the current decade than in decades past. One thing does remain true: to use a statistical application successfully, you have to understand statistics, at least a little. None of these applications will teach you statistics, so approach them with a cool head and a discerning eye. Often the best choice, if you want to choose one, is the one that your friends use, because they can help you if you run into questions. Following the crowd here can be a good thing.

These mid-level statistical applications do much more than look like a spreadsheet with panels. Their facilities for performing many different statistical analyses are generally far greater than Excel or any other spreadsheet program. It's my impression that these software tools were built specifically to enable point-and-click data analysis with a level of sophistication that spreadsheets can't approach. If you want to use a statistical technique that you can't find in Excel's menus, then you may want to level up to one of the aforementioned applications. Regression, optimization, component analysis, factor analysis, ANOVA (analysis of variance), and any number of other statistical methods are often done far better in a mid-level tool than in a spreadsheet, if it's even possible in the latter.

Beyond point-and-click statistical methods, these mid-level tools offer far greater versatility through their associated programming languages. Each of the proprietary tools I've mentioned has its own language for performing statistical analysis, which can be superior to point and click in both versatility and repeatability. With a programming language, you can do more than with clicking, and you can also save the code for future use, so you know exactly what you've done and can repeat it or modify it as necessary. A file containing a sequence of commands that can be run is generally called a *script* and is a common concept in programming. Not all languages can do this. Scripting languages are particularly useful in data science because data science is a process consisting of *steps*, actions performed on the data and models.

Learning the programming language of one of these mid-level tools can be a good step toward learning a real programming language, if that's a goal of yours. These languages can be quite useful on their own. SAS, in particular, has a wide following in statistical industries, and learning its language is a reasonable goal unto itself.

8.1.3 *Data science for the masses*

Recent years have seen much ado about bringing data science to the *analyst*, the person who can directly use the intelligence gleaned from the data science itself. I'm wholly in favor of enabling everyone to gain insight from data, but I'm still not convinced that folks not trained in statistics should be applying them. Perhaps it's the bias of a statistician's ego, but in the face of uncertainty—as always in data science—recognizing that something in the analysis is going wrong takes training and experience.

With that said, in this age of information, data, and software startups, it seems that someone is constantly claiming they make data science and analysis easy for everyone, even for beginners, and so you probably don't need to hire a data scientist. To me, this is akin to saying that a web compendium of medical information can take the place of all medical professionals. Sure, in many cases, the web compendium or the new data science product can give equal or even superior results to those of the professionals, but only the professionals have the knowledge and experience to check the necessary conditions and recognize when a particular strategy goes wrong. I've emphasized in this book that awareness of possibilities in the face of uncertainty is a key aspect of data science, and I don't think this will ever change. When the stakes matter, experience is incredibly important.

It's tempting to list a few of the new additions to the buffet of statistical applications in order to illustrate what I mean. But I'm not confident that most of them will be around in a few years, and besides that, the names don't matter. In the past decade, data science has become big business and a highly sought-after skill. Whenever a skill makes news and money is spent acquiring it, there are always companies that claim to make it easy, with varying degrees of success. I challenge you, as a data scientist, to challenge newcomers to the software product industry who claim to trivialize our work. I write while trying to transcend my own ego: do they think they can accomplish with software what we can, maybe, accomplish only with careful consideration of the needs and wants of the project at hand, plus software and statistics?

I digress, but I do want to share my (healthy, I think) skepticism for the analytic software industry. If anyone claims to have a magic pill for a seriously challenging task, please be skeptical. There are many good statistical software applications out there; it's extremely unlikely that a new one can gain a huge advantage, but hey, I've been proven wrong before. New products are almost always variations on an old theme or purpose-built tools that are very good at one thing. Both can be useful, but figuring out the true range of applicability of something new can take some effort.

8.2 Programming

When an out-of-the-box software tool can't—or doesn't—cut it, you need to make your own. I mentioned in the previous section that the most popular mid-level statistical applications possess their own programming languages that can be used to extend functionality arbitrarily. With the possible exception of SAS and its tool set, none of these programming languages is usually considered as a language independent of its parent application—the language exists because of and in tandem with the application.

There also exists a converse to this—otherwise standalone programming languages for which a GUI-based statistical application has been built. Both iPython for Python and RStudio for R are popular examples. The market of statistical applications can get a little confusing; I often see internet forum posts asking whether, for example, SPSS or R is better to learn. I can see how, maybe, the RStudio GUI and the SPSS GUI can seem roughly equivalent, but the real functionality of those two tools is vastly different. The choice between the two—or any mid-level statistical tool and a programming language—boils down to your desire to learn and use a programming language. If you don't want to write any code, don't choose any tool based on R or any other programming language.

Programming languages are far more versatile than mid-level statistical applications. Code in any popular language has the potential to do most anything. These languages can execute any number of instructions on any machine, can interact with other software services via APIs, and can be included in scripts and other pieces of software. A language that's tied to its parent application is severely limited in these capacities.

If you're intimidated by code, programming isn't as difficult as it might seem. Other than some short programs on my graphing calculator in high school, I didn't write any code until a summer internship during college, and I didn't begin in earnest until grad school. I sometimes wish I had begun earlier, but the fact remains that it isn't hard to pick up some programming skills if you're diligent.

8.2.1 Getting started with programming

I wrote my first programs on a graphing calculator during high school, but they weren't sophisticated. The only programming course I took in college was called Object-Oriented Programming; I did fine in the course, but for some reason I didn't program much at all until a summer internship at the Department of Defense, where I used MATLAB to analyze some image data. Between then and graduate school, during which I used R and MATLAB in bioinformatics applications, I slowly learned about these languages and programming in general. It's not as if there was one point in my life when I decided to learn how to program, but rather I learned various aspects of programming as I needed them for various projects.

I don't necessarily recommend this method of learning. In fact, there were plenty of times in which my lack of formal training led me to reinvent the wheel, as they say. It certainly helps to know what languages, tools, conventions, and resources are available for you to use before you begin. But there's so much available that it can be hard to know where to start if you know little about software engineering in general.

It was only after graduate school, when I started working at a software company, that I gained valuable experience with Java, object-oriented programming, several different types of databases, REST APIs, and various useful coding conventions and good practices that most software developers probably already know and that I've found helpful. And all of it was real-life data science in the wild, so to speak, so it was doubly helpful for me to learn. For those who were like me a few years ago and don't have much pure software development experience, I'll share the things that I wish I had known as I was getting started. Hopefully, this section will help beginning programmers understand how certain aspects of programming relate to others and feel more comfortable using them, discussing them, and searching for more information about them.

SCRIPTING

A program can be as simple as a list of commands to be executed in order. Such a list of commands is usually called a *script*, and the act of writing one is called *scripting*. In MATLAB (or the open-source clone GNU Octave), a script can be as simple as this:

```
filename = "timeseries.tsv";
dataMatrix = dlmread(filename);
dataMatrix(2,3)
```

The lines of this script set a variable named `filename` to the value `"timeseries.tsv"`, load the file whose name is contained in `filename` into the variable named `dataMatrix`, and then print on the screen the value contained in the second row and third column of `dataMatrix`. After installing MATLAB or Octave, there's very little preventing a beginning programmer from writing a simple script like this. The file timeseries.tsv needs to be in a particular format—in this case, tab-separated values (TSV)—in order for the built-in function `dlmread` to be able to read it properly. And you'd have to know about `dlmread` and a little about the syntax of the language, but it's easy to find good examples online and elsewhere.

My main point in showing this extremely simple example is that it's not that hard to get started with programming. If you have a spreadsheet, you can export a sheet of numeric values to TSV or CSV format and load the data as I've shown here, and you can immediately interact with the data via such a script, adding or removing commands to accomplish what you want.

An important thing to note is that the commands of such a script can be run in both an interactive language shell as well as an operating system's shell. That means you have a choice of writing a script and then telling your OS (how exactly depends on your OS) to run the whole script, or opening the interactive language shell and entering the commands directly within that shell. The OS method of running the script is generally more portable, and the interactive shell has the advantage of allowing line-by-line execution interspersed with other commands, edits, and checks that you might find helpful. For example, let's say you forgot what's in the file timeseries.tsv. In the interactive shell (to get to the interactive shell, open MATLAB, and the shell prompt appears immediately on the screen) you could run the first two lines of the previous script to load the file and then you could type `dataMatrix` at the prompt and press Enter to display the contents of that variable, which were loaded from timeseries.tsv. For a small file, this can be handy. An alternative is to open the file in Excel and look at the values there, which for some people is at least as appealing. But let's say you wanted to see the two-millionth line of a table contained in a CSV. Excel would probably have serious trouble loading the file; as of this writing, no version of Excel can handle files with two million lines. But MATLAB would have no problem with it. To inspect the two-millionth line, load the file as shown earlier, and enter `dataMatrix(2000000,:)` on the interactive shell prompt.

I spent most of my early programming years on the interactive shells of MATLAB and R. My typical workflow would be this:

1 Load some data into a variable in the interactive environment.
2 Play around with the data, inspecting and calculating some results.
3 Copy the useful commands from step 2 into a file (script) for reuse later.

As my commands became more complex, the script file became longer and more complex. Most days, as I was analyzing data, and particularly in an exploratory phase, I would end up with a script containing exactly the commands that could return me to the state I was in so that I could continue my work on a later date. The script would load into the interactive environment whatever data sets I needed, make data transformations or calculations, and generate graphs and results.

For years this is the way I wrote programs: scripts that were created almost as a side effect of poking and prodding at data in an interactive shell environment. This haphazard way of writing software isn't ideal—I'll come back to some good coding conventions later in this section. But I do still encourage beginners to use it, at least at first, because it's so easy to get started this way, and you can learn a lot about a language by trying various commands from an interactive shell.

I still use scripts quite often, but they have their limits and disadvantages. If you find yourself not being able to read and comprehend your own scripts because they're too long or complex, it may be time to use other styles or conventions. Likewise, if you're copying and pasting a section of a script into another script, you should probably look for an alternative—what happens when you make a change to a copied section of one script but forget to change the other scripts in the same section? If a script or set of scripts seem complex or difficult to manage, it's probably time to consider using functions or objects in your code; I'll discuss those later in this section.

SWITCHING FROM SPREADSHEETS TO SCRIPTS

The most common functionality of Excel and other spreadsheets can be replicated in scripting languages by using built-in commands such as `sum` and `sort` (versions of these are in every language) as well as using logical constructs involving `if` and `else` to check data for certain conditions. Beyond these, each language has thousands of functions (just like in Excel) that you can use in your commands. It's a matter of figuring out which function does what you want and how it works.

There's one basic type of command that programming languages handle well and spreadsheets don't: iteration. *Iteration* is repetition of a set of steps, possibly using different values each time. Let's say that timeseries.tsv is a table of numeric values, where each row represents the purchase of some items from a store. The first column gives the item number, ranging from 1 to some number n, which uniquely identifies which item was purchased. The second column gives the quantity of the item purchased, and the third column gives the total amount paid. The file might look like this:

```
3     1     8.00
12    3     15.00
7     2     12.50
```

But it's probably longer if the store is successful.

Let's assume you want the total quantity sold of item 12, and the file has thousands of rows. In Excel, you could sort by item number, scroll to the rows for item 12, and then use the SUM formula to add up the quantities. That might be quickest, but it's a decent amount of manual work (sorting, scrolling, and summing), particularly if you expect to do this with other items as well, after item 12. Another option in Excel is to create a new fourth column and use the IF formula in each cell of that column to test the first column for being equal to 12, giving 1 or 0 as a result (for true or false), multiplying the second and fourth columns row by row, and then adding up all the row products. This is also a fairly fast option, but if you want to see the sums for other items as well, you have to be clever about what formula you use and make sure you put the item number in a cell by itself—and refer to it in each of column 4's formulas—so that you can change the item number only in one place in order to get its total quantity.

Either of those Excel solutions can work if you want the quantity for only one or a few items, but what if you wanted total quantities for all item numbers? The sorting strategy would get quite tedious, as would the creating of extra columns, regardless of whether you created one extra column and then changed the item number or you created a new column for each item number. There's probably a better solution in Excel involving conditional lookups or searching for values, but I can't come up with it offhand. If you know Excel inside and out, you probably know much better than I do how to solve this problem. The point I'm trying to make is that this type of problem is easy to do in most programming languages. In MATLAB, for example, after reading the file into the variable dataMatrix as shown earlier, you need only write the following:

```
[ nrows, ncolumns ] = size(dataMatrix);
totalQuantities = zeros(1,1000)
for i in 1:nrows
  totalQuantities( dataMatrix(i,1) ) += dataMatrix(i,2);
end
```

This code first finds the number of rows, nrows, in dataMatrix and then initializes a vector totalQuantities of 1000 values, starting at zero, to which the quantities will be added. The kth entry in totalQuantities, accessed by the command total-Quantities(k), will give the total quantity sold of item k. If item numbers are above 1000, you'd need to make this vector longer. The for loop, which is the common name for the type of code structure between for and end, iterates through the rows of data-Matrix (in each iteration, the current row is given by the variable i) adding the value contained in row i, column 2 of dataMatrix to its proper place in totalQuantities, which is given by the value in row i, column 1 of dataMatrix.

To some people who haven't written code before, this example may seem more complicated than using Excel or some other tool they know. But I think it should be clear that almost anyone can get started with a scripting language and interactive shell and be producing results with only a bit of knowledge.

FUNCTIONS

I mentioned previously that scripts can sometimes grow long, complicated, and difficult to manage. You might also end up with multiple scripts that have some common steps or commands—if, for example, different scripts need data loaded in the same way, or different scripts load different data but process the data sets in the same way. If you find yourself copying and pasting code from one file to another and you intend to continue using both, it's time to think about creating a function.

Let's say you need to use the previous data file, timeseries.tsv, in multiple scripts. You can create a function in MATLAB by creating a file called loadData.m with the following contents:

```
function [data] = loadData()
  filename = "timeseries.tsv";
  data = dlmread(filename);
end
```

And then you can include the following line in a script

```
dataMatrix = loadData()
```

in order to load the data from timeseries.tsv into the variable `dataMatrix` as before. In my scripts, I've merely replaced two lines with one, but if you change the filename or its location, among other things, now you'll have to do that only in the function and not in various scripts. This also becomes more useful when you have more than two lines of code that you're sharing between scripts.

Functions, by design and like mathematical functions, can take inputs and give outputs. In the previous case, there are no inputs, but there is an output, the variable `data`; it's specified as the output on the first line of the function file. Within a script, functions also don't change any variables except the one to which the function output is assigned—in this case, `dataMatrix`. In that way, using functions is a good way to isolate code for the purpose of reuse between scripts.

Functions are also good for understanding what code does. Within your script, it's easy to read and understand the function call `loadData()` when most of the time you probably don't care how exactly the data is loaded, as long as it's working correctly. If loading data consisted of many steps, pushing those steps into a function would greatly improve the readability of that part of the script. If you have many chunks in your script that work together for a single purpose, like loading data, then you might want to push each of them into its own function and turn your script into a sequence of well-named function calls. Doing so is usually much easier on the eyes.

For your reference, functional programming is a somewhat popular programming paradigm—in contrast to object-oriented programming—in which functions are first-class citizens; functional programs emphasize the creation and manipulation of functions, even to the point of having anonymous functions and treating functions as variables. The main thing to know about functional programming is that, under the strict paradigm, functions have no side effects. If you call a function, there are inputs and there are outputs, and no other variables from the calling environment are affected. It's as if the inner workings of a function occur somewhere else, in a completely separate environment, until the function returns its output.

Whether or not you care about the specifics of the functional paradigm and its theoretical implications, functions themselves are useful for encapsulating generally cohesive blocks of code.

OBJECT-ORIENTED PROGRAMMING

Functions and functional programming can be said to be concerned with *action*, whereas object-oriented programming can be said to be concerned with *things*, but those things can also perform actions. In object-oriented programming, *objects* are entities that may contain data as well as their own function-like instructions called *methods*. An object usually has a cohesive purpose, much like a function would, but it behaves differently.

For example, you could create an object class called `DataLoader` and use it to load your data. I haven't used much object-oriented functionality in MATLAB, so I'm going to switch to Python here; more on Python later in this chapter. In Python, the class file named dataLoader.py might look like this:

```python
import csv

class DataLoader:

  def __init__(self,filename):
    self.filename = filename

  def load(self):
    self.data = []
    with open(self.filename,'rb') as file:
      for row in csv.reader(file,delimiter='\t'):
        self.data.append(row)

  def getData(self):
    return self.data
```

The first line imports the `csv` package that's used to load the data from the file. After that, you see the word `class` and the name of the class, `DataLoader`. Inside the class, indented, are three method definitions.

The first input for each of the methods is the variable `self`, which represents this instance of the `DataLoader` object itself. The methods need to be able to refer to the object itself because methods are able to set and change the object's attributes, or *state*, which is an important aspect of object-oriented programming, as I'll illustrate.

The first method defined, __init__, is the one that's called when the object is created, or instantiated. Any object attributes that are essential to the existence and functionality of the object should be set here. In the case of `DataLoader`, the __init__ method takes a parameter called `filename`, which is the filename from which the object will load the data. When a `DataLoader` object is instantiated in a script via a command such as

```
dl = DataLoader('timeseries.tsv')
```

the single input parameter is passed to the __init__ method for use by the object. The definition of __init__ shows that __init__ assigns this input parameter to the object attribute `self.filename`. Object attributes are set and accessed this way in Python. After instantiating the object via the __init__ method, the object, which is now called `dl` in the script (or interactive shell environment), has its `self.filename` attribute set to timeseries.tsv, but the object contains no data.

To load data from the named file into the object, you must use the `load` method via the command

```
dl.load()
```

which, according to the method definition, creates an attribute for the data as an empty list, `self.data`, opens the file named by self.filename, and then loads the data line by line into `self.data`. After this method is executed, all data from the file has now been loaded into the `self.data` attribute of the `DataLoader` object called `dl`.

If you want to then access and work with the data, you can use the third method defined, `getData`, which uses a `return` statement to pass the data as output to the calling script, much like a function.

Given the object class definition, a script that loads and gets the data for use might look like the following:

```
from dataLoader import DataLoader

dl = DataLoader('timeseries.tsv')
dl.load()
dataList = dl.getData()
```

Even though this accomplishes the same thing as my original script in MATLAB or one that uses functions, the way in which things are accomplished in this script, which uses an object, is fundamentally different. The first thing that happens after importing the class definition is the creation of a `DataLoader` object called `dl`. Inside `dl` is a separate environment where the object's attributes are preserved, conceptually out of sight of the main script. Functions don't have attributes and are therefore stateless, whereas an object's attributes—its state—can be used during method calls to affect the results or output of the method. Objects and their methods can have side effects.

Side effects and preserving state attributes can have big advantages, but they can also be dangerous if you're not careful. Functions, strictly speaking, should never change the value of an input variable, but objects and their methods can do so. On some occasions, I've constructed objects with methods that manipulated their input variables in some way that was convenient for calculating the method's output. Several times in my life, before I learned to be more careful, I didn't realize that in manipulating the values of the input within a method I was also affecting their values outside the method and object, in the calling script or environment. Mathematicians and other functionally minded people don't always consider that type of unintended side effect at first.

One big advantage of using an object is that objects offer a good way to gather a bunch of closely related data and functions into a single self-contained entity. In the case of loading data, the main script probably doesn't care where the data is coming from or how it's being loaded. In this scenario, in which certain groups of variables or values never interact directly with one another, according to the object-oriented paradigm they should probably be sequestered from each other in some way, and containing them within their own objects can be a good option to accomplish this. Likewise, any functions that deal almost exclusively with such a group of variables should probably be converted into object methods in the object that contains those variables.

The main advantages of separating program data, attributes, functions, and methods into purposefully cohesive objects are primarily in readability, extensibility, and maintenance. As with well-written functions, well-constructed objects allow code to be more easily understood, more easily expanded or modified, and more easily debugged.

Between functional and object-oriented programming, neither is absolutely better than the other. Each has advantages and disadvantages, and you can often borrow from both paradigms to write code that works best for your purposes. It's important, however, to be careful with the states of your objects, because if you're mixing functions and objects, it might be easy to treat an object method like a function when it has side effects.

One thing I'd like to note: throughout this section, I talk about a calling script or main script as if there is always one master script that makes use of a set of functions and objects. This is not always the case. I wrote that way for clarity for beginners, but in practice functions can call functions and use objects, objects can call functions and use objects, and there might not even be a script at all, which is the topic of the next section.

APPLICATIONS

In this context, I use the term *application* in contrast with *script*. A *script*, as I've discussed, is a sequence of commands to be executed. I use the word *application* to mean something that, when started or opened, becomes ready for use and to perform some task or action for the user. In that way, an application is conceptually similar to an object in programming, because an object can be created and then used in various ways by whatever created it. A script, on the other hand, is more similar to a function, because it merely completes a sequence of actions in a straightforward fashion.

Spreadsheets are applications, as are websites and apps on mobile devices. They're all applications in the sense I described earlier, because when they're started, they initialize but might not do much until the user interacts with them. It's primarily in this interaction with the user that applications are useful, unlike scripts, which generally produce a tangible result that provides some usefulness.

It would be hard to provide enough useful information here to get you started into application development. It's somewhat more complicated than scripting, so I'll point out a few concepts that might be useful to a data scientist. For more information, you'll find plenty of references and examples on the internet.

The main reason application development has become useful for data scientists is that sometimes delivering a static report to your customer isn't enough. I've often delivered to a customer reports that I feel are quite thorough, only to be asked for more detail on certain points. Sure, I could provide the customer with more detail in specific areas, maybe in an additional report, but only after going back to the data myself and extracting those details. I might have been better off delivering a piece of software that allowed my customer to delve deeper into each aspect of the report that they found interesting. I could have accomplished this perhaps by setting up a database and a web application that allowed the customer to click around through nice representations of the results and data in a standard web browser. This is precisely how most analytic software companies are delivering their product these days. All the analytics are behind the scenes, whereas a web application delivers the results in a way that's friendlier and more useful than a report.

Data scientists also create applications that consume and analyze data in real time or otherwise interactively. Google, Twitter, Facebook, and many other websites use fairly complex analytic methods that are continually delivered to the web via applications. Trending topics, top stories, and search results are all the product of data-science-heavy applications.

But, as I said, creating an application isn't as straightforward as writing a script, so I'll save the space, skip the detail here, and suggest that you consult references written by someone far better informed than I am. But if you're interested and you already have some experience with a programming language, have a look at these frameworks for building web applications in data-friendly languages:

- Flask for Python
- Shiny for R
- Node.js for JavaScript, plus D3.js for awesome data-driven graphics

8.2.2 Languages

I'll now introduce three scripting languages that I've used for data science and related programming tasks, to compare and contrast them, not to describe them in great detail. The languages are GNU Octave (an open-source clone of MATLAB), R, and Python. For these languages, I give example code, in each case using the item sales quantity example from section 8.2.1, and a timeseries.tsv data file in the same format I described. I define one function for loading the data, and then the scripts tally the quantities sold for all items (up to 1000 of them) and print to the screen the total quantity sold of item 12.

After discussing the three scripting languages, I talk a little about a language that isn't a scripting language (so an example script isn't possible) but that is important enough to software development in general and data science as well that I feel I should mention it. This language is Java.

MATLAB AND OCTAVE

MATLAB is a proprietary software environment and programming language that's good at working with matrices. MATLAB costs quite a bit—over $2000 for a single software license as of this writing—but there are significant discounts for students and other university-affiliated people. Some folks decided to replicate it in an open-source project called Octave. As Octave has matured, it has become closer and closer to MATLAB in available functionality and capability. Excepting code that uses add-on packages (a.k.a. toolboxes), the vast majority of code written in MATLAB will work in Octave and vice versa, which is nice if you find yourself with some MATLAB code but no license. In my experience, you'll most likely need to change some function calls for compatibility but not necessarily many. I once got several hundred lines of my own MATLAB code running in Octave after finding approximately 10 lines of code containing incompatibilities.

The near-total mutual compatibility, when not using add-on packages, is great, but Octave falls short in performance as well. From what I can gather from the internet, MATLAB can be two or three times faster than Octave for numerical operations, which sounds about right from my own experience, though I haven't done a direct comparison. Because both MATLAB and Octave are designed for matrix and vector operations, you have to write vectorized code if you want to take full advantage of the languages' efficiencies. Apparently, if you have code that isn't vectorized but should be, such as using for loops to multiply matrices, MATLAB is better at recognizing what's happening and compiling the code so that it's almost as fast as if it was explicitly vectorized. Octave might not be able to do this yet. In any case, making use of the efficiencies of vectorized code when working with vectors and matrices will always make your code faster, sometimes dramatically. This is true in MATLAB, Octave, R, and Python, among others.

Writing vectorized code in MATLAB and Octave is extremely easy for anyone familiar with matrix operations, because the code looks exactly like the equivalent mathematical expression. This isn't true for the other languages I discuss here. For example, if you have two matrices, A and B, of compatible dimensions, multiplying them in the standard sense (not entry-wise) can be accomplished by writing

```
A * B
```

whereas an entry-wise product for matrices A and B of identical dimensions is performed via

```
A .* B
```

Both of these operations are vectorized. Note that if the mathematical expression calls for transposing a matrix or vector, you likewise have to transpose it in the code or you may get an error or an incorrect result. The transpose operator is a single quote following the matrix, as in A'.

For reference, non-vectorized equivalents of these, matrix multiplication would probably involve at least two nested for loops over the rows and columns of the matrices. The vectorized versions are both easier to write and faster to execute, so it's best to vectorize whenever possible. Both R and Python can use vectorization as well, but multiplying matrices in those languages defaults to the entry-wise version of multiplication, though alternatives are provided for standard matrix multiplication.

As a slightly more informative introduction to MATLAB and Octave syntax, you can implement the item sales quantity example by creating a file named loadData.m containing the function loadData by writing the following lines:

```
function [data] = loadData()
  data = dlmread("timeseries.tsv");
end
```

In the same directory, create a script file named itemSalesScript.m containing the following lines:

```
dataMatrix = loadData();
[ nrows, ncolumns ] = size(dataMatrix);
totalQuantities = zeros(1,1000);
for i = 1:nrows
  totalQuantities( dataMatrix(i,1) ) += dataMatrix(i,2);
end

totalQuantities(12)
```

You can run this script in Octave from a Unix/Linux/Mac OS command line via the command

```
user$ octave itemSalesScript.m
```

and the output written to the command line should be the total quantity sold of item 12 appearing in your data file. To run the same code at the MATLAB or Octave prompt, copy and paste the contents of itemSalesScript.m to the prompt and press Enter.

I would use MATLAB or Octave in the following situations:

- If I'm working with large matrices or large numbers of matrices.
- If I know that a particular add-on package, particularly in MATLAB, will be greatly useful.
- If I have a MATLAB license and I like the matrix-friendly syntax.

I would not use MATLAB or Octave in these circumstances:

- If I have data that isn't well represented by tables or matrices.
- If I want my code to integrate with other software; it can be difficult and complicated because of MATLAB's relatively narrow set of intended applications, though many types of integrations are possible.

- If I want to include my code in a software product to be sold. MATLAB's license in particular can make this difficult legally.

Overall, MATLAB and Octave are great for engineers (in particular electrical) who work with large matrices in signal processing, communications, image processing, and optimization, among others.

For a look at some of my Octave code (ported from MATLAB once upon a time) from a few years ago, see my bioinformatics project on gene interaction on GitHub at https://github.com/briangodsey/bacon-for-gene-networks. The code is pretty messy, but please don't fault me for past sins. In a way, that code and that of my other bioinformatics projects represent a kind of snapshot of my hybrid scripts-and-functions coding style at the time.

R

My first note about R: if you want to search for help on the internet, putting the letter *R* in the search box can lead you to some funny places, though search engines are getting smarter every day. If you have trouble getting good search results, try putting the acronym *CRAN* in the box as well; CRAN is the Comprehensive R Archive Network and can help Google (and other search engines) direct you to appropriate sites.

R is based on the S programming language that was created at Bell Labs. It's open source, but its license is somewhat more restrictive than some other popular languages like Python and Java, particularly if you're building a commercial software product.

R has some idiosyncrasies and differences from the other languages I present. It typically uses the symbol < - to assign a value to a variable, though the equals sign, =, was later added as an alternative for the convenience of people who preferred it. In contrast to MATLAB, R uses square brackets instead of parentheses for indexing lists or matrices, but MATLAB is the weird one there; most languages use square brackets for indexing. Whereas both MATLAB and Python allow the creation of objects like lists, vectors, or matrices beginning with a square bracket, R does not. For example, in both MATLAB and Python, you can use the assignment A = [2 3] to create a vector/list containing a 2 and a 3, but in R, you'd need to use A <- c(2,3) to accomplish something similar. It's not a huge difference, but it's something I forget if I've been away from R for a while.

Compared to MATLAB, in R it's easier to load and handle different types of data. MATLAB is good at handling tabular data but, generally speaking, R is better with tables with headers, mixed column types (integer, decimal, strings, and so on), JSON, and database queries. I'm not saying that MATLAB can't handle these but that it's generally more limited or difficult in implementation. In addition, when reading tabular data, R tends to default to returning an object of the type data frame. *Data frames* are versatile objects containing data in columns, where each column can be of a different data type—for example, numeric, string, or even matrix—but all entries in each column must be the same. Working with data frames can be confusing at first, but their versatility and power are certainly evident after a while.

One of the advantages of R being open source is that it's far easier for developers to contribute to language and package development wherever they see fit. These open-source contributions have helped R grow immensely and expand its compatibility with other software tools. Thousands of packages are available for R from the CRAN website. I think this is the single greatest strength of the R language; chances are you can find a package that helps you perform the type of analysis you'd like to do, so some of the work has been done for you. MATLAB also has packages, but not nearly as many, though they're usually very good. R has good ones and bad ones and everything in between. You'll also find tons of R code that's freely available in public repos but that might not have made it to official package status.

During my years of bioinformatics research, R was the most commonly used language by my colleagues and our peers at other institutions. Most research groups developing new statistical methods for bioinformatics create an R package or at least make their code available somewhere, as I have for one of my projects, an algorithm called PEACOAT, on GitHub at https://github.com/briangodsey/peacoat.

You can implement the item sales quantity example in R by creating the file item-SalesScript.R containing the following code:

```
loadData <- function() {
  data <- read.delim('timeseries.tsv',header=FALSE)
  return(data)
}

data <- loadData()
nrows <- nrow(data)
totalQuantities <- rep(0,1000)
for( i in 1:nrows ) {
  totalQuantities[data[i,1]] <- totalQuantities[data[i,1]] + data[i,2]
}

totalQuantities[12]
```

You can run this script in R from a Unix/Linux/Mac OS command line via this command:

```
user$ Rscript itemSalesScript.R
```

Or from the shell prompt in an R environment, copy and paste the contents of item-SalesScript.R into the shell and press Enter.

Besides syntax and function name changes between MATLAB and R, you may notice that the basic structure is the same. R uses curly braces, { }, for function definitions and `for` loops, compared to MATLAB's use of an `end` command to denote the end of the code block. The function also uses an explicit `return` statement, which isn't present in MATLAB.

I would use R in these situations:

- If I'm working in a field for which there are many R packages.
- If I'm working in academia, particularly bioinformatics or social sciences.
- If I'd like to load, parse, and manipulate varied data sets quickly.

I would not use R in these circumstances:

- If I'm creating production software.
- If I'm creating software to be sold. The GPL license has implications.
- If I'd like to integrate my code into software in other languages.
- If I'd like to use object-oriented architecture. It's not great in R.

Overall, R is a good choice for statisticians and others who pursue data-heavy, exploratory work more than they build production software in, for example, the analytic software industry.

PYTHON

First and foremost, Python is the only one of the three scripting languages I present here that wasn't intended to be primarily a statistical language. In that way, it lends itself more naturally to non-statistical tasks like integrating with other software services, creating APIs and web services, and building applications. Python is also the only language of the three that I'd seriously consider using for creating production software, though in that respect Python still falls short of Java, which I'll discuss next.

Python, like any language, has its idiosyncrasies. The most obvious one is its lack of braces to denote code blocks, with not even an `end` command like MATLAB to say when a `for` loop or function definition has ended. Python uses indentation to denote such code blocks, to the eternal chagrin of many programmers everywhere. It's common convention to indent such code blocks, but Python is one of the only languages that forces you to do so, and it's certainly the most popular among them. The gist is that if you want such a code block to end, instead of typing `end` like in MATLAB or using a close brace, }, like in R, Java, and many others, you stop indenting your code. Likewise, you must indent your code immediately following a `for` command or a function definition line containing `def`. You'll get an error during execution otherwise.

Likely because Python was originally a general-purpose programming language, it has a robust framework for object-oriented design. By contrast, the object-oriented features of R and MATLAB seem like an afterthought. I've grown to like object-oriented design, even for simple tasks, so I use this feature quite often because Python has become my primary programming language in the last few years.

Although Python wasn't originally intended to be a heavily statistical language, several packages have been developed for Python that elevate it to compete with R and MATLAB. The `numpy` package for numerical methods is indispensable when working with vectors, arrays, and matrices. The packages `scipy` and `scikit-learn` add functionality in optimization, integration, clustering, regression, classification, and machine learning, among other techniques. With those three packages, Python rivals the core functionality of both R and MATLAB, and in some areas, such as machine learning, Python seems to be more popular among data scientists.

For data handling, the package `pandas` has become incredibly popular. It's influenced somewhat by the notion of a data frame in R but has since surpassed that in functionality. Admittedly, I had some trouble figuring out how to make profitable use of pandas when I first tried it, but after some practice it was very handy. It's my impression that pandas data frames work as in-memory, in-Python optimized data stores. If your data set is big enough to slow down calculations but small enough to fit in your computer's memory, then pandas might be for you.

One of the most notable Python packages in data science, however, is the Natural Language Toolkit (NLTK). It's easily the most popular and most robust tool for natural language processing (NLP). These days, if someone is parsing and analyzing text from Twitter, newsfeeds, the Enron email corpus, or somewhere else, it's likely that they've used NLTK to do so. It makes use of other NLP tools such as WordNet and various methods of tokenization and stemming to offer the most comprehensive set of NLP capabilities found in one place.

As for core functionality, the item sales quantity example written in Python in a file called itemSalesScript.py might look like this:

```
import csv

def loadData():
  data = []
  with open('timeseries.tsv','rb') as file:
    for row in csv.reader(file,delimiter='\t'):
      data.append(row)
  return data

dataList = loadData()
nrows = len(dataList)
totalQuantities = [0] * 1000
for i in range(nrows):
  totalQuantities[ int(dataList[i][0]) ] += int(dataList[i][1])

print totalQuantities[12]
```

You can run this script in Python from a Unix/Linux/Mac OS command line via the command

```
user$ python itemSalesScript.py
```

or copy and paste the contents of the file to a Python prompt and press Enter.

Note how indentation is used to denote the end of the function definition and for loop. Also notice that, like R, Python uses square brackets to select items from lists/vectors, but that Python uses a zero-based indexing system. To get the first item in a list called dataList in Python, you'd use dataList[0] instead of dataList[1] that you'd use in R or the dataList(1) that you'd use in MATLAB. That tripped me up a few times when I was learning Python, so watch out for it. Then again, most software developers are used to zero-based indexing in languages like Java and C, so they'd be more likely to be tripped up by R and MATLAB than by Python.

One final note about the code example: in two places I had to use the int function to coerce the given value from a string to an integer. This is because the csv package defaults to considering all values as strings unless told otherwise. There are surely better ways to handle this than the one I've used here, not the least of which is to convert the data to arrays using the numpy package, which is what I'd do anyway if I was working more intensely with the data, but I left it out for clarity of the example.

I would use Python in these situations:

- If I'm creating an analytic software application, prototype, or maybe production software.
- If I'm doing machine learning or NLP.
- If I'm integrating with another software service or application.
- If I'm doing a lot of non-statistical programming.

I wouldn't use Python in these circumstances:

- If I worked in a field where most people use another language and share their code.
- If Python's packages in my field were inferior to those of another language, like R.
- If I wanted to generate graphs and plots quickly and easily. R's plotting packages are significantly better.

I've mentioned that Python is now my language of choice, after switching from R a few years ago. I made the switch because I've been programming production proprietary software, and that involves a lot of non-statistical code, for which I find Python vastly better. Python's licenses freely allow sale of your software without having to provide the source code. Overall, I recommend Python for people who want to do some data science as well as some other pure, non-statistical software development. It's the only popular, robust language I know of that can do both well.

JAVA

Though not a scripting language and as such not well suited for exploratory data science, Java is one of the most prominent languages for software application development, and because of this it's used often in analytic application development. Many of the same reasons that make Java bad for exploratory data science make it good for application development.

For one, Java has strong, static variable typing, which means that you have to declare what type of object a variable is when you create it, and it can never change. Java objects also have many different types of methods—public, private, static, final, and so on—and choosing the appropriate type can ensure that the method gets used correctly and only at suitable times. Variable scope and object inheritance rules are also quite strict, at least compared to Python and R. All these strict rules make writing code slower, but the resulting application is typically more robust and far less prone to error. I sometimes wish I could impose some of these restrictions on my Python code, because every so often a particularly nasty bug can be traced back to a dumb thing I did that could have been prevented by one of Java's strict rules.

Java isn't great for exploratory data science, but it can be great for large-scale or production code based on data science. Java has many statistical libraries for doing everything from optimization to machine learning. Many of these are provided and supported by the Apache Software Foundation.

I would use Java in the following situations:

- If I'm creating an application that needs to be very robust and portable.
- If, being already familiar with Java, I know it has the capabilities I need.
- If I'm working on a team that uses mainly Java, and using another language would be a hardship for the overall development effort.

I wouldn't use Java in the following circumstances:

- If I'm doing a lot of exploratory data science.
- If I didn't know much about Java.
- If I don't need a truly robust, portable application.

Though I haven't provided much detail about Java, I do want to convey the popularity of this language in data science–related applications and also say that, for most experienced developers I know, it would be their first choice for attempting to build a bulletproof piece of analytic software.

Table 8.1 summarizes when I'd use each programming language for projects in data science.

Table 8.1   A summary of when I would use each programming language for projects in data science

Language	When I would use it	When I would not use it
MATLAB/Octave	If I'm working with large matrices or large numbers of matrices. If I know that a particular add-on package, particularly in MATLAB, will be greatly useful. If I have a MATLAB license and I like the matrix-friendly syntax.	If I have data that isn't well represented by tables or matrices. If I want my code to integrate with other software; it can be difficult and complicated, though there are various options. If I want to include my code in a software product to be sold. MATLAB's license in particular can make this difficult legally.
R	If I'm working in a field for which there are many R packages. If I'm working in academia, particularly bioinformatics or social sciences. If I'd like to load, parse, and manipulate varied data sets quickly.	If I am creating production software. If I'm creating software to be sold. The GPL license has implications. If I'd like to integrate my code into software in other languages. If I'd like to use object-oriented architecture. It's not great in R.
Python	If I'm creating an analytic software application, prototype, or maybe production software. If I'm doing machine learning or NLP. If I'm integrating with another software service or application. If I'm doing a lot of non-statistical programming.	If I worked in a field where most people use another language and share their code. If Python's packages in my field are inferior to those of another language, like R. If I want to generate graphs and plots quickly and easily. R's plotting packages are significantly better.

Table 8.1   A summary of when I would use each programming language for projects in data science *(continued)*

Language	When I would use it	When I would not use it
Java	If I'm creating an application that needs to be very robust and portable. If, being already familiar with Java, I know it has the capabilities I need. If I am working on a team that uses mainly Java, and using another language would be a hardship for the overall development effort.	If I'm doing a lot of exploratory data science. If I didn't know much about Java. If I don't need a truly robust, portable application.

8.3   *Choosing statistical software tools*

So far in this chapter I've talked about the basics of some statistical applications and programming and hopefully I've given you a good idea of the range of tools available for implementing the statistical methods that were discussed in the last chapter. If that chapter served its purpose, you've related your project and your data to some appropriate mathematical or statistical methods or models. If so, you can compare those methods or models with the software options available to implement them, arriving at a good option or two. In choosing software tools, there are various things to consider and some general rules to follow. I'll outline those here.

8.3.1   *Does the tool have an implementation of the methods?*

Sure, you can always code the methods yourself, but if you're using a fairly common method, then many tools probably already have an implementation, and it's probably better to use one of those. Code that's been used by many people already is usually relatively error free compared to some code that you wrote in a day and used only once or twice.

Depending on your ability to program and your familiarity with various statistical tools, you may have a readily available implementation in one of your favorite tools that you could put to use quickly. If Excel has it, then most likely every other tool does too. If Excel doesn't, then maybe the mid-level tools do, and if they don't, then you're probably going to have to write a program. Otherwise, the only remaining option is to choose a different statistical method.

If you do decide to go with a programming language, remember that not all packages or libraries are created equal, so make sure the programming language and the package that you intend to use can do exactly what you want. It might be helpful to read the documentation or some examples that are relatively similar to the analysis you want to do.

8.3.2   *Flexibility is good*

In addition to being able to perform the main statistical analysis that you want, it's often helpful if a statistical tool can perform some related methods. Often you'll find that the method you chose doesn't quite work as well as you had hoped, and what you've learned in the process leads you to believe that a different method might work better. If your software tool doesn't have any alternatives, then you're either stuck with the first choice or you'll have to switch to another tool.

For example, if you have a statistical model and you want to find the optimal parameter values, you'll be using a likelihood function and an optimization technique. In chapter 7, I outlined a few types of methods for finding optimal parameters from a likelihood function, including maximum likelihood (ML), maximum a posteriori (MAP), expectation-maximization (EM), and variational Bayes (VB). Although Excel has a few different specific optimization algorithms, they're all ML methods, so if you think you can get away with ML but you're not sure, you may want to level up to a more sophisticated statistical tool that has more options for optimization.

There are multiple types of regression, clustering, component analysis, and machine learning, among others, and some tools may offer one or more of those methods. I tend to favor those statistical tools that offer a few from each of these method categories in case I need to switch or to try another.

8.3.3   *Informative is good*

I've stressed that awareness in the face of uncertainty is a primary aspect of data science; this carries over into selection of statistical software tools. Some tools might give good results but don't provide insight into how and why those results were reached. On one hand, it's good to be able to deconstruct the methods and the model so that you understand the model and the system better. On the other hand, if your methods make a mistake in some way, and you find yourself looking at a weird, unexpected result, then more information about the method and its application to your data can help you diagnose the specific problem.

Some statistical tools, particularly higher-level ones like statistical programming languages, offer the capability to see inside nearly every statistical method and result, even black box methods like machine learning. These insides aren't always user friendly, but at least they're available. It's my experience that spreadsheets like Excel don't offer much insight into their methods, and so it's difficult to deconstruct or diagnose problems for statistical models that are more complicated than, say, linear regression.

8.3.4   *Common is good*

With many things in life—music, television, film, news articles—popularity doesn't always indicate quality, and in fact it often does the contrary. With software, more people using a tool means more people have tried it, gotten results, examined the results, and probably reported the problems they had, if any. In that way, software, notably open-source software, has a feedback loop that fixes mistakes and problems in a reasonably timely fashion. The more people participating in this feedback loop, the more likely it is that a piece of software is relatively bug free and otherwise robust.

This is not to say that the most popular thing *right now* is the best. Software goes through trends and fads like everything else. I tend to look at popularity over the past few years of use by people who are in a similar situation to me. In a general popularity contest of statistical tools, Excel would obviously win. But if you consider only data scientists, and maybe only data scientists in a particular field—excluding accountants, finance professionals, and other semi-statistical users—you'd probably see its popularity fade in favor of the more serious statistical tools.

A tool must meet these criteria if I'm going to use it:

- The tool must be at least a few years old.
- The tool must maintained by a reputable organization.
- Forums, blogs, and literature must show that many people have been using the tool for quite some time and without many significant problems recently.

8.3.5 *Well documented is good*

In addition to being in common use, a statistical software tool should have comprehensive and helpful documentation. It's very frustrating when I'm trying to use a piece of software and I have a question that I feel should have a straightforward answer, but I can't find that answer anywhere.

It's a bad sign if you can't find answers to some big questions, such as how to configure inputs for doing linear regression or how to format the features for machine learning. If the answers to big questions aren't in the documentation, then it's going to be even harder to find answers to the more particular questions that you'll inevitably run into later.

Documentation is usually a function of the age and popularity of the software. The official documentation for the tool should be on the maintaining organization's web page, and it should contain informative instructions and specifications in plain language that you can understand. It's funny to me how many software organizations don't use plain language in their documentation or make their examples overly complicated. Perhaps it's my aversion to unnecessary jargon, but I shy away from using software that has documentation I don't readily understand.

Along with determining whether a tool is common enough, I also check forums and blog posts to determine whether there are sufficient examples and questions with answers that support the official documentation. No matter how good the documentation is, it almost certainly has gaps and ambiguities somewhere, so it's helpful to have informal documentation as a backup.

8.3.6 *Purpose-built is good*

Some software tools or their packages were built for a specific purpose, and then other functionality was added on later. For example, the matrix algebra routines in MATLAB and R were of primary concern when the languages were built, so it's safe to assume that they're comprehensive and robust. In contrast, matrix algebra wasn't of primary concern in the initial versions of Python and Java, and so these capabilities were added later in the form of packages and libraries. This isn't necessarily bad; Python and Java happen to have robust matrix functionality now, but the same can't be said for every language that claims to be able to handle matrices efficiently.

In cases where the statistical methods I want to use are a package, library, or add-on to the software tool that I want to use, I place the same scrutiny on that package that I would on the tool itself: is it flexible, informative, commonly used, well documented, and otherwise robust?

8.3.7   *Interoperability is good*

Interoperability is a sort of converse of being purpose-built, but they're not mutually exclusive. Some software tools play well with others, and in these you can expect to be able to integrate functionalities, import data, and export results, all in generally accepted formats. This is helpful in projects where other software is being used for related tasks.

If you're working with a database, it can be helpful to use a tool that can interact with the database directly. If you're going to build a web application based on your results, you might want to choose a tool that supports web frameworks—or at least one that can export data in JSON or some other web-friendly format. Or if you'll use your statistical tool on various types of computers, then you'll want the software to be able to run on the various operating systems. It's not uncommon to integrate a statistical software method into a completely different language or tool. If this is the case, then it's good to check whether, for example, you can call Python functions from Java (you can, with some effort).

R was purpose-built for statistics, and interoperability was something of an afterthought, although there's a vast ecosystem of packages supporting integration with other software. Python was built as a general programming language and statistics was an afterthought, but as I said, the statistical packages for Python are some of the best available. Choosing between them and others is a matter of vetting all languages, applications, and packages you intend to use.

8.3.8   *Permissive licenses are good*

Most software has a license, either explicit or implied, that states what restrictions or permissions exist on the use of the software. Proprietary software licenses are usually pretty obvious, but open-source licenses usually aren't quite as clear.

If you're using commercial software for commercial purposes, it can be legally risky to be doing so with an academic or student license. It can also be dangerous to sell commercial software, modified or not, to someone else without confirming that the license doesn't prohibit this.

When I do data science using an open-source tool, the main question I have is can I create software using this tool and sell it to someone without divulging the source code? Some open-source licenses allow this, and some don't. It's my understanding (though I'm not a lawyer) that I can't sell to someone an application that I've written in R without also providing the source code; in Python and Java, doing so is generally permitted, and this is one reason why production applications are not generally built in R and languages with similar licenses. There are usually legal paths around this, such as hosting the R code yourself and providing its functionality as a web service or something similar. In any case, it's best to check the license and consult a legal expert if you suspect you might violate a software license.

8.3.9 Knowledge and familiarity are good

I put this general rule last, though I suspect that most people, me included, consider it first. I'll admit: I tend to use what I know. There might be nothing wrong with using the tool you know best, as long as it works reasonably well with the previous rules. Python and R, for example, are pretty good at almost everything in data science, and if you know one better than the other, by all means use that one again.

On the other hand, many tools out there aren't the right tool for the job. Trying to use Excel for machine learning, for example, isn't usually the best idea, though I hear this is changing as Microsoft expands its offerings. In cases like this one, where you *might* be able to get by with a tool that you know, it's definitely worth considering learning one that's more appropriate for your project.

In the end, it's a matter of balancing the time you'll save by using a tool you know against the time and quality of results you'll lose by using a tool that isn't appropriate. The time constraints and requirements of your project are often the deciding factors here.

8.4 Translating statistics into software

Putting math into your code is no small task. Many people seem to think that doing math on data is as easy as importing a statistics library and clicking Go. Maybe if they're lucky, it'll work, but only until the uncertainty sneaks up on them and their lack of awareness of what's going on in the statistical methods and code fails to prevent a problem of some kind. I know this is a contrived scenario, but I concoct such a heinous straw man to stress the importance of understanding the statistical methods that you've chosen and how they relate to the software that you're using or creating.

8.4.1 Using built-in methods

Any of the mid-level statistical tools should have proper instructions for how to apply their various statistical methods to your data. Although I don't have much recent experience, I expect that either the in-application guidance or documentation available online should suffice for anyone to figure out how to apply a standard statistical method.

Programming languages are usually a bit more complicated, and I've found that it's often quite hard to find bare-basics instructions and examples on how to implement and perform even the simplest statistical analyses. It's my impression that most documentation assumes a fair amount of knowledge of the language, which can make it confusing for beginners. Therefore, I'll present two examples here that illustrate how linear regression can be applied, one in R, and one in Python.

LINEAR REGRESSION IN R

R typically uses a functional style, as in this example:

```
data = data.frame(X1 = c( 1.01, 1.99, 2.99, 4.01 ),
                  X2 = c( 0.0, -2.0, 2.0, -1.0 ),
                  y  = c( 3.0, 5.0, 7.0, 9.0 ))

linearModel <- lm(y ~ X1 + X2, data)
summary(linearModel)

predict(linearModel,data)
```

First, this script creates a data frame object containing three variables, X1, X2, and y. A data frame is an object, but here it's constructed by a function called data.frame, which returns a data frame object that's stored in the variable data.

The assumed task here is that you want to perform linear regression such that X1 and X2 are inputs, and y is the output. You want to be able to use X1 and X2 to predict y, and you want to find a good linear model that can do this. The second command in the script specifies that you want to create a linear model via the function lm whose parameters are, first, a formula, y ~ X1 + X2, and second, a data frame, data, containing the data. Formulas are curious but useful constructs in R that I've hardly seen anywhere else. They're intended to represent a sort of mathematical relation between the variables. As you can probably guess, this formula tells the lm function that you want to predict y using X1 and X2. The intercept (y-value when all input variables are zero) is also automatically added, unless you explicitly remove it. You can add more input variables to the formula or add combinations of variables, such as the product of two variables, the square of a variable, and so on. You have numerous possibilities for constructing a formula in R, and it can get quite complicated, so I suggest consulting the documentation before you write your own.

The variables named in the formula must match some variables included in the data frame passed to lm. The lm function itself performs the regression and returns a fitted linear model, which is stored in the variable linearModel. It's important to note that I created the data in this example to give expected regression results. Each of the four data points has a value for X1, X2, and y. The data frame data looks like this (the > is the R prompt):

```
> data
  X1   X2   y
1 1.01  0   3
2 1.99  -2   5
3 2.99  2   7
4 4.01  -1   9
```

If you study the numbers closely, you may notice that in each row the y-value is pretty close to the corresponding result of 2*X1+1, and the X2 values don't contribute much information about what the value of y will be. You say that X1 is predictive of y, but X2 is not, so you expect your regression results to be very nearly that. You'd expect the results of linear regression to indicate this.

The command summary(linearModel) prints output to the screen, giving information about the linear model that was fit to the data, which can be seen here:

```
> summary(linearModel)

Call:
lm(formula = y ~ X1 + X2, data = data)

Residuals:
        1        2        3        4
-0.02115  0.02384  0.01500 -0.01769

Coefficients:
            Estimate Std. Error t value Pr(>|t|)
(Intercept) 1.001542   0.048723  20.556  0.03095 *
X1          1.999614   0.017675 113.134  0.00563 **
X2          0.002307   0.013361   0.173  0.89114
---
Signif. codes:  0 '***' 0.001 '**' 0.01 '*' 0.05 '.' 0.1 ' ' 1

Residual standard error: 0.03942 on 1 degrees of freedom
Multiple R-squared:  0.9999,        Adjusted R-squared:  0.9998
```

You can see in this output that the coefficient estimate for X1 is very nearly 2, that for X2 is almost zero, and that of the intercept is above 1, so the results meet your expectations.

The rest of the output—standard errors, p-values, R-squared, and so on—give the goodness of fit, significance of coefficients, and other statistics about the model that indicate whether it's a good model or not.

The final line of the script predicts y-values for the data points provided in the input data frame, which in this case is the same as the data with which you trained the model. The predict function takes the variables X1 and X2 in data and outputs y-values according to the model in linearModel. Here's the printed output:

```
> predict(linearModel,data)
       1        2        3        4
3.021152 4.976159 6.985002 9.017687
```

Each of these four values is the prediction of the model for each of the data points (rows) in data. As you can see, the values are pretty close to the y-values on which the model was trained.

LINEAR REGRESSION IN PYTHON

Python has multiple packages that offer linear regression methods, and it provides a good example of having to balance the general rules for choosing software I outlined previously. From what I've gathered, the LinearRegression object in the sklearn package might be the most popular, but the summary of the fit model isn't nearly as informative as the output from the function used in R. But the linear_model object in the package statsmodels does easily provide informative output, so I use that here.

The following code uses an object-oriented style, and the two main objects created are the linear model, which I called linearModel in the script, and a results object, which I called results. Methods of those objects are called to create the model, fit the model, summarize results, and make the same predictions you made in the R script. If you're not familiar with object-oriented coding, it can seem a bit weird at first:

```
import statsmodels.regression.linear_model as lm

X = [ [ 1.01,   0.0, 1 ],
      [ 1.99,  -2.0, 1 ],
      [ 2.99,   2.0, 1 ],
      [ 4.01,  -1.0, 1 ] ]
y = [ 3.0, 5.0, 7.0, 9.0 ]

linearModel = lm.OLS(y,X)
results = linearModel.fit()
results.summary()

results.predict(X)
```

Notice how I created the variables X and y. They're lists of values that, when fitting the model, are coerced into the appropriate array/matrix form. Data frames from the package pandas can also be used, but I elected not to use them here. I also added a column of 1s to the right of the X data because the model doesn't automatically add an intercept value. There are other, more elegant ways to add an intercept, but I didn't use them for the sake of clarity.

After creating the data objects, the script performs the same steps that the R script does: create the model, using the OLS class in the statsmodels package; fit the model, using the object method call linearModel.fit(); print a summary of results; and predict y values from the original X values.

The printed output from the method call results.summary() is shown here:

```
OLS Regression Results
==============================================================================
Dep. Variable:                      y   R-squared:                       1.000
Model:                            OLS   Adj. R-squared:                  1.000
Method:                 Least Squares   F-statistic:                     6436.
Date:                Sun, 03 Jan 2016   Prob (F-statistic):            0.00881
Time:                        13:45:54   Log-Likelihood:                 10.031
No. Observations:                   4   AIC:                            -14.06
Df Residuals:                       1   BIC:                            -15.90
Df Model:                           2
Covariance Type:            nonrobust
==============================================================================
                 coef    std err          t      P>|t|      [95.0% Conf. Int.]
------------------------------------------------------------------------------
```

It shows many of the same statistics as the summary in R plus some others. More importantly, it gives identical results.

8.4.2 Writing your own methods

As a researcher in academia, I mostly developed algorithms for analyzing various systems and data in the field of bioinformatics. Because they were new, I didn't have the luxury of applying a method in a software package, though in some cases I used some available methods to aid in things like optimization and model fitting.

Creating new statistical methods can be time consuming, and I don't recommend doing it unless you know what you're doing or it's your job. But if you must, it helps to know where to start. Generally speaking, I begin with the mathematical specification of the statistical model, which might look something like the model I described in the last chapter, which contained several specifications of the probability distributions of model parameters, such as this:

$$x_{n,g} \sim N(\mu_g , 1/\lambda)$$

If the model and all of its parameters and variables have been specified like that, then you need to convert the specification into a likelihood function that you can use to find optimal parameter values or distributions.

To get a likelihood function, which is a function of the parameter values based on the data values, you use the mathematical specification of the probability distribution functions for each individual data point and multiply them together. Or because probability densities are usually pretty small, and multiplying them together only makes for a very small number, it's usually better to take the logarithm of the likelihood functions for each data point and then add them together. Because the logarithm of a function has its maximum at the same point as the function itself, maximizing the sum of the log-likelihoods is equivalent to maximizing the product of likelihoods. In fact, most software and algorithms designed for working with probabilities and likelihoods use the advantages of taking the logarithm.

Once you have the mathematical specification of the joint likelihood and log-likelihood, you can convert this directly into software by using whatever mathematics libraries the language offers. It should be straightforward to write a software function that takes as input the parameter values and gives as output a log-likelihood based on the data. This function should do in software exactly what the log-likelihood function would do in mathematics.

Now that you have a software version of the joint likelihood function, you need to find optimal parameter values or distributions using one of the algorithms discussed in chapter 7: maximum likelihood estimation (MLE), maximum a posteriori (MAP), expectation-maximization (EM), variational Bayes (VB), or Markov chain Monte Carlo (MCMC). Most statistics software has methods for MLE, which would entail maximizing your joint likelihood function using an optimization routine. This can be easy for simple models but tricky for complex ones.

Using MAP methods would mean you'd have to go back to your model equations and calculate mathematically a specification of a posterior distribution of the parameter likelihood. Then you could maximize this posterior distribution in much the same way as you would for MLE. Formulating a posterior distribution isn't trivial, so you may want to consult a reference on Bayesian models before trying it.

EM, VB, and MCMC also typically depend on the same posterior distribution that MAP does. Many software tools have an implementation of MCMC, so you might be able to apply those directly to get an estimate of the parameter posterior distribution, but with EM and VB, you usually have to code the model-fitting algorithm yourself, though there have been efforts to create software that simplifies the process. The difficulty of developing algorithms like EM and VB is probably one of the main reasons why MCMC is so popular. It can be tricky to get MCMC to work, but once it does, it lets raw computational power take the place of the human programming required for the other two algorithms.

Exercises

Continuing with the Filthy Money Forecasting personal finance app scenario first described in chapter 2, and relating to previous chapters' exercises, try the following:

1   What are your two top choices of software for performing the calculations necessary for forecasting in this project and why? What's a disadvantage for each of these?
2   Do your two choices in question 1 have built-in functions for linear regression or other methods for time-series forecasting? What are they?

Summary

- Statistical software is an implementation of theoretical statistical models; understanding the relationship between the two is important for awareness of your project.
- A wide range of software is available for doing data science, from spreadsheets to mid-level statistical tools to statistical programming languages and libraries.
- Sometimes even spreadsheets can be useful to data scientists, for simpler tasks.
- Several good mid-level statistical tools are on the market, each with strengths and limitations.
- Programming isn't that hard, but it does take some time to learn, and it offers maximum flexibility in doing statistics on your data.

Supplementary software: bigger, faster, more efficient

This chapter covers

- Non-statistical software that can help you do statistics more efficiently
- Some popular and ubiquitous software concepts related to analytic software
- Basic guidelines for using supplementary software

Figure 9.1 shows where we are in the data science process: optimizing a product with supplementary software. The software tools covered in chapter 8 can be very versatile, but there I focused mainly on the statistical nature of each. Software can do much more than statistics. In particular, many tools are available that are designed to store, manage, and move data efficiently. Some can make almost every aspect of calculation and analysis faster and easier to manage. In this chapter I'll introduce some of the most popular and most beneficial software for making your life and work as a data scientist easier.

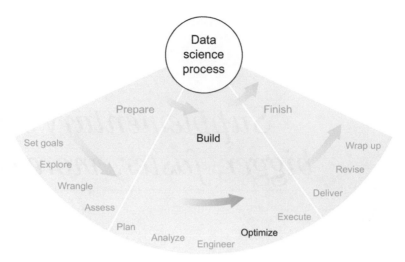

Figure 9.1   An important aspect of the build phase of the data science process: using supplementary software to optimize the product

9.1   *Databases*

I discussed the concept of a database in chapter 3 as one form of data source. Databases are common, and your chances of running across one during a project are fairly high, particularly if you're going to be using data that's used by others quite often. But instead of merely running into one as a matter of course, it might be worthwhile to set up a database yourself to aid you in your project.

9.1.1   *Types of databases*

Many types of databases exist, each designed to store data and provide access to it in its own way. But all databases are designed to be more efficient than standard file-based storage, at least for some applications.

More types (and subtypes) exist, but the two most common categories of databases today are *relational* and *document-oriented*. Though I'm certainly not an expert in database models and theory, I will attempt to describe the two types as I see them from the perspective of how I typically think about them conceptually and interact with them.

RELATIONAL

Relational databases are all about tables. A *table* in a relational database can usually be visualized as a two-dimensional sheet such as those found in spreadsheets: the sheet contains rows and columns, with data elements in the cells.

The powerful thing about relational databases is that they can hold many tables and can, behind the scenes, relate the tables to each other in clever ways. This way, even the most complicated queries from multiple tables and data types can be executed in an optimal way, often saving enormous amounts of time when compared with a primitive scan-the-tables approach to find data that matches a query.

Among relational databases, which have been popular for decades, one dominant language has emerged for formulating queries: *structured query language* (SQL, usually pronounced "sequel"). SQL is practically ubiquitous, though other query languages for relational databases do exist. In short, you can use SQL to query many different kinds/brands/subtypes of relational databases; so if you're familiar with SQL, you can begin to work with an unfamiliar database without learning a new query syntax. On the other hand, not all SQL-based databases use exactly the same syntax, so some relatively minor adaptations to a specific query may be necessary for it to work on a new database.

DOCUMENT-ORIENTED

In some sense, *document-oriented* databases are the antithesis to relational databases. Whereas relational databases have tables, document-oriented databases have, well, documents. No surprise there.

A *document* in this case can be a set of so-called *unstructured* data, like the text of an email, along with a set of structured identifying information, such as an email's sender and time sent. It's closely related to the *key-value* concept of data storage, wherein data is stored and catalogued for easy retrieval according to a set of a few keys. *Keys* are usually chosen to be the fields of a data point by which you would find it when querying—for example, ID, name, address, date, and so on. The *values* of a data point can be thought of as a sort of payload that's stored alongside the keys but that generally isn't used to find the data point in a query. It can be a messy pile of data if you want because you're not usually querying the data using the value (for a notable exception, keep reading).

Things like raw text, lists of unknown length, JSON objects, or other data that doesn't seem well suited for fitting into a table can usually fit easily into a document-oriented database. For efficient querying, each piece of unstructured data (a possible value) would ideally be matched with a few bits of structured identifying information (potential keys), because almost without exception databases handle structured data much more efficiently than unstructured.

Because document-oriented databases are a sort of antithesis of relational databases and tables, the term *NoSQL* is often applied to them. You'll find other types of NoSQL databases, but document-oriented is the largest subclass.

Besides being generally more flexible and probably less efficient than relational databases, document-oriented databases can have their own strengths. An example of such a strength can be seen in the popular Elasticsearch data store. Elasticsearch is an open-source document-oriented database built on top of the (also open-source) Apache Lucene text search engine. Lucene and Elasticsearch are good at parsing text, finding certain words and word combinations, and generating statistics about the occurrences of those words. Therefore, if you're working with a large number of text documents, and you'll be studying the occurrence of words and phrases, few if any databases (relational or not) will be as efficient as Elasticsearch.

Querying an Elasticsearch (or similar) database by raw text is a notable exception to the general rule that you should query by key and not by value. Because Lucene does such a good job of indexing text, querying by terms in the text behaves more like searching by key than in most other databases.

OTHER DATABASE TYPES

If you're working with a specific type of data that can't be represented easily as a set of tables or documents—and so isn't ideal for either a relational or document-oriented database—it might be worth searching for a database that suits that data type. For instance, graph data such as I've used in social-network analysis projects can often benefit from the efficiencies of a graph database. Neo4j is a popular *graph database* that represents connections between things (such as people in a social network) in a way that makes storage, querying, and analysis of graph data easier. There are many other examples of databases that cater to very specific data types, but I won't attempt to survey them here. A quick online search should lead you in the right direction.

9.1.2   *Benefits of databases*

Databases and other related types of data stores can have a number of advantages over storing your data on a computer's file system. Mostly, databases can provide arbitrary access to your data—via queries—more quickly than the file system can, and they can also scale to large sizes, with redundancy, in convenient ways that can be superior to file system scaling. Here I give brief descriptions of some of the major advantages that databases can offer.

INDEXING

A database *index* is a set of software tricks that generate a sort of map of all the data so that anything can be found quickly and easily. *Indexing* is the process of building such a map. Often indexing makes efficient use of hardware—disk and memory—to improve overall efficiency.

The price of having an index (versus no index) is some disk and memory space, because the index itself takes up room. Usually you have a choice of creating a very efficient index that takes up more space or a less efficient index that takes up less space. The optimal choice depends on what you're trying to accomplish.

CACHING

Caching, in the general sense, is the holding aside of certain data that's accessed very often with the goal of gaining efficiency overall because that often-used data is readily available in a special location. When certain bits of data are accessed often, you can decrease the overall average access time by holding the often-used data close at hand in some sense (various aspects of system architecture make this possible). If the often-used data has very short access times, it doesn't matter if the occasional rarely accessed data takes a bit longer to find. Databases often try to recognize the data that's used most often and hold it close instead of putting it back among the rest of the data. Like indexing, caching takes up space, but you usually have a choice of how much space you'd like to dedicate to the cache, which in turn determines how effective it is.

SCALING

Many types of databases in existence today can be distributed over many machines. Obviously, this isn't a direct advantage over storing your data in files on a disk, because if you have access to many machines, you have access to many disks. The advantage, then, of a distributed database over a distributed file system is the coordination.

If you have data on many disks on many machines, you have to keep track of what you're keeping where. Distributed databases are designed to do this automatically. Distributed databases typically consist of *shards,* or chunks of data that each exist in a single location. A central server (or multiple servers) manages access and transfer between shards. Additional shards can be used to increase the potential size of the database or to replicate data that exists elsewhere, according to the chosen database configuration.

CONCURRENCY

If two different computer processes try to change the same data point at the same time, the changes are said to be *concurrent,* and the issue of finding the proper final state is generally referred to as *concurrency.* Databases generally handle this better than the file system. Specifically, if two different processes are trying to create or edit the same file at the same time, any number of errors may occur, or none at all, which is sometimes a bigger problem. Generally speaking, you want to avoid concurrency at all costs on a file system, but certain types of databases provide convenient solutions for resolving any conflicts.

AGGREGATIONS

A database's index can be applied in tasks other than finding data matching a query. Often databases provide functionality for performing *aggregations* of the data matching a query or all data. A database might be able to add up, multiply, or summarize data much faster than your code would, and so it could be helpful to push this summarization to the database and increase overall efficiency.

For example, Elasticsearch makes it easy to calculate the frequency of certain search terms within a database. If Elasticsearch didn't provide this functionality, you'd have to query for all occurrences of the term, count the number of occurrences, and divide by the total number of documents. That may not seem like a problem, but if you're doing this thousands or millions of times, allowing the database to calculate the frequencies in an optimized, efficient way can save a considerable amount of time.

ABSTRACTED QUERY LANGUAGE

Querying a database for certain data involves formulating the query in a query language, such as SQL, that the database understands. Although it can be annoying to have to learn a new query language for a new database, these languages offer abstraction from the search algorithm that underlies the query. If your data was stored in files on the file system and you weren't using a database, every time you wanted to search for data points meeting certain criteria, you'd have to write an algorithm that goes through all your files—all the data points—and checks to see if they meet your criteria. With a database, you don't have to worry about the specific search algorithm because the database handles it. The query language provides a concise, often readable description of what you're looking for, and the database finds it for you.

9.1.3   *How to use databases*

Most software tools, Excel included, can interface with databases, but some are better at it than others. The most popular programming languages all have libraries or packages for accessing all the most popular databases. Learning how it's done is a matter of checking the documentation. Generally speaking, you'll have to know how to do the following:

- Create the database.
- Load your data into the database.
- Configure and index the database.
- Query the data from your statistical software tool.

Each database is a bit different, but once you get used to a couple of them, you'll see similarities and learn more of them quickly. It seems that today there's a book in publication for every type of database out there, so it's a matter of finding it and putting it to use. For NoSQL databases, the offerings can be particularly broad, diverse, and overwhelming, so a book like *Making Sense of NoSQL* (McCreary and Kelly, Manning, 2013) can help you sort through all the capabilities and options.

9.1.4   *When to use databases*

If accessing your data from the file system is slow and awkward, it's probably time to try a database. It can also depend on how you're accessing your data.

   If your code is often searching for specific data—thousands or millions of times—a database can greatly speed up access times and the overall execution time of your code. Sometimes code can become orders of magnitude faster upon switching from file system storage to a database. One of my projects once sped up by 1000 times when I first made the switch.

   If you have data on the file system and you mostly proceed through it top to bottom, or if you don't search often, then a database might not help you much. Databases are best for finding on-demand data that matches specific criteria, and so if you don't need to query, search, or jump around in the data, the file system might be the best choice.

   One reason why I sometimes resist using a database is that it adds some complexity to the software and the project. Having a live, running database adds at least one more moving part to all the things you need to keep your eye on. If you need to transport your data to multiple machines or locations, or if you worry that you don't have the time to configure, manage, and debug yet another piece of software, then maybe creating a database isn't the best idea. It certainly requires at least a little maintenance work.

9.2   *High-performance computing*

High-performance computing (HPC) is the general term applied to cases where there's a lot of computing to do and you want to do it as fast as possible. In some cases you need a fast computer, and in others you can split up the work and use many computers to tackle the many individual tasks. There is also some middle ground between these two.

9.2.1   *Types of HPC*

Beyond the question of having one computer or many, you may also consider using computers that are good at certain tasks or compute clusters that are configured and organized in particularly useful ways. I describe a few of the options here.

SUPERCOMPUTERS

A *supercomputer* is an extremely fast computer. There's something of a worldwide competition for the fastest supercomputer, a title that carries more prestige than anything else. But the technological challenges for taking the title are not small, and neither are the results.

A new supercomputer is millions of times faster than a standard personal computer — it could probably compute your results millions of times faster than your PC. If you have access to one—and not many people have such access—it might be worth considering.

Most universities and large, data-oriented organizations with an IT department may not have a supercomputer, but they have a powerful computer somewhere. Computing your results 100x or 1000x faster might be possible, if only you ask the right people for access.

COMPUTER CLUSTERS

A *computer cluster* is a bunch of computers that are connected with each other, usually over a local network, and configured to work well with each other in performing computing tasks. More so than with a supercomputer, computing tasks may need to be explicitly parallelized or otherwise split into separate tasks so that each computer in the cluster can perform some part of the work.

Depending on the cluster, the various computers and the tasks they're executing may be able to communicate with each other efficiently, or they may not. Some types of commodity computer clusters (HTCondor is a popular software framework for unifying them) focus less on optimizing the individual machines and more on maximizing the total amount of work the cluster can do. Other cluster types are highly optimized for performance that, in aggregate, resembles a supercomputer.

One shortcoming of a cluster when compared to a supercomputer is usually the available memory. In a supercomputer, there's usually one giant pool of available memory, and so extremely large and complex structures can be held in memory — which is much, much faster than trying to store that structure on a disk or in a database. In a cluster, each computer has only its own available memory, so it might be able to load only a small piece of a complex structure at one time. Writing and reading to disk can cost time and overall performance, but it depends highly on the specific calculations that are being done. Highly parallel calculations are more suitable for clusters.

GPUs

Graphics processing units (GPUs) are circuits that are designed to process and manipulate video images on a computer screen. The video card on every computing device with a screen has a GPU.

The nature of video manipulation has resulted in GPU designs that are very good at performing highly parallelizable calculations. In fact, some GPUs are so good at certain types of calculations that they're preferred over standard CPUs. For a while, several years ago, researchers were buying and building clusters out of video game systems such as the Sony PlayStation because the computing power available from the systems' GPUs was greater than that of other computers of similar price.

9.2.2 Benefits of HPC

The one and only benefit of HPC is quite simple to state: speed. HPC can do your computing faster than standard computing, also known as low-performance computing. If you have access—and this is a big *if*—then HPC is a good alternative to waiting for your PC to calculate all the things that need to be calculated. *Cloud computing*, which I discuss later in this chapter, makes HPC available to everyone—for a price. The benefit of using a cloud HPC offering—and some pretty powerful machines are available—must be weighed against the monetary cost before you opt in.

9.2.3 How to use HPC

Using a supercomputer, computer cluster, or GPU can be quite similar to using your own personal computer, assuming you know how to make use of multiple cores of your machine. The statistical software tools and languages that you're using typically have a method to use multiple cores of a personal computer, and these methods usually transfer nicely to HPC.

In the R language, I used to use the `multicore` package for parallelizing my code and using multiple cores. In Python, I use the `multiprocessing` package for the same purpose. With each of these, I can specify the number of cores I'd like to use, and each has some notion of sharing objects and information between the processes running on the various cores. Sharing objects and information between processes can be tricky, so you, particularly as a beginner, should shy away from doing it. Purely parallel is much easier on the code and on the brain, if you're able to implement your algorithm that way.

In my experience, submitting my code to a computer cluster was similar to running it on my own machine. I asked my colleagues at the university where I was working what the basic command was for submitting a job to the cluster queue, and then I adapted my code to conform. I could specify the number of computer cores I would like as well as the amount of memory, both of which affected my status in the queue. The cluster at this particular university, as at most, was in high demand, and queuing was both a necessity and a bit of a game.

Sometimes, particularly with GPUs, it's necessary to modify your code to make explicit use of special hardware capabilities. It's usually best to consult an expert or wade through the documentation.

9.2.4 When to use HPC

Because HPC is faster than the alternative, the rule is: if you have access, use it. If there's no cost to you, and you don't have to change your code much to take advantage of it, the question is a no-brainer. But it isn't always that simple. If I have the option of using some HPC solution, I think first about the code changes and other legwork I'll have to do in order to use HPC and then I compare that to the computing time I'll save. Sometimes, if you're not in a hurry, HPC isn't worth it. Other times, it can give you results in an hour that would have otherwise taken a week or longer.

9.3 Cloud services

Cloud services were all the rage a few years ago. They're still very popular, but they're growing more mature and becoming less of a novel technology. It's safe to say, however, that they're here to stay. In short, cloud services provide, rentable by the hour, the capabilities you could otherwise get only by buying and managing a rack of servers yourself.

The largest providers of cloud services are mostly large technology companies whose core business is something else. Companies like Amazon, Google, and Microsoft already had vast amounts of computing and storage resources before they opened them up to the public. But they weren't always using the resources to their maximum capacity, and so they decided both to rent out excess capacity and to expand their total capacity, in what has turned out to be a series of lucrative business decisions.

9.3.1 Types of cloud services

Services offered are usually roughly equivalent to the functionality of a personal computer, computer cluster, or local network. All are available in geographic regions around the world, accessible via an online connection and standard connection protocols, as well as, usually, a web browser interface.

STORAGE

All the major cloud providers offer file-storage services, usually paid per gigabyte per month. There are often also various tiers for storage, and you may pay more if you want faster reading or writing of your files.

COMPUTERS

This is probably the most straightforward of cloud offerings: you can pay by the hour for access to a computer with given specifications. You can choose the number of cores, the amount of machine memory, and the size of the hard disk. You can rent a big one, fire it up, and treat it like your supercomputer for a day or a week. Better computers cost more, naturally, but the prices are falling every year.

DATABASES

As an extension to the storage offered by cloud providers, there are also cloud-native database offerings. This means you can create and configure databases without ever having a sense of which computers or disks the database is running on.

This machine agnosticism can save some headaches when maintaining your databases, because you don't have to worry about configuring and maintaining the hardware as well. In addition, the databases can scale almost infinitely; the cloud provider is the one that has to worry about how many machines and how many shards are involved. The price, a literal one, is that you will often be charged for each access to the database—reads and writes—as well as for the volume of data stored.

WEB HOSTING

Web hosting is like renting a computer and then deploying a web server to it, but it comes with a few more bells and whistles. If you want to deploy a website or other web server, cloud services can help you do so without worrying much about the individual computers and machine configurations. They typically offer platforms under which, if you conform to their requirements and standards, your web server will run and scale with usage without much hassle. For example, Amazon Web Services has platforms for deploying web servers using Python's Django framework as well as the Node.js framework.

9.3.2 *Benefits of cloud services*

There are two major benefits of using cloud services, as compared to using your own resources, particularly if you'd have to purchase the local resources. First, cloud resources require zero commitment. You can pay only for the amount that you use them, which can save tons of money if you're not sure yet how much capacity you'll need. Second, cloud services have a far greater capacity than anything you might buy yourself, unless you're a Fortune 500 corporation. If you're not yet sure about the size of your project, cloud services can give you extreme flexibility in the amount of storage and computer power, among other things, that you can access at a moment's notice.

9.3.3 *How to use cloud services*

With an incredible variety of cloud services, you have almost unlimited combinations of ways you might use them together. The first step is always to create an account with the provider and then to try out the basic level of the service, which is usually offered for free. If you find it useful, then scaling up is a matter of using it more and paying the bill. Note that it's often worth comparing similar services before diving in.

9.3.4 *When to use cloud services*

If you don't own enough resources to adequately address your data science needs, it's worth considering a cloud service. If you're working with an organization that has its own resources, it may be cheaper to exhaust the local options before paying for the cloud. On the other hand, even if you have considerable resources locally, the cloud certainly has more; if you continually run into local resource limits, remember that the cloud provides virtually limitless capacity.

9.4 Big data technologies

If, in the analytic software industry, there was a phrase more often spoken than *cloud computing* in the last 10 years, it was *big data*. It's a shame that the phrase and the technologies it describes were understood far less often than the phrase was spoken.

I'm going to take some liberties in talking about big data because I don't feel that it ever possessed anything resembling a concrete definition. Everyone in the software industry from developers to salespeople used the phrase to pump up the impression of the software they were building or peddling, and not all the usages agreed with each other. I'm going to describe here not what I think every single person means when they use the phrase *big data* but what I mean when I say it. I think my own meaning is important because I tried to distill the concept down to the core ideas and technologies that were somewhat revolutionary when they came to market in the mid-2000s.

I don't use *big data* to mean "lots of data." Such a usage is doomed to become obsolete, and quickly, as we argue about what *lots* means. In my personal experience, 10 years ago 100 gigabytes was a lot of data; now 100 terabytes is routine. The point is that the word *big* will always be relative, and so any definition I concoct for *big data* must likewise be relative.

Therefore, my own personal definition of *big data* is based on technologies, not necessarily the size of data sets: *big data* is a set of software tools and techniques that was designed to address cases in which data transfer was the limiting factor in computational tasks. Whenever the data set is too big to move, in some sense, and special software is used to avoid the necessity of such data movement, the phrase *big data* is applicable.

Perhaps an example can illustrate the concept best. Google, arguably one of the first forces behind big data technologies, processes a tremendous amount of data on a regular basis in order to support its main business: a search engine that's supposed to find anything on the internet, which is obviously a vast place, and systems that place advertisements intelligently onto web pages. Maintaining the best search results involves analyzing the number and strength of links from all pages on the internet to all other pages. I don't know how big this data is right now, but I know it's not small. Certainly, the data is spread across many servers, probably in many different geographic locations. Analyzing all the data in order to generate a basis for internet-wide search results is a task of complex coordination among all the data servers and data centers, involving a huge amount of data transfer.

Google, being smart, realized that data transfer was a major issue that was slowing down its calculations considerably. It figured minimizing such transfer was probably a good idea. How to minimize it, however, was a different question. The following explanation of what Google did, and most of the preceding description as well, is what I've inferred from Google's release, years ago, of information regarding its MapReduce technology and other technologies it inspired, such as Hadoop. I don't know what happened at Google, and I can't claim to have read all papers and articles that have been published on the topic, but I do think the following hypothetical explanation is enlightening for anyone wondering how big data technologies work. It definitely would have been enlightening to me a few years ago.

In retrospect, what I would have done, had I worked at Google when it realized data transfer was killing analytic efficiency, was design a three-stage algorithm with the goal of minimizing data transfer while still performing all the calculations I wanted to perform.

The first step in the algorithm was to perform an initial calculation on each of the data points on the servers local to each of the databases. This local calculation resulted in, among other things, an attribute that indicated to which group of data points this particular data point belonged. In online search terms, this attribute corresponded to the corner of the internet in which this data point, probably a web page, would be found. Web pages tend to link to other pages within the same corner and not as much to pages in other corners of the internet. For each data point, once attributes specifying the corner(s) of the internet were determined, Google's algorithm proceeded to the second step. Within the MapReduce framework, this is the *map* step.

Step two surveyed the new attributes for the data points and minimized the transfer of data from one geographical place to another. If most of Corner X's data was on Server Y, step two would send all Corner X data to Server Y, so only a fraction of Corner X data would need to be transferred at all; most of the data was already there. This step is colloquially referred to as the *shuffle* step and, if done cleverly, provides one of the major advantages of using the most popular big data technologies.

Step three, then, is to take all the data points with a common attribute and analyze them all at once, generating some common results and/or some individual results that take into account the other data with the same attribute. This step analyzes all the web pages in Corner X and gives results not only about Corner X but also about all the pages in Corner X and how they relate to each other. This is called the *reduce* step.

The general summary of the three steps is this: some calculations are done locally on each data point, and data is mapped to an attribute; for each attribute, all data points are collected, while data transfer/shuffling is minimized; finally, all data points for each attribute are reduced to a set of useful results. Conceptually, the MapReduce paradigm, which is the basis for many other big data technologies, but certainly doesn't include all of them.

9.4.1 Types of big data technologies

Hadoop is an open-source implementation of the MapReduce paradigm. It has been very popular but seems to have lost steam in the last couple of years. Hadoop was originally a tool for batch processing, and since its maturity other big data software tools that claim to be real time have begun to supplant it. They all have in common the notion that too much data transfer is detrimental to the process, so data local computation should be favored whenever possible.

Some big data concepts have led to the development of databases that make explicit use of the MapReduce paradigm and its implementations like Hadoop. The Apache Software Foundation's open-source projects HBase and Hive, among others, rely explicitly on Hadoop to power databases that are designed to function well at extremely large scales, whatever that means to you in whatever year you're reading this.

9.4.2 Benefits of big data technologies

Big data technologies are designed not to move data around much. This saves time and money when the data sets are on the very large scales for which the technologies were designed.

9.4.3 How to use big data technologies

This varies greatly depending on the technology. But they generally mimic the non–big data versions, at least at small scales. You can get started with a big data database much as you would a standard database, but perhaps with a bit more configuration.

Other technologies, including Hadoop in particular, require a little more effort. Hadoop and other implementations of MapReduce require specifications for mappers in step one and reducers in step two. Experienced software developers won't have a problem coding basic versions of these, but some tricky peculiarities in implementation and configuration might cause problems, so take some care.

9.4.4 When to use big data technologies

Whenever computational tasks are data-transfer bound, big data can give you a boost in efficiency. But more so than the other technologies described in this chapter, big data software takes some effort to get running with your software. You should make the leap only if you have the time and resources to fiddle with the software and its configurations and if you're nearly certain that you'll reap considerable benefits from it.

9.5 Anything as a service

This obviously isn't a real thing, but I often feel that it is. It's sometimes hard to read software descriptions without coming across the phrase *software as a service* (SaaS), *platform as a service* (PaaS), *infrastructure as a service* (IaaS), or any other *something* as a service. Though I make fun of it, it's very much a boon to the software industry that so many things are offered as a service. The purpose of services for hire is to replace the things that we would do ourselves, and it's our hope that the service provided is better or more efficient than what we would have done ourselves.

I'm a big fan of letting other people do any standard task that I don't want to do myself, in real life as well as in software. An increasing number of such tasks are available as a service in today's internet-connected economy, and I see no reason to expect that trend to slow down any time soon. Though I won't discuss any specific technologies in this section, I emphasize that you may be able to simplify greatly your software development and maintenance tasks by hiring out some of its more common aspects. From hardware maintenance to data management, application deployment, software interoperability, and even machine learning, it's possible to let someone else handle some of the less-concerning aspects of whatever you're building. The caveat is that you should trust those you hire to do a good job, and that trust may take some effort to build. A simple online search can provide some worthwhile candidates for offloading some of your work.

Exercises

Continuing with the Filthy Money Forecasting personal finance app scenario first described in chapter 2, and relating to previous chapters' exercises, try these:

1 What are three supplementary (not strictly statistical) software products that might be used during this project, and why?

2 Suppose that FMI's internal relational database is hosted on a single server, which is backed up every night to a server at an offsite location. Give a reason why this could be a good architecture and one reason why it might be bad.

Summary

- Some technologies don't fall under the category of statistical software, but they're useful in making statistical software faster, scalable, and more efficient.

- Well-configured databases, high-performance computing, cloud services, and big data technologies, all have their place in the industry of analytical software, and each has its own advantages and disadvantages.

- When deciding whether to begin using any of these auxiliary technologies, it's usually best to ask the question: are there any gross inefficiencies or limitations in my current software technologies?

- It takes time and effort to migrate to a new technology, but it can be worth it if you have a compelling reason.

- There's been a lot of hype surrounding cloud services and big data technologies; they can be extremely useful but not in every project.

Plan execution:
putting it all together

Figure 10.1 shows where we are in the data science process: executing the build plan for the product. In the last three chapters, I covered statistics, statistical software, and some supplemental software. Those chapters provide a survey of technical options available to data scientists in the course of their projects, but they don't continue along the data science process from the previous chapters. Because of this, in this chapter I bring you back to that process by illustrating how you can go from the formulation of a plan (chapter 6) to applying statistics (chapter 7) and software (chapters 8 and 9) in order to achieve good results. I point out some helpful strategies as well as some potential pitfalls, and I discuss what it might mean to have good results. Finally, I give a thorough case study from a project early in my career, with a focus on applying ideas from the current chapter as well as the previous few.

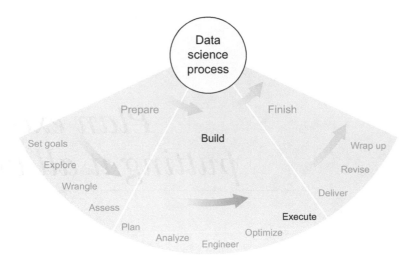

Figure 10.1   The final step of the build phase of the data science process: executing the plan efficiently and carefully

10.1   *Tips for executing the plan*

In chapters 8 and 9, I discussed various software related to statistical applications, when and where different types might be best used, and how to think about ways that the software relates to the statistics that you intend to do. But the process of building that software is another story. Even if you know exactly what you want to build and how you want the result to look, the act of creating it can be fraught with obstacles and setbacks, particularly the more complicated the tool that you're trying to build.

Most software engineers are probably familiar with the trials and tribulations of building a complicated piece of software, but they may not be familiar with the difficulty of building software that deals with data of dubious quality. Statisticians, on the other hand, know what it's like to have dirty data but may have little experience with building higher-quality software. Likewise, individuals in different roles relating to the project, each of whom might possess various experiences and training, will expect and prepare for different things. As part of the project awareness that I've emphasized throughout this book, I'll consider briefly the types of experiences and difficulties that different people might have and a few ways that problems can be prevented. I don't presume to know what others are thinking, but in my experience people with similar backgrounds tend to make similar mistakes, and I'll describe those here with the hope that they're helpful to you.

10.1.1   *If you're a statistician*

If you're a statistician, you know dirty data, and you know about bias and overstating the significance of results. These things are familiar to you, so you innately watch out for them. On the other hand, you may not have much experience building software for business, particularly *production* software—by which I mean software that's used directly by a customer to gain insight into their data. Many things can go wrong with production software.

CONSULT A SOFTWARE ENGINEER

Statisticians are smart people; they can learn and apply a lot of knowledge in a short time. To every smart person, it can be tempting to learn a new technology as you need it and to trust your own ability to use it properly. This is great if you're creating something that you'll use yourself or that's primarily a prototype. But in cases where bugs and mistakes will have a significant negative impact for your project and your team, it's best to at least consult a software engineer before, during, and after building an analytic software tool. If nothing else, the software engineer will give you a thumbs-up and tell you your design or your software is great. More likely—if the engineer is paying attention—they'll be able to point out a few areas where you can improve in order to make your software tool more robust and less likely to fail for unknown reasons. If you're not a software engineer, building a piece of production software yourself is like building a deck for your house when you have no training in carpentry or construction. You can learn most of what you need to know from books and other references, in theory, but putting the wood and the nails and the joints together can get a little messy. It can be very helpful to ask someone who has some hands-on experience, to make sure.

HAVE SOMEONE TEST YOUR SOFTWARE THOROUGHLY

If you plan on handing software to a customer and letting them use it directly, you can bet they'll find a dozen ways to break it. It's difficult to eliminate all bugs and handle all possible edge-case outcomes in a nice way, but you can find the most obvious bugs and problems if you give the software to a co-worker—ideally one who has a background similar to the customer's—and tell them to use all aspects of the tool and to try to break it. Better still, give the software to several people and have them all use it and try to break it. This is often called a *bug bash*, but it can extend beyond bugs into the realm of user experience as well as the general usefulness of the tool. Feedback here should not be taken lightly, because if your co-workers can find a bug in a few hours, I can almost guarantee that the customers will find it twice as fast, and that can cost you time, money, and reputation.

CUSTOMERS TAKE A LOT OF TIME

If you've never delivered software to a customer before, it may come as a surprise that an astonishingly large number of customers won't use your software without significant prompting—and customers who *do* use your software will bombard you with questions, problems, and insinuations that you did everything wrong.

Presuming that you want people to use your software, it can be worth spending time with customers to make sure that they're comfortable with using the software and that they're using it correctly. This means you may need to send some emails, make phone calls, or show up in person, depending on your situation. Projects in data science often depend on successfully using this new piece of software, and in the common case where the customer may not fully understand what the future impact is of your new data-centric solution, you may have to guide them down the right path.

Customers bombarding you is a good sign. It means they're already engaged and they really want the software to work. The downside is that either there are many problems with it or they don't know how to use it properly. Both of these can presumably be fixed by you or others on your team. Be aware ahead of time that customers can require maintenance at least as much as the software.

10.1.2 *If you're a software engineer*

If you're a software engineer, you know what a development lifecycle looks like, and you know how to test software before deployment and delivery. But you may not know about data and all the ways it can break your beautiful piece of programmed machinery. As I've mentioned before, uncertainty is the absolute enemy of the software engineer, yet uncertainty is inevitable in data science. No matter how good you are at software design and development, data will eventually break your application in ways that had never occurred to you. This requires new patterns of thought when building software and a new level of tolerance for errors and bugs because they'll happen that much more often.

CONSULT A STATISTICIAN

Software engineers are smart people; they can follow the flow of logic and information through complex structures. Data and statistics, though, introduce a level of uncertainty that logic and rigid structure don't handle well innately. Statisticians are well versed in foreseeing and handling problematic data such as outliers, missing values, and corrupted values. It can be helpful to have a conversation with a statistician, focusing on the sources of your data and what you intend to do with it. A statistician might be able to provide some insight into the types of problems and edge cases that may occur once you get your software up and running. Without consulting a statistician or a statistics-oriented data scientist, you run the risk of having overlooked a potentially significant special case that can break your software or otherwise cause problems for it.

DATA CAN BREAK YOUR SOFTWARE

Software engineers are good at connecting disparate systems and making them work together. A critical part of getting two software systems to work together is the agreement, or contract, between the two systems that states how they communicate with one another. If one of those systems is a statistical system, the output or state often can't be guaranteed to meet a specific set of contractual guidelines. Special and edge cases of data values can make statistical systems do weird things, and when software components are asked to do weird things, they often break. When dealing with data and statistics, it's best to forgive them in advance. Consider the broadest possible set of outcomes or states, and plan for that. If you're feeling particularly magnanimous, you may want to enclose statistical statements in try-catch blocks (or similar) such that nothing breaks in the strict sense, and then weird or unacceptable outcomes can be handled, logged, reported, or raised as an exception, whatever seems appropriate.

CHECK THE FINAL RESULTS

This may seem obvious to most of you, but in a shortage of time it's incredible how often this step gets skipped. I suggest to statisticians that they ask some people to try to break their software, and I strongly suggest to software engineers that they run through a few full examples of whatever data they're analyzing and make sure the results are 100% correct. (Really, everyone should do this, but I hope that statisticians are trained well enough to do this by default.) It can be a tedious process to begin with a small amount of raw data and trace it all the way through to an outcome, but without doing an end-to-end correctness test, there's no way to guarantee that your software is doing what it's supposed to do. Even performing a few such tests doesn't guarantee perfect software, but at least you know that you're getting *some* correct answers. If you want to take your testing to the next level, translate your end-to-end tests into formal integration tests so that if you make changes to your software in the future, you'll know immediately if you've made a mistake, because the integration test will fail.

10.1.3 *If you're a beginner*

If you're starting out in data science, without much experience in statistics or software engineering, first of all, good for you! It's a big step into a broad field, and you need a good amount of courage to take it. Second, be careful. You can make many mistakes if you go in without the awareness I've emphasized throughout this book. The good news is that there are many people around who can help you; if they're not at your company, find them elsewhere, such as at other similar companies, local technology organizations, or anywhere on the internet. For some reason, people in the software industry love to help others out. Anyone with some experience can probably give you some solid advice if you can explain your project and your goals to them. More specifically, though, it's best to follow the advice I give in this chapter to both statisticians and software engineers. As a beginner, you have double duty at this stage of the process to make up for lack of experience.

10.1.4 *If you're a member of a team*

If you're merely one member of a team for the purposes of this project, communication and coordination are paramount. It isn't necessary that you know everything that's going on within the team, but it *is* necessary that goals and expectations are clear and that someone is managing the team as a whole.

MAKE SURE SOMEONE IS MANAGING

I've seen some odd cases in which a team had no manager or leader. On exceptional teams, this can work. Sometimes everyone understands the problem, handles their part, and gets the job done. This is rare. But even in these rare cases, it's usually inefficient if everyone on the team is keeping track of everything everyone else is doing. It's usually better if one person is keeping track of all of the things that are happening, and this person can answer any questions about the status of the project that may come from anyone on the team or someone outside the team—for instance, a customer. It's not necessary, but it's usually advisable to have a team member designated as the one who keeps track of all things related to project status. This role may be as simple as taking notes, or it may be as complex as an official manager who holds formal meetings and sets deadlines. As a member of the team, you should know who this person is and the extent of their management role. If some aspect of management is lacking, you may want to bring it up with your own boss or another person of authority.

MAKE SURE THERE'S A PLAN

Everyone who has held more than a couple jobs has most likely had a boss who didn't do a good job. Some bosses are nice but not effective, and some are the opposite. In chapter 6, I discussed how to make a plan for your project; if you're working on a team, you probably didn't make the plan yourself, but you probably participated in a discussion of what should be done, when, and by whom. This should have resulted in some sort of plan, and you should know who is keeping track of this plan. If that's not the case, there may be a problem. Probably the group leader or manager has a plan, and that person should be able to describe or outline it on demand; if this plan is nonexistent, incoherent, or bad, you may want to start a serious and probably difficult conversation with team leadership. It may not be your personal responsibility to manage the plan, but it benefits the whole group to make sure that someone is handling it in a reasonable way.

BE SPECIFIC ABOUT EXPECTATIONS

Personnel issues aside, there's almost nothing worse when working on a team than having unclear direction with your own work. If you don't know exactly what you're supposed to be doing and what the expectations are for your results, it's tough to do a good job. On the other hand, it's OK to have some open-ended goals as long as everyone is aware of that. In any case, if your part of the project isn't quite clear to you, make sure to ask someone (or everyone) in order to get the issue settled.

10.1.5 *If you're leading a team*

If, as in the previous section, you're part of a team that's taking on a data science project, all of those suggestions still apply. But if in addition to that you have a position of leadership, there are a few more to add.

MAKE SURE YOU KNOW WHAT EVERYONE IS DOING

A team is nothing if it doesn't know what it's doing, cohesively. Not everyone needs to know everything, but at least one person should know almost everything that's going on, and if you're the team leader, that person should be you. I'm not suggesting that you be a micromanager, but I am suggesting that you take an active interest in the status of each part of the project. This active interest should result in an awareness of the team and project status such that you can answer most general questions about the project status without consulting anyone else. If you can't answer questions about project timelines and whether you think you'll meet certain deadlines, your interest in team activities probably isn't active enough. For more specific questions, such as implementation details, it's probably OK to ask the relevant team member. If you're the team leader and manager, it's part of your job to be the representative of the team in front of non–team members, such as customers.

BE THE KEEPER OF THE PLAN

In chapter 6, I discussed the process of making a plan for your project, with different paths and alternatives for different intermediate outcomes. If you have a reasonably sophisticated project, you probably have developed a plan that takes some time to understand. It would likely be inefficient if everyone on the team took the time to consult and understand the plan every time they had to make a decision. It's a good idea, as team leader, to take responsibility for the plan and field all questions related to the plan over the course of the project. That is not to say that the plan belongs to you and you alone; quite the contrary. The plan should have been developed with the input of the whole group, and certain aspects of the plan might still be owned by the most appropriate members of the group. But it might be a good idea that you, as the team leader, are the only one who is thoroughly familiar with the plan as a whole, as well as the team's status within it. If a customer asks, "Where are you in the development process?" you should be able to explain the plan summary to them and then say where the team is within the framework of the plan.

DELEGATE WISELY

Beyond having a plan, a team that's taking on a data science project needs to work together in such a way that work is distributed relatively evenly and to the people who are best suited to the given tasks. Software engineers should handle the more programming- and architecture-oriented aspects, data scientists should be concerning themselves more with data and statistics, subject matter experts should be handling anything related directly to the project domain, and anyone else with a certain set of skills should be handling the tasks most relevant to those skills. I don't suggest that anyone should be pigeonholed based merely on what they're good at, but each team member's expertise and limitations are relevant to the division of tasks. I've worked on teams where the few data scientists were treated like the many software engineers, and the results were not positive. Considering the people on the team against the tasks to be done should be enough.

10.2 Modifying the plan in progress

In chapter 6, I discussed formulating a plan for completing your data science project. The plan should contain multiple paths and options, all depending on the outcomes, goals, and deadlines of the project. No matter how good a plan is, there's always a chance that it should be revised as the project progresses. Even if you thought of all uncertainties and were aware of every possible outcome, things outside the scope of the plan may change. The most common reason for a plan needing to change is that new information comes to light, from a source external to the project, and either one or more of the plan's paths change or the goals themselves change. I'll briefly discuss these possibilities here.

10.2.1 Sometimes the goals change

When the goals of the project change, it can have large implications for the plan. Usually goals change because the customers have either changed their mind about something or they've communicated information that they didn't mention before for one reason or another. It's a common phenomenon—discussed in chapter 2—that customers may not know which information is important to you, a data scientist, so information gathering and goal setting can seem more like elicitation than business. If you've done a good job asking the customer the right questions along the way, you probably aren't far from a good, useful set of goals. But if new information enters the picture, changing the plan may be necessary.

Because you're already part of the way through the original plan, you probably have something to show for it: preliminary results, some software components, and the like. If the change in goals is dramatic, these things may no longer be as useful as they were, and it can be hard to convince yourself to jettison them. But the previous costs of having built something should not inherently be considered in making decisions for the future; in the finance industry, this is called a *sunk cost*, and it's a cost you can't recover; it's lost forever, no refunds. Because the money and time have already been spent, any new plan (for the future) shouldn't consider them. But whatever you've already produced can certainly be useful, and so that definitely should be taken into account when formulating a new plan. For example, if you've already built a system to load and format the raw data you intend to use, this system is probably going to be useful no matter what the new goals are. On the other hand, if you've built a statistical model that answers questions that are particular to the original goals but not the new ones, you might want to throw out that model and start over.

The main focus when goals change is to go through the process of making a plan again, like in chapter 6, but this time around you have some additional resources—whatever you've already produced from the completed part of the original plan—and you have to be very careful not to let sunk costs and other inertia prevent you from making the right choices. It's usually worth it to formally run through the planning process again and make sure that every ongoing aspect of the project is in the best interest of the goals and the new plan that you formulate.

10.2.2 Something might be more difficult than you thought

This happens to me a lot. I remember setting out in 2008 to use MapReduce on Amazon Web Services (AWS) to compute the results of a rather hefty algorithm for bioinformatics that I had written in R. Documentation, tutorials, and simple tools for AWS were rather sparse back then, and the same was true for the MapReduce-related packages in R. I was also rather naïve, I must confess. To make a long story short, many hours later, I knew neither how to set up a cluster on AWS nor how to use one with R. Needless to say, I changed my plan.

When a step within your plan that you thought would be reasonably simple turns into a nightmare, that's a good reason to change the plan. This doesn't usually have as large of an impact on the overall plan as a change in goals would, but it can still be significant. Sometimes you might be able to swap out the difficult thing for an easier one. For instance, if you can't figure out how to use MapReduce, you might gain access to a compute cluster and do your analysis there. Or if a piece of analytic software is overly complex, you might trade it for a simpler one.

If the difficult thing isn't easily avoided—such as when there's no comparable software tool to replace the one that has proven difficult to use—you may have to change the plan entirely based on the fact that a particular step must either be left out or changed. The key to making this decision is recognizing early—and correctly—that figuring out how to do the difficult thing is much more costly than doing something else.

10.2.3 Sometimes you realize you made a bad choice

I do this a lot, too. There are any number of reasons why a plan that seemed good when you made it would begin to seem less good as you make some progress. You might not have been aware of certain software tools or statistical methods, for example, and you realize that those are better choices. Or after beginning to use a certain tool, you realize that it has a limitation that you weren't aware of before. Another possibility is that you had incorrect assumptions or got bad advice about which tools to use.

In any case, if you start to realize that a previous choice, and its inclusion in the plan, was a bad idea, it's never too late to reevaluate the situation and reformulate a plan based on the most current information. It's advisable to take into account all the progress up to that point, ignoring purely sunk costs.

10.3 Results: knowing when they're good enough

As a project progresses, you usually see more and more results accumulate, giving you a chance to make sure they meet your expectations. Generally speaking, in a data science project involving statistics, expectations are based either on a notion of statistical significance or on some other concept of the practical usefulness or applicability of those results or both. Statistical significance and practical usefulness are often closely related and are certainly not mutually exclusive. I'll briefly discuss the virtues of each and their relationship with one another.

Note that throughout this section, I use the term *statistical significance* loosely to mean the general levels of accuracy or precision, ranging from the concept of p-values to Bayesian probabilities to out-of-sample accuracies of machine learning methods.

10.3.1 Statistical significance

I mentioned statistical significance in chapter 7 but provided relatively little guidance about choosing a particular significance level. That's because the appropriate level of significance depends greatly on the purpose of the project. In sociological and biolog-ical research, for example, significance levels of 95% or 99% are common. In particle physics, though, researchers typically require a 5-sigma level of significance before accepting results as significant; for reference, 5-sigma (five standard deviations from the mean) is approximately 99.99997% significance.

Depending on the type of statistical model you're using and the statistical approach, there are different formal notions of significance, ranging from *confidence* to *credibility* to *probability*. I don't want to discuss the nuances of each of these here, but I will high-light that significance can take many forms, though all of them indicate that if you repeat the analysis or gather more data that's similar, you'll see the same results with a certainty level matching the significance level. If you use a 95% significance level, 19 out of 20 comparable analyses would be expected to give the same result. This inter-pretation doesn't formally match every type of statistical analysis, but it's close enough for the discussion here.

Let's say you're doing a project in genomics, and you're trying to find genes that are related to metabolism. Given a good statistical model that you developed for this proj-ect, and using the previous notion of repeated analyses with a 95% significance level, you'd expect that any gene that meets this significance level would also meet that signif-icance level in 19 out of 20 repeated experiments. That clearly leaves one experiment in which it wouldn't meet the significance level. Assuming that the gene truly is involved with metabolism, this one non-significant result would be considered a *false negative*, meaning that the result was negative (not significant) but it shouldn't have been. If you analyzed data from thousands of genes, you'd expect to see many false negatives.

On the other hand, because you did only one experiment and subsequent analysis for each gene, surely there are some genes that are not involved in metabolism but that met the 95% significance level. In theory, these genes should most of the time not give significant results, but you were lucky enough to conduct one of the rare experi-ments whose data makes them significant. These are called *false positives*.

In practice, choosing a significance level means choosing the right balance between false negatives and false positives. If you absolutely need almost all of your positives to be true, then you need a very high significance level. If you're more concerned with cap-turing nearly all of the true things (for example, all true metabolism-related genes) in your set of positives, then a lower significance level is more appropriate. This is the essence of statistical significance.

10.3.2 *Practical usefulness*

What I'm calling *practical usefulness* is very much like statistical significance as I've described it, but with more of a focus on what you intend to do with the results instead of a purely statistical notion of confidence. What you plan to do next with the results should play a large role in how significant you need them to be.

In the example of metabolism-related genes, a possible next step would be to take the set of significant genes and to run a specific experiment on each of those genes in order to verify at a much higher level of precision whether they're truly involved with metabolism. If these experiments are costly in terms of time and/or money, then you'll probably want to use a high level of significance in your analyses so that you perform relatively few of these follow-up experiments, only on the genes that you're certain about.

In some cases, possibly even this example, the specific level of significance is almost irrelevant because you know that you want to take some fixed number of the most significant results. You could, for example, take the 10 most significance genes and perform the follow-up experiment on them. It might not matter whether you make the cutoff 99% or 99.9% if you're not going to take more than 10 anyway. A significance level of less than 95%, though, is probably not advisable, and if there aren't 10 genes meeting that level, it might be best to focus only on the ones that have statistical evidence in their favor, that meet at least a minimal level of significance.

You can begin to decide on a significance level by first asking yourself the question, what am I going to do next with the significant results? Considering the specific things you intend to do next with the set of significant results, answer these questions:

- How many significant results do you want or need?
- How many significant results can you handle?
- What is your tolerance for false negatives?
- What is your tolerance for false positives?

By answering these questions and combining the answers with your knowledge of statistical significance, it should be possible to select a set of significant results from your analyses that will serve the purposes of your project.

10.3.3 *Reevaluating your original accuracy and significance goals*

As part of your plan for the project, you probably included a goal of achieving some accuracy or significance in the results of your statistical analyses. Meeting these goals would be considered a success for the project. In light of the previous section on statistical significance and practical usefulness, it's worth reconsidering the desired level of significance of the results at this stage of the process, for a few reasons that I outline here.

YOU HAVE MORE INFORMATION NOW

You didn't have as much information when you began the project as you do now. The desired accuracy or significance may have been dictated to you by the customer, or you may have chosen it yourself. But in either case, now that you're getting to the end of the project and you have some real results, you're arriving at a position from which you can better determine whether that level of significance is the most effective.

Now that you have some results, you can ask yourself these questions:

- If I give a sample of results to the customer, do they seem pleased or excited?
- Do these results answer an important question that was posed at the beginning of the project?
- Could I—or the customer—act on these results?

If you can answer yes to these questions, then you're in good shape; maybe you don't need to adjust your significance levels. If you can't answer yes, it would be helpful to reconsider your thresholds and other aspects of how you select important results.

THE NUMBER OF RESULTS MIGHT NOT BE WHAT YOU WANT

No matter how you chose your significance levels previously, you might end up with more significant results than you can handle or too few results for them to be useful. The solution to too many results is to raise the threshold for significance, and for too few results, the solution might be to lower the threshold. But you should be careful of a few things.

Raising or lowering the threshold because you'd like more or fewer results can be a good idea as long as this doesn't violate any assumptions or goals of your project. For example, if you're working on a project involving the classification of documents as either relevant or not relevant to a legal case, it's important that you have few false negatives. Classifying an important document as not relevant can be a big problem. If you happen to realize that your classification algorithm missed an important document or two, lowering the significance threshold of the algorithm to include these documents will indeed lower the number of false negatives. But it will also presumably increase the number of false positives, which in turn will require more time to subsequently review all the positive results manually. Here, decreasing the level of significance directly increases the amount of manual work that needs to be performed later, which can be costly in legal contexts. Rather than merely change the threshold, it might be better to go back to the algorithm and model and see if you can make them better for the task at hand.

The main point is that it can be a good idea to increase or decrease significance thresholds in order to decrease or increase arbitrarily the number of significant results, but only if it doesn't adversely affect the project's other assumptions and goals. It's good to think through all possible implications of a threshold change so that you can avoid problems.

THE RESULTS MIGHT NOT BE QUITE WHAT YOU EXPECTED

Sometimes, despite all your best intentions, and after considering all the uncertainties, you end up with results that don't seem like what you'd expect. You might have a set of significant results that, generally speaking, don't seem to be what you're looking for. This is obviously a problem.

One potential solution is to raise the significance threshold and make sure the most significant results, the very top, do indeed meet your expectations. If they look good, then you can possibly use the new threshold as long as the change doesn't adversely affect anything else in the project. If they don't look good, you likely have a bigger problem than significance. You may have to go back to the statistical model and try to diagnose the problem.

Generally speaking, as you increase the threshold for the level of significance, the better your set of results should match what you expect. For example, documents should be more relevant in the legal example, genes should be more obviously related to metabolism in the genomics example, and so on. If this isn't the case, it would be best to investigate the cause.

10.4   Case study: protocols for measurement of gene activity

I'll illustrate the concepts from this and the previous few chapters by giving an in-depth explanation of a project from early in my career. With a master's degree and two years of work experience, I decided to go back to school to get a PhD. I soon joined a research group in Vienna whose focus was the development of effective statistical methods for applications in bioinformatics.

I hadn't worked in bioinformatics before, but I'd long had an interest in the primary language of biology—DNA sequences—and so I was looking forward to the challenge. I would have to learn about bioinformatics and relevant biology as well as some software and programming tools because my prior programming experience consisted mainly of MATLAB and a little C. But I had the support of two advisers and a small group of other researchers working in my lab, each with varied experience in bioinformatics, statistics, and programming.

Soon after getting settled at my new desk, one of my advisers came to me with a prospective first project and asked me to have a look. The general idea was to compare laboratory protocols for microarrays in a rigorously statistical manner. My adviser had already considered the experimental setup as well as a possible mathematical model that could be applied to the resulting data, so the first step had already been taken, which was probably good for me as a beginner. As the outcome of the project, we wanted to know which lab protocol was the best, and we intended to publish the result in a scientific journal not only for the laboratory implications but also for the statistical ones.

As I worked on this project, I learned a lot about bioinformatics, mathematics, statistics, and software, all of which, when put together, fit squarely in the field we now know as data science. In the rest of this section, I describe this project in terms of concepts from preceding chapters in this book, with the hope that this case study illuminates how they might work in practice.

10.4.1 The project

The goal of the project was to evaluate and compare the reliability and accuracy of several laboratory protocols for measuring gene expression. Each protocol is a chemical process by which RNA extracted from biological samples can be prepared for application to a microarray. Microarray technologies, which in the last decade have largely been replaced by high-throughput genetic sequencing, can measure the expression level (or activity level) of tens of thousands of genes in an RNA sample. The protocols that prepared the RNA for microarrays varied in their complexity as well as the required amount of RNA input needed for each microarray. The amount of RNA input needed for the protocols ranged from about a microgram down to a few nanograms, according to the developers of the protocols, which were often private companies that probably had reasons to mislead researchers about the reliability of their protocols in order to sell more of the required kits. Nonetheless, it would be beneficial to be able to use less RNA per microarray, because maintaining and extracting biological samples can be expensive. We wanted to hold a head-to-head competition between the protocols as they'd be used in the lab to see if any of the promises held up and in order to get the most out of our limited lab budgets.

We had four protocols in total, and one of them was well known to be quite reliable, so it was the closest thing to a gold standard that we had. For each protocol, we would run four microarrays whose putative experimental goal was to compare gene expression between male and female fruit flies—*Drosophila melanogaster*, a common model organism that's better understood than most organisms. There are some large differences between expression in male and female flies in some genes, particularly those known to be associated with sexual development and function, and in other genes there shouldn't be much of a difference. Each set of four microarrays would be run in a *dye-swap* configuration, which means that male RNA is dyed with the green radioactive dye on two arrays and with the red radioactive dye on the other two arrays; female RNA is dyed in the opposite color on each array. In the end, each microarray, for each of about 10,000 genes, gives a measurement of the ratio of gene expression in males to that in females.

Because we were using one of the protocols as a sort of gold standard, we ran two sets of four microarrays using it. Beyond having two sets of a reliable protocol available for comparison with other protocols, we could compare the two sets with each other to get an idea of the reliability of this protocol. If the two sets gave widely differing results, that would be evidence that even this gold standard protocol wasn't reliable.

In addition to all of that, for two of the four protocols we ran experiments using less RNA than what the protocol usually requires, so that we could compare these protocols with other protocols that typically require less RNA, in a sort of fair-fight scenario. A set of microarrays, one for each protocol, for four protocols, plus an extra set of the gold standard and two sets for the two low-RNA versions give 28 microarrays in total. This was the entire data set we would be using.

10.4.2 *What I knew*

Upon starting this project, I knew mathematics and statistics—at least to the master's degree level—and a fair amount of MATLAB. I knew the basics of DNA and RNA transcription and the general principles about how genes are translated and expressed within cells. In a relatively short time, I also learned the basics regarding the project description, including the foundations of how microarrays work and how the experiments are configured.

10.4.3 *What I needed to learn*

I had a lot to learn about bioinformatics, but strangely that wasn't the bulk of what I had to learn. It seemed like I learned the relevant knowledge about genes and microarrays in a relatively short time, but there were specific aspects of the mathematics and statistics that I hadn't seen before, and I also didn't know R, which was the preferred programming language of the lab because of its strengths specific to bioinformatics.

On the mathematics side, although I was very familiar with probability and statistics, I hadn't ever formulated and applied a mathematical model to data. I was a Bayesian-leaning mathematician with a fully Bayesian adviser, and so I needed to commit to learning all the implications of formulating and applying a Bayesian model.

On the programming side, I was a complete beginner with R, but on the advice of my advisers, that's the language I would use. The R libraries for loading microarray data are very good, and the statistical libraries are comprehensive as well, so I'd need to learn a lot of R in order to use it on this project.

10.4.4 *The resources*

Beyond my two advisers, I had several colleagues with varied experience in bioinformatics, mathematics, and programming in R. I was definitely in a good environment in which to learn R. When I encountered a problem or a weird error, I had to ask aloud, "Has anyone had this problem before?" and someone usually had a helpful comment or even a solution to my problem. My colleagues were certainly helpful. I tried to pay back my knowledge debt by telling the rest of the group whenever I discovered a programming trick that I thought they might not have seen before.

Beyond human resources, we also had some technological ones. Most important, my group had a lab capable of performing microarray experiments from beginning to end. Though microarrays aren't cheap, if it seemed prudent we could create any amount of data that we wanted for the analysis.

On the computational side, I had access to two university-owned servers, each of which had many computing cores and therefore could compute results several times faster than I could on my local machine. I kept this in mind while writing my code and made sure that everything I did could run in parallel on multiple cores.

10.4.5 *The statistical model*

Quite a few variables might come into play in this project. First and foremost among them was true gene expression. The main goal of the project was to evaluate how closely the measurements for each protocol matched the true gene expression level. We would want a variable in the model representing the true gene expression. We didn't have any perfect measurements of this—the best we had was the gold standard protocol that we knew was less than perfect—so this true gene expression variable would have to be a latent one. In addition to the true gene expression, we would need variables representing the measurements that the protocols produced. These are obviously measured quantities because we had the data for them, and there might be an associated error term because measurements on a genetic level are often noisy.

In addition to the true gene expression values and their various measurements, several types of variance were involved. Usually, we'd be looking at RNA samples from various individual flies, and there would be a variance between individuals depending on their own genetic composition. But in this case we mixed all the samples of female flies together, and likewise for the males, so there would be no biological variance among individuals. Microarrays notoriously don't produce the same results every time you run one with the same biological sample. That's why we were running four microarrays per protocol: to get an estimate of the technical variance resulting from each of the protocols. Lower technical variance is generally better, because it means that multiple measurements of the same thing will give results that are close to each other. On the other hand, lower technical variance isn't always better; a protocol that totally fails and always reports a measurement of zero for every gene will have perfect technical variance of zero but would be completely useless. We would want a notion of technical variance somewhere in our model as well.

The model formulation that we ultimately settled on assumed that the measurements reported by the microarrays for each protocol were normally distributed random variables based on the true gene expression values. Specifically, for each gene g, the measurement $x_{n,g}$ indicates the gene expression value reported by microarray n from the gold standard protocol, and $y_{m,g}$ represents the expression value reported by microarray m from another protocol. The formulation is as follows:

$$x_{n,g} \sim N(\mu_g, 1/\lambda)$$

$$y_{m,g} \sim N(\mu_g + \beta, 1/(\alpha\lambda))$$

Here μ_g is the true gene expression value of gene g, λ is the technical precision (inverse variance) of the gold standard protocol. The variables β and α represent inherent differences between a protocol and the gold standard. β allows for a possible rescaling of expression values; in case one protocol tends to have lower or higher values across all genes, we wanted to allow for that (and not penalize) because it doesn't directly imply that the rescaled numbers are wrong. Lastly, α represents the protocol's technical variance relative to the gold standard's. A higher α means that protocol's technical variance is lower.

I've mentioned that I like to consider every variable a random variable until I've convinced myself that I'm allowed to fix the values in place. Therefore, parameters in the aforementioned probability distributions need to have their distributions specified as well, as in the following:

$$\mu_g \sim N(0, 1/(\gamma\lambda))$$

$$\beta \sim N(0, 1/(\nu\lambda))$$

$$\lambda \sim \text{Gamma}(\varphi, \kappa)$$

A gamma distribution is related to the normal distribution in such a way that makes it useful and convenient to use for variance parameters of normal distributions. The rest of the yet-undiscussed model parameters appearing in the equations—γ, ν, φ, and κ— I didn't treat as random variables, but I was careful about it.

Each of these model parameters is at least two steps away from the data—by that, I mean that none of them appears directly in one of the equations describing the observed data, $x_{n,g}$ or $y_{m,g}$. Because of this removal, such parameters are often called hyper-parameters. In addition, these parameters can be used in a non-informative fashion—meaning that their values can be chosen so as not to exert too much influence on the rest of the model. I attempted to make the hyper-parameters almost irrelevant to the rest of the model, but I checked to make sure this was the case. After finding the optimal parameter values (see the section on model fitting in this chapter), checking to make sure that the value of a hyper-parameter is almost irrelevant to the model and the results involved a sort of sensitivity analysis wherein I changed the values of the parameters dramatically and looked to see if the results changed at all. In this case, the hyper-parameters, even if I multiplied them by 10 or 1000, didn't affect the conclusions in a significant way.

I've described a fairly complex model with several paragraphs and equations, but I'm a visual person, so I like to make diagrams of models. A good visual representation of a mathematical or statistical model comes in the form of a *directed acyclic graph* (DAG). Figure 10.2 shows the DAG for the model of multi-protocol measurement of gene expression. In the DAG, you can see all of the variables and parameters that I've discussed, each inside its own circle. The gray shaded circles are observed variables, whereas the unshaded circles are latent variables. An arrow from one variable to another indicates that the origin/first variable appears as a parameter in the distribution of the target/second variable. The rectangles, or sheets, in the background show that there are multiple genes *g* and microarray replicates *n* and *m*, each of which possesses a different instance of each of the variables contained in the sheet. For example, for each gene *g*, there is a different true gene expression value μ_g as well as a set of gold standard measurements $x_{n,g}$ and a set of measurements by another protocol $y_{m,g}$. Such a visual representation helps me keep all the variables straight.

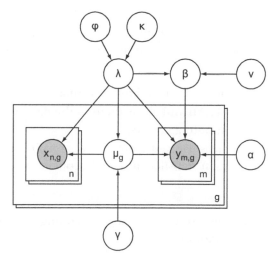

Figure 10.2   A directed acyclic graph (DAG) representing a model of the comparison of gene expression measurements based on different laboratory techniques

10.4.6 *The software*

I was learning and using the R language while working on this project. R has a bunch of great bioinformatics packages, but I used only the `limma` package, which is handy for loading and manipulating microarray data, among other things. Being a beginner with R, I decided to use it only to manipulate the data into a familiar format: a tab-separated file containing gene expression values.

After manipulating and formatting the raw data in R, I wrote the code that fit the statistical model in MATLAB, a language that was more familiar to me and one that is very good at performing operations on large matrices, an important computational aspect of my code.

I had R code that processed and reformatted the microarray data into a familiar format, and then I had a considerable amount of MATLAB code that loaded the processed data and applied the statistical model to the data. At this point in my career, this was the most complex piece of software I had written.

10.4.7 *The plan*

Academic timelines are usually rather slow. There was no real deadline for this project, except for an upcoming conference for which I might apply to give a talk. The conference application deadline was a few months away, so I had a good amount of time to make sure everything was in order before submitting.

The main goal of the project, as with most academic projects, was to have a paper accepted into a good scientific journal. In order to have a paper accepted, the research must be original, meaning it contains something no one has done before, and it must be rigorous, meaning the paper shows that the author didn't make any mistakes or fallacies.

Therefore, my first primary goal was to make sure that the main scientific results were rock solid. The next goal was to compile additional statistics and supporting evidence that the methods used in the project were consistent with the common knowledge and methods of bioinformatics. Finally, I would write a compelling scientific paper based on the research and submit it to the conference and/or a good scientific journal.

My plan, therefore, was a relatively simple one. Given my level of knowledge at the time, the plan was approximately the following:

1 Learn R and use it to manipulate the data into a familiar format.
2 Write the statistical methods in MATLAB and apply them to the data using one of the university's high-powered computing servers.
3 Compile a set of known statistics measuring microarray data quality and compare them to the results from the main statistical model. Reconcile any discrepancies as necessary.
4 Write a compelling paper.
5 Show the paper to my adviser, and go around and around editing and improving it. Some iterations may require additional analysis.

6 Once the paper is good enough, submit it to the conference and/or a journal.

7 If rejected, edit the paper based on feedback from journal reviewers and submit again.

This was a fairly straightforward plan, without too many competing interests or potential roadblocks. The most time was spent on developing the sophisticated statistical model, building the software, and iteratively checking and improving various aspects of the analysis.

One problem that we did run into during the course of this project was that the data quality seemed very poor for one of the microarray protocols. After weeks of investigation, our laboratory researchers figured out that one of the chemical reagents used in the protocol expired much sooner than expected. It became ineffective after only a few months, and we hadn't realized that—probably because we weren't using the original packaging and were sharing the reagents with nearby labs. Once we figured that out, we ordered some new reagent and reran the affected microarray experiments, with better results.

Other than the reagent snafu, there were no major issues, and everything ran according to plan. The biggest uncertainty at the beginning was in how good the results would be. Once I had calculated them and compared them to the known statistics for microarray data quality, that obstacle had largely been overcome. On the other hand, there was considerable discussion between my advisers and me about what exactly constitutes good results and what additional work, if any, would improve them.

10.4.8 *The results*

The purpose of this project was to compare objectively the fidelity of several microarray protocols in the laboratory and to decide which protocols and which amounts of RNA are required to produce reliable results. The main results were from the statistical model described earlier, but as in most bioinformatic analyses, no one trusts a novel statistical model unless one can prove that it doesn't contradict known applicable models. I calculated four other statistics that measured the different aspects of the fidelity that we intended to measure with the main statistical model. If these other statistics generally supported the main statistical model, other researchers might be convinced that the model is a good one.

The results table excerpted from a draft of the scientific paper can be seen in figure 10.3. The descriptions of the other statistics are given in the original, clipped caption, but the specifics aren't important here. What is important is that in the combination of the four other statistics—technical variance (TV), correlation coefficient (CC), gene list overlap (GLO), and the number of significant genes (Sig. Genes)—there was ample evidence that the log marginal likelihood from our statistical model (log ML) was a reliable measure of protocol fidelity. These supplementary statistics and analyses functioned like descriptive statistics—they're much closer to the data—and provided easy-to-interpret results that are hard to doubt. And because they generally supported

Protocol	Log ML	TV	CC	GLO	Sig. genes
Direct 50 μg, set 2	−69,534	0.0949	0.9945	0.91	3099
Indirect 20 μg	−82,713	0.1352	0.9767	0.88	1562
Indirect 2 μg	−87,275	0.0665	0.9192	0.75	1781
Klenow 2 μg	−107,687	0.3196	0.9344	0.74	858
Direct 2 μg	−115,913	0.3834	0.9283	0.77	177
Smart 2 μg	−121,727	0.0602	0.8434	0.18	7624

Comparing protocols using various statistics. For each labeling/amplification protocol: based on a reference data set utilizing direct labeling with 50 μg (set 1, not listed in the table), the log marginal likelihood (log ML) of the data having been generated by the process assumed by our model (greater, or less negative, values are preferred), the technical variance (TV) of the microarray replicates, the correlation coefficient (CC) of the protocol with the reference data, and the gene list overlap (GLO) of the top 100 genes of the protocol with the top 100 genes from the reference. The final column, "Sig. genes," contains the number of genes found to be significantly differentially-expressed for that protocol. In addition to the four experimental protocols, for comparison we include a data set that is a technical replicate of the reference, direct 50 μg set 2, and a third alternative reference data set, indirect 20 μg.

Figure 10.3   The main table of results for the microarray protocol comparison project, as clipped from a draft submitted to a scientific journal

the results from the statistical model, I was confident that others would see the value in a statistical model that considers all of these valuable aspects of fidelity at once.

10.4.9   Submitting for publication and feedback

In scientific research, as in data science in industry, what you know to be true because you've proven it through rigorous research may not be accepted by the community at large. It takes most people some time to accept new knowledge into their canon, and so it's rarely surprising to experience some resistance from people whom you think would know better.

A few weeks after submitting a version of my research paper to the bioinformatics conference, I received an email informing me that it was not accepted to be the topic of a talk at the conference. I was disappointed—but not too disappointed—because the acceptance rate at this particular conference was known to be well under 50%, and a first-year PhD student is probably at a distinct disadvantage.

The rejection letter came with minimal feedback from scientists who had read my paper and had judged its worthiness. From what I could tell, no one had questioned the rigor of the paper, but they thought it was boring. Exciting science definitely gets more attention and press, but someone does need to do the boring stuff, which I fully acknowledge I was doing.

After the rejection, I went back to the later steps in my plan, focusing on how to make the paper more compelling (and exciting, if possible) before submitting the paper again to a scientific journal.

10.4.10 How it ended

Not every data science project ends well. The initial rejection by the conference was the beginning of an extended phase of redefining the exact goals of the paper that we would resubmit to a scientific journal. From shortly before the initial submission until the end of the project (well over a year later), some of the goals of the project and paper were continually moving. In that way, this academic experience was a lot like my later experiences at software companies. In both cases, goals rarely stayed in one place throughout a project. In software and data science, business leadership and customers often modify the goals for business reasons. In my microarray protocol project, the goals were changing because of our impression of what good results might mean to potential paper reviewers.

Because the end goal of the project was to get a paper published in a scientific journal, we needed to be aware of what the journal's reviewers might say. Each step of the way, we looked for holes in our own arguments and gaps in the evidence that our research provided. In addition to that, we needed to take into consideration feedback from other researchers who weren't involved in our project, because these researchers are peers of those who would eventually become our reviewers.

It can be frustrating to have goals that move constantly. Thankfully, there were no large goal changes, but there certainly were dozens of small ones. Because of the goal changes, progress through the project was riddled with small plan changes, and I spent several months juggling and prioritizing the changes that might have the most significant impact on our chances of acceptance into a good journal.

Ultimately, no paper based on this research was ever published. The project leadership was quite fickle and couldn't settle on a single set of goals, and they were never satisfied with the state of the research and paper no matter how many modifications they or I made. I was also rather inexperienced in working with a research team and publishing an academic paper, and no matter how much I pushed for it, without the approval of all authors, a paper generally can't be published at all.

This is certainly not a tale of happily ever after, but I think the project as a whole provides examples of both good and bad things that can happen during a data science project. Things were going rather well until the later stages of the project—I think the analysis and results of the project were good—but I was forced to make some tough decisions when put in a difficult spot, and the plan was modified several times before being thrown out the window. Data science is not, as the press sometimes seems to believe, always sunshine and rainbows, but it can help solve many problems. Don't let the possibility of failure prevent you from doing good work, but be aware of signs indicating that the plan and the project might be running off track; catching it early can give you the opportunity to correct the problems.

Exercises

Continuing with the Filthy Money Forecasting personal finance app scenario first described in chapter 2, and relating to previous chapters' exercises, try these:

1. List three people (by role or expertise) at FMI with whom you will probably be talking the most while executing your project plan and briefly state why you will probably talk to them so much.

2. Suppose that the product designer has spoken with the management team, and they all agree that your statistical application must generate a forecast for all user accounts, including ones with extremely sparse data. Priorities have shifted from making sure the forecasts are good to making sure that every forecast exists. What would you do to address that?

Summary

- A project plan can unfold in a number of ways; maintaining an awareness of outcomes as they occur can mitigate risk and problems.
- If you're a software engineer, be careful with statistics.
- If you're a statistician, be careful with software.
- If you're a member of a team, do your part to make a plan and track its progress.
- Modifying a plan in progress is an option when new, external information becomes available, but make modifications deliberately and with care.
- Good project results are good because they're useful in some way, and statistical significance might be a part of that.

Finishing off the product and wrapping up

O nce a product is built, as in part 2, you still have a few things left to do to make the project more successful and to make your future life easier. Previous chapters focused more on what I might call raw results, or results that are good in a statistical sense but may not be polished enough for presenting to the customer.

Part 3 first looks at the advantages of refining and curating the form and content of the product with the express purpose of concisely conveying to the customer the results that most effectively solve problems and achieve goals of the project. This and some other aspects of product delivery are covered in chapter 11. Chapter 12 discusses some of the things that can happen shortly after product delivery, including bug discovery, inefficient use of the product by the customer, and the need to refine or modify the product. Chapter 13 concludes the book with some advice for storing the project cleanly and carrying forward lessons from the project in order to improve your chances of success in future projects.

Delivering a product 11

This chapter covers

- Understanding what the customer wants to see in results
- Various forms that results can take, from a simple report to an analytical application
- Why some content should or should not be included in the results product

Figure 11.1 shows where we are in the data science process: product delivery. Previous chapters of this book discuss setting project goals, asking good questions, and answering those questions through rigorous analysis of data. After all this is done, if you're the lead data scientist you probably know more about every aspect of the project than anyone else, and you're in a position to answer all sorts of questions about the project, ranging from the methods and tools used to the significance and impact of the results. But it's not usually a good idea to stay in this position in perpetuity, making yourself the only possible source of information about the project and its results. Not only would you become the single point of failure (if you're not available for some reason, what happens?), but you also would have created perpetual work for yourself, whenever questions come up. Because of these possibilities, it's usually good to create something that summarizes or catalogs your results so

239

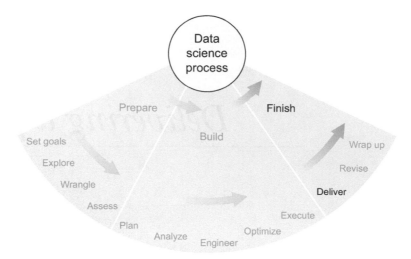

Figure 11.1   **The first step of the finishing phase of the data science process: product delivery**

that customers and other people can have their questions—at least the most common ones—answered without involving you.

In order to create an effective product that you can deliver to the customer, first you must understand the customer perspective. Second, you need to choose the best media for the project and for the customer. And finally, you must choose what information and results to include in the product and what to leave out. Making good choices throughout product creation and delivery can greatly improve the project's chances for success.

11.1   *Understanding your customer*

In chapter 2, I discussed listening to customers and asking them questions that can help you understand their problems, as well as providing information relevant to the questions they have. Hopefully, some of the strategies I presented led to good outcomes in data gathering, exploration, design and implementation of statistical methods, and overall results. I'll revisit that idea of understanding the customer again here, with a focus on creating a product that will most efficiently make those good results available to the customer.

11.1.1   *Who is the entire audience for the results?*

You probably know the customer very well by now, but there may be people other than customers who might also be interested in results. If the customer is a leader of a group or organization, other members of that group might also be part of the audience for your results. If the customer is an organization, certain departments or individuals within that organization may be part of the audience, but others may not. If the customer is an individual or a department, results may be passed up the hierarchy, to bosses or executives, so decisions can be made. In any case, it's best not to assume that the customer you've dealt with regularly is the only audience for the results you've generated. Consider the network of people surrounding the customer and whether they're part of the audience. If you're not sure, ask the customer, "Who do you foresee wanting to see these results, and why?" Hopefully, you can assemble a good idea of who the audience is.

11.1.2 *What will be done with the results?*

Once you know the audience for your results, you'll want to figure out what they're going to do with them. This is often more difficult than you would think.

In chapter 2, I wrote briefly about how you might discuss deliverables with the customer, so you may already have a good idea about what types of things the customer wants to see in the results and what they might do with them. In bioinformatics, for example, a customer might intend to take the top-10 candidate genes from your results and run extensive experiments on them. If you've built a beer-recommendation algorithm, the customer may intend to have their friends use the algorithm and then drink the recommended beers. There are many possibilities.

In a project involving organizational behavior for which you used some techniques in social network analysis, the customer may be interested in exploring each individual's contacts and seeing how those contacts are similar or different from the individual. This example is less of an action than an interest. If a customer begins a sentence beginning with

- "We would be interested in..."
- "We want to see..."
- "We would like to know..."

or similar, be sure to pursue the issue further and find out how exactly they intend to take action on this new knowledge. The actions they intend to take are far more important than what they're interested in.

If, for example, the customer intends to make business decisions based on what they find out, then you should probably figure out what their tolerance is for error and incorporate that into the tailored results you present to them. Misunderstanding the intended action and its consequences can cause bigger problems later. The example at the end of this chapter gives one instance when miscommunication while delivering a product may have caused a problem.

There are an uncountable number of ways that a customer might act on the results that you deliver, so it's best so spend some time trying to pin those down before you finalize them and their format. You might try having the customer run through a hypothetical scenario involving various types of results that are appropriate for the project, or you might even want to visit them in their workplace, observe their workflows, and witness personally how they make decisions. Talking to multiple people is also a good idea, particularly if your audience is composed of individuals with varying experience, knowledge, and interests in results. Overall, you'd like to understand as thoroughly as possible the perspective of the customer and audience and what they expect and intend with respect to the results that you'll deliver. This understanding can help you create and deliver a product that helps the customer accomplish their goals.

11.2   Delivery media

The thing that you create and deliver to customers—the product—can take many forms. In data science, one of the most important aspects of a product is whether the customer passively consumes information from it, or whether the customer actively engages the product and is able to use the product to answer any of a multitude of possible questions. The most common example of a *passive* product is a report or white paper; the customer can find in this only the answers that are in the text, tables, and figures present in the document. The most common example of an *active* product is an application that allows customers to interact with data and analysis in order to answer some questions on their own. Various types of products can fall anywhere along the spectrum between passive and active. Each of these types has strengths and weaknesses, which I discuss in the following sections.

11.2.1   Report or white paper

Probably the simplest option for delivering results to a customer, a report or white paper includes text, tables, figures, and other information that address some or all of the questions that your project was intended to answer. Reports and white papers might be printed on paper or delivered as PDFs or other electronic format. Because a report is a passive product, customers can read it when delivered and can consult the report as needed in the future, but the report will never be able to provide any new answers that weren't included when it was written—this is an important distinction between reports and more active product types. On the other hand, reports and white papers are some of the simplest and most easily digestible product types.

STRENGTHS

Some strengths of a report or white paper are these:

- On paper or in electronic form, reports and white papers are portable and don't require any special technology or knowledge in order to use them, except some general domain knowledge of the report's topic.
- Reports and white papers can provide the simplest and quickest way for the customer to find answers if the desired answers are present and if the report is concise and well organized. For most people, finding and reading an answer on a page is easier than, for example, opening an application or interpreting data in a spreadsheet.
- Reports also offer the ability to construct a narrative that can be useful for effective delivery of answers, information, caveats, and impact. Some product types provide data and answers out of context, but a narrative can establish contexts

that help the readers of the report make better use of the results therein. For example, classifications generated by a machine learning algorithm can be far more useful to customers if they understand the accuracies and limits of applicability of that algorithm. A narrative can provide context prior to stating results in order to prevent misinterpretation and misuse of results.

LIMITATIONS

Some limitations of a report or white paper are these:

- The biggest limitation of reports and white papers is that they're fully passive. You need to know before you write the report which questions the customer wants to have answered, and you need to answer these questions in a way that's easily comprehensible. If you're not successful in writing a good report, the customer will return to you with questions or, even worse, dismiss the project as a failure and lose confidence in you and/or your team, even if the results themselves are quite good.
- It can be tough to include the right amount of detail so that all the major points are covered and the most important questions are answered, while avoiding details that distract from the important points.
- Reports and papers can answer questions only at the current time and may not apply to future times or other data sets outside the current set of data. If it's likely that the customer will want to revisit the project's questions in the future or use another data set, a report might not be the best choice.
- Some people don't like reading reports. People of various learning and leadership styles may prefer to see results in a different format, and if these people are stubborn and in a position of authority, writing a report would be a waste of time.

WHEN TO USE IT

A report or white paper can be a good product to deliver when

- Your project involves a few key questions that can be answered completely and succinctly in a written report that may include tables, graphics, or other figures.
- The main goals of your project involve answering a few questions one time, and these answers are useful by themselves, without an ongoing need to update or expand the answers.
- The customer would like a written report, and you don't feel that that's an inappropriate request.

11.2.2 Analytical tool

In some data science projects, the analyses and results from the data set can also be used on data outside the original scope of the project, which might include data generated after the original data (in the future), similar data from a different source, or other data that hasn't been analyzed yet for one reason or another. In these cases, it can be helpful to the customer if you can create a tool for them that can perform these analyses and generate results on new data sets. If the customer can use this analytical tool effectively, it might allow them to generate any number of results and continue to answer their primary questions well into the future and on various (but similar) data sets.

A simple example of such an analytical tool is a spreadsheet that makes projections based on the current financial situation and expectations of a company and its industry. Theoretically, a customer could enter a range of values into such a spreadsheet and see how the projections change if the company's financial situations change. Customers might not be able to create the spreadsheet themselves if it consists of complicated formulas and statistical methods, but they can understand the intent and the meaning of the results if they, for example, conform to generally accepted financial-modeling principles.

An analytical tool that you might deliver as a product of your data science project might also be a software script that accepts a data set and analyzes it, generating results that can be used by the customer in a specific, useful way. It might also be a highly specialized database query that addresses some of the project's questions. An analytical tool delivered as a product can take many forms, but it needs to fulfill some criteria:

- The analytical tool needs to generate reliable results within the boundaries of the types of data sets for which it was intended.
- The set of applicable data sets must be well specified.
- The customer must be able to use the analytical tool correctly.

If all three of these criteria are met, then you might have a good product to deliver. The usefulness of the tool also depends on how many of the project's questions it can answer and how important those questions are to the project's goals and to the customer.

STRENGTHS
Some strengths of analytical tools are these:

- Analytical tools allow the customer to answer some of their own questions quickly and without involving you. This saves time and effort for everyone involved.
- Within the intended scope of answerable questions, an analytical tool is more versatile than a report. Even within a narrow scope, analytical tools can usually give an unlimited number of results as inputs and data sets vary. It would be impossible to provide such unlimited results in a report.

LIMITATIONS
Some limitations of analytical tools are these:

- It's often difficult to build an analytical tool that's good at answering important questions reliably and concisely for a customer. If at some point the tool runs into an edge case and gives incorrect or misleading results, the customer may not realize it.
- Customers need to be able to understand the basics of how the tool works in order to know its limitations and interpret the results correctly.

- Customers need to be able to use the tool properly, or they'll risk getting incorrect results. If you're not available to assist them, you need to have reasonable guarantees that they won't mess something up.

- If there are bugs or other problems with the tool, the customer may need support from you. Even if the analysis is good, things like data formatting, computer compatibility, and third parties whom the customer invited to share the tool can all cause unexpected problems that require your attention and slow the customer down.

- Because it's so hard to create a foolproof analytical tool, such a tool can typically replicate only the absolute clearest of the project's analyses. Accuracy, significance, and impact must all generally be high, and so the scope of an analytical tool must be reduced to only those analyses and results that meet these stringent criteria.

WHEN TO USE IT

An analytical tool can be a good product to deliver when

- The analysis completed within your project is conducive to being converted into such a tool, specifically that it can be made relatively easy to use and its results can be expected to be reliable.

- The customers can be expected to understand the tool to a point that they can use it correctly and interpret results correctly.

- A passive product such as a report isn't sufficient for the customer's needs, such as the case where the customer intends to replicate the project's analysis for new data sets.

11.2.3 *Interactive graphical application*

If you want to deliver a product that's a step more toward active than an analytical tool, you'll likely need to build a full-fledged application of some sort. Although it can be argued that analytical tools like scripts and spreadsheets are also applications, I'll draw a fuzzy distinction here between command-line-style, numbers-in-numbers-out analytical tools and graphical user interface (GUI) point-and-click-style applications. These aren't well-defined categories, but I think the loose conceptual descriptions suffice here, because you can combine the two types in any number of ways and consider both sets of strengths and limitations listed here as appropriate. The former type (command-line style) I consider to fall into the analytical tool category of the previous section. In this section, I consider mainly GUI-based applications.

GUI-based applications, these days, are typically built on web frameworks, which I discussed earlier in this book. They don't have to be web applications, but that type is most common right now. Such an interactive graphical application that you might deliver to your customer might include the following:

- Graphs, charts, and tables
- Drop-down menus that enable different analyses

- Interactive graphics, such as a timeline with movable endpoints
- The ability to import or select different data sets
- A search bar
- Results that can be filtered and/or sorted

None of these is required, but each of them enables the user (the customer) to answer more project-related questions at their leisure.

The most important thing to remember about interactive graphical applications, if you're considering delivering one, is that you have to design, build, and deploy it. Often, none of these is a small task. If you want the application to have many capabilities and be flexible, designing it and building it become even more difficult. Software design, user experience, and software engineering are each full-time jobs at software companies, and so if you have little experience with delivering applications, it's probably best to consult someone who does and to consider carefully the time, effort, and knowledge required before you start.

The strengths and limitations of interactive graphical applications include those of analytical tools discussed in the previous section, but I'll add more specific ones here.

STRENGTHS

Some strengths of interactive graphical applications include the following:

- If it's well designed, an interactive graphical application can be the most powerful tool that you can deliver to a customer in terms of the information and answers it can convey.
- A well-designed and well-deployed interactive graphical application is easy to access and easy to use. It can be made clear within the application itself how to use the application properly and effectively.
- An interactive graphical application can be made portable and scalable if it's built and deployed using common frameworks. This can be useful if you expect the number of users to grow or if you think another customer will want to use it as well.

LIMITATIONS

Some limitations of interactive graphical applications are these:

- Interactive graphical applications are hard to design, build, and deploy. Not only are the tasks difficult, but they also can take a lot of time.
- Interactive graphical applications often require ongoing support. The potential for bugs and problems increases with the complexity of the software and the deployment platform, and supporting the application and fixing bugs may take a considerable amount of time and resources.
- Customers might not use the application properly. If proper use isn't clear, or if a user isn't careful, misleading conclusions might be drawn.

WHEN TO USE IT

An interactive graphical application can be a good product to deliver when

- The guidelines from the previous section for when to use an analytical tool apply.
- A point-and-click GUI is strongly preferred over other types of analytical tools, either for ease of use or for the effectiveness of results delivery.
- You have the time and resources to design, build, deploy, and support such an application.

11.2.4 Instructions for how to redo the analysis

Whether or not you've already elected to create and deliver one of the products I've discussed, it can be a good idea to record the steps that you took to perform the project's final analysis and to package it into an instruction book for the customer's use or even for your own.

If you're dealing with a smart and capable customer, possibly even a data scientist of some sort, they may be able to replicate your analysis if given instructions. This can be helpful for them if they want to analyze new data or other similar data in the future. As with building an analytical tool, the goal is to enable the customer to ask and answer some of their own questions without requiring much of your time. Giving them detailed instructions can accomplish this without requiring you to create and deliver a high-quality, relatively bug-free software application. If you're giving them any code, there's still the possibility of encountering bugs, but in this case there's a reasonable expectation that the customer can read, edit, and fix the code themselves if they need to. You may still need to provide support sometimes, but this arrangement shifts a large part of the support burden away from you, assuming the customer is capable.

On the other hand, delivering an instruction set to a customer can create all sorts of problems if they aren't familiar with some of the steps or if they don't have much experience with the tools you're using.

STRENGTHS

Some strengths of delivering a set of instructions are these:

- It's usually pretty easy to write down what you did, bundle it with your code or other tools, and deliver it to a customer.
- A set of instructions can be extremely useful to you in the future, if you ever return to this project and need to analyze data in a similar way again.

LIMITATIONS

Some limitations of delivering a set of instructions are these:

- The customer needs to understand everything you deliver, and they need to be able to replicate it, possibly with changes in data sets or other aspects, without encountering many problems that they can't solve.

- Delivering instructions requires a lot of time and effort on the part of the customer, because they will have to read and understand some complex analyses and tools.
- Unclear instructions or messy code can make it nearly impossible to replicate the analysis reliably. You need to take care to avoid this possibility.

WHEN TO USE IT

A set of instructions for performing the analysis can be a good product to deliver when

- The exploratory work was the challenging part, and applying the statistical methods is relatively easy for the customer to do.
- The customer is smart and capable and shouldn't have many problems working with the instructions, tools, and/or code that you deliver.
- You think there's even a remote possibility that you'll return to this project in the future—hold onto the instructions for yourself.

11.2.5 *Other types of products*

There are many other products that might also fit your project and your customer well. Here are some:

- *A web-based API that, when queried in a certain way, returns answers and information pertaining to the query*—This can be useful when a customer wants to be able to integrate your analysis into an existing piece of software.
- *A software component that's built directly into the customer's software*—This takes more coordination than a web-based API because you have to understand the architecture of the existing software, but it can still be a good idea depending on how the software will be used and deployed.
- *An extended development project in which you work with the customer's own software engineers to build a software component that they will then maintain themselves*—If you have the time now, letting others build and maintain software based on your analysis can save you a lot of time later.
- *A database populated with the most useful data and/or the results of some analyses*—For customers who regularly work with databases, giving them one can sometimes be more convenient for them to work with than an API or other component, if you can figure out an efficient and relatively foolproof way to structure the database so that it's useful and is used properly.

Each of these has its own set of strengths and limitations, many of which correspond to those I listed for other products earlier. If you're considering a product that doesn't fit in any of the categories I've described in detail, perhaps thinking through it in much the same way that I have will lead you to your own conclusions. In particular, it's important to consider whether a particular product is more passive or active and what the time requirements will likely be for you, both in the near future and in the long term if you'll need to provide support. Beyond that, every project and every specific potential product will have its own nuanced situations, and if you find yourself even a little unsure of what the ramifications are, it can be very helpful to consult someone with experience and ask their opinions. The internet can also be a good source of guidance if you can distinguish the good from the bad.

11.3 Content

In addition to deciding the medium in which to deliver your results, you must also decide which results it will contain. Once you choose a product, you have to figure out the content you'll use to fill it.

Some results and content may be obvious choices for inclusion, but the decision may not be so obvious for other bits of information. Typically, you want to include as much helpful information and as many results as possible, but you want to avoid any possibility that the customer might misinterpret or misuse any results you choose to include. This can be a delicate balance in many situations, and it depends greatly on the specific project as well as the knowledge and experience of the customer and the rest of the audience for the results. In this section, I provide some guidance on how to make decisions about inclusion and exclusion, and I also discuss how user experience can make products more and less effective.

11.3.1 Make important, conclusive results prominent

If there are critical questions that your project was intended to answer, and you now have conclusive answers to these questions, these answers should be prominent in your product. If you're delivering a report, a summary of these important, conclusive results should appear in the first section or on the first page, and a more thorough discussion of methods and impact should be given later in the paper. If you're delivering an interactive graphical application, these results should appear either on the main page of analytical results, or they should be very easily accessible through a few clicks, searches, or queries.

In general, it's best to put the most important, conclusive, unmistakable, straightforward, and useful results front and center in whatever product you're delivering so that the customer and the rest of the audience can find them without having to look for them and immediately understand the results and their impact.

11.3.2 Don't include results that are virtually inconclusive

It can be tempting to tell the customer about all of the planned analyses that didn't work alongside all of those that did. In a research setting, this might be a good idea, because failed experiments can sometimes give insight into how a system works and why other positive results turned out the way they did. But in non-academic data science, including in a report, the stories of the things that you tried that didn't work can distract from the important, actionable information in the report.

Most people don't need distractions from their work; they can find them on their own. If a piece of information doesn't support valuable intelligence that can be used directly to make business decisions or otherwise help achieve any of the stated goals of a project, it's usually best to leave it out. Feel free, however, to make note of any interesting tidbits for your own records or a supplementary report that isn't the primary product for the customer; sometimes these can come in handy later if a project's direction changes or if a new, related project is begun.

11.3.3   *Include obvious disclaimers for less significant results*

You probably have some results that fall between the labels *conclusive* and *inconclusive*. Deciding what to do with these can be tough, and there can be many reasons both for including them and for excluding them. It's certain, though, that you wouldn't want the customer to confuse results that are absolutely conclusive with those that are only partially so. Therefore, both as insurance for your own reputation and as a step toward making sure that the customer understands how best to use the information you're providing, I highly recommended including disclaimers and caveats next to every result that's less than 99.9% statistically significant or otherwise is not quite conclusive.

For example, let's say you're trying to detect fraudulent credit card transactions, and the customer is immediately going to reject the transactions that your software labels as fraudulent. If your software is 99.9% accurate, the customer probably won't complain about the 0.1% of cases that were falsely rejected. But if your software has a false positive rate of 10%, the customer might complain very strongly. In similar situations, if you do have a 10% false positive rate, it's definitely better to communicate that rate to the customer along with its potential implications before you deliver them the results and before they act on them. If there were any misunderstandings at all, and they acted on your results before they fully understood their implications and limitations, that could be bad for the customer, bad for the project, and possibly bad for you.

If you want to deliver some results that aren't conclusive but that still might be helpful and informative, make sure you include a disclaimer stating exactly how significant the results are, what the limitations are, and what the positive and negative impacts are if the customer uses those results in certain ways. Overall, though, the customer needs to understand fully that you're not 100% sure about these results and that acting on them might have unexpected consequences. If you can communicate this effectively, the customer will be in a good position to make good decisions based on your results, and you'll be in a position to have a successful project.

11.3.4   *User experience*

Most people who use the phrase "user experience" refer to the ways that a person might interact with a piece of software. Within the software industry, user experience (UX) designer has become a lucrative career and rightly so. Understanding how people might interact with a piece of software is not an easy task, and it has been demonstrated in many contexts that how people interact with software has a large influence on whether that software is ultimately effective. User experience makes the difference between good analytical software that's used effectively and good analytical software that most people can't figure out how to use.

User experience can also refer to a report, an analytical tool, or any other product that you might deliver to a customer. The experience that the customer or audience has with your product is the user experience, and the principal goal is to ensure that these users use the product properly in order to draw correct conclusions from it and make good business decisions. If a customer isn't using the product properly, you might reconsider the user experience. The goal is to enable and encourage the customer and the audience to do the right thing.

INVERTED PYRAMID OF JOURNALISM

The popular concept of an inverted pyramid, as illustrated in figure 11.2, shows how a journalistic news story might be represented in order to be most effective to the reader. The implicit assumption is that a reader might not read the whole article, or at least that the reader might not read the whole article with their full attention. Based on this assumption, the most important information, the *lede* (or lead), should be at the very beginning of the article, followed by the body that supports the lede, and finally the tail that adds to the rest but isn't absolutely necessary for the story to be complete.

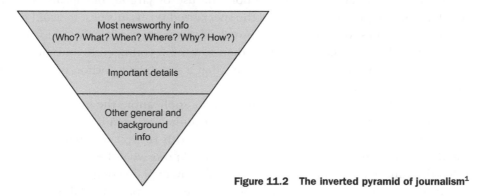

Figure 11.2   The inverted pyramid of journalism[1]

For reports on data science projects, this means that it might be most effective to follow the same pattern to deliver results to a customer: lead with the most important, most impactful results in clear language, then include details that directly support those results, and finally include other auxiliary results that are useful but not necessary.

For analytical tools and interactive graphical applications (and other products), it can be helpful to consider the concept of the inverted pyramid when designing and building. The most important results and information should be in the user's face as soon as they start using the application. Supporting details might take a little more effort, but not too much, and then users might need to look around a bit before they find the less important, extra information.

---

[1] From https://en.wikipedia.org/wiki/Inverted_pyramid, public domain image

Although it certainly shouldn't be a hard rule of data science projects, following the inverted pyramid from journalism can be helpful in writing a report or designing an application that delivers the most important information to the customer first and the less important but still helpful information second.

PLAIN LANGUAGE WITH NO JARGON

Jargon is confusing to people who don't work in the field from which it comes. You shouldn't use jargon in your reports or your applications or any of your products. If you do use it, you should make the definitions clear to the customers, the audience, or the users of the product you're delivering.

The term *jargon* is hard to define. For our purposes, *jargon* is a set of terms or phrasing that's familiar to people of a specific training, experience, or knowledge but that isn't familiar to people working in substantially different fields. Because you can rarely guarantee that the people you're speaking with are people with similar backgrounds to you, it's generally best to assume that they don't know your jargon.

I admit to being wholly anti-jargon, but I also see the value in using jargon in highly specialized conversations and writing. Jargon allows people to communicate efficiently within their fields—or at least within the subfields for which that jargon is valid. In those situations, I fully support the use of jargon, but in any situation in which people might not understand the specialized terms, it's best to avoid them.

When it comes to presenting your work, if you must speak with or in front of people, it's helpful to speak more plainly than you think you need to and more slowly as well. It's rarely advantageous to use terms that a significant portion of your audience doesn't understand.

When you're writing a report or text for an application, the same rules apply: the text should be comprehensible by most of the audience, even if they don't have experience in some related areas. Most important, with respect to language and understanding, using jargon isn't proof that someone knows what they're talking about. It's often the contrary, in my experience. The ability to explain complex concepts in plain language is a rare talent and in my opinion a far more valuable skill than explaining anything using jargon.

VISUALIZATIONS

Like the field of user experience design, data visualization improves your application or other product greatly, but it isn't usually a main focus of that product. Data visualization is also very well studied, and it's usually best to heed the warnings and follow the best practices of those who have studied and thought a lot about data visualization.

Edward Tufte's *The Visual Display of Quantitative Information* is a must-read book for people who want to get their data visualization absolutely right. There are other great references on the topic as well, but Tufte is usually the best place to start. Not only will you learn about when it's best to use bar charts or line graphs, but you'll also discover some key principles that apply to any visualization—maps, timelines, scatter plots, and so on—such as "encourage the eye to compare different pieces of data" and "be closely integrated with the statistical and verbal descriptions of a data set."

Tufte's books are packed with such tenets and plenty of examples that show exactly what he means.

Visualizations of data and results can be helpful in reports and applications, but if they're not designed well, they can be detrimental to the product's intent. It's often worth taking some time to study and consider the assumptions and implications of any visualizations that you're trying to create. Consulting some data visualization references, like Tufte's books, or someone with experience can have large benefits later, as the visualizations continue to serve their purpose as clear, concise conveyors of useful information.

THE SCIENCE BEHIND USER EXPERIENCE

The study of user experience is a science, though some people don't treat it as such. I didn't realize that it was or could be more science than art until a few years ago, when I witnessed experience studies and evaluations in action. There are many well-studied principles regarding what makes an application easy to use, or powerful, or effective, and if you're building a complex application, employing these principles can make a huge difference in the success of your project. I encourage you to consult an experienced UX designer if you're building an application. Sometimes even a short conversation with a UX designer can lead to great improvements in your application's usability.

11.4 *Example: analyzing video game play*

While working with Panopticon Laboratories, an analytic software company whose goal is to characterize and detect suspicious in-game behavior in multiplayer online video game environments, we delivered a preliminary report to a customer (a video game publisher) that included a survey of the state of their in-game community as well as a list of some of the more suspicious players. To do this, as we did with all customers, we fit a proprietary statistical model to their data; this model assigned scores to each player, indicating how suspicious or fraudulent the player appeared to be in various categories. We were highly confident that the players with the highest scores were indeed fraudulent players, but the farther we progressed down the list of the most suspicious players, the less sure we were. We were contractually obligated to deliver to the customer a list of suspicious players, and we knew that we had to convey along with this list some notion of this uncertainty.

The customer didn't employ any data scientists in the security department with which we were dealing, so we had to be careful not to mince words about statistical significance or uncertainty. The main thing we had to decide was how many suspicious players to include on the list. If we provided a relatively short list, we would likely be leaving out some very suspicious players who would continue to cost the video game publisher money. If we included too many players in the report, we would be pointing the finger at innocent players (with a not-insignificant false positive rate) and possibly misleading the video game publisher into thinking the problem was bigger than it was and possibly also causing them to take action against those innocent players, such as banning them from game play.

To resolve the decision, we worked with the customer to determine that they did indeed intend to ban players who were highly suspicious and that they were willing to accept a false positive rate of less than 5%. In order to establish a false positive rate, the customer planned to sample randomly from our initial list of suspicious players and check each one manually. We could then use the feedback to reinforce the statistical models and subsequently generate a new, more accurate report. Two or three rounds of this is usually enough to obtain high accuracy.

We had a minor setback when, after using the first-round feedback to generate another report but before we were quite ready to say that the behavior models were 100% done, the customer indicated that they were ready to begin banning the suspicious players from the game based on our lists. Luckily, before they acted, we had the chance to talk with them about how the most recent report still wasn't necessarily actionable and that their feedback on this report would be crucial to gaining the requisite actionable intelligence from the next phase of reporting (meeting the <5% false positive rate requirement) and the subsequent software deployment. This was a classic case of not knowing what the customer was going to do with the product we were delivering. I'm not sure they would have admitted their intent beforehand (maybe they didn't even realize it themselves), and so any line of questioning may have been fruitless anyway, but it was worth trying and worth being vigilant. The only thing worse than delivering something that isn't entirely effective is delivering something that is effective but that is then misused, to much detriment.

After the next round of feedback, we delivered a report for which we expected a false positive rate of well under 5% (to give ourselves a cushion), and we made sure that the customer understood that the list still wasn't perfect and that they could expect that a small percentage of the players on that list weren't bad guys. If they took action against all of those players, they should expect some adverse effects.

After delivery of the final report, we began hooking up their data source to our real-time analytic engine that powers an interactive graphical web application that provides the same information as the reports, plus the ability to interact with and learn far more about players and their behavior. The application allows the customer to see the same curated lists of suspicious players and allows them to click players' names and get more information about them—in particular, more information about why they're considered suspicious. In many ways, the application is superior to the reports because of the increased amount of information available, the multiple ways and formats in which the results can be viewed, and the interactive nature of the application that lets users find the answers they need when they want them. Also, the application has informative graphics and a well-designed user experience, which makes interacting with data and results both easier and more intuitive. Supporting a customer deployment of a live application is a considerable amount of work, but the app seems to be far more useful to customers than the reports have been.

Exercises

Continuing with the Filthy Money Forecasting personal finance app scenario first described in chapter 2, and relating to previous chapters' exercises, try these exercises:

1 Suppose your boss or another management figure has asked for a report summarizing the results of your work with forecasting. What would you include in the report?

2 Suppose the lead product designer for the FMF web app asks you to write a paragraph for the app users, explaining the forecasts generated by your application, specifically regarding reliability and accuracy. What would you write?

Summary

- The product is, in a sense, the thing that you've been working toward for the entire duration of the project; it's important to get the format and content right.
- The format and medium of the product should, as much as possible, meet the customer's needs both now and in the foreseeable future.
- The content of products should focus on important, conclusive results and not distract the customer with inconclusive results or other trivia.
- It's best to spend some time thinking formally about user experience (UX) design in order to make the product as effective as possible.
- Consider in advance whether the product will need ongoing support and plan accordingly.

After product delivery: problems and revisions

This chapter covers

- Diagnosing problems with the product after it's delivered to the customer
- Finding remedies to product problems
- Getting and using feedback from customers
- Revising the product based on known problems and feedback

Figure 12.1 shows where we are in the data science process: revising the product after initial feedback. The previous chapter covered the delivery of a product to your customer. Once the customer begins using the product, there's the potential for a whole new set of problems and issues to pop up. In this chapter, I discuss some of these problem types and how to deal with them, and I talk about customer feedback and revising the product based on the problems you encounter and the feedback you receive.

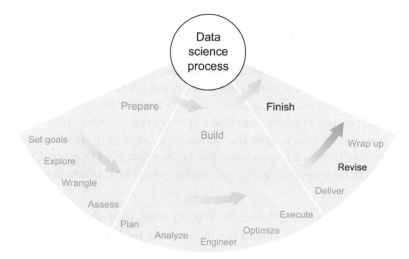

Figure 12.1   The second step of the finishing phase of the data science process: revising the product after initial delivery to the customer

12.1 *Problems with the product and its use*

Despite your best efforts, you may not have anticipated every aspect of the way your customers will use (or try to use) your product. Even if the product does the things it's supposed to do, your customers and users may not be doing those things and doing them efficiently. In this section, I discuss a few causes for the product not to be as effective as you would hope, and I give some suggestions for how to recognize and remedy them.

12.1.1 *Customers not using the product correctly*

Customers tend to use new products in every way except the way that was intended. Sometimes they misunderstand where to type which text and which buttons to press, either because they haven't put a lot of effort into figuring out the correct way or because it's difficult to figure out. Sometimes customers try to use a product to do something it wasn't intended to do, usually either because they think the product is supposed to do that thing or because they're trying to be clever and twist the product's capabilities into doing an extra thing it shouldn't be doing.

In either case, and in others, customers not using the product in the intended ways is problematic because it can lead to false or misleading results or no results at all. Misleading results are probably worse, because the customer might gain false confidence and act on those results, potentially leading to poor business decisions.

If the customer can't get any results at all, then hopefully they'll come back to you to ask for help, which is far better than the alternative: they'll give up and stop using the product altogether.

HOW TO RECOGNIZE IT

If you deliver a product to a customer and forget about it, you'll never know how it worked out for them. Maybe it was great; maybe it wasn't. Therefore, the first step in recognizing improper use of your product is to talk to the customer about it. You talked to the customer at the time of product delivery, and presumably you provided instructions for use, but, like the product itself, instructions may be used incorrectly, partially, or not at all. At least one follow-up is usually in order.

It's usually best to give the customer a bit of time to try out the product before you pester them with questions, but before that it's OK to reaffirm that you're there to help if they need it. When you do follow up with questions, you should ask things like this:

- Are you getting the results you expected from the product?
- Have you been able to use the product to address the intended business needs?
- Is the product falling short in any way?
- How often and by how many people is the product used?
- Can you describe the typical use of the product?

If they describe any problems, bad results, or something unexpected, it would be good to explore these further and try to find out what the trouble is.

In addition to finding out if the customer is experiencing problems, it's important to notice if the customer isn't able to give a complete answer to any of your questions. This can be a sign that the customer you're talking to isn't the main person who is using product or isn't being completely informed by the person using the product, or that no one is using the product. Your role as a data scientist may not be to force the customer to use your product, but it is (usually) part of your job to help them use it properly. If they're not using it properly because they can't figure it out, a little encouragement may be good.

Sometimes talking with the customer isn't enough. If you want to get to know how they're using the product, you may need to spend some time with the customer while they're working. As they work with the product, it might be enough to observe—you certainly don't want to interfere with how they normally use the product—but it can be good to ask them questions as they go along. Particularly if they do something unexpected, you might want to ask them why they performed that action, but it's important not to direct them or otherwise show them how to do anything until you fully understand why they've performed the action they did. With understanding, you may be able to fix a root cause of the misuse instead of a symptom.

For instance, if the customer clicks the wrong button in the product, instead of saying, "I think you clicked the wrong button," it would be better to ask, "Why did you click that button?" and try to understand their reasoning. Let's say the customer is clicking a button labeled SUBMIT in order to make changes to a name-address pair inside a database, when you think they should be clicking a button labeled UPDATE. If you ask them why they clicked SUBMIT instead of UPDATE, they might say that they thought UPDATE was for the special case when they wanted to change only the address of an existing entry but leave the name unchanged.

You designed the application so SUBMIT adds a new entry and UPDATE changes an existing one. Because the customer wanted to change an existing entry, they should have clicked UPDATE instead of SUBMIT. If you had instructed them to click the other button, you would have learned little, but now you know the reasoning behind their actions. You might then explain that SUBMIT is for creating new name-address entries, whereas UPDATE is for modifying existing entries no matter which part of the entry they want to change. By clicking SUBMIT they've created a new, correct entry, but the old, incorrect entry still exists. More important, you've learned that the words *SUBMIT* and *UPDATE* aren't clear enough to the customers, so it might be worth changing them or further educating the customers about the differences between the two buttons.

How to remedy it

Once you've recognized and diagnosed the root causes of improper use of the product, there are two ways to remedy them:

- Educate and encourage the customers to use the product in the correct way.
- Modify the product so that it is clearer which actions are correct.

Further educating customers might include writing new documentation and delivering it to them. It might also include holding seminars, workshops, or one-on-one sessions in which you personally guide them through the proper protocols for product use. Which way will be more effective will depend highly on the situation.

Modifying the product to encourage proper use is a question of user experience (UX), which I cover next. A UX problem might be causing improper product use, but there's always a gray area between "the UX isn't very good" and "the users are using it wrong." In the end, the goal is to make the product effective, so UX changes that enable that can be a good idea, even if they seem wrong for other reasons. When in doubt, consult a UX expert.

12.1.2 UX problems

Beyond the case of customers using the product incorrectly in some way, they may be using it inefficiently. They can use the product to do the things they need to do, and they can solve problems with it, but it's taking more time or effort than it should. Addressing the user experience directly can help improve inefficiency.

A product can be inefficient in a few ways. One such way is having extraneous steps in a workflow. Let's say that your customer typically performs a query within the product and then always sorts the results in a particular way. If the results weren't sorted that way by default, then the customer would need to perform the sort step in addition to the query. The extra time and effort can add up if the customer performs the query tens or hundreds of times per day. Changing the default sort method could make the product more efficient.

The product could also be inefficient, in some sense, if it was designed to do many things, but the customer uses only a couple of those things often. For example, perhaps you performed some complex genetic analyses of several stages of fruit fly development from embryo to adult, and you delivered to the customer a report as well as a multisheet spreadsheet containing results from each of those stages. You then find out that 95% of the time the customer finds a specific entry in the adult data and then cross-references it with the other stages of development. It wasn't clear to you before you designed the spreadsheet that the customer would be spending so much time specifically on the adult stage, but now it's clear that you could save the customer some time by adding an additional page that contains all the cross-references the customer would typically do. Adding even more pages for more cross-referencing might also make sense, but only if the customer might use them and there are few enough to keep the spreadsheet a manageable size.

The appearance or arrangement of a product and its interface might also lead to inefficiencies. These are some of the most straightforward questions in UX and UI design:

- Is the text easy to read and well formatted?
- Are the buttons and text boxes in places that make them easy to use?
- Are keyboard shortcuts available for commonly performed actions?
- Is everything easy to find and easy to use?

UX and UI design extend far beyond these questions in both scope and detail, though the last question is something of a catchall in looking for UX issues. Beyond the most obvious cases, it's often best to consult a UX expert.

HOW TO RECOGNIZE THEM

It can be easy to miss some UX problems, particularly if you've designed and built the product yourself. You may have to give the product to someone else before you realize that the interface has significant flaws.

One strategy is to diagnose UX flaws through the customer. You might ask them questions such as the following:

- Have you found the product easy to use?
- Is there anything in the product you found difficult to do?
- What are the most common tasks you find yourself doing?
- How often do you use each part of the product?

If, given the answers you receive, you still suspect that that there may be some UX issues, it might be good to spend some time with the customer observing how they work, as I described previously.

For a more thorough treatment of the UX and your customer's workflows, you can bring in a UX professional. Their education and experience lie somewhere in the areas of technology, design, and psychology, and they'd likely want to work directly with the customer to learn everything they can about product use and workflows before making recommendations about what is good, what is bad, and what improvements might be made.

As with most product-related problems, you can either deal with a UX problem or change the product. Assuming that the problem doesn't make the product unusable, it's a viable option to educate customers about how to work around the issue, or they may be able to figure it out for themselves. The other option, changing the product, presumably involves more of your time for redesign and development, and the choice of remedy involves weighing the time-and-effort benefits of changing the product against the customer's time and effort saved when compared to the workaround. See section 12.3, later in this chapter, for more on what that process entails.

12.1.3 Software bugs

A bug is something that's wrong with the software. This is in contrast with a UX problem, which causes a product to be unintuitive but not necessarily wrong. Examples include the following:

- Incorrect numerical results from calculations
- Error messages or crashes in the software
- Improperly displayed text, tables, images, and the like
- Buttons or other action-based objects that do nothing

This is obviously not an exhaustive list, but it should be illustrative for those who have little experience dealing with software bugs.

HOW TO RECOGNIZE THEM

Many software development teams, before they deliver software to their customers, conduct a bug bash in order to find and later fix bugs in the software. In a *bug bash*, several people—perhaps the whole development team plus some product-oriented people not on the team—take an hour (or some fixed amount of time) to bash on the software, trying to break it. Bug bashers might click every button in the software, enter crazy values into text boxes (negative numbers, absurdly large numbers, words where numbers should be, and so on) and see if they can make the software crash, give an unwanted error message, or otherwise do something it's not supposed to do. Each time they succeed in finding a bug, they record the details so that it can be fixed before the software is released to the customer.

If you and your colleagues don't find bugs yourself, your customers will probably do it for you. They're good at that. By that, I mean that because they haven't been involved with the product from design to development, they have far fewer prejudices and conformant behaviors than you do. Therefore, they'll try to do things with the software that you didn't foresee, opening up the range of activities in which bugs might be discovered.

HOW TO REMEDY THEM

Because bugs, by definition, are mistakes in software, you usually have little choice but to fix them. On the other hand, if a bug is hard to fix and customers rarely encounter it, you might be able to justify not fixing it. This is more common than I'd like to admit. If you have a favorite piece of widely used software that has a public bug-reporting system (Ubuntu and Bitbucket are good examples), you can find some examples of bugs that are years old, because they're reasonably hard to fix and they affect few users. Though bugs are generally taken more seriously than UX flaws, the decision about whether to fix a bug comes down to comparing the time and effort to fix it with the cost to the customer of leaving it in.

12.1.4 *The product doesn't solve real problems*

This might be one of the worst outcomes for a product: you've spent time designing and developing a product that meets all the customer's descriptions of what they do, what they want, and what the problems are, but for some reason the product that you made isn't helping the customer achieve their goals. It's not a good feeling to have this happen. Assuming that the mismatch between the product and the goals isn't caused by incorrect use, UX problems, or software bugs, the product must fall short in some more profound way.

For example, while working at a startup analyzing organizational communications within financial firms subject to SEC regulation, my team developed statistical methods for detecting risky behaviors and incorporated them into the software product. Our customers wanted to find bad or suspicious employees who may be involved in illegal trafficking of privileged information, internally or externally, such as that which might be used for insider trading of securities. We built a framework for creating behavioral profiles for combinations of suspicious activity that compliance officers might be looking for in a potential lawbreaker. These profiles could be translated into the risky behaviors that the statistical models could detect, and a list of the most suspicious employees was generated for each behavioral profile.

We thought this would answer many questions that financial regulatory compliance departments had, and all potential-customer feedback to that point seemed in agreement with that assumption. But when the initial set of compliance officers got their hands on it, they were underwhelmed with the behavioral profiling and detection of risky behaviors. Many of them continued to use their old tools for compliance, which mostly comprised scanning a random sample of internal communications looking for suspicious words and phrases. There didn't seem to be any significant flaws in UX or any major bugs, but the customers didn't feel the product answered their main questions.

In retrospect, I'm convinced that the product made it most of the way to the answers the customers wanted but fell short of satisfactory in the minds of the compliance officers. It seems that they wanted one of two things:

- Statistical methods that tell them, without much doubt, who the bad guys are
- A better way to search and filter communications and employees

Unfortunately our statistical methods weren't good enough yet to fulfill the first item, and having complex statistical methods facilitate a better filter as in the second seemed to create cognitive dissonance between trusting those statistical methods and the expectation of deterministic behavior in searches and filters. Said another way, if the customers couldn't trust the statistical methods completely, they would rather use methods that they understand completely, such as simple searches and filters. This wasn't entirely obvious to anyone involved with the project until after the product had been built and delivered.

The good news—if it can be called that—is that we learned a lot by delivering the product and getting reactions from the customers. The reactions, and the fact that more than one customer had the same reaction, taught us more about our customers and the industry we were selling to than any other interactions with customers that we'd had before.

All wasn't lost; large parts of the software product were usable even without the behavioral profiling, in particular the pieces that managed, stored, and queried data. But with respect to the product interface, the development team had to perform one of the fabled pivots for which startups are so famous. The UI, which had been built around behavior profiles, had to be redesigned to something the customers were interested in using. Thankfully, we knew a lot more about our customers at this point than we had only a few months before, due mainly to the delivery of the product and the subsequent rejection of it.

Each case like this, in which a product fails to achieve its main goals, can be quite different from the others. A large number of variables come into play. Sometimes you can bridge the gap by educating the customers and convincing them that—as in my example—the statistical models are trustworthy for filtering and sorting. Sometimes you have to make dramatic changes in the product. But assuming that customers have started using the product, recognizing that there is a problem isn't difficult.

HOW TO RECOGNIZE IT

This one is easy: when the customer starts using the product, if there's a problem, they will either complain or stop using the product. Once you've talked to the customer long enough to rule out improper use, UX, and significant bugs, you'll soon realize if your product has missed its goals.

HOW TO REMEDY IT

This one is tough. Every case is different, but you can use the newfound knowledge about what the customer wants to make your most informed product decisions yet. Options usually include further education of the customer, changing the product, building a new product, and finding a different kind of customer for the product you already have. Depending on your situation, some of these may make more sense than others, but one thing is certain: you should consider all options thoroughly before making a decision.

12.2   Feedback

Getting feedback is hard, and I mean that in both senses of the phrase. On the one hand, it's often difficult to get constructive feedback from customers, users, or anyone else. On the other hand, it can be hard to listen to feedback and criticism without considering it an attack on—or a misunderstanding of—the product that you've spent a lot of time and effort building. In this section, I discuss how any feedback, except in rare cases, is a good thing, and I share some advice about making the most of the feedback that you get.

12.2.1   Feedback means someone is using your product

If you're getting feedback on the product, someone is using the product, which is good. It's surprising to me how many times in my life I've seen someone build a product that doesn't get used. The reasons it wasn't used vary, but they include the following:

- Customers didn't have the time to learn to use the product.
- The customer who asked for the product wasn't a user, and the users resisted integrating the product into their workflow or weren't satisfied by it.
- The product addressed a moving goal, and by the time it was developed, the goal had moved too far for the product to be useful.

Whatever the reasons why customers might not use the product, if you're receiving feedback from someone, those reasons don't apply, which is good.

12.2.2   Feedback is not disapproval

Unless a person is being unconstructive or downright mean, their feedback should not be taken as an insult to you or your product. Most people on this Earth love to make suggestions for how other people can do things better; in my experience, this is particularly true of engineers, software or otherwise. They don't mean any harm, and some of their suggestions might be useful.

This probably has more to do with business etiquette than it does data science, but you can learn much useful information if you can listen to feedback without taking it personally. It's difficult, though, to spend months building something and then hear someone tear it down after using it for 10 minutes, and I've seen more than one developer or data scientist vehemently defend a product against the smallest of suggestions; that's why I'm mentioning this here. In these situations, I stand by the maxim "Cooler heads prevail."

You don't have to take every comment and every suggestion to heart, but it's usually worth it to listen. Afterward, you might consider the person's knowledge and expertise before deciding whether to take their feedback seriously. I probably wouldn't take the CEO's advice on statistical methods unless they had a statistics degree, and likewise I wouldn't take a statistician's advice in business matters unless they had some relevant experience. Anyone and everyone might have some suggestions that could improve the product, and someone who can listen and consider calmly has a much better chance of achieving product greatness than those who can't.

12.2.3 Read between the lines

While you're busy listening to anyone and everyone's feedback, there's a sort of post-processing step you can use to gain even more information. It's not completely precise, but it can be boiled down to a few concepts that should be considered together:

- What people say isn't always precisely what they mean.
- What people say is a reflection of who they are and what experiences they have.
- What people say about a situation is based on their own perceptions and not necessarily on reality.

These are nebulous statements, I know, and they don't apply strictly to data science, but they are worth considering. Any time you're considering taking someone's suggestion to change a product, it can be valuable to consider who they are and where they're coming from before devoting time and effort to the change. I explain these three points in the following subsections.

WHAT THEY MEAN

If someone uses your web application and they say, "You should add a tab called Search and it should search all the available data," taking their suggestion literally may not be the best idea. Probably they mean to say, "I would like to be able to search all the data," but they may not be concerned about the search functionality coming in the form of a tab, a page, or a page header. Taking the person's suggestion literally without considering which parts of the suggestion are important may be a mistake. They may not have considered all potential UX solutions before suggesting an extra tab, even if the suggestion of a search capability is a good one.

Similarly, when I was working at the startup developing a product analyzing organizational communications within financial firms, discussed earlier in this chapter, we often heard the suggestion that the users shouldn't have to define behavioral profiles for the suspicious types they were looking for. The need for the user to define these profiles was a hindrance to the use of the product, and we received requests for a set of generic profiles that could be used without user input. We came to understand after a short time that it was too much effort for users to construct profiles, despite the fact that the typical users of the product knew far more about the suspicious types they were looking for than we did as data scientists and software developers. We began interpreting "You should include a set of generic behavioral profiles" as "We don't want to put time and effort into developing behavioral profiles." The latter statement is more definitive and direct, and understanding it that way prevented us from developing the requested generic profiles that we knew wouldn't be specific enough to give acceptable results.

It's more art than science, but being able to distinguish what a customer says from what they mean can save significant time and effort in product revisions.

WHO THEY ARE

It may be obvious that a person's identity and experience affect the things they say. In software-related industries, I've noticed a few patterns in how people in certain roles think. Certainly not everyone conforms to these descriptions, but for whatever reason—common basis of education, experience, objectives, and so on—people in the following roles generally tend to share a few opinions and biases:

- *Salespeople and business developers* want everything to be easier and more clear-cut. Their feedback might seem to trivialize statistics and software engineering in favor of making everything easier to understand. They want the product to solve the customer's problem directly, in one step (which is rarely possible).

- *Software engineers* want to make everything more efficient, and they want to add every capability. Their feedback might include phrases like "You could make it faster if...," "If you just _____, it could also do...," and "Does it do _____? Why not?" They want the product to handle all of the edge cases of every potential user and with exabytes of data.

- *Other data scientists* want to make the analytics smarter and the data-driven graphics impossibly informative. Their feedback might include "Which statistical methods did you use? Oh." and "You could probably visualize that by...." They want the product to give academic-quality results for every use case and to have enough flexibility for powerful statistical analysis.

- *Subject matter experts* mainly want their problem solved; they have little experience with software or data science but are willing to learn what they need, to an extent. Their feedback is usually reserved and inquisitive, such as "Can I do _____?" and "How do I _____?" Because they want their problem solved, they're open to almost any strategy or method unless they realize the product can't solve their problem.

I hope that these are useful lenses through which you can consider feedback from people in various business roles, even though they obviously aren't perfect. All feedback can be important, but the question of whether to act on it depends heavily on whether your goals align with the giver of the feedback.

THEIR PERCEPTION

It's important to consider what someone observed about the product and the addressable problem before they gave their feedback.

While working with a startup recently, an adviser suggested that, for the complex analytic component that I built, we should stop using the file system for intermediate storage and instead put intermediate and final results into a database. I understood his thinking: clearly, databases are faster than a file system for all but the simplest reads and writes, so it would be an obvious improvement to switch to a database, regardless of which type. In addition to that, we were working with many terabytes of data, which was a lot in 2015. This wasn't the first time that I'd received this advice, so I had experience dealing with the arguments on both sides. Given my experience, I wasn't tempted to follow it. My reasons for not following the advice at the time were these:

- A database is a software component that must be configured and managed on every environment, whether during testing or during a live customer deployment. That's a significant amount of work and maintenance.
- I was the only person who was developing or maintaining the code for this analytic software component, and I didn't have a lot of experience with multiple deployments of databases.
- The file system storage was working quite efficiently.
- I performed some code profiling and found that the majority of the time was spent calculating things and not on storage. Switching to a database would entail, at best, less than a 2x efficiency improvement.

The startup adviser who had recommended that we switch to a database—any database—didn't know any of these facts. As the data scientist and developer, I was privy to these facts, and I knew he wasn't, so I was able to consider his comments in the context of what he knew and what he didn't. I knew it would be a lot more work for me during each deployment if we switched to a database, and we didn't have the money to hire anyone else, so it was more sustainable to go without. Many software engineers might disagree with me, but I was laser focused on getting the correct results from the software and less concerned with whether it took 1.5x longer than it could.

It would be incredibly difficult to characterize *how* every person's perception might differ from yours, but I'd like to stress that every person's perception differs from yours, at least a little. Their feedback should be viewed through the lens of what they know about the product and the situation.

12.2.4 Ask for feedback if you must

Some data scientists deliver products and forget about them. Some data scientists deliver products and wait for customers to give feedback. Some data scientists deliver products and bug those customers constantly. I don't want to imply that the last category is the best, but it's often a good idea to follow up with your customers to make sure that the product you delivered addresses some of the problems that it was intended to address. There are two main reasons why you might want to do this.

REPUTATION

The first reason you might want to follow up with your customer is that, presumably, it's good for your reputation and that of your team and employer (if any) that your projects are successful and that your customers are satisfied. Certainly, it's not fun to spend weeks or months building something that isn't useful, which is a shame. But far more important than that, the project was a crucial part of your work and should reflect the quality of work that you do in general and what customers can expect in the future. Following up with customers allows you to address any concerns—in particular, the easy-to-solve ones—and greatly improve customer satisfaction.

LEARNING OPPORTUNITY

In asking for feedback from your customers—playing the long game—you can improve yourself and your skills in data science. When delivering a product to a customer, there aren't many ways in which you can figure out where you went wrong and where you were successful without talking to that customer. Asking them how things went—thoroughly, as described throughout this chapter—provides one of the only insights to the success or failure of the product that you designed and built.

12.3   *Product revisions*

Every product developer wishes they could deliver their product to the customer, the product solves all of the customer's problems, and everyone lives happily ever after. That rarely happens. As with every step of the data science process, the initial phase of product usage is subject to uncertainty. Usually there are problems. Sometimes, as discussed earlier in this chapter, those problems can be fixed or alleviated by working with the customer to help them use the product more effectively. But in other cases, problems arise that are either difficult or impossible to solve by training the customer to work around them. Revising or changing the product in some way then becomes the best—or only—option.

Earlier in this chapter, I discussed different types of problems with the product that might occur and how they might be fixed. In some cases, I suggested that the problems could be fixed by changing or revising the product itself. Making product revisions can be tricky, and finding an appropriate solution and implementation strategy depends on the type of problem you've encountered and what you have to change to fix it. In this section, I discuss product revisions as a direct result of prior uncertainty about some aspects of the project, the processes of designing and engineering revisions, and the decision of which product revisions to make in order to maximize the project's chance of success.

12.3.1   *Uncertainty can make revisions necessary*

If, throughout the project, you've maintained awareness of uncertainty and of the many possible outcomes at every step along the way, it's probably not surprising that you find yourself now confronting an outcome different from the one you previously expected. But that same awareness can virtually guarantee that you're at least close to a solution that works. Practically speaking, that means you never expected to get everything 100% correct the first time through, so of course there are problems. But if you've been diligent, the problems are small and the fixes are relatively easy.

It might even be the case that you knew that there was some chance that these exact problems would arise, and you may have even planned for that possible outcome. If this is true, you must have maintained incredible awareness throughout the project, and now you're in an excellent position to find and enact tenable solutions to the problems. If you didn't foresee these problems, you're in the vast majority; knowing that there is uncertainty isn't the same as knowing which outcomes might come to be. But now that you know which problems did pop up (and which successes) after product delivery, you're in a better, more informed position than ever from which to achieve the project's main goals. It will, however, take further effort from you to design and build the necessary product revisions.

12.3.2 Designing revisions

By *designing revisions* I mean the process of figuring out what product revisions are necessary and what form they should take. The design process conceptually identifies and imagines product changes without making them.

Designing a revision is largely the same as designing a product in the first place, except that there's already a product in existence, hopefully most of which you can still use. But although you may be able to continue to use large parts of the existing product, it may be best not to. To borrow a term from finance, the time and effort spent on anything that you've already built are *sunk costs*, so the costs of building the existing product shouldn't be considered when making future decisions. You can consider the existing product as an asset at your disposal when making those decisions.

Earlier in this chapter, I talked about recognizing and finding a remedy for various types of problems with a product. At this point you should know generally what the problem is and how to fix it, but I didn't give many specifics about the remedy itself. Here I'll say a bit more about designing these remedies in the form of product revisions for three types of problems.

BUGS

From a design perspective, fixing a bug is trivial. Within a certain context, the software does something when it's obvious it should be doing something else. The design of the revision is to make the software stop doing the former and do the latter. The engineering of the revision, however, may not be so trivial.

UX PROBLEMS

UX problems are all about design. Tricky ones may require the help of a UX expert. Given that the first version of the product contained a UX problem, unless the problem and the specific solution are now obvious (which they sometimes are), it's entirely likely that a second try at a UX design will also be problematic. For nontrivial problems, it's probably worth putting more effort into a UX redesign than was put into the original design, and this usually requires the help of someone with UX experience. At the least, it's worth spending some time with the users to get a good impression of how they're using the product and how the problems arise.

PROBLEMS WITH FUNCTIONALITY

With respect to analytic software applications, I use the term *functionality* to mean any actions taking place behind the scenes—data collection, data flow, computation, storage, and so on—as well as the application's general ability to deliver information and results to a user. A problem with functionality can therefore be, for example, the application taking excessive time to deliver a result to a UI, an improper statistical model being used, or a crucial piece of data not being used properly.

Making revisions to a product's functionality often requires architectural changes, which can have consequences for many other aspects of the application. Such revisions shouldn't be taken lightly. It's often best to have discussions with everyone involved in the design and engineering of the product in order to run through the repercussions of making the revisions under consideration. For more complex analytic applications, it may not be entirely clear how dramatic and far-reaching any revisions might be, and it may take some investigation to find out.

When designing significant revisions in functionality, I typically gather all members of the team with key knowledge about the product and its architecture and follow these steps:

1. Plainly state a best-case revision, with respect to the end result for a user.
2. Get feedback from everyone present regarding the repercussions within the application.
3. Consider whether the best-case revision can be achieved or if some aspect of it is untenable.
4. Get estimates on time and effort required to make the desired changes.

These steps can be repeated for any number of suggested revisions. Then the revisions can be compared with each other based on time and effort required, closeness to the best case the revision was intended to achieve, and the overall impact to the product and the project's success.

12.3.3 Engineering revisions

By *engineering revisions* I mean the process of taking a revision design and building it into the product. For analytic applications, this means coding or incorporating new tools.

Like a product design, a product architecture can have considerable inertia, but it should be considered both a sunk cost and an asset. Many parts of the product's architecture may still be useful, but some of them may not. Deciding when to throw out a significant chunk of code can be a tough call, but it's sometimes the right thing to do.

On the other hand, there may be clever ways to use your current architecture to fulfill the requirements of a revision design. Use these clever solutions at your own risk. They may save you time now but may cost you significant time and effort later, should you ever need to make further revisions or additions to the product. If you find yourself considering a clever solution—a solution that cobbles together existing software components in a way that wasn't originally intended—it can be good to ask yourself and your team these questions:

- If I rebuilt the entire product, would I build it this way?
- Why not?
- Do the reasons why not apply to the current situation and indicate that I'm taking undue risk by engineering this clever solution?

A little bit of foresight here can go a long way. A single clever revision is usually OK, but a second round of revisions on top of a clever revision almost guarantees more, cleverer revisions, and the cycle of revisions can continue until the entire code base is so clever that no one knows how to fix or revise anything without unraveling the application like a ball of yarn.

Clever solutions notwithstanding, I'll say a bit more about engineering revisions based on a few types of problems.

BUGS

The lifecycle of a software bug is finding it, diagnosing it, and fixing it. Finding it is the easy part. Diagnosing the root cause of the bug can go either way, easy or hard, depending on how deep and how interrelated the bug is with respect to the application. Fixing the bug can also be easy or hard, and this level of difficulty can be independent of whether the bug was difficult to diagnose. Some bugs are diagnosed easily, but their fixes are anything but easy, and the opposite can also be true.

In most cases, making a product revision that includes bug fixes is straightforward. You diagnose and fix the bugs. Little design is involved, and there's barely a question of whether or how a bug should be fixed. But in some unfortunate cases, the diagnosis or fix for a bug is so incredibly complicated that it can't be accomplished in a reasonable timeframe, if at all. In these cases, you must make important decisions about the impact of the bug and whether you can work around it in some useful way. Tolerating a bug is never fun, but some bugs are stubborn enough that you have to let them stick around for a while—or forever—if for no other reason than business pressures dictate that the project must be brought to a close. Minimizing the impact of the bug then becomes the goal of the revision.

UX PROBLEMS

Revisions intended to fix UX problems are design heavy. Figuring out what to do is usually much harder than engineering the revision itself. Certainly some UX aspects require sophisticated engineering, but most don't. Many UI frameworks exist that enable various standard behaviors, and the vast number of software applications in existence makes it likely that someone has already built a UX similar to yours. Be sure to have your UX designer inspect your revisions thoroughly before you deliver them to the customer.

PROBLEMS WITH FUNCTIONALITY

Revisions addressing problems with functionality can have far-reaching consequences within your application. My comments on such revisions in section 12.3.2 also hold true here. It's best to gather the team and run through all consequences and repercussions of making various desired revisions.

Beyond the known or foreseen repercussions, other unexpected effects might appear as well. Changing an object in your software so that it has a new capability can change application behavior in every place in the code in which that object is used. Object-oriented programming is notorious (and beloved) for relying on side effects to get things done, some of which may not be obvious on first reading the code. For complex applications, software developers rely on unit tests and integration tests (among other types of tests) to help ensure that new bugs aren't introduced by software changes. If you're worried about introducing bugs during a revision (or even if you're not), it can be a good idea to include tests in your code.

Many software engineers argue (and I agree with them) that this is a late time to begin formal testing of your application code. Ideally you would have written tests as soon as you wrote any code, and you would always have 100% test coverage for your application. But being a data scientist and not a software developer, I rarely write tests as I write code for the first time. I usually adapt experimental or research code to make application code, and testing is an afterthought. It's only when I realize that I'll be making a series of revisions, and I worry that I'll break something in the process, that I begin writing tests. It may not be an ideal workflow, but it's what I tend to do. In any case, it's better to write tests late than to write them never, and this point in the process is a good time to include them if you haven't already. Ask an experienced software engineer or consult any popular software testing reference for more information on using testing to help prevent the introduction of bugs during development or revision of your product.

12.3.4 *Deciding which revisions to make*

Once you recognize a problem with the product and figure out how it can be fixed, there remains the decision of whether to fix it. The initial inclination of some people is that every problem needs to be fixed; that isn't necessarily true. There are reasons why you might not want to make a product revision that fixes a problem, just as there are reasons why you would. Here are some examples.

Here are some possible reasons in favor of making a revision:

- You'll have a better product, a more satisfied customer, and a more successful project.
- You're contractually obligated to make certain types of fixes or improvements.
- Future projects, products, or revisions depend on this one, and making a revision now will improve the quality of those.
- The customer is willing to pay more for the revision.
- The customer is asking for a revision, and granting the request will help you maintain or improve your relationship with the customer.

And here are some possible reasons against making a revision:

- The revision doesn't improve the product much.
- The revision is difficult or time consuming to make.
- Your contractual obligations have already been fulfilled, and you feel that the product is, as they say, "good enough for government work."
- You suspect the customer won't notice the problem or won't be significantly affected by it.

Here are some variables that you should generally take into account:

- Time and effort required to make the revision
- The real impact of the revision on the product and its efficacy
- Contractual obligations
- Other possible revisions and their impacts, time, and effort
- Conflicting obligations of the development team

The final decisions, like many decisions, boil down to weighing the pros and cons for each side and then making the call. In my experience in software development and data science, the important thing is to stop and consider the options rather than blindly fixing every problem found, which can cost a lot of time and effort.

Exercises

Continuing with the Filthy Money Forecasting personal finance app scenario first described in chapter 2, and relating to previous chapters' exercises, try these:

1 Suppose that you've finished your statistical software, integrated it with the web app, and most of the forecasts appearing in the app seem to be incorrect. List three good places to check to try to diagnose the problem.

2 After deploying the app, the product team informs you that it's about to send selected users a survey regarding the app. You may submit three open-ended questions that will be included in the survey. What would you submit?

Summary

- Customers tend to find completely new ways to break your product.
- The process of recognizing, diagnosing, and fixing problems in the product should be undertaken deliberately and carefully.
- Getting feedback is helpful, but it shouldn't be taken at face value.
- Product revisions should be designed and engineered with the same level of care (or more) as when you designed and built the product itself.
- Not every problem needs fixing.

Wrapping up:
putting the project away

This chapter covers

- Cleaning up, documenting, and storing project materials
- Making sure you or someone else can find and restart the project later
- Project postmortem reflection and lessons
- A project as data science experience and its products as tools

Figure 13.1 shows where we are in the data science process: wrapping up the project. As a project in data science comes to an end, it can seem like all the work has been done, and all that remains is to fix any remaining bugs or other problems before you can stop thinking about the project entirely and move on to the next one (continued product support and improvement notwithstanding). But before calling the project done, there are some things you can do to increase your chances of success in the future, whether with an extension of this same project or with a completely different project.

There are two ways in which doing something now could increase your chances of success in the future. One way is to make sure that at any point in the future you

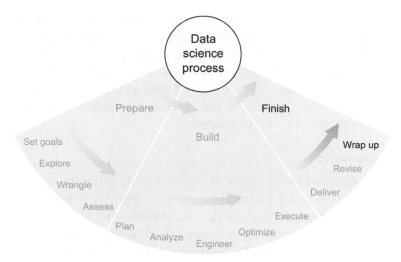

Figure 13.1   The final step of the finishing phase and the final step overall of the data science process: wrapping up the project neatly

can easily pick up this project again and redo it, extend it, or modify it. By doing so you will be increasing your chance of success in that follow-on project, as compared to the case when a few months or years from now you dig up your project materials and code and find that you don't remember exactly what you did or how you did it. Another way to increase your chances of success in future projects is to learn as much as possible from this project and carry that knowledge with you into every future project. This chapter focuses on those two things: packing away a project neatly and reusably and learning as much as possible from the project as a whole.

13.1   Putting the project away neatly

It can be tempting to put a project out of your mind after your to-do list is done and there are no more tasks on the horizon. You usually have other projects pending, and you'd rather use your time to make progress with those instead of dwelling on a project that has been completed. But there are three future scenarios, among others, in which you'll be happier if you take the time now to make sure project materials are organized and in a safe place:

- Someone has a question about the project, its data, its methods, or its results.
- You begin an extension or a new project based on this project.
- A colleague begins an extension or new project based on this project.

None of these cases appears daunting if it occurs immediately after the project in question. But if some time has passed—months or years—it becomes increasingly challenging to remember details. If you can't remember them, you'll need to consult the project materials to find answers. How much time and effort it takes you to do this depends entirely on how organized you were when wrapping up the project.

In this section, I'll discuss thinking ahead to these future scenarios, but first I'll cover the two practical concepts most relevant to putting a project away neatly: documentation and storage. To save yourself time and effort in the future scenarios I mentioned, you should make sure your project materials are easy to find (storage) and easy to understand (documentation).

13.1.1 Documentation

Project documentation can be thought of in three levels, depending on who might use it and how much technical expertise is required to understand it. Customers or users see the top-level documentation, whereas only software engineers building the product generally see the bottom-most level of documentation, and in the middle is technical documentation for folks who need to know how the software works but won't need to modify it. Much like in designing and building a product, knowing your audience is helpful in creating documentation.

USER DOCUMENTATION

The top level, *user documentation*, is what a customer would see in the product or in materials accompanying the product. This includes any reports, results summaries, and text and descriptions in any applications you built and delivered. User documentation should contain whatever information is necessary for someone to use your product in the way you intended. It's the conceptual equivalent of the information needed to drive a car, without any reference to car maintenance or how to build a car.

User documentation might include the following:

- How to use the product
- The product's main capabilities and limitations
- Any non-obvious information that might help the user
- Warnings against using the product in ways known to cause problems

Typically, user documentation appears either in the product itself or in materials that accompany the product. Some common forms of user documentation include the following:

- A help page within a web application
- A written document that's given to all users explaining how to use the product
- A wiki or other resource provided for users

In general, the scope of user documentation doesn't extend past the user interface or anything else that wasn't explicitly intended for the customers and users to see. Information about how the product works behind the scenes should be reserved for lower-level documentation.

DEVELOPER DOCUMENTATION

The middle level, *developer documentation*, consists of information that a software developer would want to know if they were going to integrate with or programmatically use the product, or if they were going to build something similar themselves. Developer documentation should describe architecture and interfaces without delving too much into specific software implementations. It's a complete surface-level description plus a conceptual internal description, of the same nature as the information needed to perform an oil change or replace the brakes on a car, without being too concerned with how the car was built. When changing the oil, it might be helpful to know that there is an engine inside the car and that the engine is connected to the gas tank, but the specific construction of these—including timing belts, pistons, valves, and more—is largely irrelevant to the task.

Developer documentation might include the following:

- Thorough descriptions of APIs and other points of integration
- Specific statistical methods that were implemented
- High-level descriptions of software architecture or object structure
- Data inputs and outputs, with content and format descriptions

Developer documentation doesn't usually appear within the product itself, except when the product's users are software developers. Here are some common forms of developer documentation:

- A wiki, a Javadoc, a pydoc-generated document, or other document describing an API
- A README file in the code repository
- A diagram or other description of the software architecture or object model
- A technical report describing the statistical methods used
- A written or graphical description of data sources and formats
- Examples of code that integrates or programmatically uses the software product

In general, developer documentation, as I'm using the term here, describes the inner workings of the software product or methods without necessarily getting into the product code and detailed structure.

CODE DOCUMENTATION

The lowest level of documentation, *code documentation*, tells a software developer on the product development or maintenance team how the code works at the lowest level, so that they can fix bugs, make improvements, or extend the capabilities of the product. In the context of my earlier automotive comparisons, the equivalent of code documentation explains how to fix, disassemble, reassemble, and tune any part of the car, inside and out. A funny but apt aspect of this comparison is that this low-level documentation says nothing about how to drive the car. Driving a car and fixing a car require nearly mutually exclusive sets of knowledge, though admittedly they aid one another. The same is true for code documentation and user documentation. There may be a little overlap, but generally speaking they'll be different.

Code documentation may include the following:

- Descriptions of objects, methods, functions, inheritance, usage, and so on
- Highly detailed descriptions of object structure and architecture
- Explanations about why certain implementation choices were made

Code documentation usually accompanies the code itself or is somewhere close by. Some common forms of code documentation are these:

- Comments in the code alongside the thing they're describing
- READMEs or other documents in the code repo
- Software architectural diagrams
- Documentation generated automatically using Javadoc, pydoc, or other similar application

In general, code documentation should provide enough information for any developer on the product team to navigate, understand, and work with the code base in a reasonably efficient manner. Without good code documentation, such a developer would have to figure out how the code works the hard way: by reading the code itself. For sufficiently complex software products or code that isn't inherently readable, this is a rabbit hole no one wants to find oneself in.

13.1.2 Storage

By *storage*, I mean the ways in which you might store all material—code, documentation, data, results, and the like. More convenient and navigable locations make it easier to find answers to questions that pop up later or to revive the project entirely if need be. In addition, safer, more reliable locations help ensure the continued existence of the materials well into the future.

In this section, I consider both the location in which the materials are stored and the format in which they're stored. Because I'm mixing these two concepts, the alternatives listed might not be direct replacements for one another, but it's often difficult to separate the location from the format—for example, with remote Git repos—so I outline the capabilities of each so that it's clear which alternatives can be used for what purpose.

LOCAL DRIVE

Usually the easiest place to store your code, data, and other files, your local computer is a reasonable choice for projects that aren't that important. But there are serious risks and limitations when you're using only one machine and not backing up your files anywhere else. See table 13.1 for a summary of when and why to use a local drive.

Table 13.1 Benefits and risks of using a local drive for storage

Advantages	Disadvantages	Best for
Easy Convenient Can store any file formats You have complete control.	Limited disk space Single point of failure or loss in case you break or lose the computer No one else can access it without you.	Personal projects that are easy to redo Whenever you have a backup somewhere else

NETWORK DRIVE

A shared network drive at your place of work is often bigger than your local computer's drive, and it may also have regular backups to another location by the IT department. Usually you can connect to such a drive either by logging into the system or by using a computer that has been explicitly connected to the network and the drive. See table 13.2 for a summary of when and why to use a network drive.

Table 13.2 Benefits and risks of using a network drive for storage

Advantages	Disadvantages	Best for
Can store any file formats Managed internally, for example, by an IT department There is often plenty of space. Other people can access your files if you choose.	Limited access There may be a single point of failure if not backed up elsewhere. Can get disorganized if many people are using it	Projects shared between people Saving all of your files in one place without extra work

CODE REPOSITORY

I've mentioned source code repositories previously in this book, in conjunction with version control tools like Git. For anything but the most trivial coding projects, committing your code to a repo and pushing it to a remote location is strongly recommended. You or your organization can manage your own repo server, or you can use one of the popular web-based remote repo providers such as Bitbucket or GitHub. Not only does this provide a duplicate, managed location for your code to reside in, but it also provides a central location for viewing and sharing the code. See table 13.3 for a summary of when and why to use a code repository.

Table 13.3 Benefits and risks of using a code repository for storage

Advantages	Disadvantages	Best for
Great for sharing code and working on it together Remote servers function as both version control and as a backup copy.	It's not great for anything but code and other plain-text-based file formats. Repo software like Git can take some time to learn.	All code Plain-text-based files Whenever the history of changes may be important

READMEs

Though not technically a location or a format, a README is a text-based file that accompanies an application or code, typically residing in the same folder. Its format is generally some kind of markup language that can be read directly in any text editor or by an interpreter of the markup language. There can be multiple READMEs, one in each folder in the code or project structure, each describing what's in that folder. They can be committed to code repos as well, and both Bitbucket and GitHub provide nice facilities for viewing READMEs in certain formats (for example, the Markdown markup language, among others) directly in a web browser. I highly recommend providing READMEs with your code, including important developer- and code-level documentation. See table 13.4 for a summary of when and why to use READMEs.

Table 13.4   Benefits and risks of using READMEs

Advantages	Disadvantages	Best for
Lightweight format Resides in the same place as code Saved in all the same places as the code Markup languages enable reasonably good formatting.	The text-based format isn't as flexible as wikis and other more sophisticated document types. It's part of the code base and not that shareable without including code.	Documentation that isn't within the code itself but should always accompany the code

WIKI SYSTEM

Wikis are web-based systems designed for multiple, shared, interrelated documents that may be updated and expanded repeatedly. Wikipedia is the canonical example of a large system of wikis. Documents can be related to each other through links, and good wiki systems update all relevant links whenever a document's location changes, something you'd have to do by hand if you tried to use a less-sophisticated documentation system. See table 13.5 for a summary of when and why to use a wiki system.

Table 13.5   Benefits and risks of using a wiki system for documentation and storage

Advantages	Disadvantages	Best for
Handles links and references between documents better than other media Wiki markup languages allow fairly sophisticated formatting and page structure.	They can be tedious to set up and manage. Few good wiki products are free to use. Without active maintenance, wikis can get disorganized or cluttered.	Extensive non-code documentation with many links and references between documents Documents requiring more formatting or structure than plain text generally provides

WEB-BASED DOCUMENT HOSTING

Google (Drive/Docs) and Microsoft (Office 365), among others, offer online document and file hosting. These can be helpful for organizing files and documentation, as well as offer a browser-based document editor that's accessible from any computer. The documents hosted are generally in a few familiar formats: word-processing-style documents, spreadsheets, diagrams, graphics, and so on. You may also be able to upload other file types but not work with them through a browser. In that way, these can act as a plain remote backup server that's managed by the hosting company. See table 13.6 for a summary of when and why to use a web-based document hosting.

Table 13.6   Benefits and risks of using web-based document hosting for storage

Advantages	Disadvantages	Best for
Sophisticated word processing and spreadsheets Handles many file types Collaborative editing The major companies offer near-flawless reliability.	Not good for storing code Can get messy without some effort toward organization These systems have some quirks, for example, in the conversion from file to web version and vice versa.	Documents of the sort you might want to print or turn into a PDF Spreadsheets, diagrams, graphics, and some other specialized file types Printable user documentation

13.1.3   *Thinking ahead to future scenarios*

Now that I've talked about some available types of documentation and storage, I'll return to the three future scenarios I listed at the beginning of this section and discuss the implications of each on the choices you might make at the end of a project.

SOMEONE HAS A QUESTION ABOUT THE PROJECT

If you finished a project a while ago and someone comes to you with a question about the data, methods, or results and you don't know the answer offhand, you'll have to go fishing through the old materials. The questions to ask yourself, in order, are these:

1 Did you save the relevant materials somewhere?
2 If yes, can you find those materials now?
3 If you find the materials, can you find the answer to the question within them?

For the first question, let's hope the answer is yes. If you didn't save the materials, then you'll have little hope of answering the question. The lesson here is that you should always save your project materials in a safe place whenever there's any chance you'll need them in the future.

Question 2 deals with your ability to find everything you need to answer the question. Beyond the fact that you did save the materials, hopefully you saved them in a place that you remember (or can locate) and that's relatively convenient to access. If not, that's something to think about the next time you're finishing a project. Consider choosing one of the storage options I mentioned previously or another that has the reliability and convenience for keeping your project materials safe for years to come.

The organization and documentation of your materials is the crux of the third question. If all you have is a pile of files in your project folders and no document that describes them, you might have a tough time finding what you're looking for. And next time consider using a storage location and format that are appropriate for the types of materials you have. In addition, good user and developer documentation is crucial to being able to navigate project materials and to find definitive answers about details of the project. Without such documentation, some details of the project are bound to be forgotten. Some of them might be able to be inferred from code and tangential details, but some won't. To avoid loss of significant knowledge, it's best to capture whatever knowledge you can into documentation at the end of a project. Not only might it save you time and effort, but it may also ensure that customers and others don't lose faith in your work if they come back to you with questions later.

YOU BEGIN AN EXTENSION OR A NEW PROJECT BASED ON THIS PROJECT

As in the previous scenario, in which someone asks you a question about the completed project, this scenario requires that you can find and sort through all of your old materials. But here you'll need to be able to understand the materials on a deeper level. You'll need to understand the code or other aspects of the statistical software well enough to modify it or integrate something with it. This is a much bigger challenge than figuring out what was done and what the results were.

Specifically, knowing *what* code does and knowing *how* it does it are different things. If you're going to work with existing code, you'll need to know how the code works—or at least how part of the code works. User and developer documentation won't help much, but code documentation will. Without good code documentation or a reliable memory of how the code works, you'll have to read the code and decipher it yourself.

When finishing up a project, put yourself in the shoes of your future self and ask, "What parts of the code and software functionality might I find confusing in a year or two?" Be generous in your answer. Some things that seem obvious now might not seem obvious after you've been away from the project for a while.

At the least, you should go through each of the major parts of the code and document the first things that jump out at you as possibly becoming confusing later. A detailed set of instructions on how to use the product as well as a description of the overall software architecture can also be immensely useful.

A COLLEAGUE BEGINS AN EXTENSION OR NEW PROJECT BASED ON THIS PROJECT

If you can imagine what it would be like for you to revive your project at some point in the not-so-near future, think what it would be like for someone else to do the same—without you. What would happen then? In my experience, they would falter in the same points that you would, plus a few more because they weren't working on the project the first time around.

Put yourself in their shoes. What would they need to know in order to follow in your footsteps? You could comb through your code, find any examples of code that might be confusing, and write a comment about why you did it that way. That's the brute-force method, and it's not necessarily recommended unless you have exceptionally poorly readable code or you have a ton of time. More efficient and probably more helpful would be to think about which parts of the software are novel and would seem confusing to a completely unfamiliar eye. Do you do anything unconventional, like coding style, complex statistical methods, or any algorithmic tricks that improve performance in a non-obvious way? If so, you should document them.

Documenting your work for someone else is a far more thorough affair than documenting it for yourself. You have to think beyond your own conventions and your own perspectives. It might be a new colleague who is tasked with taking over the project. Maybe they know almost nothing about the history of the project, and they're suddenly supposed to understand it all and make some use of it.

Like working on the user experience of a piece of software, creating documentation is an exercise in empathy. If you can imagine what someone might not understand about the project and the code, you can write much better documentation on all levels by helping them understand. Imagine any software developers at your current employer—senior and junior—the data scientists who might come after you, the person at the next desk over; these people have any number of reasons not to understand your project, your documentation, or your code. But if you can put yourself in their shoes, you can begin to see which parts of your work they might not understand, and you can create the documentation that addresses that. Write the documentation—user, developer, and code—as if you were never going to return to the project, but someone else will. Create the documentation that they would need to continue with it without your input. If someone can take over the project without you helping, based on your documentation, you've succeeded.

13.1.4 *Best practices*

I take the following steps when documenting and storing project materials:

1 Skim the code, editing for organization and readability and adding comments for my future self and for others who might have to read it.
2 Write high-level READMEs for each major component of the code, explaining basic functionality and usage; include these with the code.
3 Commit the code to a Git repo and push it to a remote host such as Bitbucket.
4 Collect all project results, reports, and other non-code materials, and place them in a shared, reliable storage location; also include raw data if it's not too big.
5 Leave myself breadcrumbs to help find all the pieces again; for example, the main README could contain links to the locations of all the materials. Or I sometimes email myself all the information so that all links are in one place.
6 If I'm working on a team, I document the location of all the materials on the team's main documentation system, such as a shared wiki, where everyone can find it easily.

Much of this chapter was written as if documentation and storage are something you handle at the end of a project. It's better and easier (in the long run) to concern yourself with both starting from day one of the project. Documentation in particular will most likely be far better if you've been documenting things from the beginning. Here are a few things that I do throughout every project to improve the state of documentation and storage at the end:

- I commit all code and push it to a remote host as soon as the code is nontrivial.
- I don't write user or developer documentation until I'm fairly certain they won't need to be completely rewritten in the near future (documentation has a nasty habit of becoming obsolete).
- When I'm fairly certain that the user and developer experiences are stable, I write quick-and-dirty documentation for them.
- Every time I'm reading my code and I find a section that confuses me, even a little, I write a comment explaining the confusing part to myself.
- I put user and developer documentation either into READMEs or on a wiki, depending on their complexity and the other particulars of the situation.

Following these general guidelines has saved me much time and effort whenever I've had to return to an old project.

13.2 *Learning from the project*

I've covered some ways in which you can improve your chances of success if at some point in the future you have to revisit that project. Obviously, knowledge you gain from a project will help if you revisit that same project. But that same knowledge can also help you with other data science projects. To that end, it can be helpful to formally consider all the things you've learned from the project and then extract from these things some new knowledge that's applicable not only to this project.

Such knowledge might concern the technology you used. Was a piece of software better or worse than you expected? Did you use infrastructure that ended up causing you problems? The new knowledge could also relate to surprises you may have found in the data. Were your preliminary analyses and descriptive statistics thorough enough? Did your software crash because of unexpected values in data? In any case, there are things that you've learned and probably things that you'd do differently if you started the project again. Some of these are project specific, and some of them can be treated as lessons to be applied in future projects. By conducting a project postmortem, you can hope to tease out the useful lessons from the rest.

13.2.1 *Project postmortem*

A *project postmortem* is a formal consideration, after the project is over, of everything that happened during the course of the project, with the intent of learning some things that will help in future projects.

A funny thing about memory is that if you know a particular fact now, it can be hard to remember what it was like before you knew that fact. Figuring out what you've learned since the beginning of a project is not always easy. If you've been making notes throughout, though, the task can be much easier. In particular, the goals you set and the plan you made way back in chapter 6 can now provide a lot of insight into what you knew and what you thought you knew back then. Chapter 2 framed some questions whose answers would fulfill some fundamental goals of the project; these can be helpful as well.

REVIEW THE OLD GOALS

The goals that you stated in chapters 2 or 6 were based on the knowledge you had back then; you had no choice. If you can't remember what you didn't know then, maybe your goals from back then will betray your ignorance.

Let's revisit the beer-recommendation algorithm project from chapters 2 and 6. The main goal was to be able to recommend beers a user of the application would like, and to do that, you'd have to predict the score that a user of the application would give a particular beer they tried. Assume that you stated specific goals of achieving 90% accuracy on recommendations and a 10% standard error in score predictions and that you achieved neither of these.

What are some reasons why you failed to achieve those goals? One possibility is that the data set wasn't large enough or was too sparse to support such high accuracy. Perhaps there were hundreds of beers and hundreds of users, but the typical user had rated only 10–20 beers on average. It would be hard to predict the rating of a beer that few people had rated. Another possibility is that human taste and preference have a large variance and are inherently not predictable to the degree stated. Research supports this theory to an extent—unrecorded factors such as the context in which the person tried the beer and what they ate or drank beforehand can influence ratings beyond the 10% error rate you were striving for.

In any case, every goal that wasn't achieved has some main suspects for its demise. Pinning down a few of these can show you what you didn't know before and hence what you've learned since you stated the goal. Can what you've learned be applied to future data science projects? In the case where the data was too sparse, you might be more wary in the future of the promises of data sets and be less optimistic about the accuracy of results until you've proven them possible. In the case where you realized that human preference is fickle, you learned that some factors can't—or won't—be measured such that you can make use of them, and these factors can limit your accuracy and success. In future projects, you might be less ambitious or at least acknowledge the possibility that inherent and insurmountable variances might prevent you from achieving the goals.

REVIEW THE OLD PLAN

Like old goals, an old plan can tell you a lot about what you knew and what you were thinking at the time you made it. It can be helpful to look at it again to filter out what you've learned since then and again to consider whether what you've learned constitutes a lesson that you can carry into future projects.

Consider the plan for the beer-recommendation algorithm project that appears in figure 6.2 of chapter 6. This plan has two outcomes: either the accuracy goals were met or they weren't, and the user interface would depend on that outcome. One aspect of that plan that now seems a bit naïve is that it seems to imply that accuracy of the algorithm is by far the most important thing in the application. The entire product design depends on the accuracy achieved by the algorithm. There's nothing inherently wrong with this perspective, but it relies heavily on the data and the math. Good algorithms don't guarantee that users will show up in the application, and maybe there's another option that can make the application a success without requiring high accuracy predictions.

If the main goal of the project is to make an app that engages users and keeps them coming back, then it may not be entirely necessary for the algorithm to have near-flawless accuracy. Perhaps there's another way to engage users, and it might become obvious after releasing the app, but it wasn't obvious before. A more flexible plan that included as an option redesigning the app may have been a better choice. Market research wasn't part of the plan, but maybe it should have been; you can carry that lesson into future projects.

REVIEW YOUR TECHNOLOGY CHOICES

Beyond deviations from the goals and plans that you set earlier in the project, you may have learned something new about the technologies that you chose to use. Did the programming language you used cause problems at any point? Did you elect to use a database that caused more problems than it was worth? Were the statistical methods and the requisite software tools the right choice, or is it now clear that you should have chosen something else?

Sometimes software tools fulfill the promise of what you wanted them to do, but sometimes they fall short. Maybe you tried to use the Perl language to do some text parsing but then found it inordinately difficult to integrate the results with the rest of your application, which is written in Java. You ditched Perl and tried Python instead, finding that Python isn't quite as easy to use for text parsing, but it integrates more easily with Java applications. Your experience with each of these languages depends entirely on your knowledge and expertise with them, but in this scenario, you've learned about advantages and disadvantages of both languages.

Likewise, you may have included big data software like Hadoop or Spark in your original implementation, but did you need it? For experts, it's no problem to include these technologies in an application, but for others it's an additional workload to use these specialized tools in their applications. Was the extra effort in development and maintenance worth it?

Whenever you include new or somewhat unfamiliar technologies in a project, you stand to learn something about those technologies. In future projects, whatever you learn can be used to make better decisions about which tools to use for which task and why. It can be helpful to ask yourself now, "Did I make good technology choices, or do I now realize I could have done better?"

DO IT DIFFERENTLY NEXT TIME

Unless you're perfect, there probably was a time during the project when you realized you should have done something differently. It can be a learning experience to realize that another choice would have been better, but in many cases this realization is based on knowledge that you didn't have at the time you made the decision. If you can generalize that realization and carry it into future projects, it might be helpful.

It's tough to formalize the process of generalizing lessons from a specific project to the set of all future projects. If the lesson deals with software or other tools that you used, you can certainly apply that knowledge to future projects; for example, if a software tool turned out not to be as good as you thought, you probably shouldn't use it next time you're in a similar situation. But if the lesson concerns something more specific to the project, such as the data or the goals, it may not be easy to apply it in the future.

For example, it may have been impossible to know that people's preferences were too fickle to support 90% accuracy in beer recommendations, but for future projects it's possible to generalize that lesson and recognize that some accuracy benchmarks are unattainable. Assuming that better statistical analysis will give better results, to an arbitrarily accurate degree, is a fallacy. It's best to learn from lessons like that early and to proceed cautiously (but ambitiously) into future projects, when merely the awareness of the possibility of the same type of outcome can help you in your planning and execution.

Whether there's a specific lesson you can apply to future projects or a general lesson that contributes to your awareness of possible, unexpected outcomes, thinking through the project during a postmortem review can help uncover useful knowledge that will enable you to do things differently—and hopefully better—next time.

13.3 Looking toward the future

The project is over, all the materials are documented and in safe places, and a postmortem review unveiled a few lessons you can take with you into projects yet to come. Regardless of how successful the project was—let's hope it was a resounding success—one thing is certain: you have more experience in the field of data science.

It's clearly a truism: the more data science you do, the more experience you have. None of it guarantees that you've done good work or that you will in the future. But more experience does directly imply that you have more projects to learn from. Doing good data science depends highly on the experiences you've had and what you've learned from them. This is true for all scientific fields. You can know everything there is to know about statistics and software development, but with little experience it's hard to anticipate any of the multitude of uncertainties that affect every project in data science. If you can use all your past experience to foster an awareness of all the things that might go wrong in a given project, your chances of success in that project increase dramatically. You can plan a full set of alternatives and hedge your bets.

On the other hand, no matter how much you learn, you can't foresee everything. Data is unpredictable, or perhaps it's better to say that data always offers the possibility of something unexpected. Even if you can make accurate predictions 9 times out of 10—or 99 out of 100—things might change. The underlying system might start behaving differently, or maybe the data source could become less reliable. In either case, your experience might be able to help you figure out what the problem is, particularly if you can connect the current situation with any of your past projects and set a strategy accordingly.

Along with all the uncertainties in data science, one certainty is that software and other tools will continue to change. Every year, and practically every month, new and improved software tools appear on the market. Some of them are great; some are not. I'm a fan of staying with tools that have been proven to work for the task at hand; there are fewer uncertainties and generally more people who can help out when problems arise. New tools might be able to do something that nothing else can, but only in exceptional circumstances are exceptional tools necessary. If you stay up to date on new developments, though, and you utilize all your experience, you might recognize the moment when you need something entirely new and specialized. That isn't a common situation, but it does happen, and when it does it can lead to significant breakthroughs in analytical technologies. But that's the exception and not the rule.

Given the excitement surrounding many new software tools, the more difficult challenge is often to resist using them until they have an established track record. It's usually the cool thing to do to use the newest, most exciting software, but unless you can foresee the state of the industry in a few years, you might want to wait until you're sure that a particular tool is reliable and durable before you use it in your project. Unlike statistical methods, which can be proven correct or not, software is shown to be good or bad only through use. It's best to choose your software based on what you know and not on what you hope is true. With both statistics and software, you have to take care in what you choose, because both have a large effect on a project's results. New developments can affect your choices, but it's important to remember a fundamental difference between the two main aspects of data science: software changes all the time, but statistics are forever.

If you take away only one lesson from each project, it should probably relate to the biggest surprise that happened along the way. Uncertainty can creep into about every aspect of your work, and remembering all the uncertainties that caused problems for you in the past can hopefully prevent similar ones from happening again. From the data to the analysis to the project's goals, almost anything might change on short notice. Staying aware of all of the possibilities is not only a difficult challenge but is near impossible. The difference between a good data scientist and a great data scientist is the ability to foresee what might go wrong and prepare for it.

Exercises

Reflect on your past and present projects, and try these exercises:

1 Think of a project (data science or otherwise) you've worked on in the past, preferably more than a year ago. Where are the materials and resources related to that project? If someone asked you to repeat, restart, or continue that project today, would you be able to? Could you have done anything back then to make it easier today?

2 Consider your current job and place of employment. Where are shared resources kept? Can you find what you're looking for easily? If it were your job to come up with a detailed plan and policy for archiving completed projects, what would you include?

Summary

- Organizing project materials and storing them in a reliable place can spare you from headaches later if you have to revive the project for any reason.
- It's important to document the software and the methods so that you and your colleagues can understand every aspect of the project and work with it in the future.
- Documentation is an exercise in empathy; you have to imagine what you and others might not understand in the future and write explanations accordingly.
- Conducting a formal project postmortem can reveal many lessons that may not have been obvious otherwise.
- Every project offers many lessons to be learned, and many of them can be generalized to apply to almost any future data science project.
- Data science is mostly about recognizing when something unexpected might occur, and awareness of such uncertainties can make the difference between success and failure in future projects.

exercises:
examples and answers

Answers are listed by chapter below.

Chapter 2

1. What are three questions you would ask the product designer?

Some questions you might want to ask the product designer before getting started include:

- What are some examples of forecasts that you would like to be able to provide to FMI's app users?
- How do you imagine the users interacting with the forecasts?
- How do the forecasts fit in with the rest of the components in the app?

2. What are three good questions you might ask of the data?

Some example questions include:

- Is it possible to make reliable forecasts into the future?
- If so, how far into the future are the forecasts reliable?
- Is it possible to classify transactions such as withdrawals, purchases, and so on into various grades of "good" and "bad" in terms of their effect on the user's financial health, and to show how they affect forecasts?

3. What are three possible goals for the project?

Possible goals might include:

- A forecast that can reliably inform the user when an account balance will probably reach a certain level—for example, a bank account being empty, hitting a savings goal, or a credit card hitting the credit limit.

- Providing the users with suggestions for financial behavior changes to improve their forecasts.
- A visualization that conveys forecasts clearly and concisely.

Chapter 3

1. List three potential data sources that you expect would be good to examine for this project. For each, also list how you would expect to access the data (for example, database, API, and so on).

Data sources may include:

- FMI's internal databases; I would guess they are relational, SQL-based databases, but they could also be NoSQL as well.
- The APIs of the banks and other financial institutions from whom FMI originally pulls its data; these are probably XML- or JSON-based APIs.
- Users might provide some helpful data voluntarily, such as transactions, categories, or other attributes; these must be designed into the product, would originally be web actions, and could be put into FMI's internal database.

2. Consider the three project goals you listed in exercise question 3 in the last chapter. What data would you need in order to achieve them?

The goals would require, respectively:

- Making reliable forecasts would require several months (minimum) of complete transaction data for each relevant account, plus enough transaction attributes to classify them into various categories such as "repeating" or "one-time" transactions, in order to improve the accuracy of the forecasts.
- Providing suggestions to users would require the same as forecasts (previous bullet item), plus a more stringent requirement for transaction attributes and the ability to classify them. A longer history of data (one year?) might also be required.
- A data visualization may not have any special data requirements, but reliable transaction attributes would certainly help in cases where, for example, spending categories or transaction types are part of the visualizations.

Chapter 4

1. You're about to begin pulling data from FMI's internal database, which is a relational database. List three potential problems that you would be wary of while accessing and using the data.

It would be good to watch out for, for example:

- Missing, invalid, or incorrect values in the database.
- Names and other identifier-type strings that don't always match up between fields or tables—for example, having "John Public" in one place and "John Q

Public" in another. These are unequal strings that may or may not represent the same people.

- If you have to join some database tables, it's best to make sure that the field you are joining on matches the records well. I would check to see how many records from each table have properly matching records from the other table, and vice versa.

2. In the internal database, for each financial transaction you find a field called `description` containing a string (plain text) that seems to provide some useful information. But the string doesn't seem to have a consistent format from entry to entry, and no one you've talked to can tell you exactly how that field is generated or any more information about it. What would be your strategy for trying to extract information from this field?

My strategy would be something like:

a   Pull a manageable collection (a few hundred?) of transactions (a random set would be good) from the database, examine the description fields, and try to notice any patterns.

b   Ask myself: does the string seem to be mainly comma-separated, semicolon-separated, pipe-separated, JSON, or free-form? What characters or terms are repeated from entry to entry?

c   If I've diagnosed a format after all, check to make sure it applies to the whole collection I'm working with.

d   If there still doesn't seem to be a common format, focus on the aspects of the string that are most interesting to me. For example, if I am interested in the ZIP code of the transactions (and they appear nowhere else in the database), I examine how the ZIP codes are represented in the string. If each description string contains a substring such as `"ZIP code: XXXXX"`, then I could write a script that searches for the substring `"ZIP code:"`, captures the next characters, and records them as the ZIP code. I would try to use context (text around desired data) for all interesting nuggets I find within the description string.

e   If none of the above suffices to extract some specific information from the description string, I would begin to expand the elements of context and format that I use to detect and capture data within the string. If there isn't an obvious context such as a substring `"ZIP code:"`, I would try to figure out a combination of punctuation, separators, whitespace, and other format elements that distinguish the data from its neighbors. Perhaps the ZIP code is always the first five-digit number that always appears between two commas, as in `",XXXXX,"` or maybe it always appears directly after a two-letter state abbreviation, such as `"OH,XXXXX,"`. A script can easily find substrings meeting these patterns, but they might also capture unwanted data if I'm not careful.

Chapter 5

1. Given that a main goal of the app is to provide accurate forecasts, describe three types of descriptive statistics you would want to perform on the data in order to understand it better.

Some useful descriptive statistics might be:

- The typical, minimum, and maximum number of transactions per month for the set of financial accounts you intend to forecast. More transactions would be more informative for statistical forecasting methods.
- The variances or some other measures of fluctuation of account balances. Smaller variances likely make it easier to forecast.
- A set of plots of account balances over time for randomly chosen accounts. Looking at plots can provide far more information than mean and variance. It can also give you a good feeling for account balance behavior and get you thinking about statistical methods that might be helpful for forecasting.

2. Assume that you're strongly considering trying to use a statistical model to classify repeating and one-time financial transactions. What are three assumptions you might have about the transactions in one of these two categories?

Some possible assumptions are:

- Repeating transactions occur weekly, monthly, or on some other regular interval.
- Repeating transactions have the same label, name, or other identifying attribute in every instance.
- One-time transactions are usually larger than the average transaction, in cases such as vacations, large purchases, windfalls, and so forth.

Chapter 6

1. Suppose that your preliminary analyses and descriptive statistics from the previous chapter lead you to believe that you can probably generate some reliable forecasts for active users with financial accounts that have many transactions, but you don't think you can do the same for users and accounts with relatively few transactions. Translate this finding into the "What is possible? What is valuable? What is efficient?" framework for adjusting goals.

A possible translation:

- *What is possible?* It is probably possible to make reliable forecasts for users with the highest-quality data, but almost certainly not possible for users with the lowest-quality data.
- *What is valuable?* It is most valuable to provide reliable forecasts for the most active app users. Less active users may not care as much, and if they do, they might be enticed to become more active in the interest of getting access to good forecasts.

- *What is efficient?* It is probably most efficient to start with the user accounts with high-quality data, generate reliable forecasts, and then to try to apply the methods to lower-quality account data, tweaking/improving the methods as much as possible until some kind of inflection point in which the work needed to (maybe) make the methods work for lower-quality data is too much to justify.

2. Based on your answer to the previous question, describe a general plan for generating forecasts within the app.

One possible basic plan is:

a Work with the highest-quality account data to develop a statistical method and software for generating reliable forecasts.

b If you are unsuccessful at (a), revisit the goals and consider whether it is worth spending more time on this one.

c If you are successful with (a), apply the methods and software to lower-quality data and find a sort of minimum quality level for reliable forecasts.

d Optionally, improve the forecasting methods to better handle lower-quality data, but weigh the time spent against the marginal benefit. Discuss with the product designer and jointly decide how much work to put in.

e When everyone is satisfied with the success, scope, and reliability of the forecasts, refine and prep your software for integration with the web app. Be sure to include some notion of not having enough high-quality data; for example, the software should tell the web app `"NOT ENOUGH DATA; NO FORECAST GENERATED"` whenever the established data-quality threshold is not met.

Chapter 7

1. Describe two different statistical models you might use to make forecasts of personal financial accounts. For each, give at least one potential weakness or disadvantage.

Possible statistical models include:

- Linear regression on end-of-month account balances for the past six months. This would capture the general trajectory of the account, but weaknesses include: it doesn't capture fluctuations in balances very well, in case spending varies widely; and, if, for example, a large monthly check (income) does not arrive on time, it might fall into the following month, potentially throwing off the end-of-month balance—and thus the regression results—by a lot.

- Estimate average monthly income and average monthly expenses for the account for the past six months; assume future months will have approximately the same levels of income and expenses. This model likely avoids the preceding problem of a check not arriving on time, but a weakness is that six individual months is not many data points, and the model would be susceptible to large one-time or abnormal transactions anywhere.

2. Assume you've been successful in creating a classifier that can accurately put trans-actions into the categories *regular, one-time*, and any other reasonable categories you've thought of. Describe a statistical model for forecasting that makes use of these classi-fications to improve accuracy.

I would also try to create a category for *normal* expenses, which represents day-to-day expenses like coffee, groceries, dinner, or cocktails but which may not strictly fall into the other two categories previously mentioned, *repeating* and *one-time. Normal* expenses probably aren't as large as *one-time* transactions, but aren't considered *repeating*, either. For example, if I go out to eat a couple of times per week, it's not really a one-time expense because I do it (predictably) every week, and it's not repeating, either, because I go to different places and on different days of the week.

I would use monthly amounts falling into each of these three categories to calculate baselines for each of them. For repeating transactions, I would use six to nine months of data, placing higher weight on more recent months. So, I would have a weighted average monthly amount for repeating transactions and normal expenses, butI would leave out one-time transactions. My forecasts would be based on assuming that the sum of *repeating* transactions and *normal* expenses would continue into the near future, with the intention of somehow showing the user how *one-time* transactions can affect their forecasts and their financial situation (but this is more a UX and product question than a statistical one).

Because I am such a fan of acknowledging uncertainty when it exists, I would also likely calculate for my forecasts a notion of variance, with more variance for forecasts far-ther into the future, and also for accounts with more erratic income and expenses.

Chapter 8

1. What are your two top choices of software for performing the calculations necessary for forecasting in this project and why? What's a disadvantage for each of these?

My top two choices would be:

- *Python*—I can easily do calculations in Python, but a disadvantage is that if my code is going to be deployed with the live Filthy Money Forecasting app, it will have to be relatively bulletproof and bug-free; I'd probably try to recruit a pro-duction developer to help with that. I would also have to find a way to make Python interface well with existing code if it doesn't already.

- *Whatever language/tool is already doing some calculation in the existing app*—I can probably just add a component to the code, but the disadvantages might be, depending on the language, that it might not have good built-in statistical libraries, and I might not know this language yet, so I'd have to learn it.

2. Do your two choices in question 1 have built-in functions for linear regression or other methods for time-series forecasting? What are they?

Respectively:

- Python does. Between the packages `numpy`, `scikit-learn`, and others, Python has some of the best statistical functionality among programming languages.

- It depends on the language; I would consult the internet before committing.

Chapter 9

1. What are three supplementary (not strictly statistical) software products that might be used during this project, and why?

Some products might include:

- A relational database, because FMI already has one and it contains most of the data you will need.
- A high-performance compute server or cluster, because there is a lot of data and a lot of computation to do.
- Cloud computing services, because FMI might not already have the computing resources necessary to perform the forecasting calculations within a reasonable time.

2. Suppose that FMI's internal relational database is hosted on a single server, which is backed up every night to a server at an offsite location. Give a reason why this could be a good architecture and one reason why it might be bad.

The good: if the single server is powerful enough and the total data set is small enough for the server to handle everything quickly and efficiently, this architecture is probably easier to manage than a larger, distributed system.

The bad: data sets grow, and at some point the server will be overwhelmed either by the sheer size of the data or by the computational cost of managing and querying it; also, a single server is probably a single point of failure.

Chapter 10

1. List three people (by role or expertise) at FMI with whom you will probably be talking the most while executing your project plan and briefly state why you will probably talk to them so much.

I would guess that I would talk to these people the most:

- *The web app developer responsible for the FMF app*—Integrating the statistical software with the app will probably take significant communication, negotiation, and agreement to make sure the two pieces align properly.
- *The product designer responsible for the app*—They will probably have many questions about how to interpret output from your statistical application, and you will want to have a good idea of how they expect the user to interact with the data in order to make sure your statistics are applicable.
- *An internal database expert*—If you haven't already used the database extensively, there are likely nuances in structure, access, and efficiency that may not be immediately clear and that may be very helpful to you.

2. Suppose that the product designer has spoken with the management team, and they all agree that your statistical application must generate a forecast for all user accounts, including ones with extremely sparse data. Priorities have shifted from making sure the forecasts are good to making sure that every forecast exists. What would you do to address that?

If a forecast must exist no matter what, then I would probably assume that low-data-quality accounts will stay at their current (or month-end) balances for the near future. Without the data to justify forecasting a move up or down, the status quo is probably the best choice. I would, however, talk this through with the product designer and others before implementing it.

Chapter 11

1. Suppose your boss or another management figure has asked for a report summarizing the results of your work with forecasting. What would you include in the report?

I would include, first, a summary of expected forecast accuracies for user accounts with high-quality data, and follow it with results from lower-quality data. This frames the results in terms of what is possible when users are fully engaged (which is an issue for all of FMI and not just for you) with the main application and also highlights one of the biggest successes of your project. Second, I would discuss the distribution of high- and low-quality data in user accounts in order to illustrate to what extent data quality issues affect the app. Lastly, I would provide a few specific examples (with data) of how the forecasts can be used to influence user behavior, such as warning about a bank account that will soon be empty or a credit limit that might be reached soon. This connects the forecasting project directly to user engagement, which is often the most important thing to management types working with app development.

2. Suppose the lead product designer for the FMF web app asks you to write a paragraph for the app users, explaining the forecasts generated by your application, specifically regarding reliability and accuracy. What would you write?

Forecasts generated by this app are based on your recent spending and earning habits, as well as on any other transactions or events occurring within any of your accounts that are connected to FMF. The more consistent you are in your financial habits, the better our forecasts become—yet another reason to be in control of your finances! Unfortunately, in some cases we may not have enough data to make a forecast at all; in these cases, you may want to connect more accounts to FMF and engage with the app more regularly in order to have these powerful forecasts at your fingertips and maximize your financial well-being. Thanks for making FMF the most powerful personal finance site on the web!

Chapter 12

1. Suppose that you've finished your statistical software, integrated it with the web app, and most of the forecasts appearing in the app seem to be incorrect. List three good places to check to try to diagnose the problem.

I'd check these first:

- The output from the statistical application. If it's outputting correct results, then the problem lies in the app that is making use of them. If not, then the problem is in the statistical part.

- If the problem seems to be in the web app, I'd check the database internal to that app. If the data is stored incorrectly, then there is likely a problem between data intake and when it is stored. If it is stored correctly, then there is a problem in the way the data is handled between when it is pulled from the app's internal storage and shown on the screen.
- If the problem seems to be in the statistical application, I would think about the way the data flows through the statistical model and examine results coming directly out of the statistical model, but before they are transformed into the format in which it is sent to the web application.
- *BONUS 4th ANSWER*—Check the initial data going into any part of your application. If there's something wrong with the database query, nothing that comes after will be correct.

2. After deploying the app, the product team informs you that it's about to send selected users a survey regarding the app. You may submit three open-ended questions that will be included in the survey. What would you submit?

I would probably submit the following questions:

- Have the financial forecasts in the app been informative to you? In what ways?
- Have you acted upon information within the financial forecasts? How?
- Do you feel that the financial forecasts are accurate? Why or why not?

Chapter 13

1. Think of a project (data science or otherwise) you've worked on in the past, preferably more than a year ago. Where are the materials and resources related to that project? If someone asked you to repeat, restart, or continue that project today, would you be able to? Could you have done anything back then to make it easier today?

This is mainly a thought experiment. It depends entirely on where you work and what you're working on.

2. Consider your current job and place of employment. Where are shared resources kept? Can you find what you're looking for easily? If it were your job to come up with a detailed plan and policy for archiving completed projects, what would you include?

This is another thought experiment, but useful for improving the outcomes of future projects. Solid plans for documenting and storing projects can be incredibly helpful.

index